Volume One

by
Amy Reeder Hadley

D1113708

HAMBURG // LONDON // LOS ANGELES // TOKYO

Fool's Gold Vol. 1
Created by Amy Reeder Hadley

Layout - Erika Terriquez
Production Artist - Fawn Lau
Cover Design - Anne Marie Horne
Copy Editor - Peter Ahlstrom

Editor - Lillian Diaz-Przybyl
Digital Imaging Manager - Chris Buford
Production Manager - Elisabeth Brizzi
Managing Editor - Lindsey Johnston
Editorial Director - Jeremy Ross
Editor in Chief - Rob Tokar
VP of Production - Ron Klamert
Publisher - Mike Kiley
President and C.O.O. - John Parker
C.E.O. and Chief Creative Officer - Stuart Levy

A TOKYOPOP Manga

TOKYOPOP Inc.
5900 Wilshire Blvd. Suite 2000
Los Angeles, CA 90036

E-mail: info@TOKYOPOP.com
Come visit us online at www.TOKYOPOP.com

ISBN: 1-59816-585-2

First TOKYOPOP printing: July 2006
10 9 8 7 6 5 4 3 2 1
Printed in the USA

FOOL'S GOLD
Table of Contents

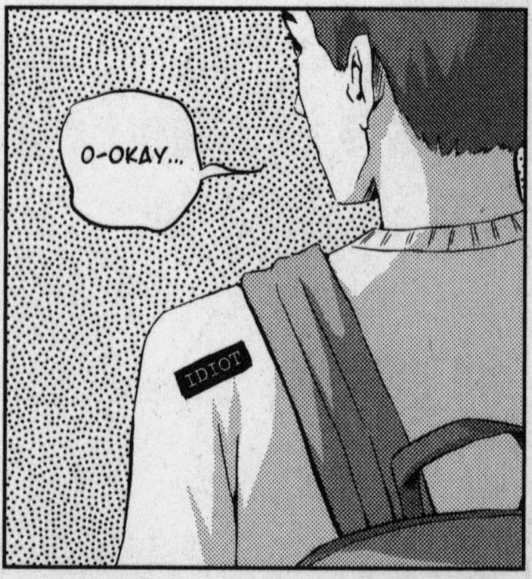
O-OKAY...
IDIOT

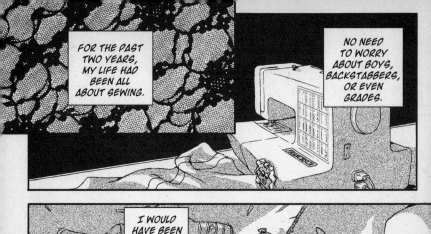

FOR THE PAST TWO YEARS, MY LIFE HAD BEEN ALL ABOUT SEWING.

NO NEED TO WORRY ABOUT BOYS, BACKSTABBERS, OR EVEN GRADES.

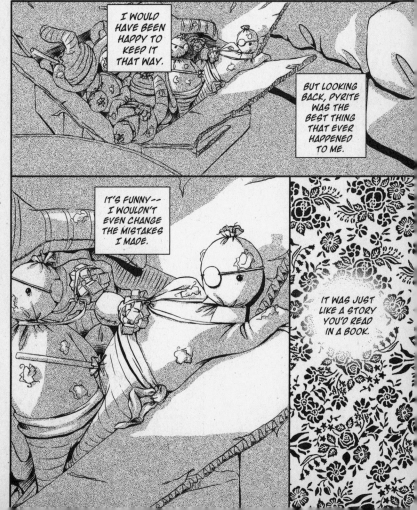

I WOULD HAVE BEEN HAPPY TO KEEP IT THAT WAY.

BUT LOOKING BACK, PYRITE WAS THE BEST THING THAT EVER HAPPENED TO ME.

IT'S FUNNY-- I WOULDN'T EVEN CHANGE THE MISTAKES I MADE.

IT WAS JUST LIKE A STORY YOU'D READ IN A BOOK.

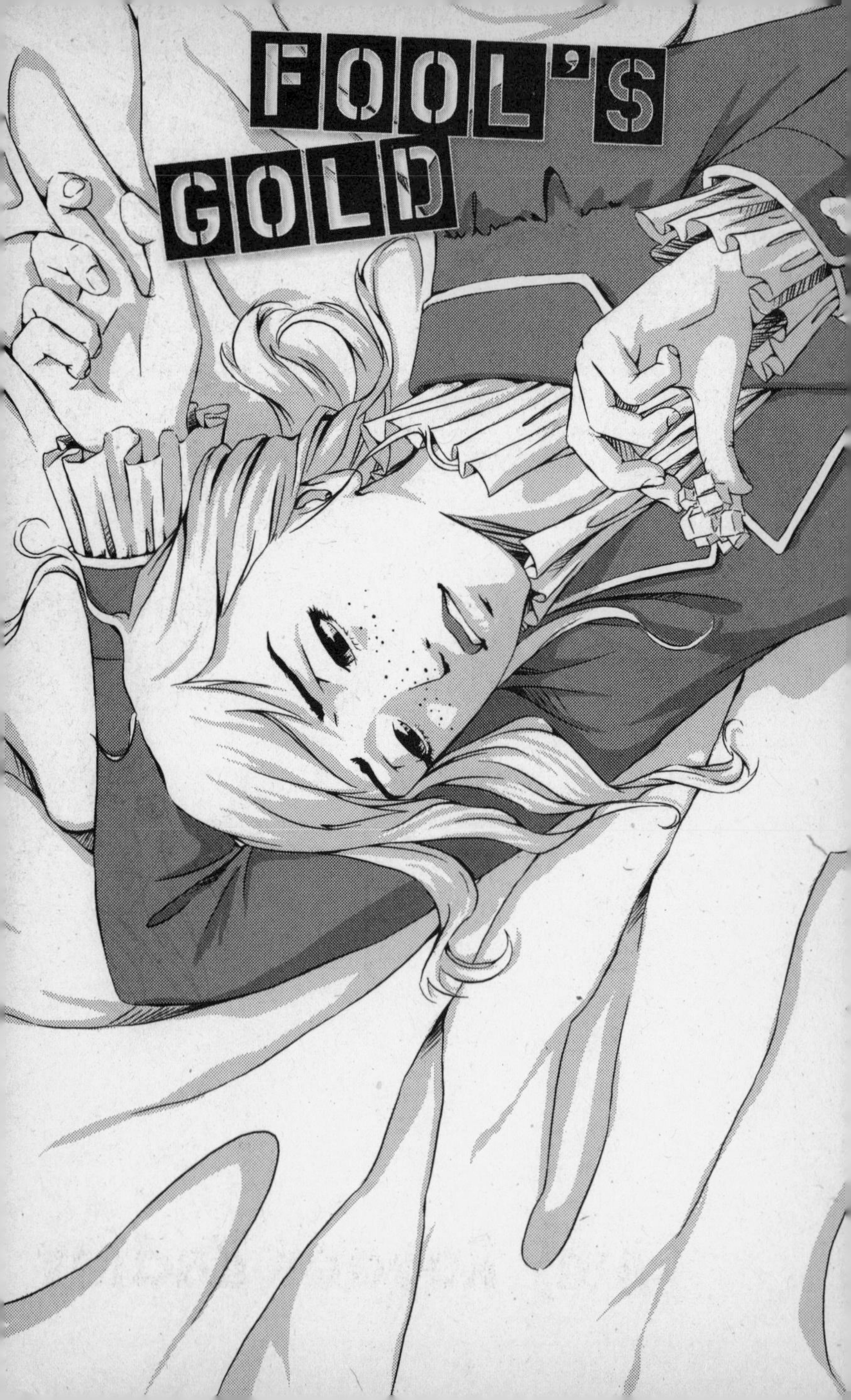
FOOL'S
GOLD

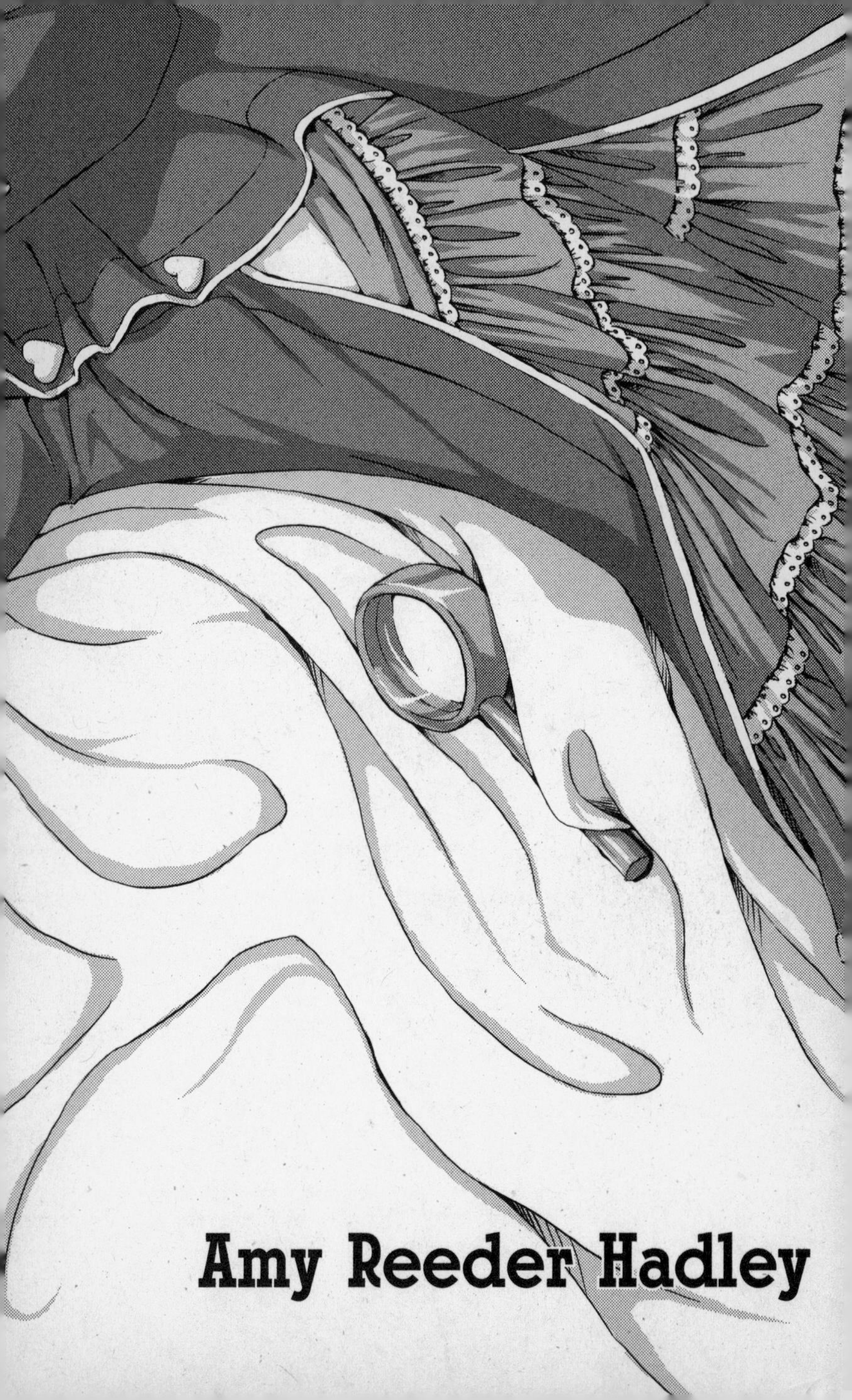
Amy Reeder Hadley

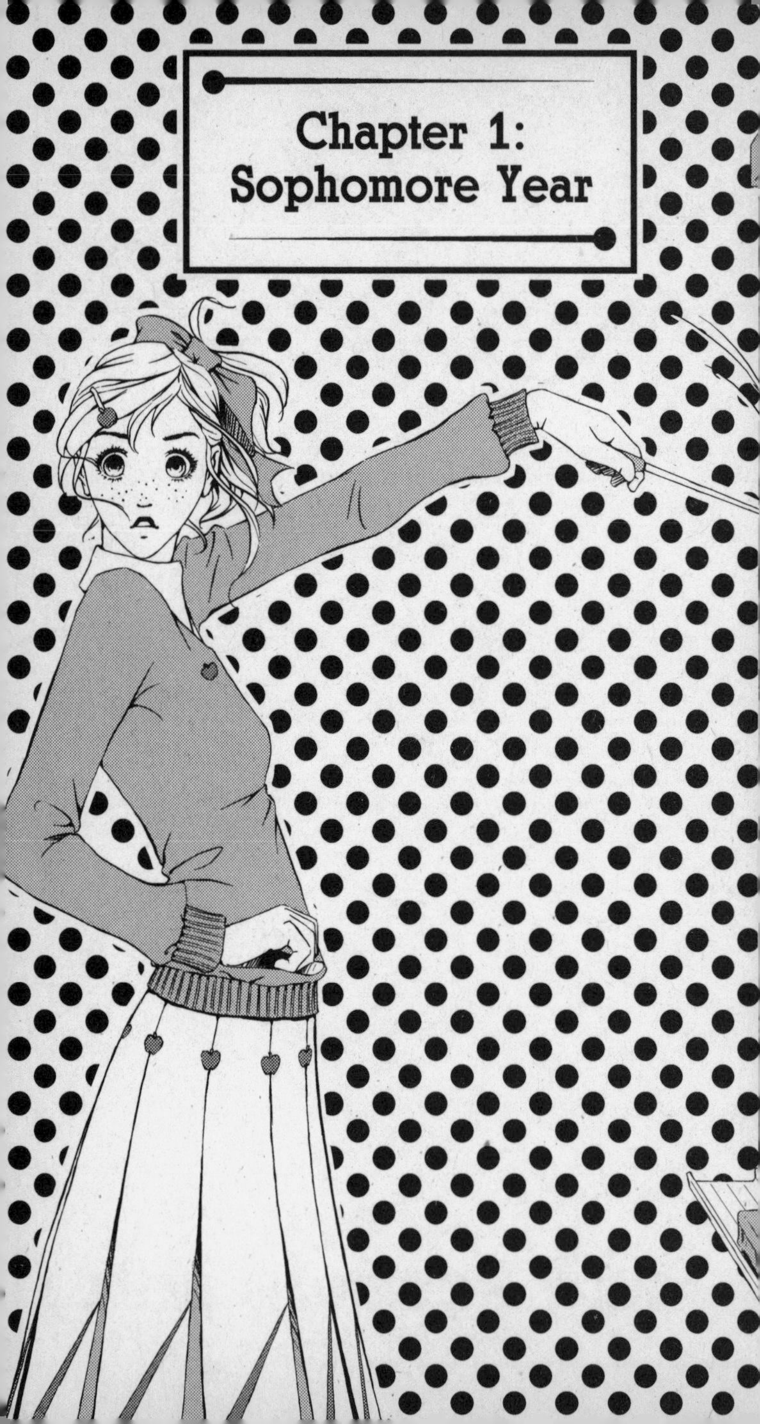
Chapter 1:
Sophomore Year

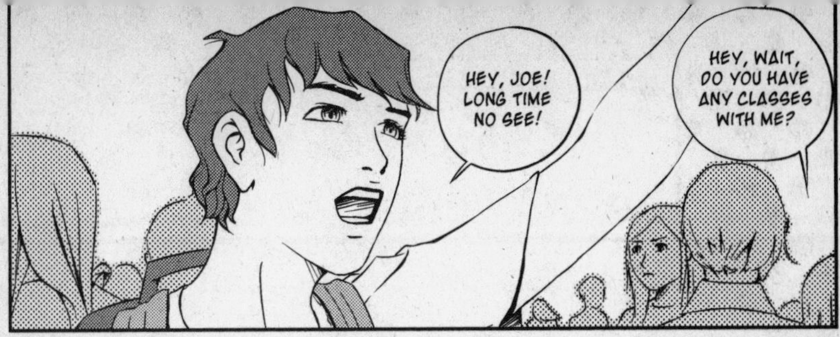
HEY, JOE! LONG TIME NO SEE!
HEY, WAIT, DO YOU HAVE ANY CLASSES WITH ME?
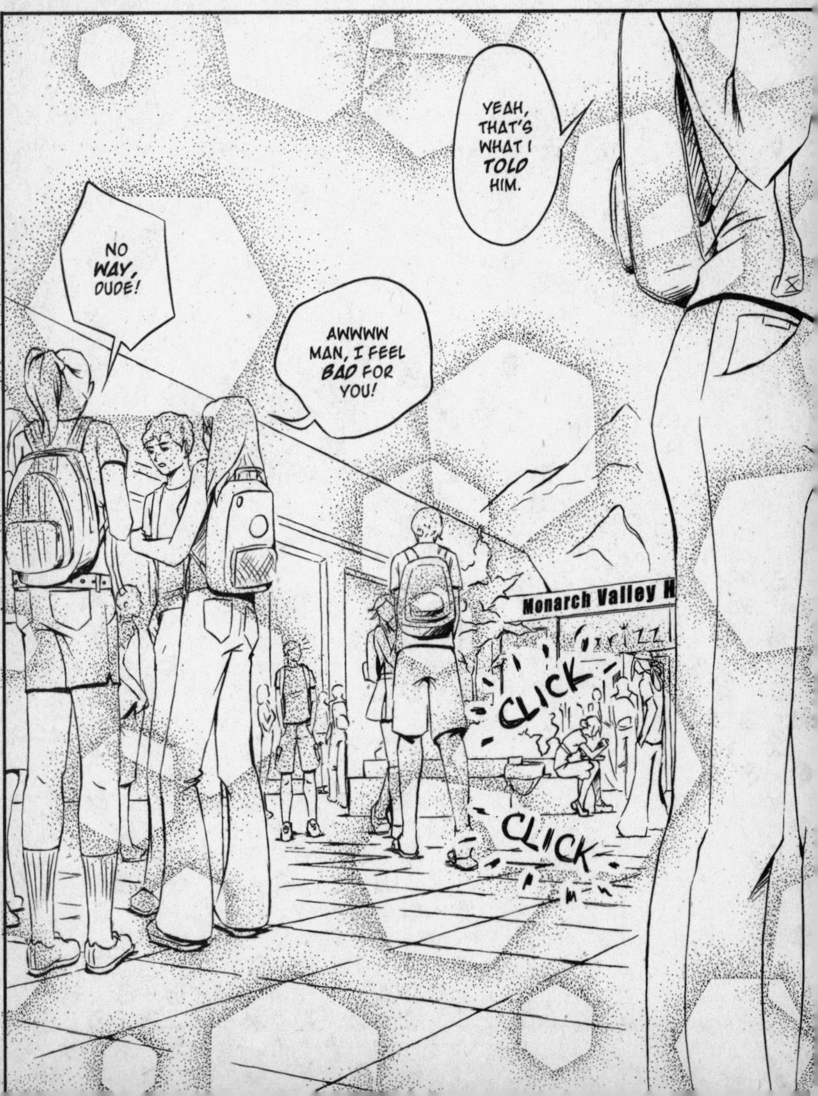
YEAH, THAT'S WHAT I *TOLD* HIM.
NO *WAY,* DUDE!
AWWWW MAN, I FEEL *BAD* FOR YOU!
Monarch Valley H
CLICK
CLICK

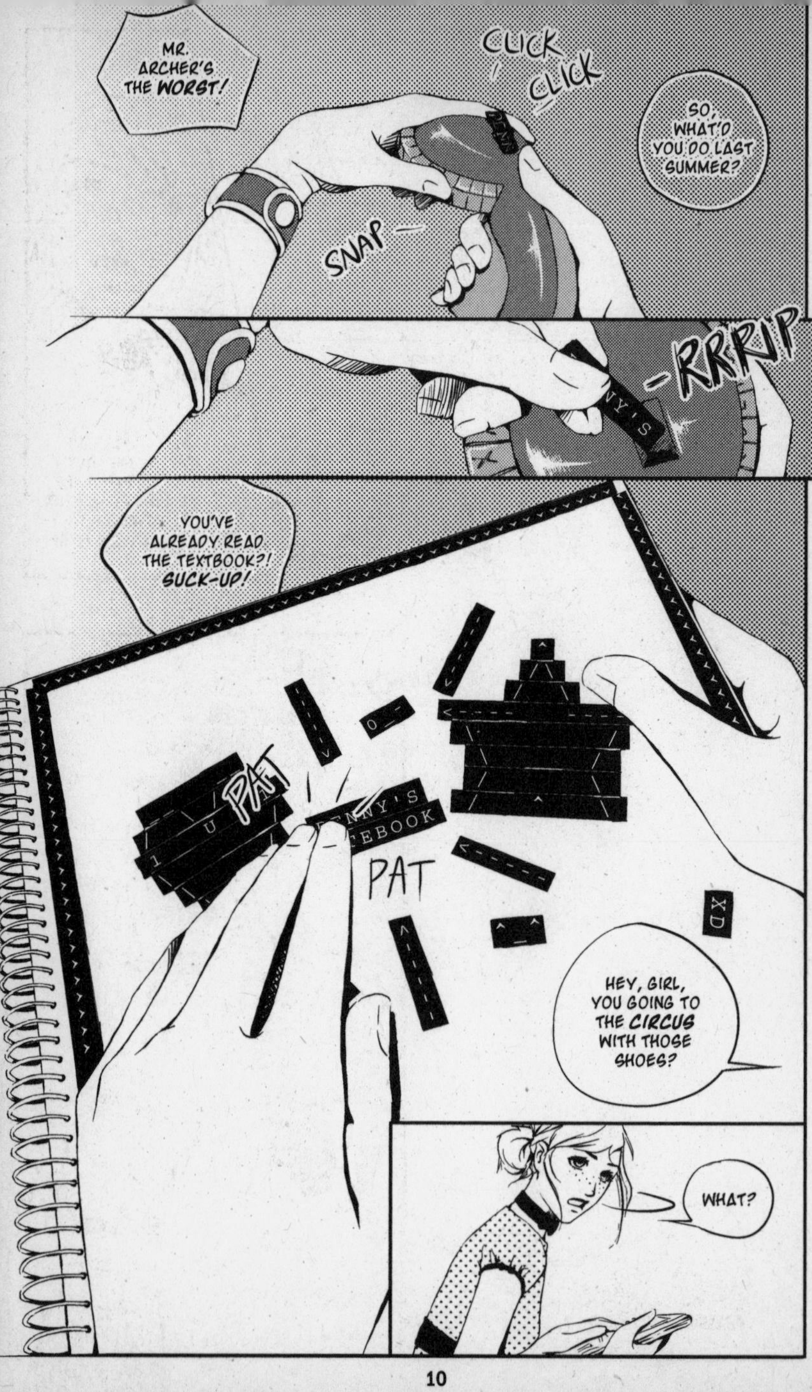
MR. ARCHER'S THE WORST!
CLICK
CLICK
SO, WHAT'D YOU DO LAST SUMMER?
SNAP—
-RRRIP
YOU'VE ALREADY READ THE TEXTBOOK?! SUCK-UP!
PAT
PAT
XD
HEY, GIRL, YOU GOING TO THE CIRCUS WITH THOSE SHOES?
WHAT?

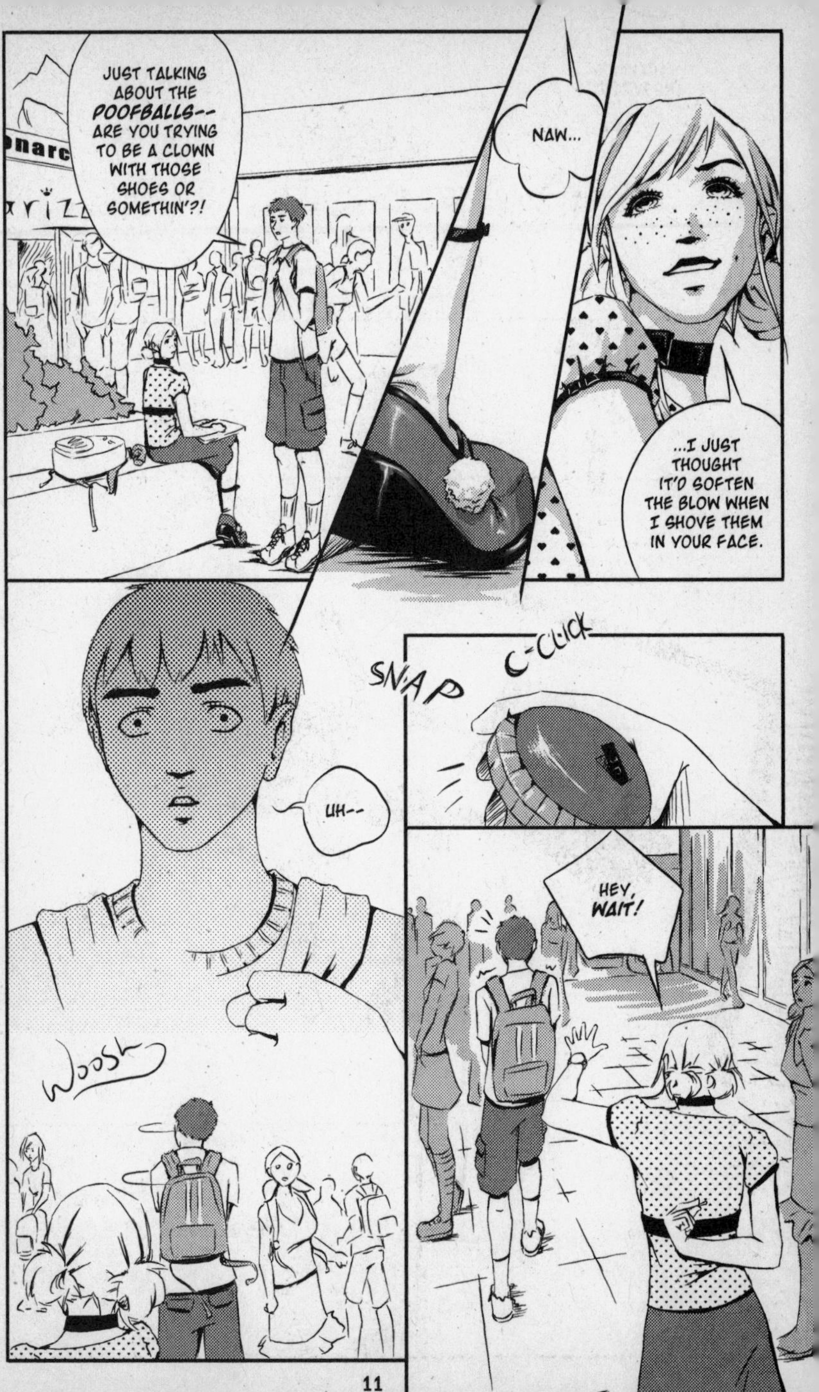
JUST TALKING ABOUT THE POOFBALLS-- ARE YOU TRYING TO BE A CLOWN WITH THOSE SHOES OR SOMETHIN'?!
NAW...
...I JUST THOUGHT IT'D SOFTEN THE BLOW WHEN I SHOVE THEM IN YOUR FACE.
UH--
SNAP
C-CLICK
WOOSH
HEY, WAIT!

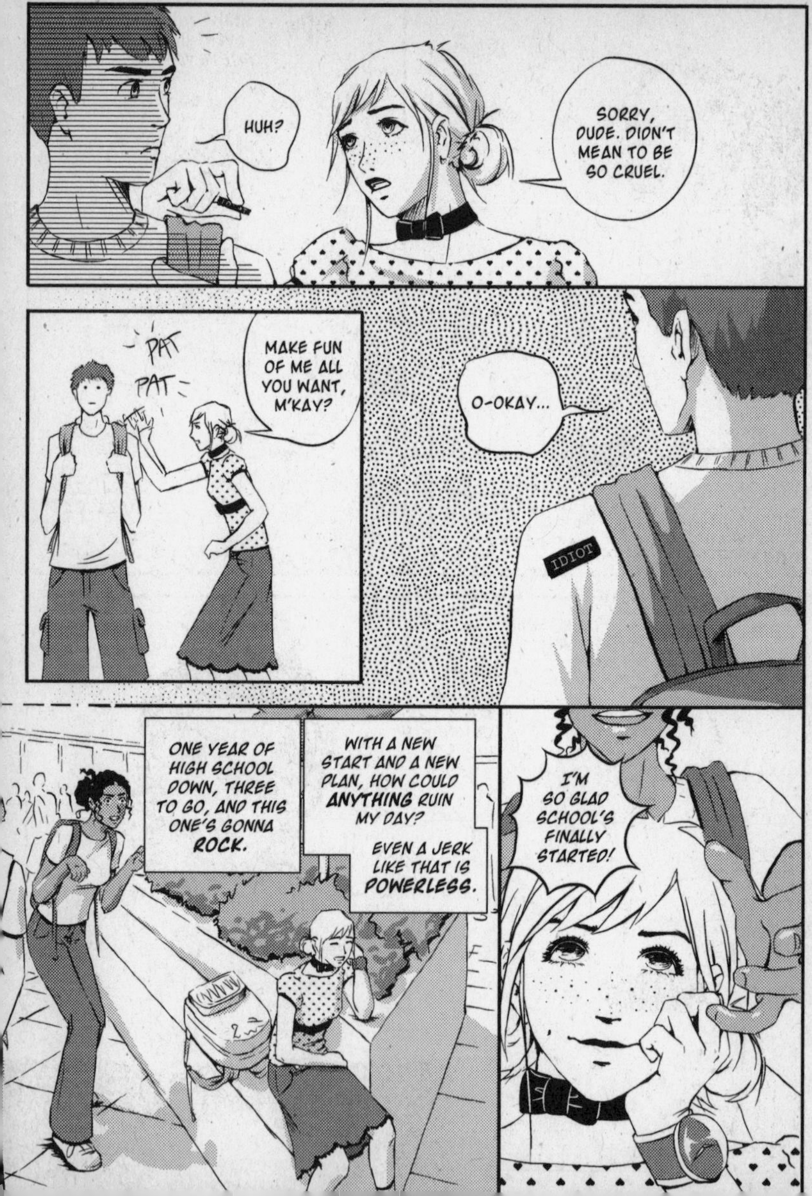
HUH?
SORRY, DUDE. DIDN'T MEAN TO BE SO CRUEL.
PAT
PAT
MAKE FUN OF ME ALL YOU WANT, M'KAY?
O-OKAY...
IDIOT
ONE YEAR OF HIGH SCHOOL DOWN, THREE TO GO, AND THIS ONE'S GONNA ROCK.
WITH A NEW START AND A NEW PLAN, HOW COULD ANYTHING RUIN MY DAY?
EVEN A JERK LIKE THAT IS POWERLESS.
I'M SO GLAD SCHOOL'S FINALLY STARTED!

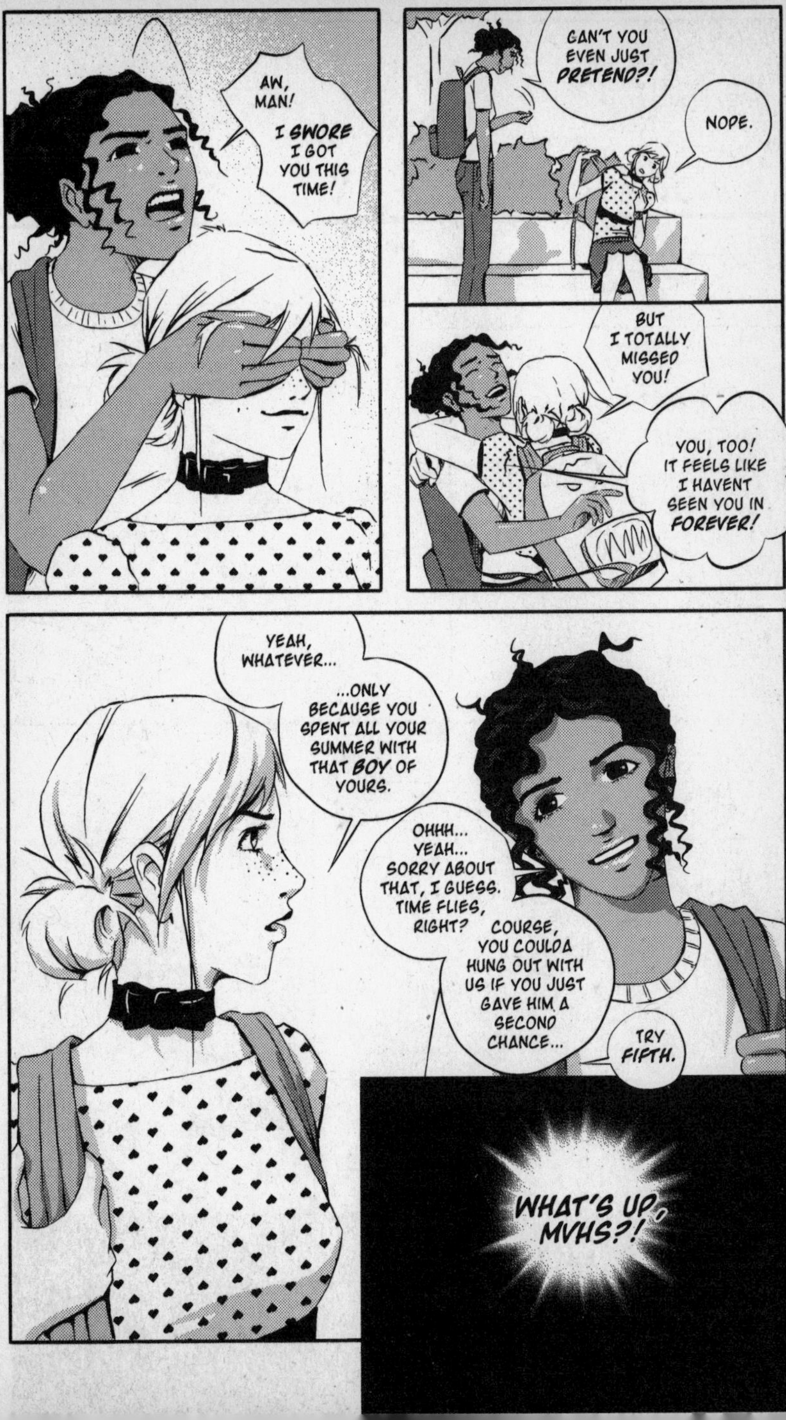
AW, MAN!
I SWORE I GOT YOU THIS TIME!
CAN'T YOU EVEN JUST PRETEND?!
NOPE.
BUT I TOTALLY MISSED YOU!
YOU, TOO! IT FEELS LIKE I HAVENT SEEN YOU IN FOREVER!
YEAH, WHATEVER...
...ONLY BECAUSE YOU SPENT ALL YOUR SUMMER WITH THAT BOY OF YOURS.
OHHH... YEAH... SORRY ABOUT THAT, I GUESS. TIME FLIES, RIGHT?
COURSE, YOU COULDA HUNG OUT WITH US IF YOU JUST GAVE HIM A SECOND CHANCE...
TRY FIFTH.
WHAT'S UP, MVHS?!

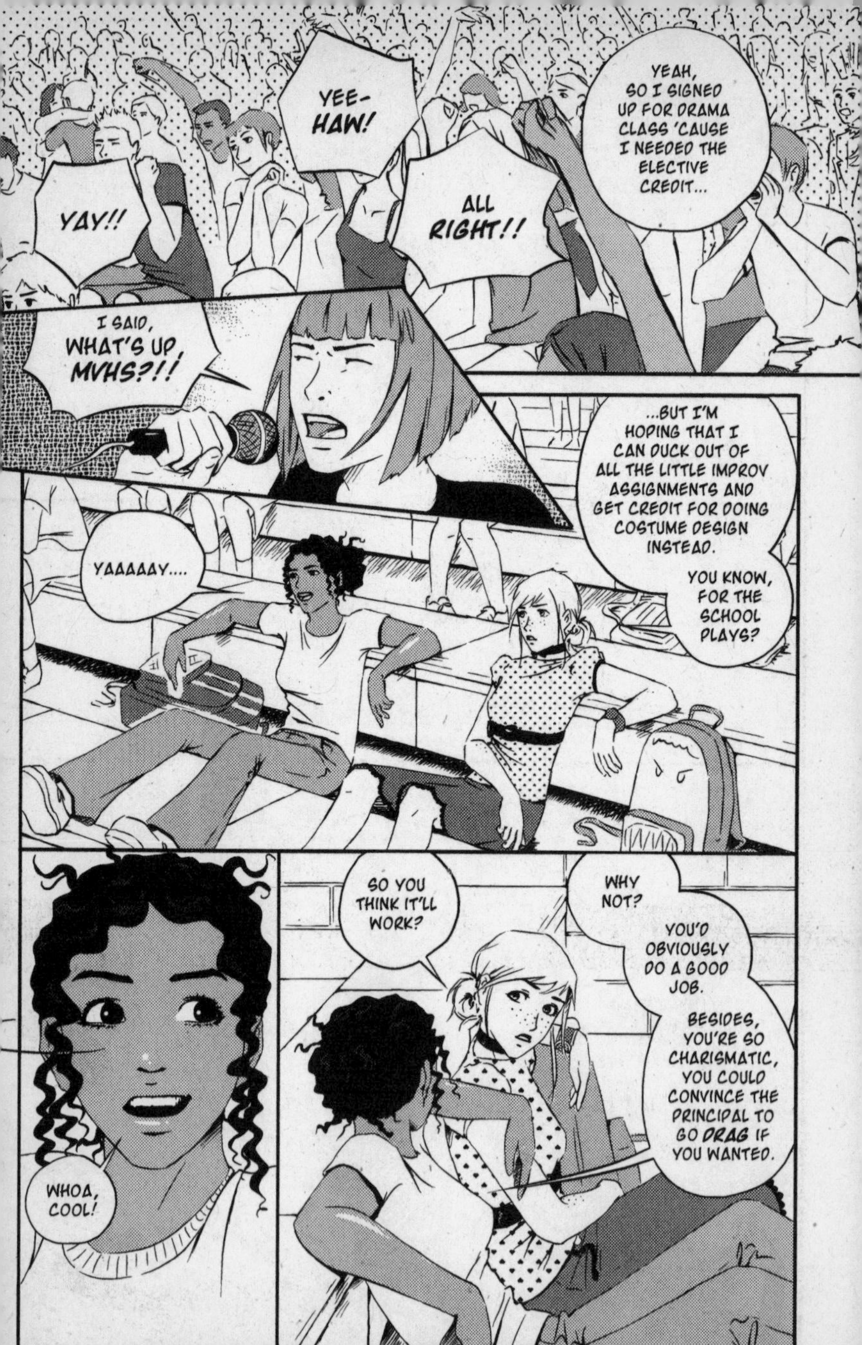
YAY!!
YEE-HAW!
ALL RIGHT!!
YEAH, SO I SIGNED UP FOR DRAMA CLASS 'CAUSE I NEEDED THE ELECTIVE CREDIT...
I SAID, WHAT'S UP, MVHS?!!
...BUT I'M HOPING THAT I CAN DUCK OUT OF ALL THE LITTLE IMPROV ASSIGNMENTS AND GET CREDIT FOR DOING COSTUME DESIGN INSTEAD.
YOU KNOW, FOR THE SCHOOL PLAYS?
YAAAAAY....
WHOA, COOL!
SO YOU THINK IT'LL WORK?
WHY NOT?
YOU'D OBVIOUSLY DO A GOOD JOB.
BESIDES, YOU'RE SO CHARISMATIC, YOU COULD CONVINCE THE PRINCIPAL TO GO DRAG IF YOU WANTED.

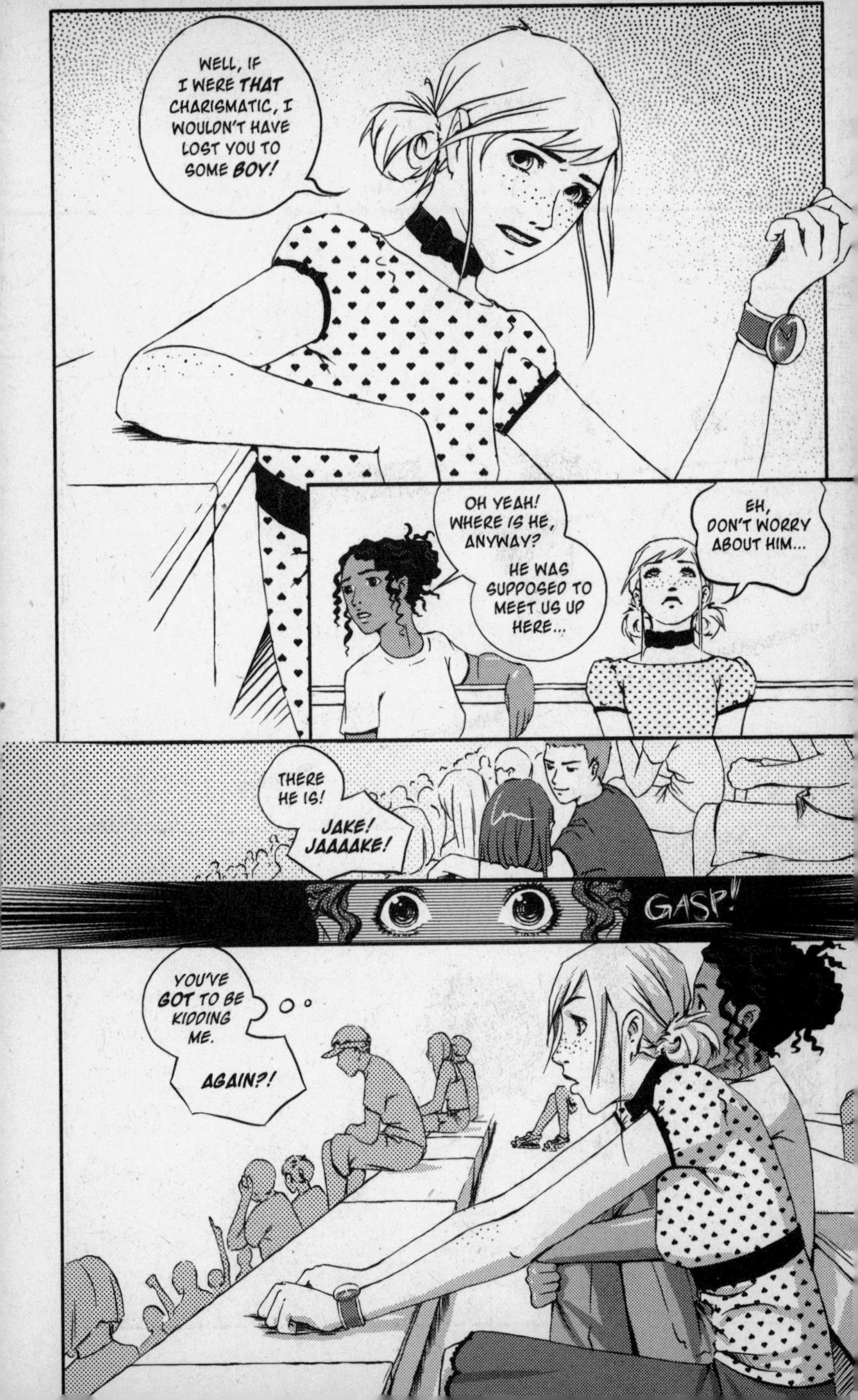
WELL, IF I WERE THAT CHARISMATIC, I WOULDN'T HAVE LOST YOU TO SOME BOY!
OH YEAH! WHERE IS HE, ANYWAY?
HE WAS SUPPOSED TO MEET US UP HERE...
EH, DON'T WORRY ABOUT HIM...
THERE HE IS!
JAKE! JAAAAKE!
GASP!
YOU'VE GOT TO BE KIDDING ME.
AGAIN?!

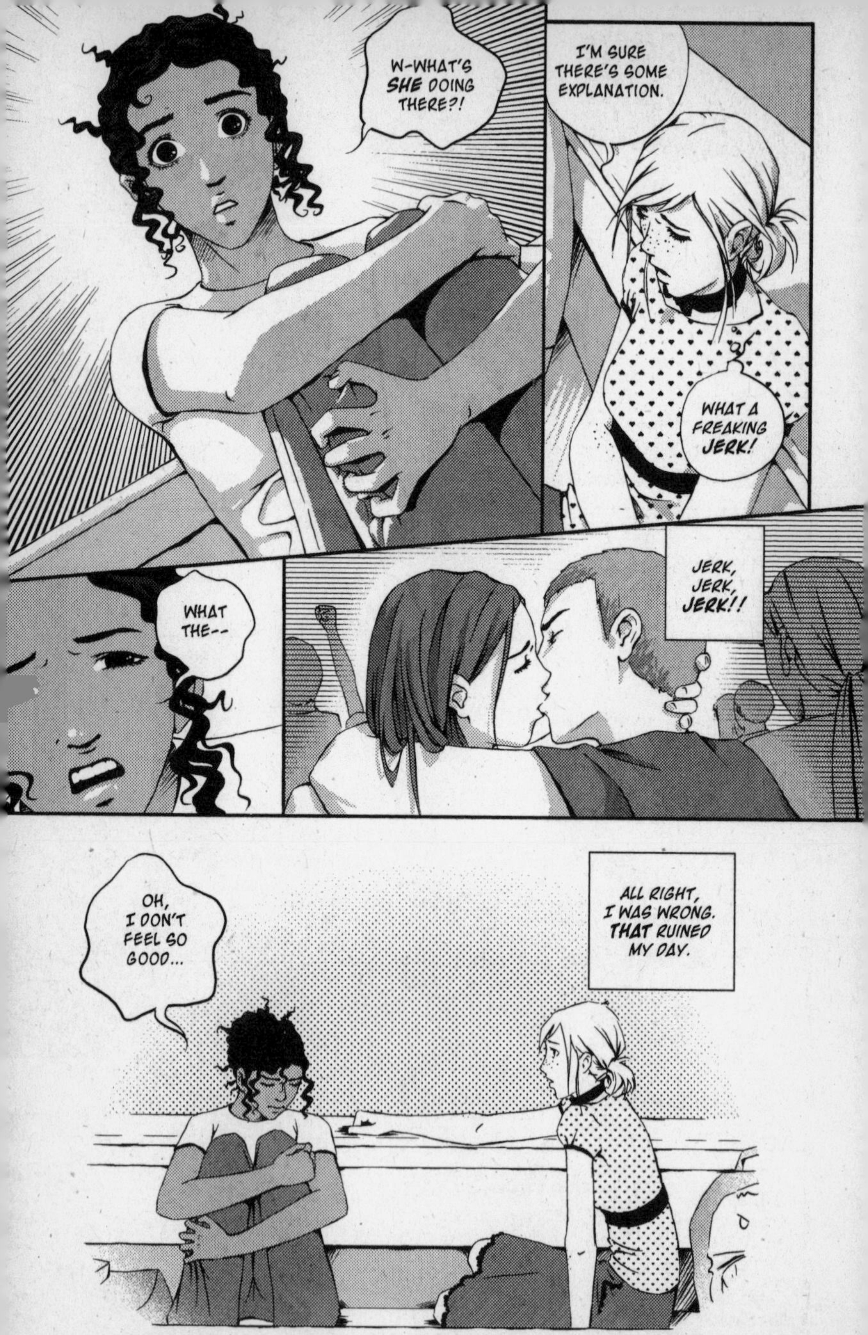
W-WHAT'S **SHE** DOING THERE?!
I'M SURE THERE'S SOME EXPLANATION.
WHAT A FREAKING **JERK!**
WHAT THE--
JERK, JERK, **JERK!!**
OH, I DON'T FEEL SO GOOD...
ALL RIGHT, I WAS WRONG. **THAT** RUINED MY DAY.

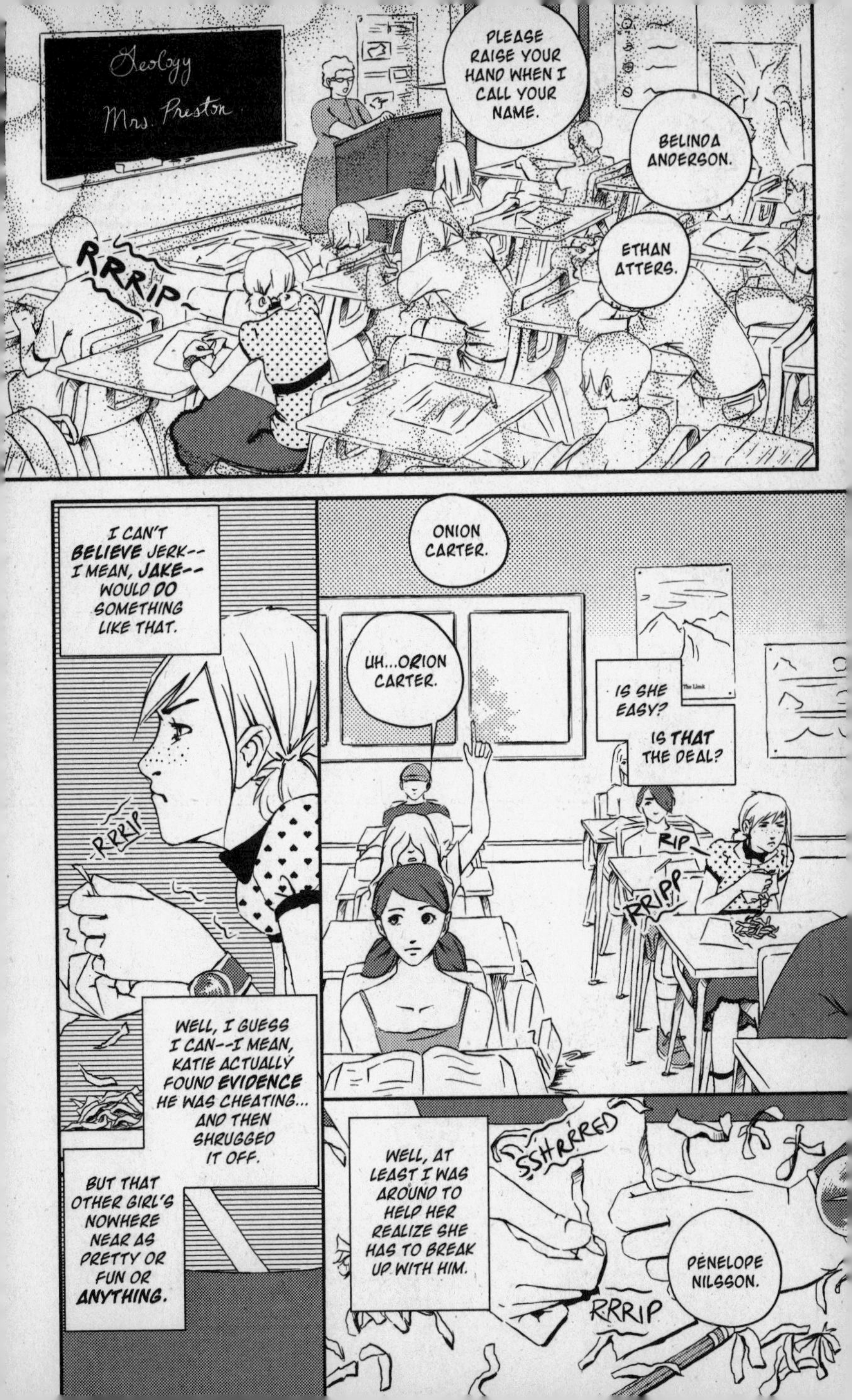

Geology
Mrs. Preston
PLEASE RAISE YOUR HAND WHEN I CALL YOUR NAME.
BELINDA ANDERSON.
RRRIP
ETHAN ATTERS.
I CAN'T BELIEVE JERK--I MEAN, JAKE--WOULD DO SOMETHING LIKE THAT.
RRRIP
ONION CARTER.
UH...ORION CARTER.
IS SHE EASY?
IS THAT THE DEAL?
RIP
RRIPP
WELL, I GUESS I CAN--I MEAN, KATIE ACTUALLY FOUND EVIDENCE HE WAS CHEATING... AND THEN SHRUGGED IT OFF.
BUT THAT OTHER GIRL'S NOWHERE NEAR AS PRETTY OR FUN OR ANYTHING.
WELL, AT LEAST I WAS AROUND TO HELP HER REALIZE SHE HAS TO BREAK UP WITH HIM.
SSHRRRED
RRRIP
PENELOPE NILSSON.

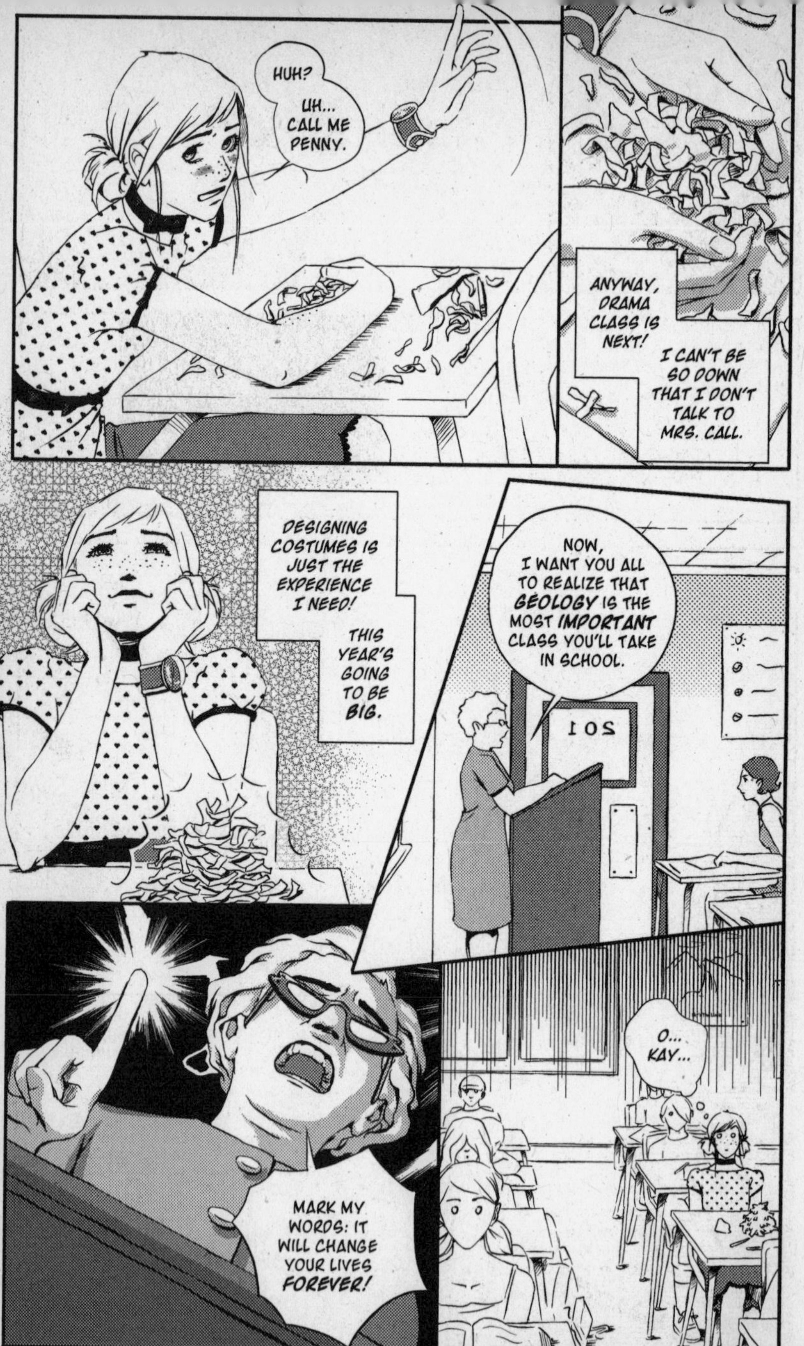
HUH?
UH... CALL ME PENNY.
ANYWAY, DRAMA CLASS IS NEXT!
I CAN'T BE SO DOWN THAT I DON'T TALK TO MRS. CALL.
DESIGNING COSTUMES IS JUST THE EXPERIENCE I NEED!
THIS YEAR'S GOING TO BE BIG.
NOW, I WANT YOU ALL TO REALIZE THAT GEOLOGY IS THE MOST IMPORTANT CLASS YOU'LL TAKE IN SCHOOL.
201
MARK MY WORDS: IT WILL CHANGE YOUR LIVES FOREVER!
O... KAY...

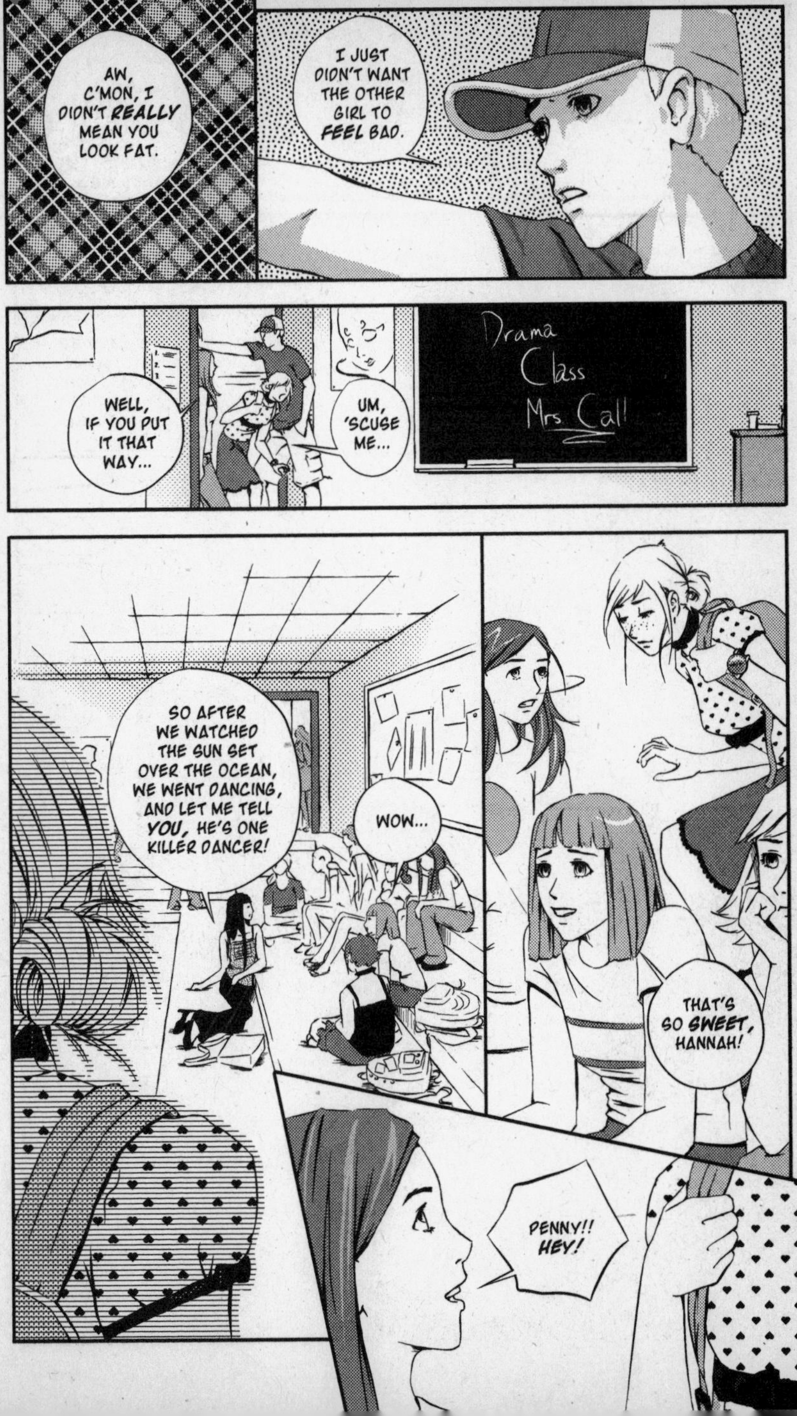
AW, C'MON, I DIDN'T REALLY MEAN YOU LOOK FAT.
I JUST DIDN'T WANT THE OTHER GIRL TO FEEL BAD.
WELL, IF YOU PUT IT THAT WAY...
UM, 'SCUSE ME...
Drama Class Mrs. Call
SO AFTER WE WATCHED THE SUN SET OVER THE OCEAN, WE WENT DANCING, AND LET ME TELL YOU, HE'S ONE KILLER DANCER!
WOW...
THAT'S SO SWEET, HANNAH!
PENNY!! HEY!

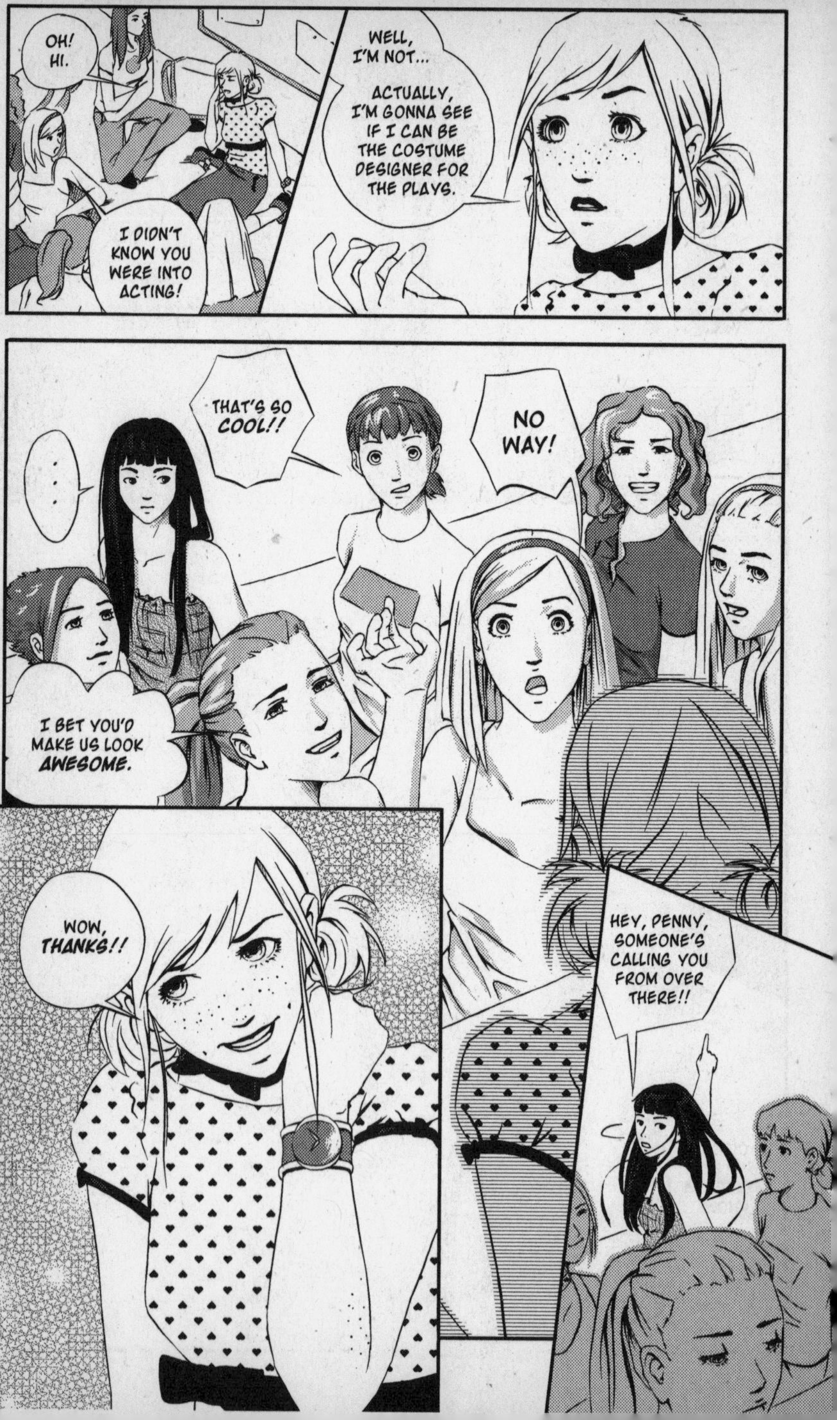
OH! HI.
I DIDN'T KNOW YOU WERE INTO ACTING!
WELL, I'M NOT... ACTUALLY, I'M GONNA SEE IF I CAN BE THE COSTUME DESIGNER FOR THE PLAYS.
...
THAT'S SO COOL!!
NO WAY!
I BET YOU'D MAKE US LOOK AWESOME.
WOW, THANKS!!
HEY, PENNY, SOMEONE'S CALLING YOU FROM OVER THERE!!

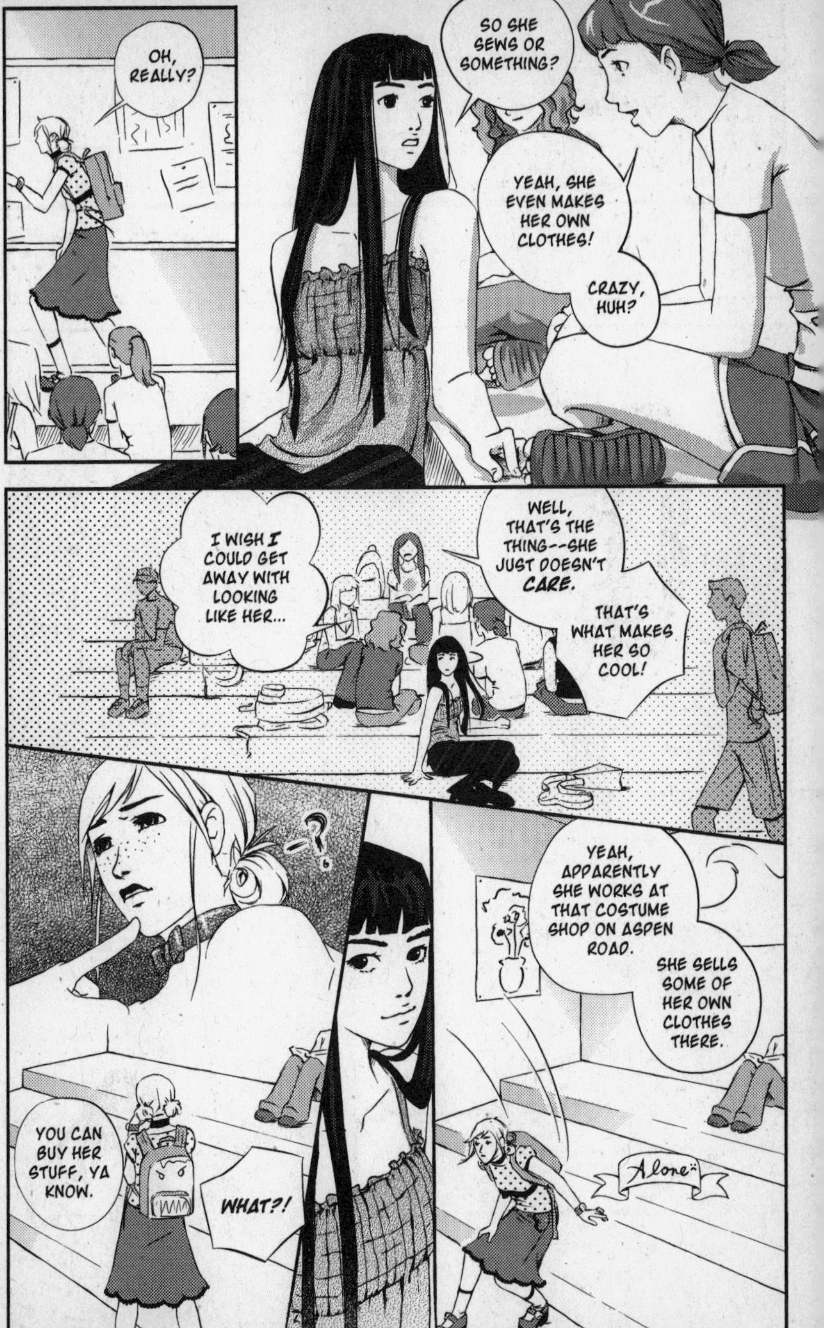
OH, REALLY?
SO SHE SEWS OR SOMETHING?
YEAH, SHE EVEN MAKES HER OWN CLOTHES!
CRAZY, HUH?
I WISH I COULD GET AWAY WITH LOOKING LIKE HER...
WELL, THAT'S THE THING--SHE JUST DOESN'T CARE.
THAT'S WHAT MAKES HER SO COOL!
YOU CAN BUY HER STUFF, YA KNOW.
WHAT?!
YEAH, APPARENTLY SHE WORKS AT THAT COSTUME SHOP ON ASPEN ROAD.
SHE SELLS SOME OF HER OWN CLOTHES THERE.
Alone

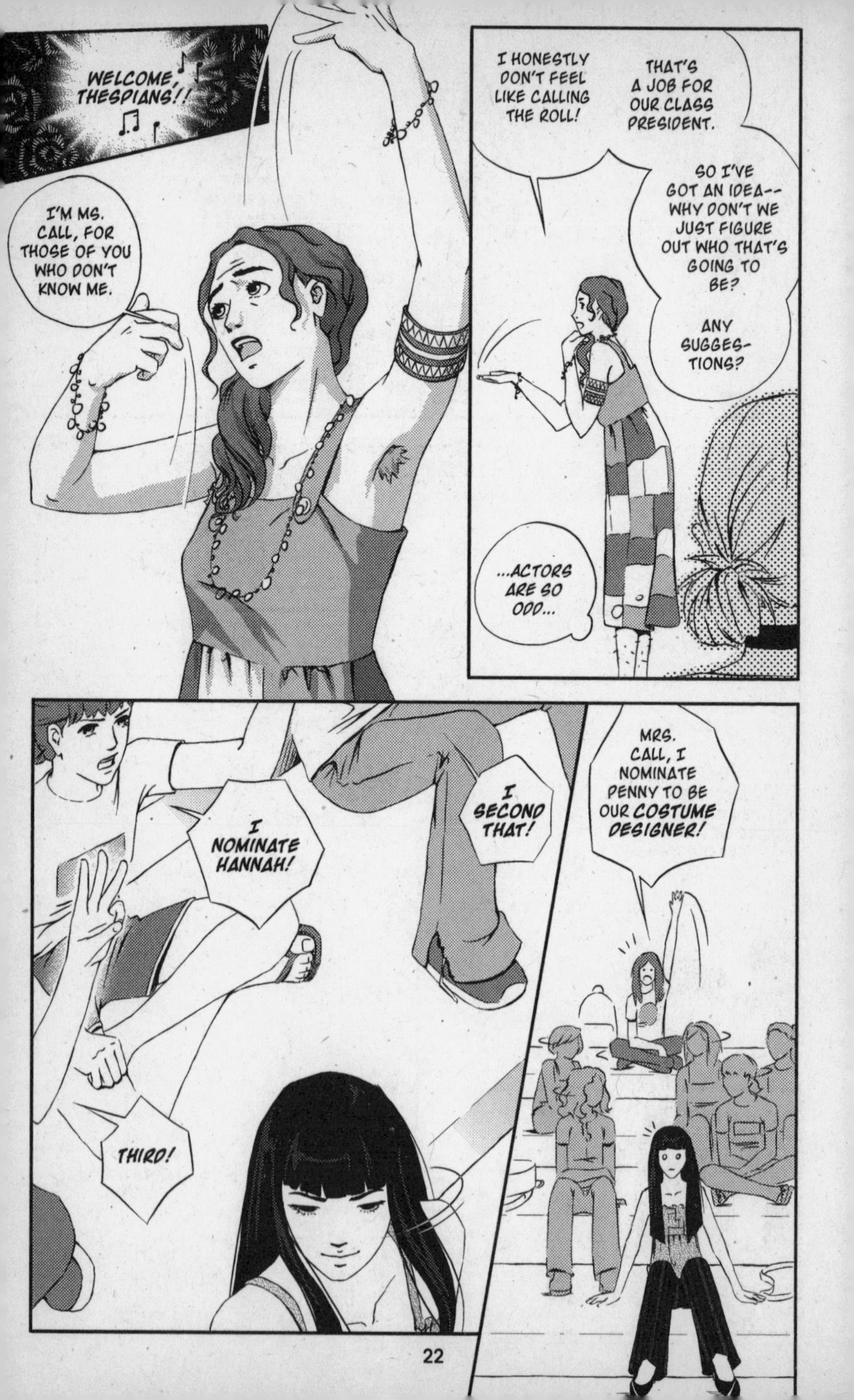

WELCOME, THESPIANS!!
I'M MS. CALL, FOR THOSE OF YOU WHO DON'T KNOW ME.
I HONESTLY DON'T FEEL LIKE CALLING THE ROLL!
THAT'S A JOB FOR OUR CLASS PRESIDENT.
SO I'VE GOT AN IDEA-- WHY DON'T WE JUST FIGURE OUT WHO THAT'S GOING TO BE?
ANY SUGGES-TIONS?
...ACTORS ARE SO ODD...
I NOMINATE HANNAH!
I SECOND THAT!
THIRD!
MRS. CALL, I NOMINATE PENNY TO BE OUR COSTUME DESIGNER!

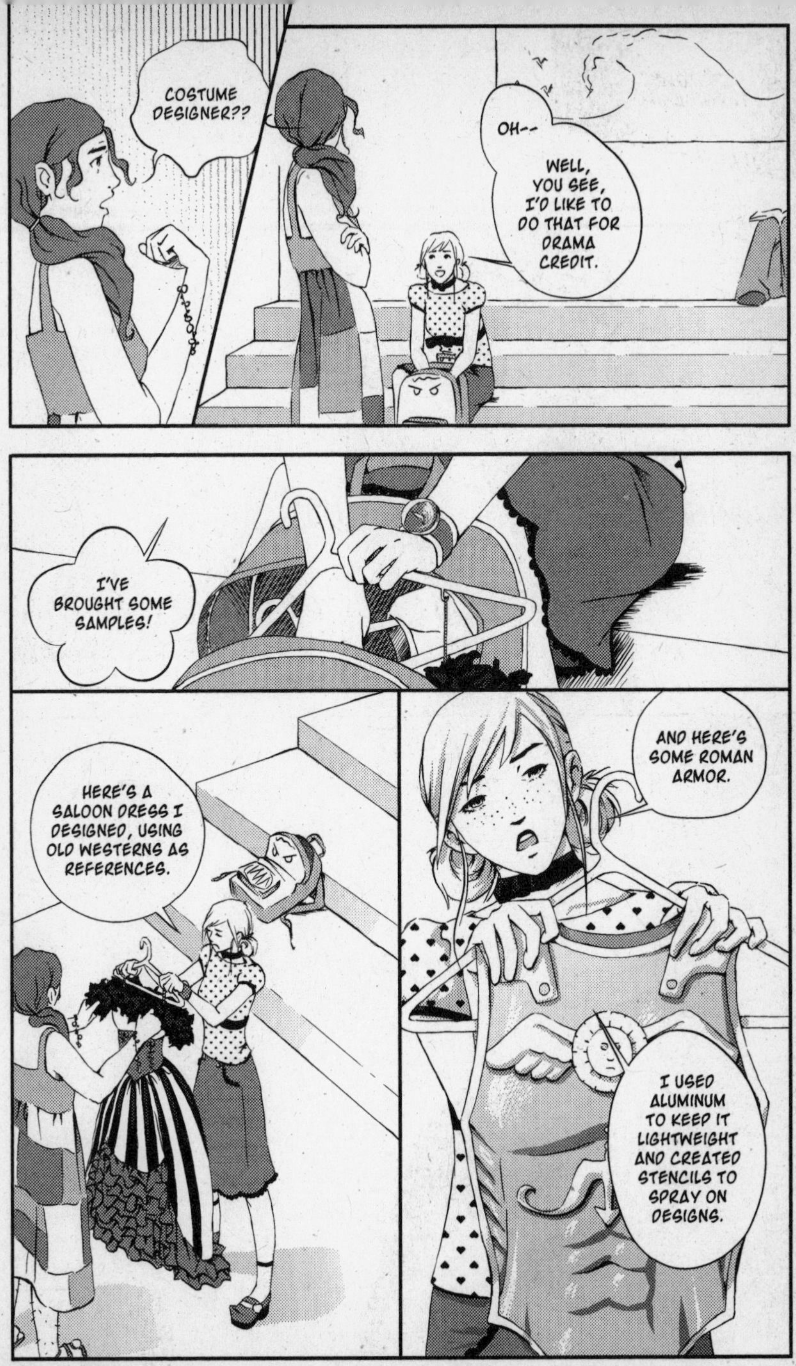
COSTUME DESIGNER??
OH--
WELL, YOU SEE, I'D LIKE TO DO THAT FOR DRAMA CREDIT.
I'VE BROUGHT SOME SAMPLES!
HERE'S A SALOON DRESS I DESIGNED, USING OLD WESTERNS AS REFERENCES.
AND HERE'S SOME ROMAN ARMOR.
I USED ALUMINUM TO KEEP IT LIGHTWEIGHT AND CREATED STENCILS TO SPRAY ON DESIGNS.

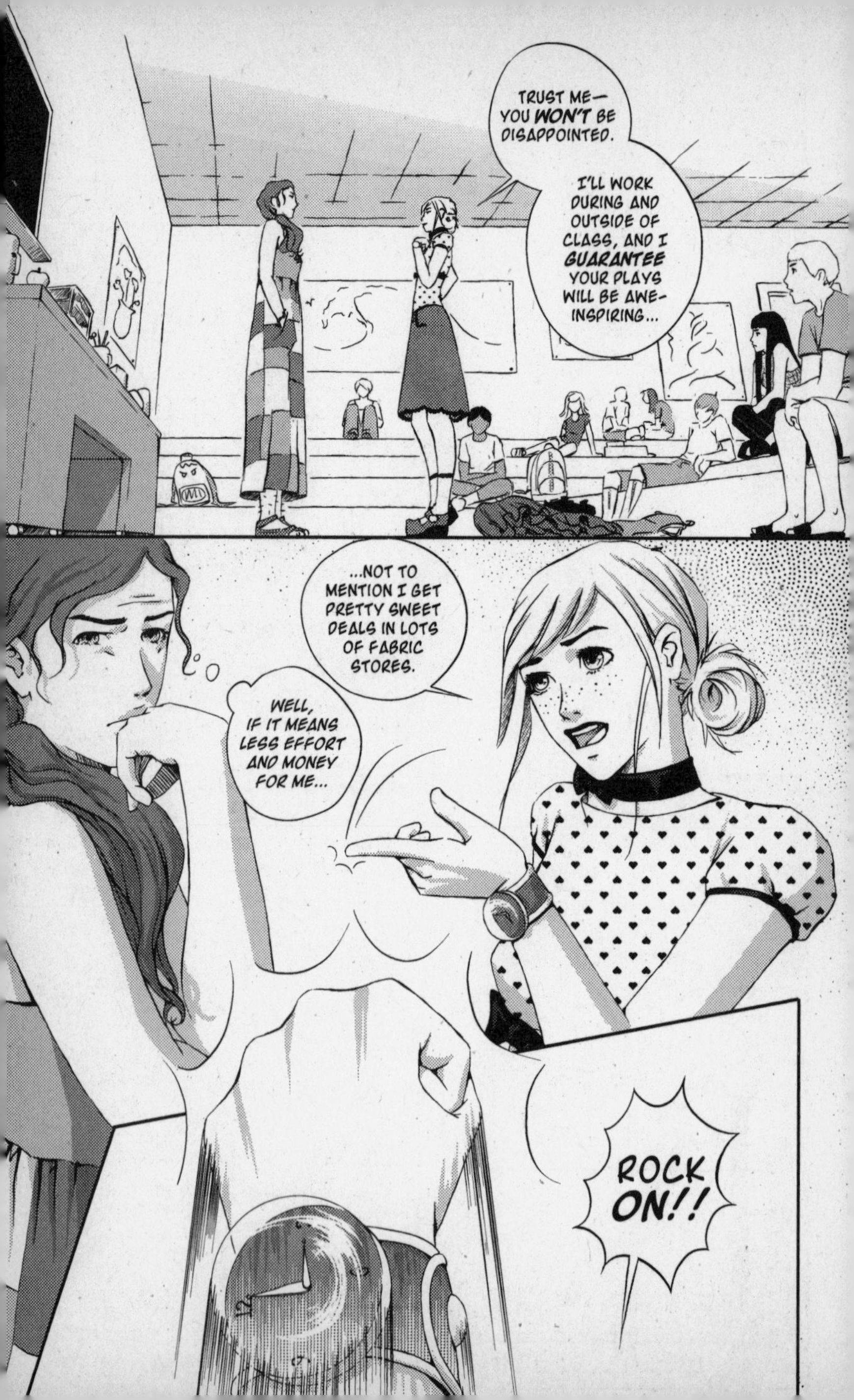

TRUST ME— YOU **WON'T** BE DISAPPOINTED.
I'LL WORK DURING AND OUTSIDE OF CLASS, AND I **GUARANTEE** YOUR PLAYS WILL BE AWE-INSPIRING...
...NOT TO MENTION I GET PRETTY SWEET DEALS IN LOTS OF FABRIC STORES.
WELL, IF IT MEANS LESS EFFORT AND MONEY FOR ME...
ROCK ON!!

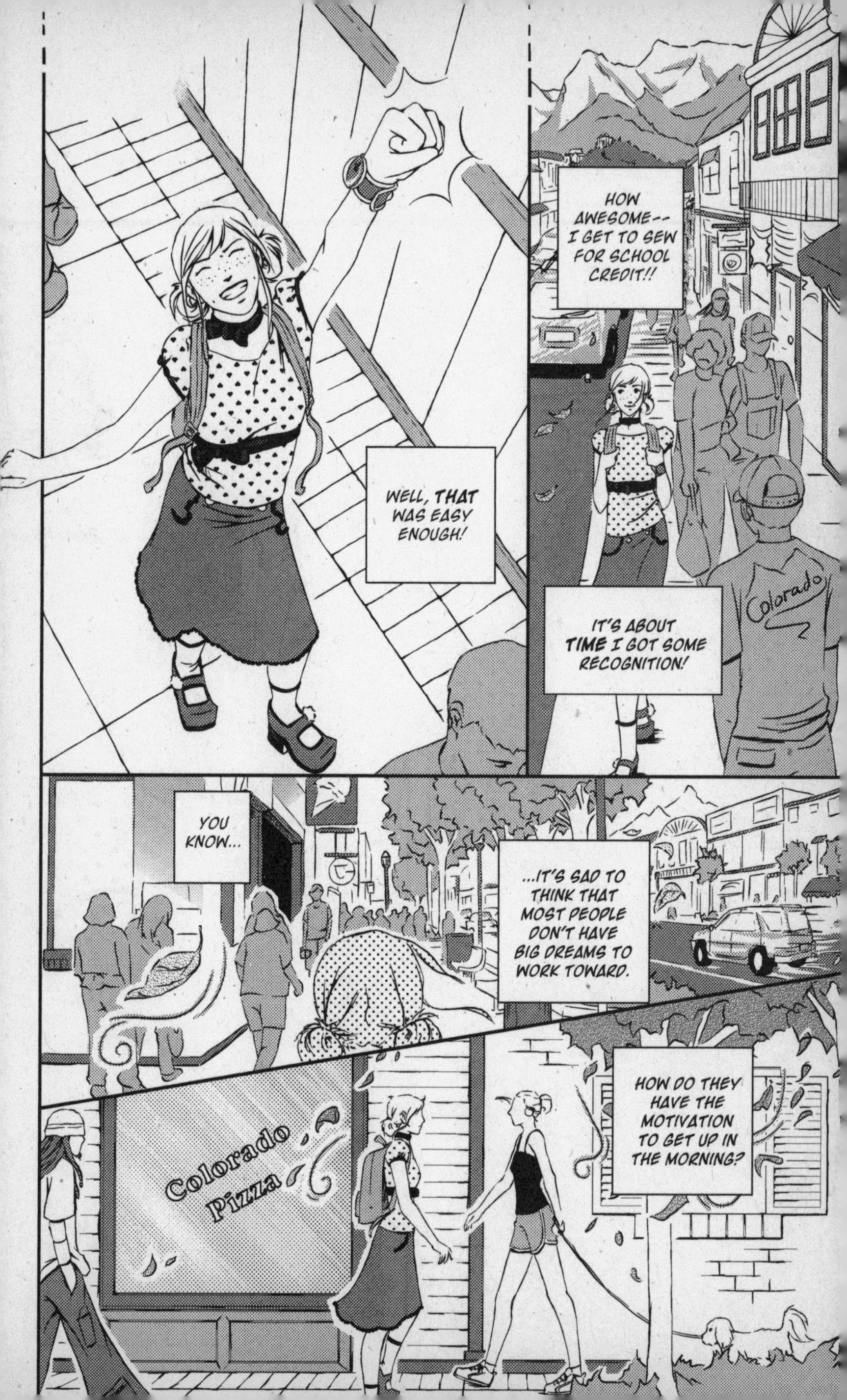
WELL, THAT WAS EASY ENOUGH!
HOW AWESOME--I GET TO SEW FOR SCHOOL CREDIT!!
Colorado
IT'S ABOUT TIME I GOT SOME RECOGNITION!
YOU KNOW...
...IT'S SAD TO THINK THAT MOST PEOPLE DON'T HAVE BIG DREAMS TO WORK TOWARD.
Colorado Pizza
HOW DO THEY HAVE THE MOTIVATION TO GET UP IN THE MORNING?

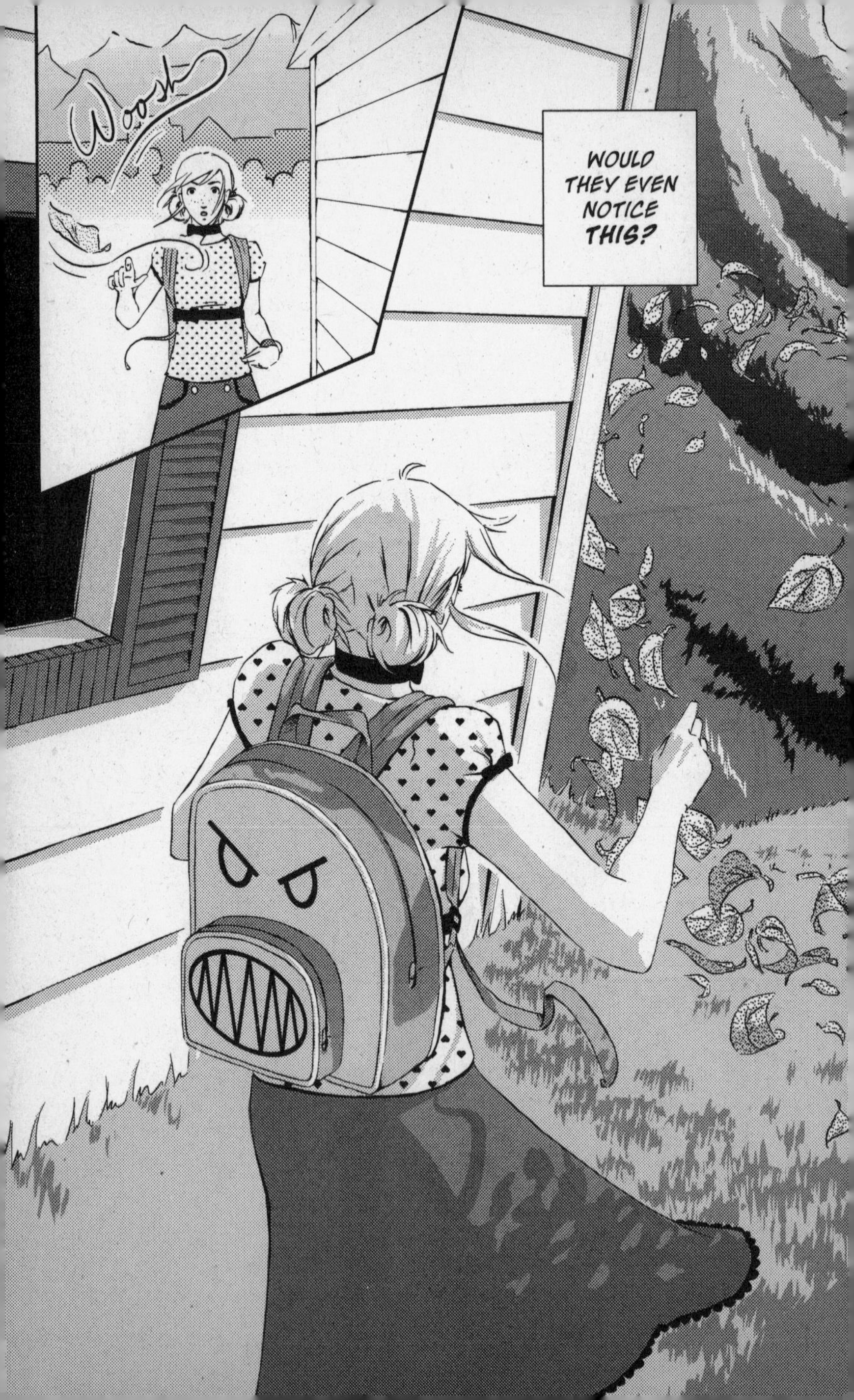
Woosh
WOULD THEY EVEN NOTICE THIS?

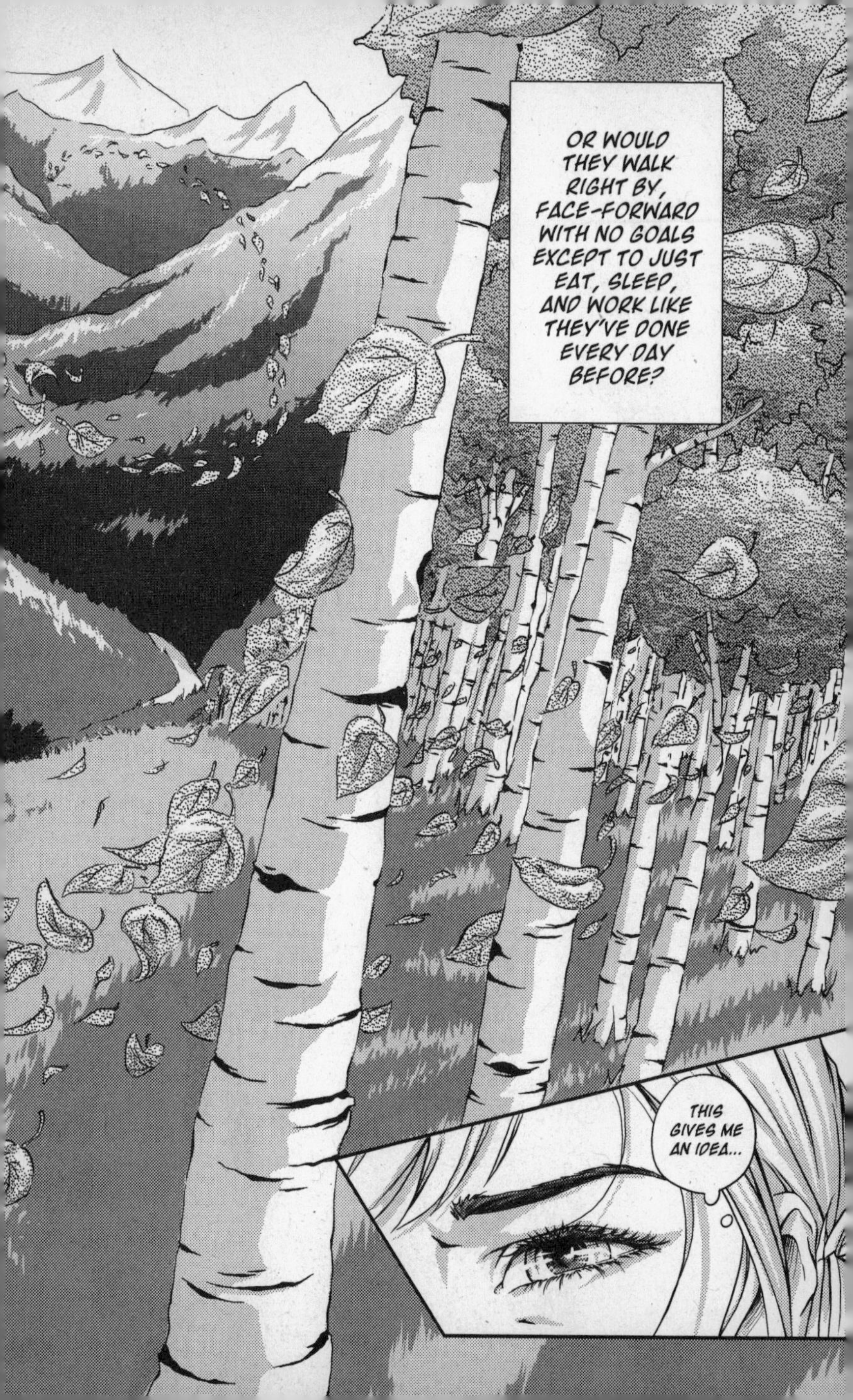
OR WOULD THEY WALK RIGHT BY, FACE-FORWARD WITH NO GOALS EXCEPT TO JUST EAT, SLEEP, AND WORK LIKE THEY'VE DONE EVERY DAY BEFORE?
THIS GIVES ME AN IDEA...

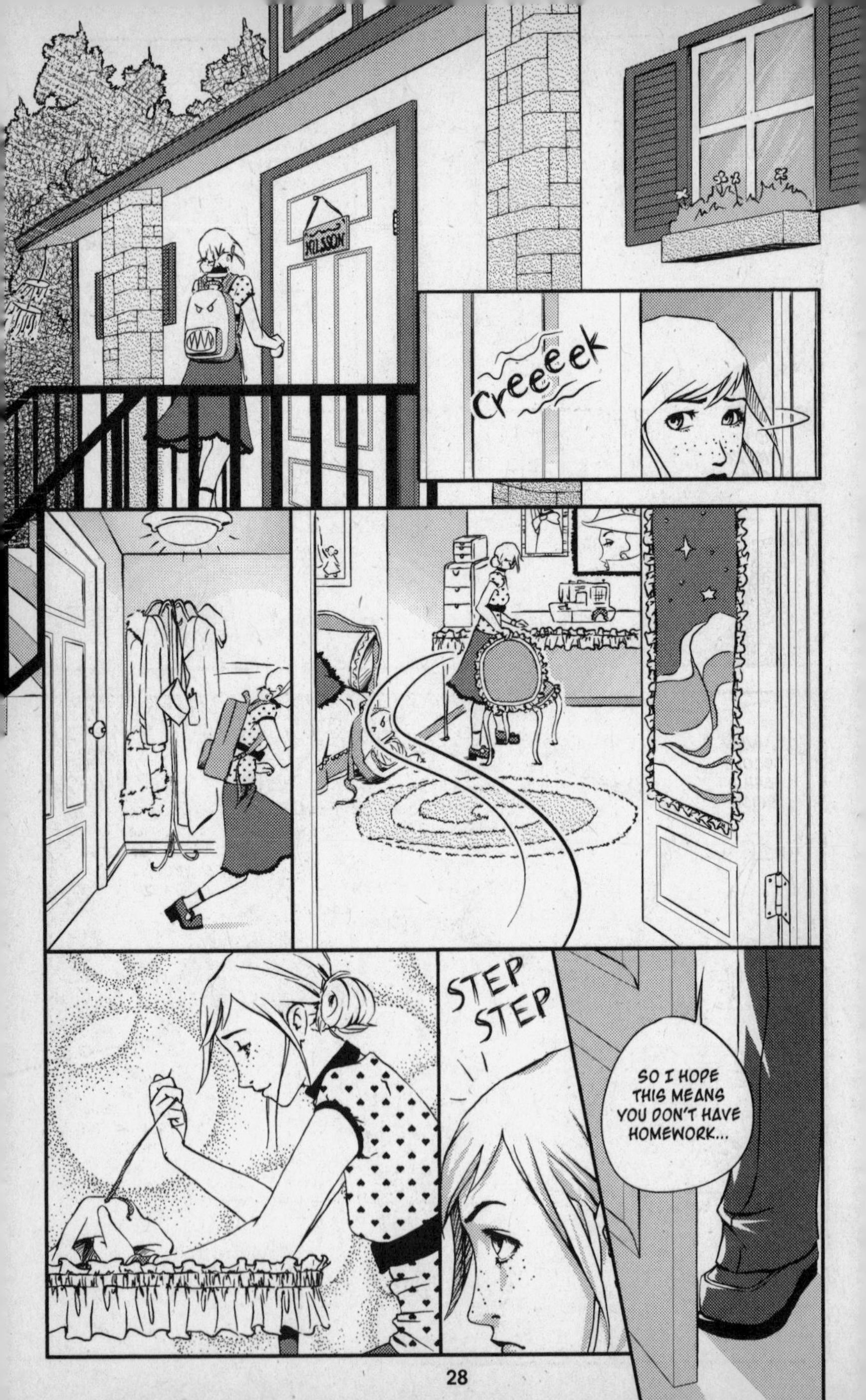
NILSSON
creeeek
STEP STEP
SO I HOPE THIS MEANS YOU DON'T HAVE HOMEWORK...

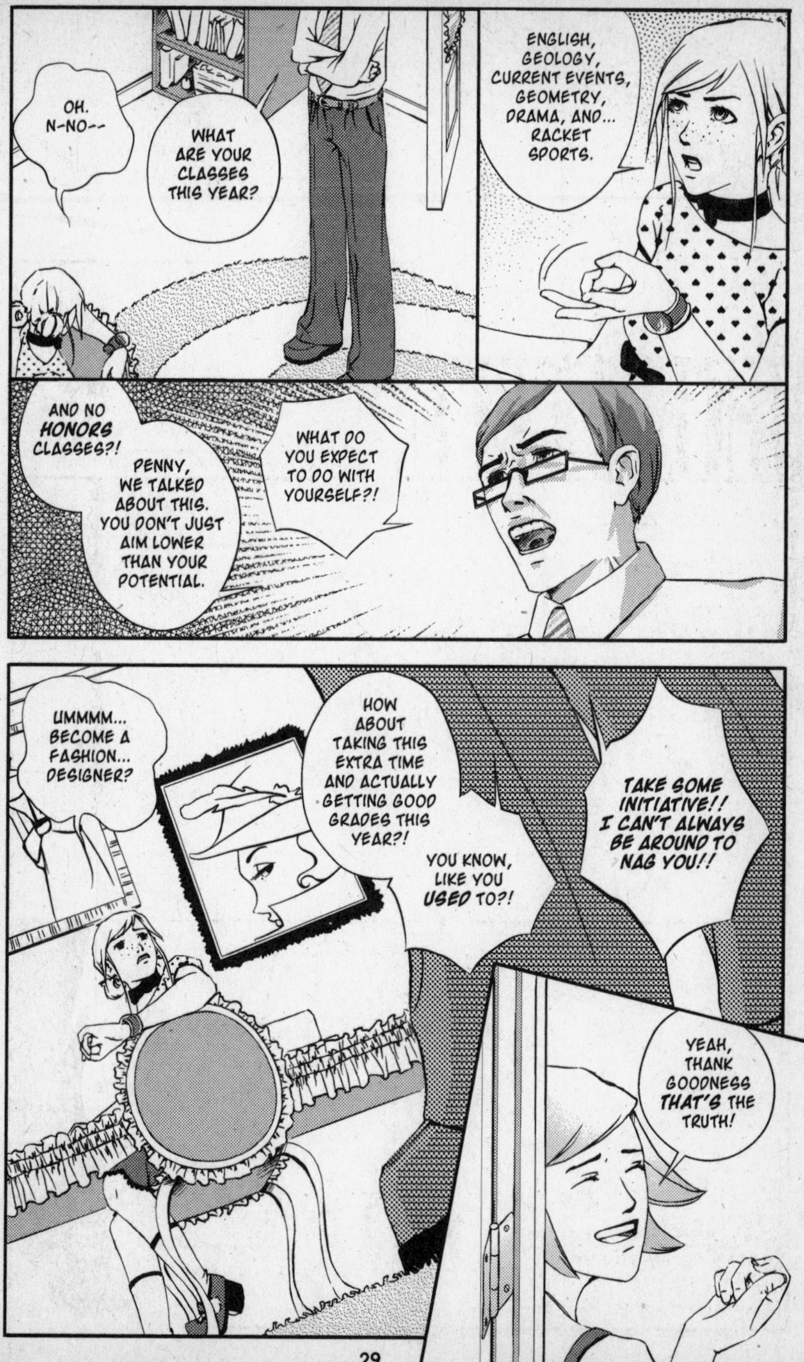
OH. N-NO--
WHAT ARE YOUR CLASSES THIS YEAR?
ENGLISH, GEOLOGY, CURRENT EVENTS, GEOMETRY, DRAMA, AND... RACKET SPORTS.
AND NO **HONORS** CLASSES?!
PENNY, WE TALKED ABOUT THIS. YOU DON'T JUST AIM LOWER THAN YOUR POTENTIAL.
WHAT DO YOU EXPECT TO DO WITH YOURSELF?!
UMMMM... BECOME A FASHION... DESIGNER?
HOW ABOUT TAKING THIS EXTRA TIME AND ACTUALLY GETTING GOOD GRADES THIS YEAR?!
YOU KNOW, LIKE YOU **USED** TO?!
TAKE SOME INITIATIVE!! I CAN'T ALWAYS BE AROUND TO NAG YOU!!
YEAH, THANK GOODNESS **THAT'S** THE TRUTH!

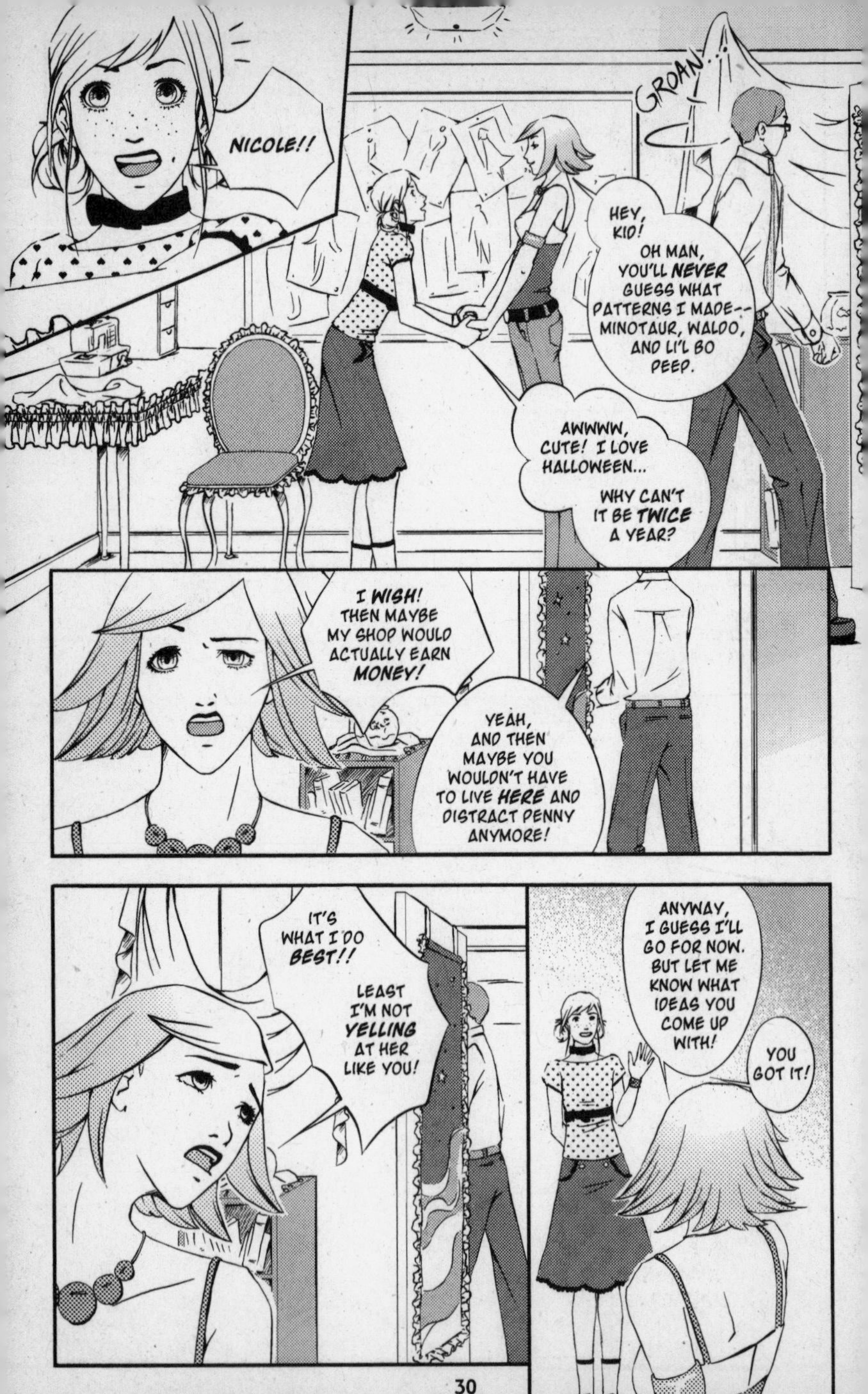
NICOLE!!
GROAN...
HEY, KID!
OH MAN, YOU'LL NEVER GUESS WHAT PATTERNS I MADE--MINOTAUR, WALDO, AND LI'L BO PEEP.
AWWWW, CUTE! I LOVE HALLOWEEN...
WHY CAN'T IT BE TWICE A YEAR?
I WISH! THEN MAYBE MY SHOP WOULD ACTUALLY EARN MONEY!
YEAH, AND THEN MAYBE YOU WOULDN'T HAVE TO LIVE HERE AND DISTRACT PENNY ANYMORE!
IT'S WHAT I DO BEST!!
LEAST I'M NOT YELLING AT HER LIKE YOU!
ANYWAY, I GUESS I'LL GO FOR NOW. BUT LET ME KNOW WHAT IDEAS YOU COME UP WITH!
YOU GOT IT!

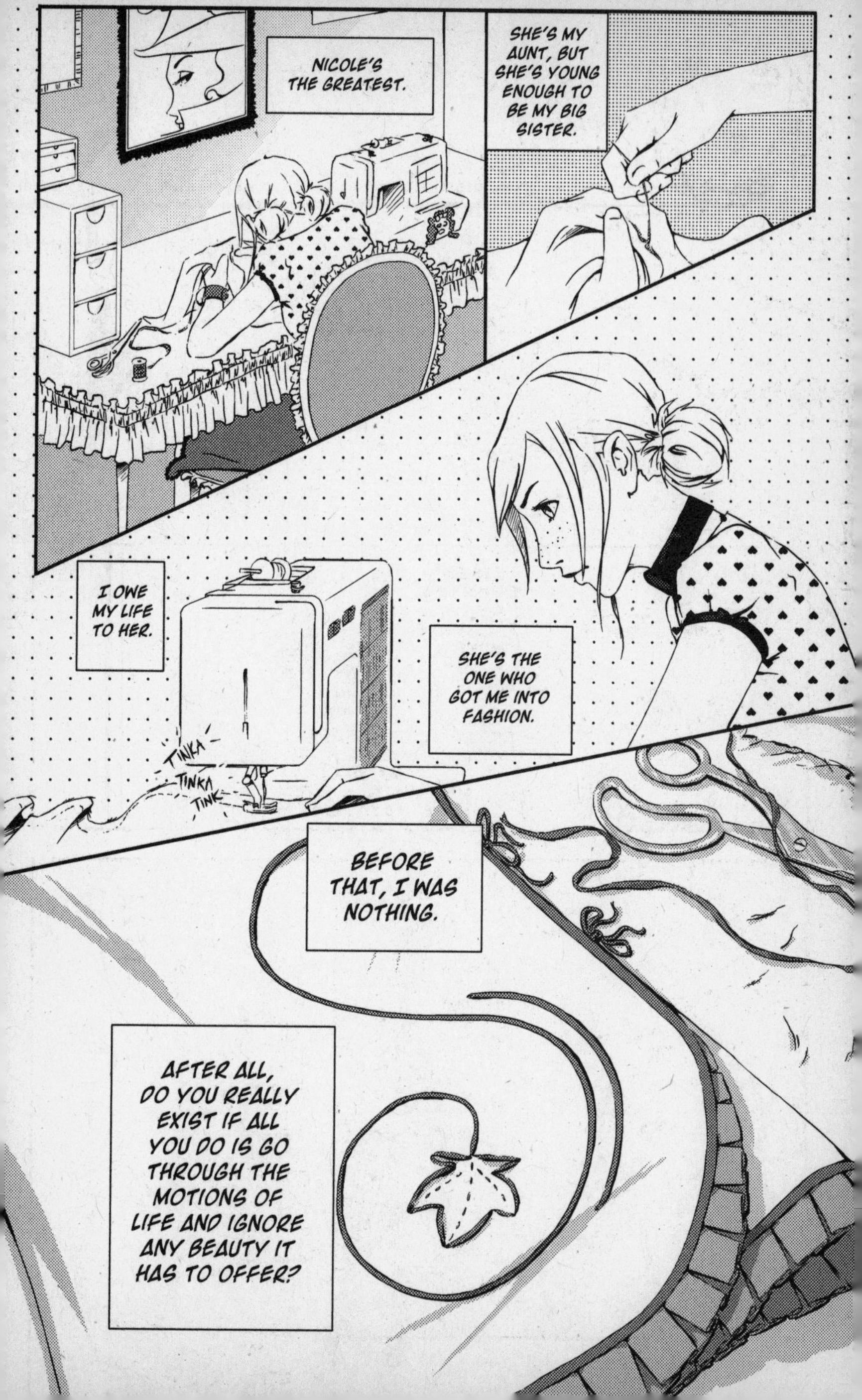
NICOLE'S THE GREATEST.
SHE'S MY AUNT, BUT SHE'S YOUNG ENOUGH TO BE MY BIG SISTER.
I OWE MY LIFE TO HER.
SHE'S THE ONE WHO GOT ME INTO FASHION.
TINKA TINKA TINK
BEFORE THAT, I WAS NOTHING.
AFTER ALL, DO YOU REALLY EXIST IF ALL YOU DO IS GO THROUGH THE MOTIONS OF LIFE AND IGNORE ANY BEAUTY IT HAS TO OFFER?

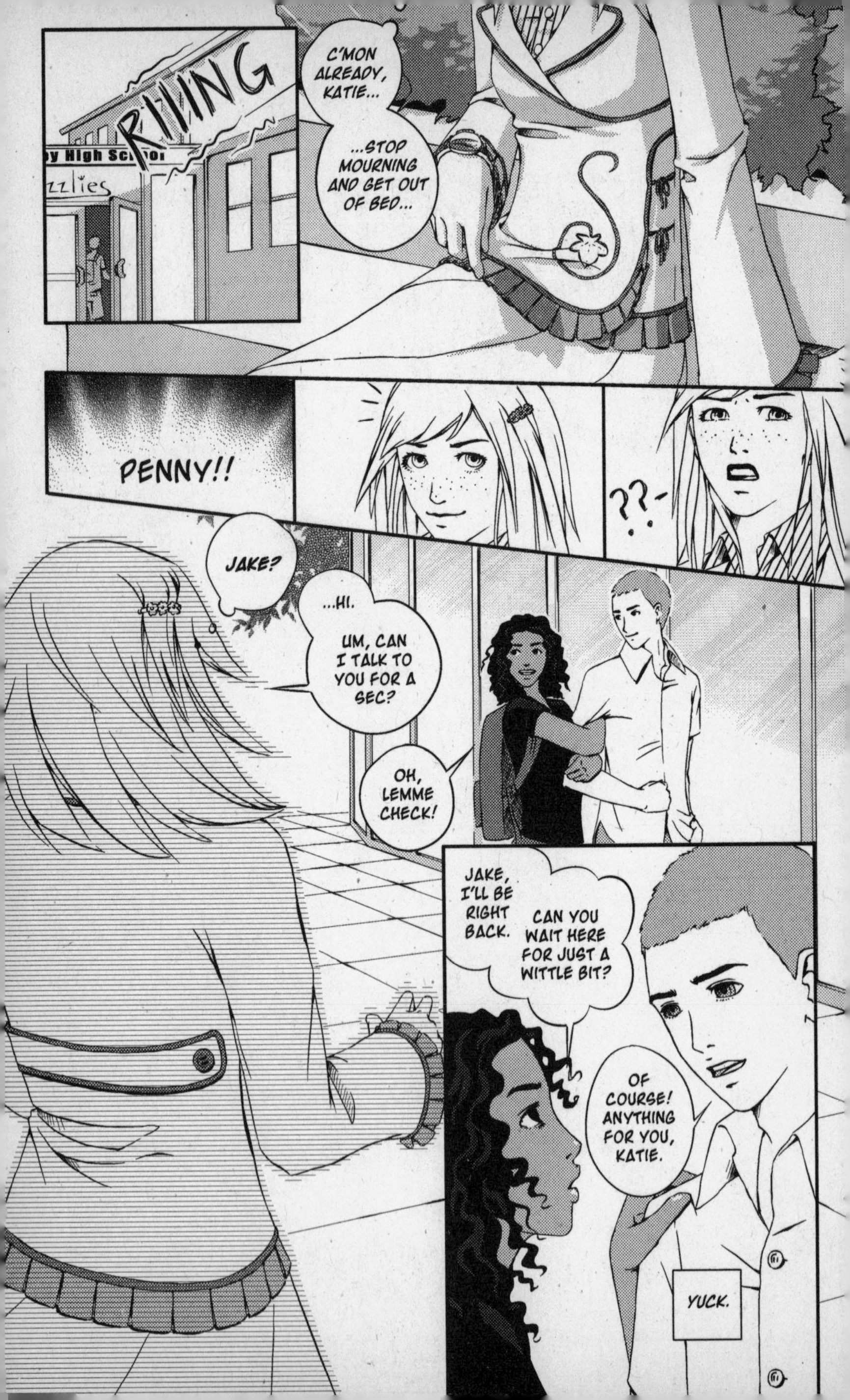
RIIING
C'MON ALREADY, KATIE...
...STOP MOURNING AND GET OUT OF BED...
PENNY!!
??-
JAKE?
...HI.
UM, CAN I TALK TO YOU FOR A SEC?
OH, LEMME CHECK!
JAKE, I'LL BE RIGHT BACK.
CAN YOU WAIT HERE FOR JUST A WITTLE BIT?
OF COURSE! ANYTHING FOR YOU, KATIE.
YUCK.

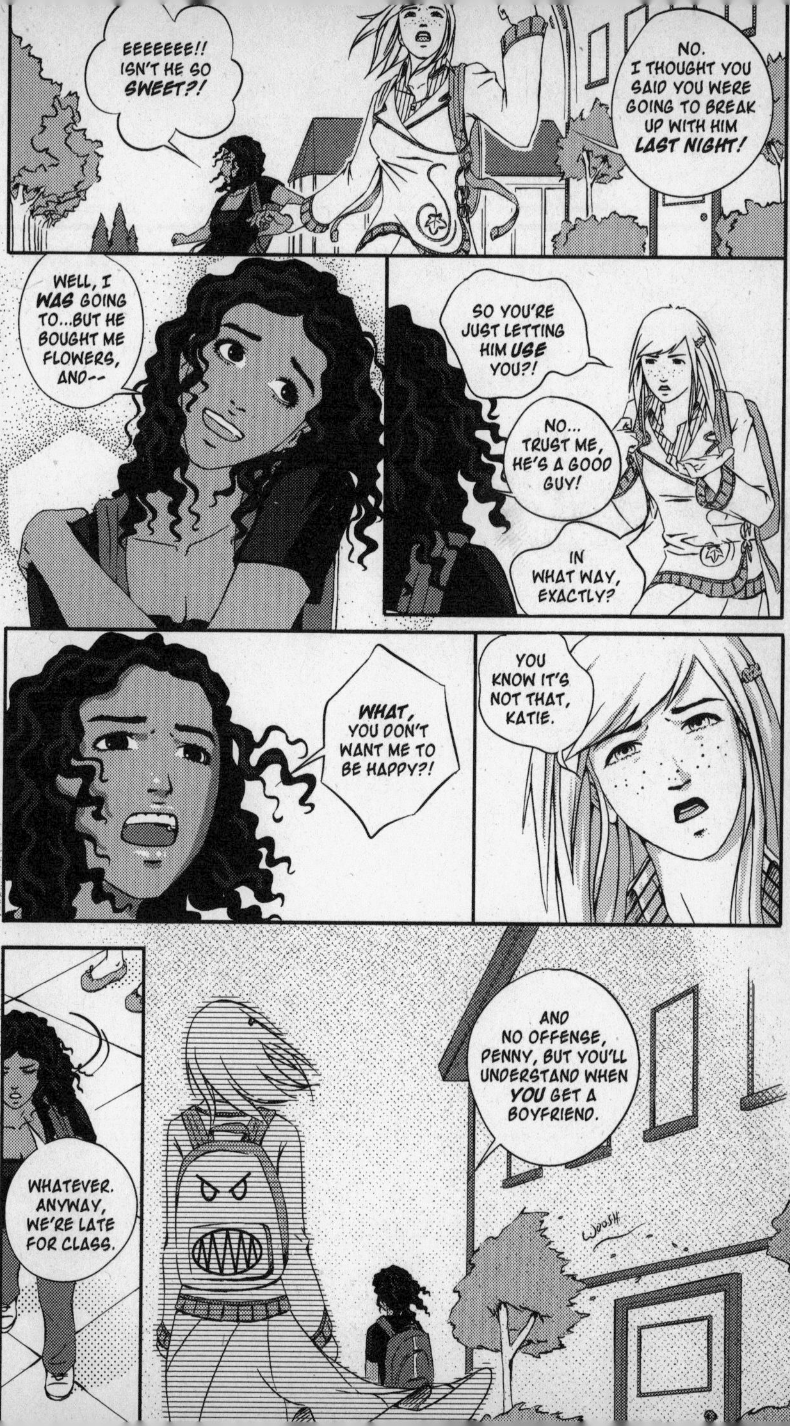
EEEEEEE!! ISN'T HE SO SWEET?!
NO. I THOUGHT YOU SAID YOU WERE GOING TO BREAK UP WITH HIM LAST NIGHT!
WELL, I WAS GOING TO...BUT HE BOUGHT ME FLOWERS, AND--
SO YOU'RE JUST LETTING HIM USE YOU?!
NO... TRUST ME, HE'S A GOOD GUY!
IN WHAT WAY, EXACTLY?
WHAT, YOU DON'T WANT ME TO BE HAPPY?!
YOU KNOW IT'S NOT THAT, KATIE.
WHATEVER. ANYWAY, WE'RE LATE FOR CLASS.
AND NO OFFENSE, PENNY, BUT YOU'LL UNDERSTAND WHEN YOU GET A BOYFRIEND.
WOOSH

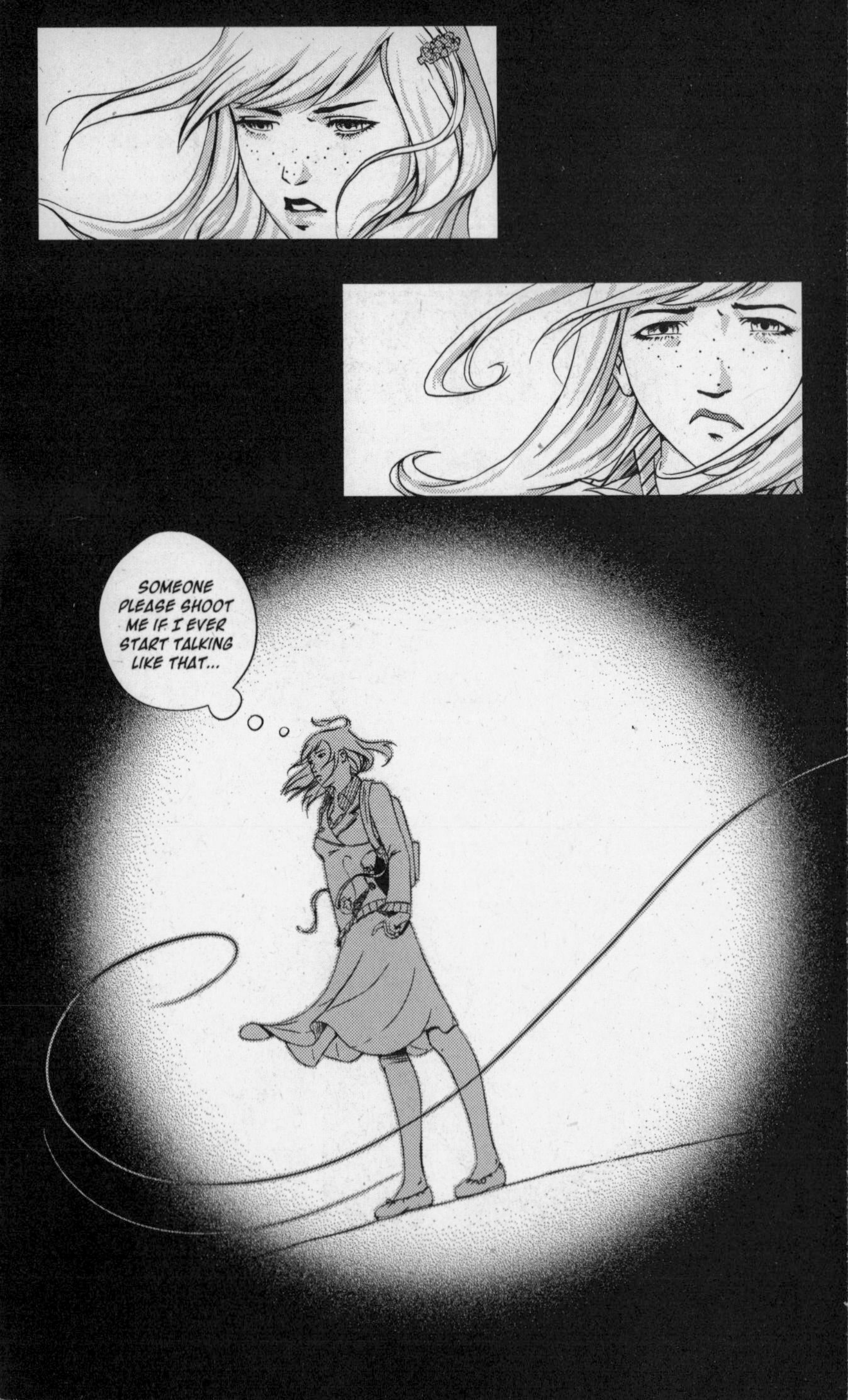
SOMEONE PLEASE SHOOT ME IF I EVER START TALKING LIKE THAT...

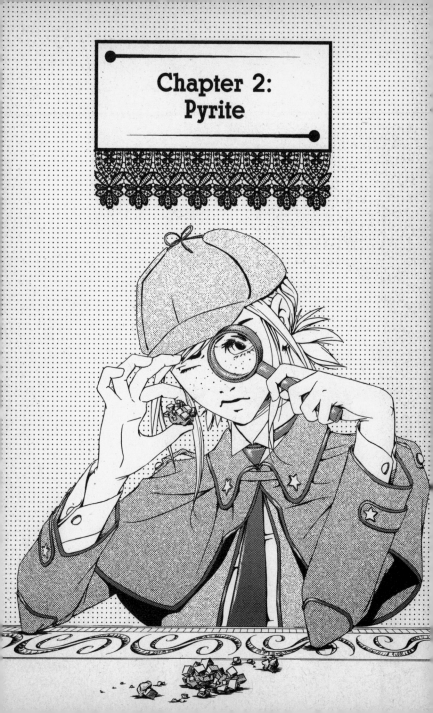

Chapter 2: Pyrite

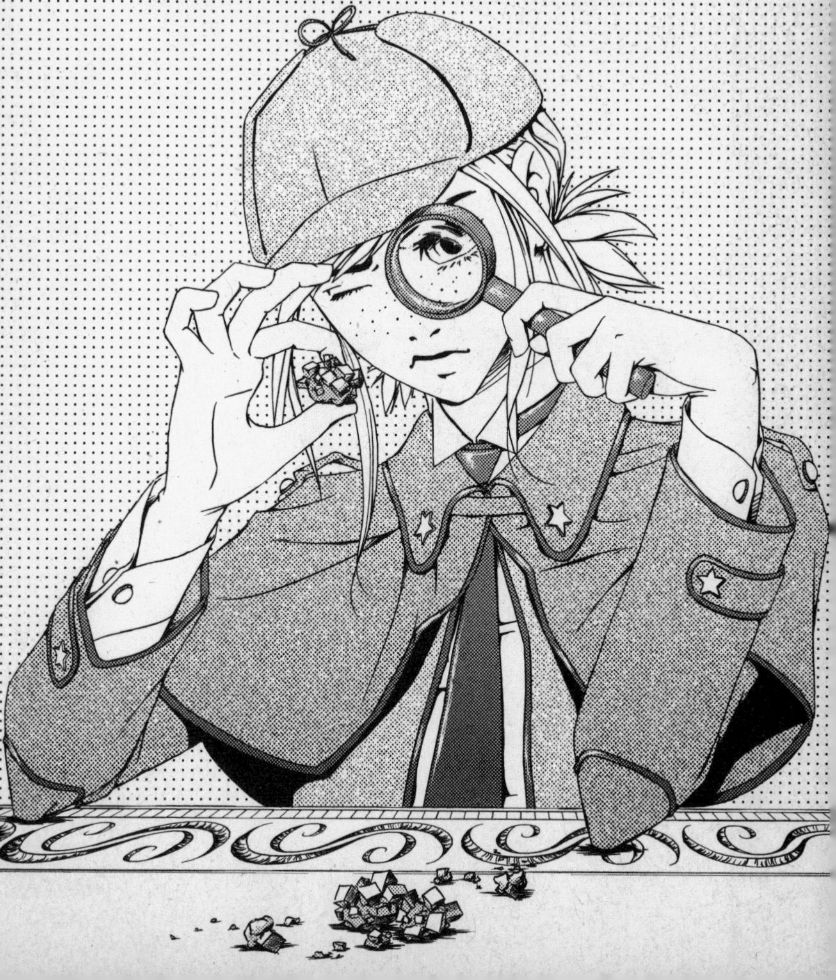

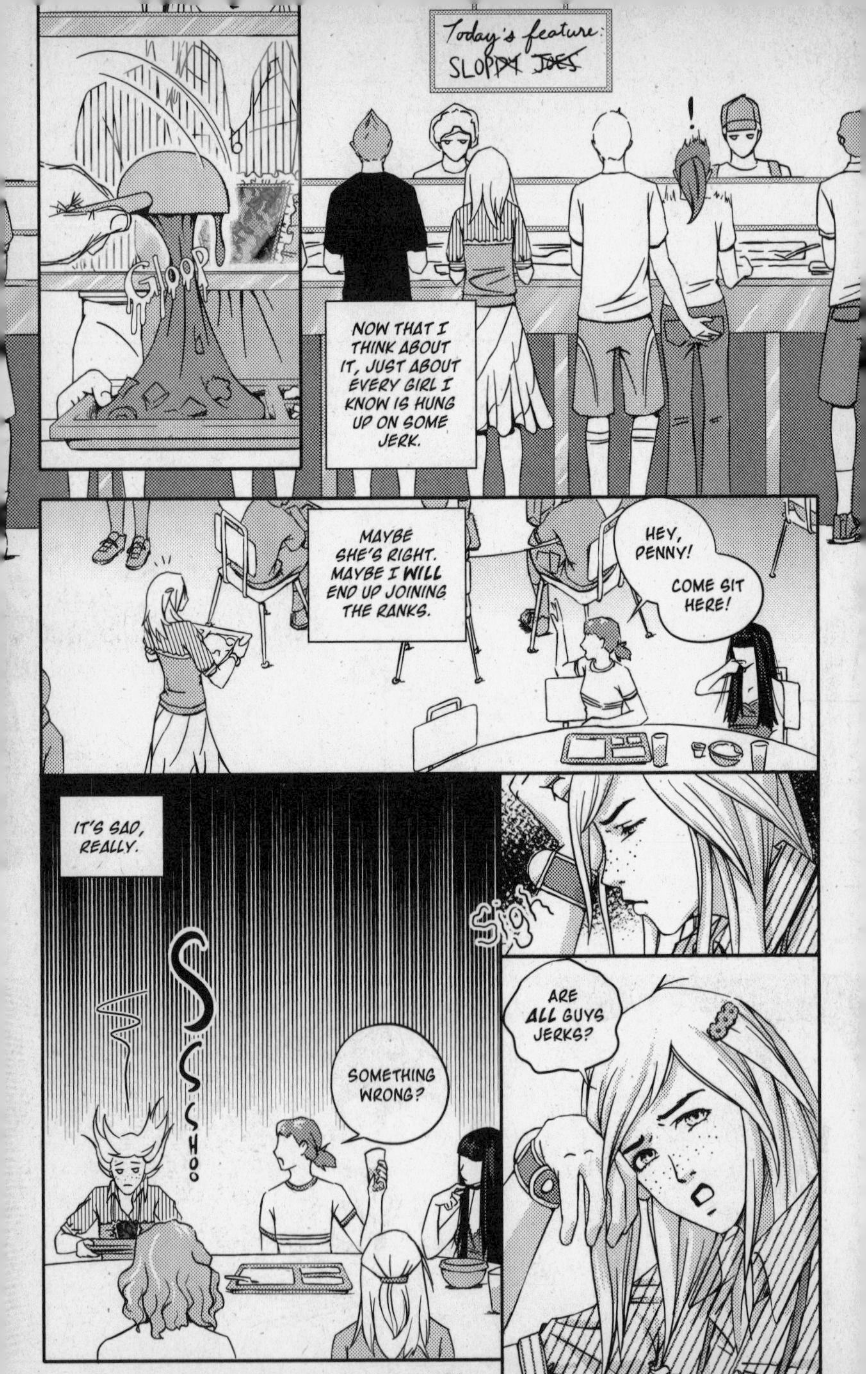
GLOOP
Today's feature:
SLOP~~PY JOES~~
!
NOW THAT I THINK ABOUT IT, JUST ABOUT EVERY GIRL I KNOW IS HUNG UP ON SOME JERK.
MAYBE SHE'S RIGHT. MAYBE I **WILL** END UP JOINING THE RANKS.
HEY, PENNY!
COME SIT HERE!
IT'S SAD, REALLY.
SSHOO
SOMETHING WRONG?
SIGH
ARE **ALL** GUYS JERKS?

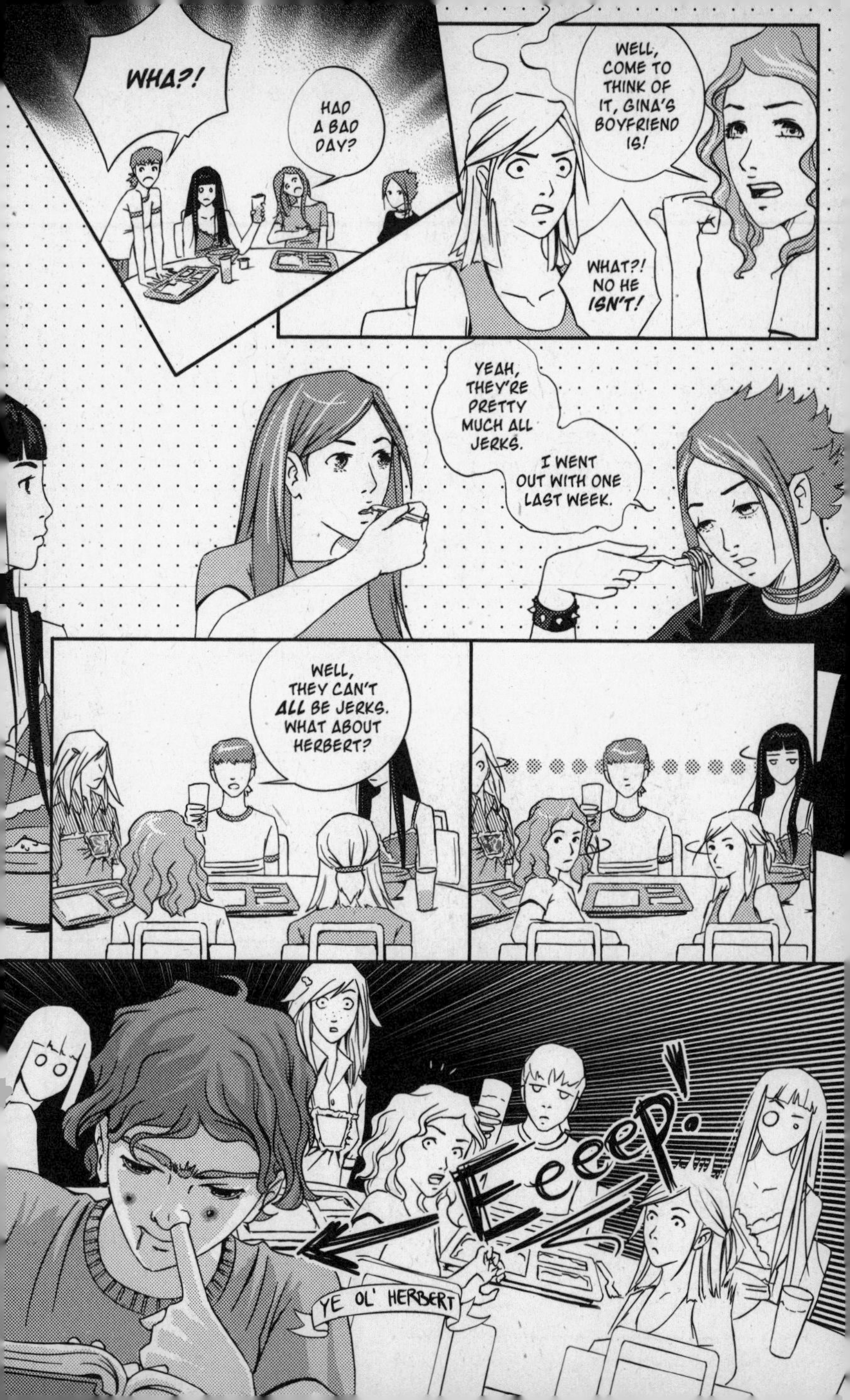
WHA?!
HAD A BAD DAY?
WELL, COME TO THINK OF IT, GINA'S BOYFRIEND IS!
WHAT?! NO HE ISN'T!
YEAH, THEY'RE PRETTY MUCH ALL JERKS.
I WENT OUT WITH ONE LAST WEEK.
WELL, THEY CAN'T ALL BE JERKS. WHAT ABOUT HERBERT?
EEEEP!
YE OL' HERBERT

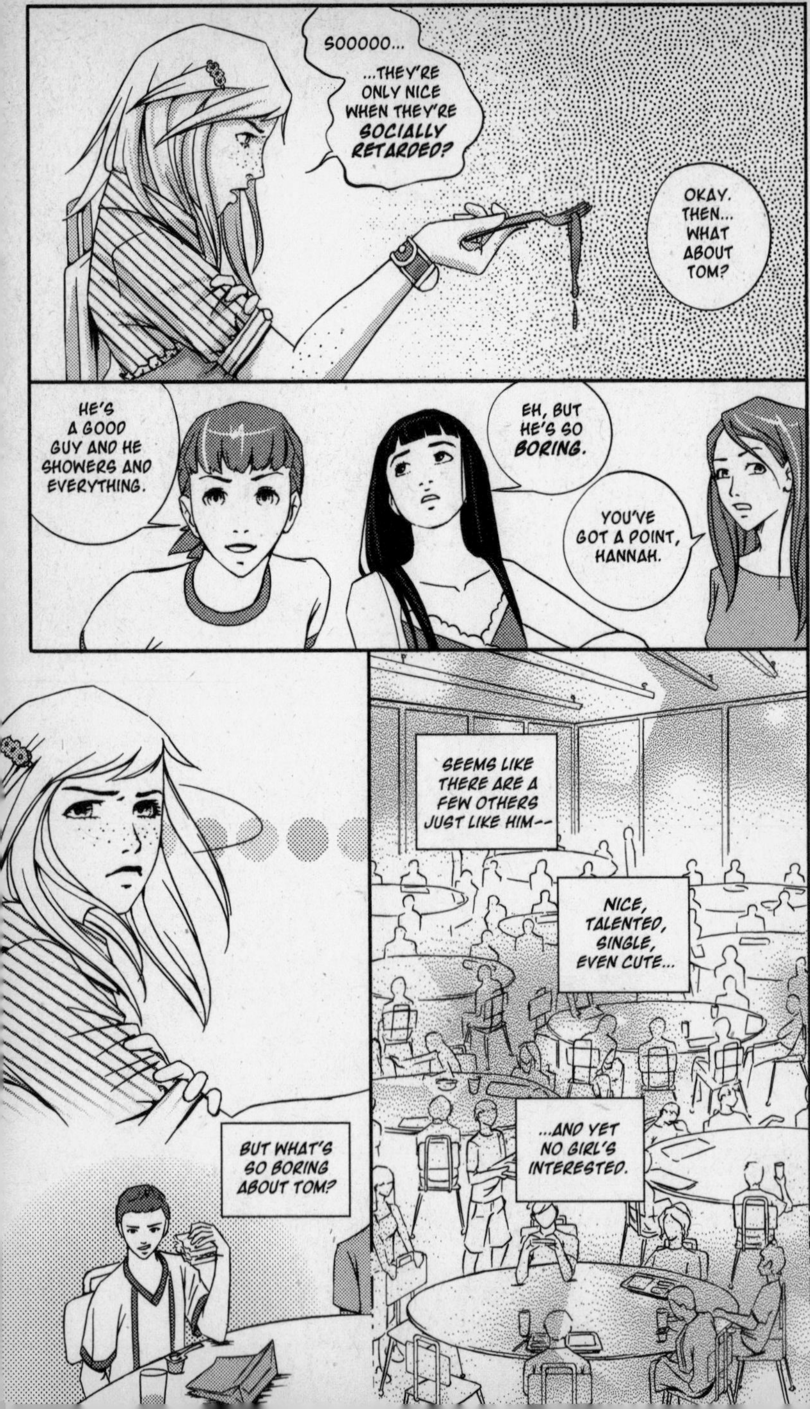
SOOOOO...
...THEY'RE ONLY NICE WHEN THEY'RE SOCIALLY RETARDED?
OKAY. THEN... WHAT ABOUT TOM?
HE'S A GOOD GUY AND HE SHOWERS AND EVERYTHING.
EH, BUT HE'S SO BORING.
YOU'VE GOT A POINT, HANNAH.
BUT WHAT'S SO BORING ABOUT TOM?
SEEMS LIKE THERE ARE A FEW OTHERS JUST LIKE HIM--
NICE, TALENTED, SINGLE, EVEN CUTE...
...AND YET NO GIRL'S INTERESTED.

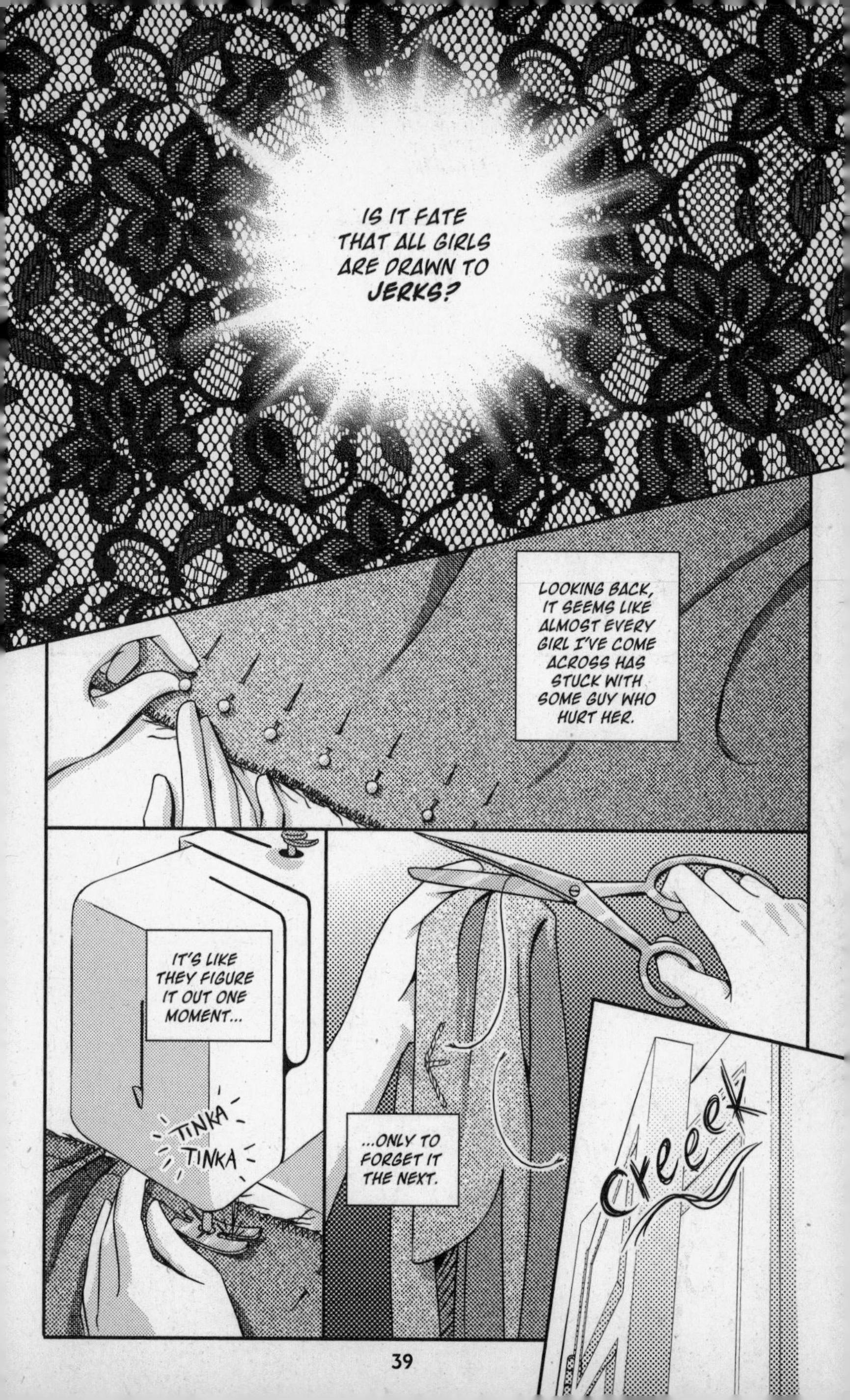
IS IT FATE THAT ALL GIRLS ARE DRAWN TO JERKS?
LOOKING BACK, IT SEEMS LIKE ALMOST EVERY GIRL I'VE COME ACROSS HAS STUCK WITH SOME GUY WHO HURT HER.
IT'S LIKE THEY FIGURE IT OUT ONE MOMENT...
TINKA TINKA
...ONLY TO FORGET IT THE NEXT.
creeek

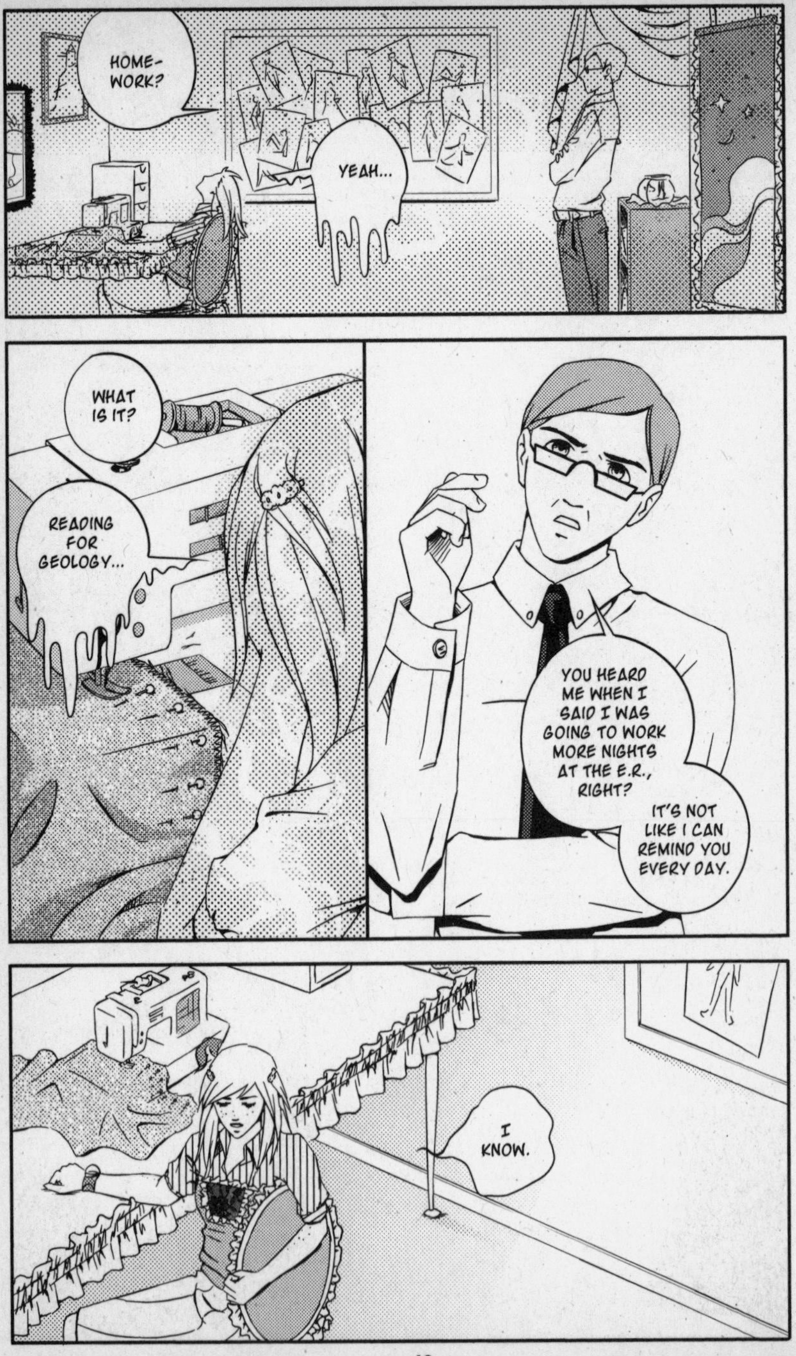
HOME-WORK?
YEAH...
WHAT IS IT?
READING FOR GEOLOGY...
YOU HEARD ME WHEN I SAID I WAS GOING TO WORK MORE NIGHTS AT THE E.R., RIGHT?
IT'S NOT LIKE I CAN REMIND YOU EVERY DAY.
I KNOW.

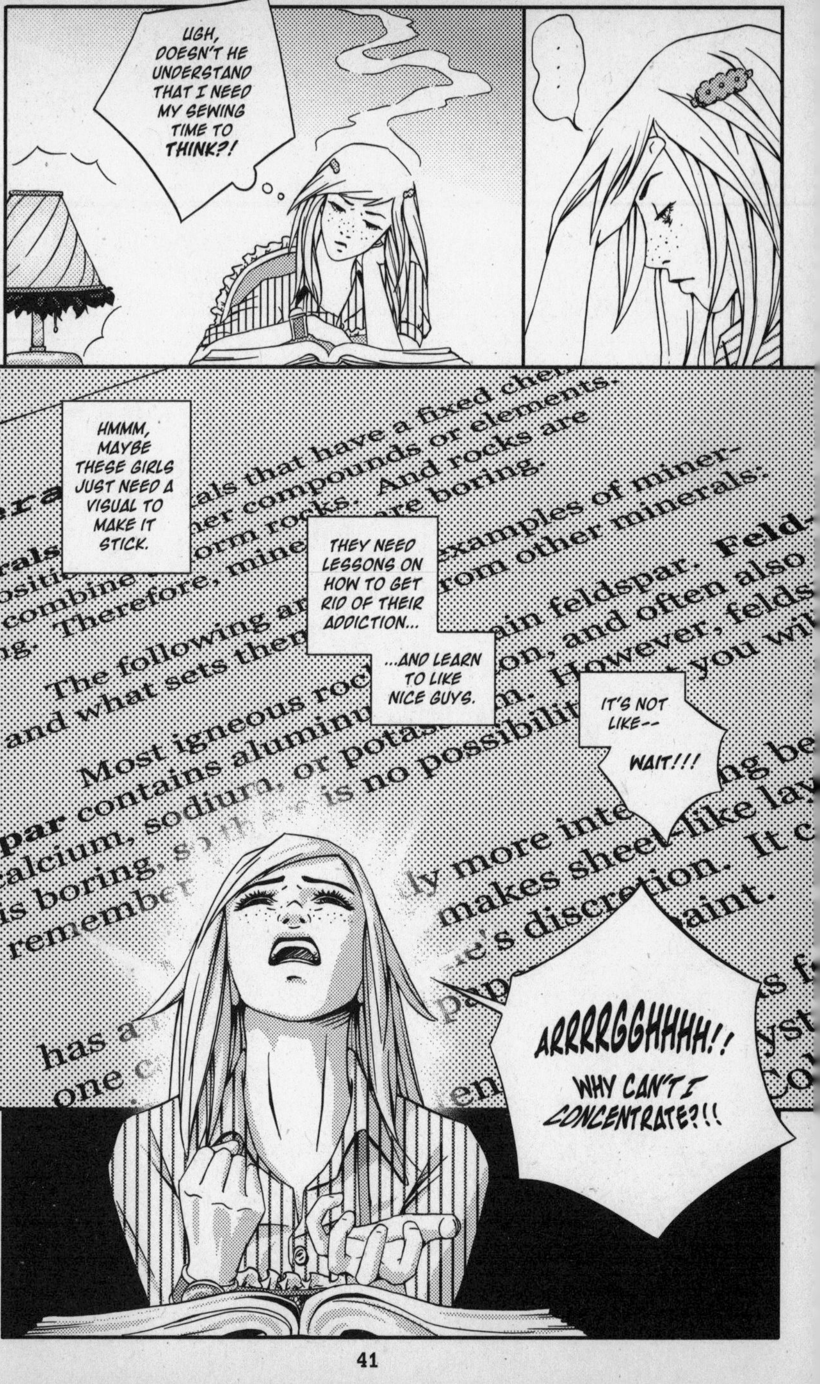
UGH, DOESN'T HE UNDERSTAND THAT I NEED MY SEWING TIME TO THINK?!
...
HMMM, MAYBE THESE GIRLS JUST NEED A VISUAL TO MAKE IT STICK.
THEY NEED LESSONS ON HOW TO GET RID OF THEIR ADDICTION...
...AND LEARN TO LIKE NICE GUYS.
IT'S NOT LIKE--
WAIT!!!
ARRRRGGHHHH!!
WHY CAN'T I CONCENTRATE?!!

ANYWAY, I'VE GOTTA DO **SOMETHING** TO STOP THIS.

n feldspar. **Feld-**

Mica is ... teresting because it ... et-like layers that has a nice name and makes ... one can pee ... ff at one's discretion. It can be used for insulatio ... paper, and paint.

WHAT'S SO EXCITING ABOUT A JERK, ANYWAY?

Pyrite, often referred to as fool's gold, ha a gold-like appearance, large crystals, and is ofte mistaken as gold. During the Colorado Gold Ru many miners believed they had discovered nounds of gold, only to learn that it was in act ty pyrite. Despite th ... mineral's appearance, i irtually worthless.

WHY DOES SOMETHING SO **WORTHLESS** SEEM SO **ATTRACTIVE?**

... ue can strike the ... and cre

Pyrite ... old-like appearance ... staken as gold. During the ... ny miners believed they had dis ... unds of gold, only to learn that it was i ... pyrite. Despite the mineral's appearance, it ... Only ... ally worthless. ... mai

THAT'S IT!

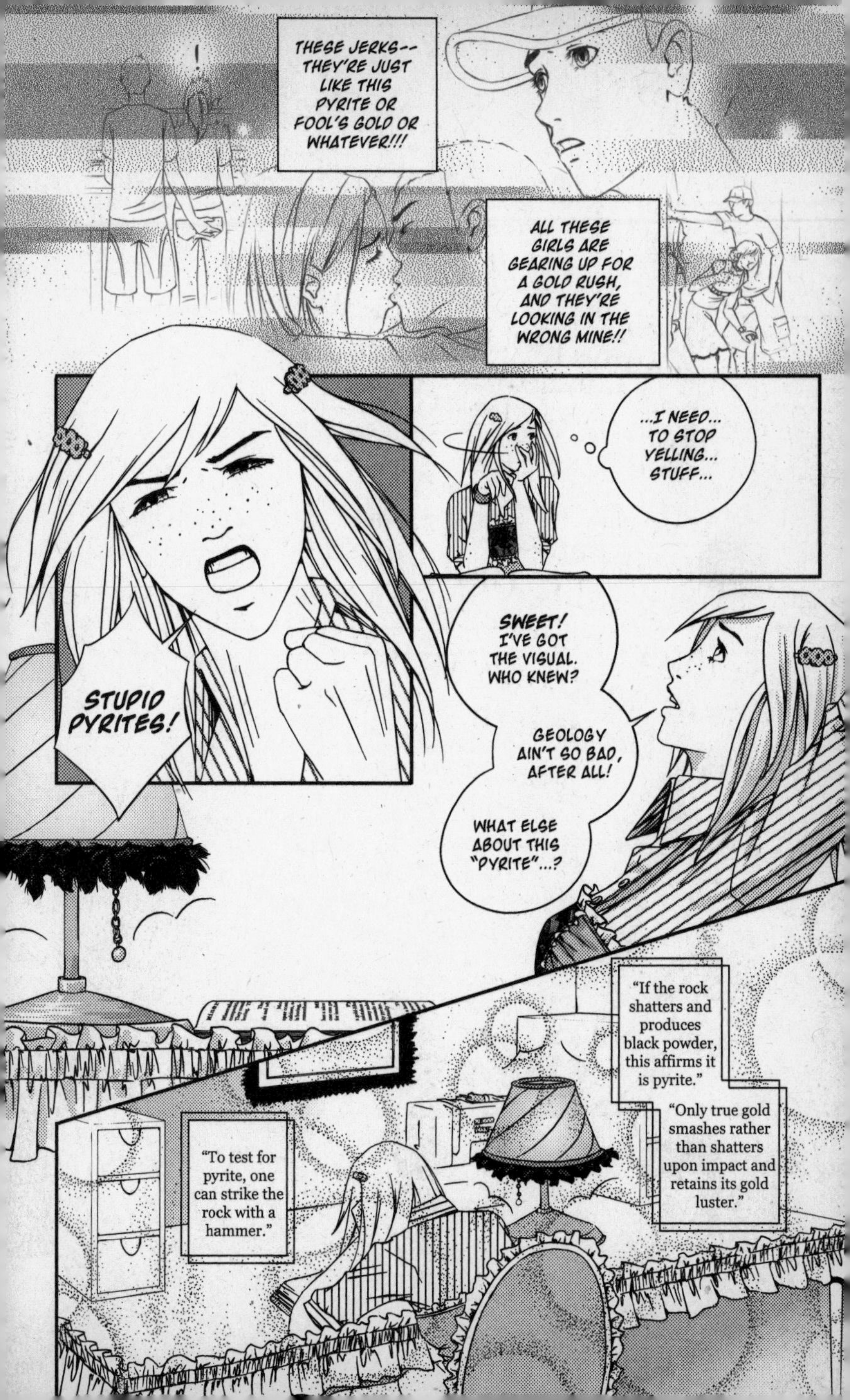

THESE JERKS--THEY'RE JUST LIKE THIS PYRITE OR FOOL'S GOLD OR WHATEVER!!!
ALL THESE GIRLS ARE GEARING UP FOR A GOLD RUSH, AND THEY'RE LOOKING IN THE WRONG MINE!!
STUPID PYRITES!
...I NEED... TO STOP YELLING... STUFF...
SWEET! I'VE GOT THE VISUAL. WHO KNEW?
GEOLOGY AIN'T SO BAD, AFTER ALL!
WHAT ELSE ABOUT THIS "PYRITE"...?
"To test for pyrite, one can strike the rock with a hammer."
"If the rock shatters and produces black powder, this affirms it is pyrite."
"Only true gold smashes rather than shatters upon impact and retains its gold luster."

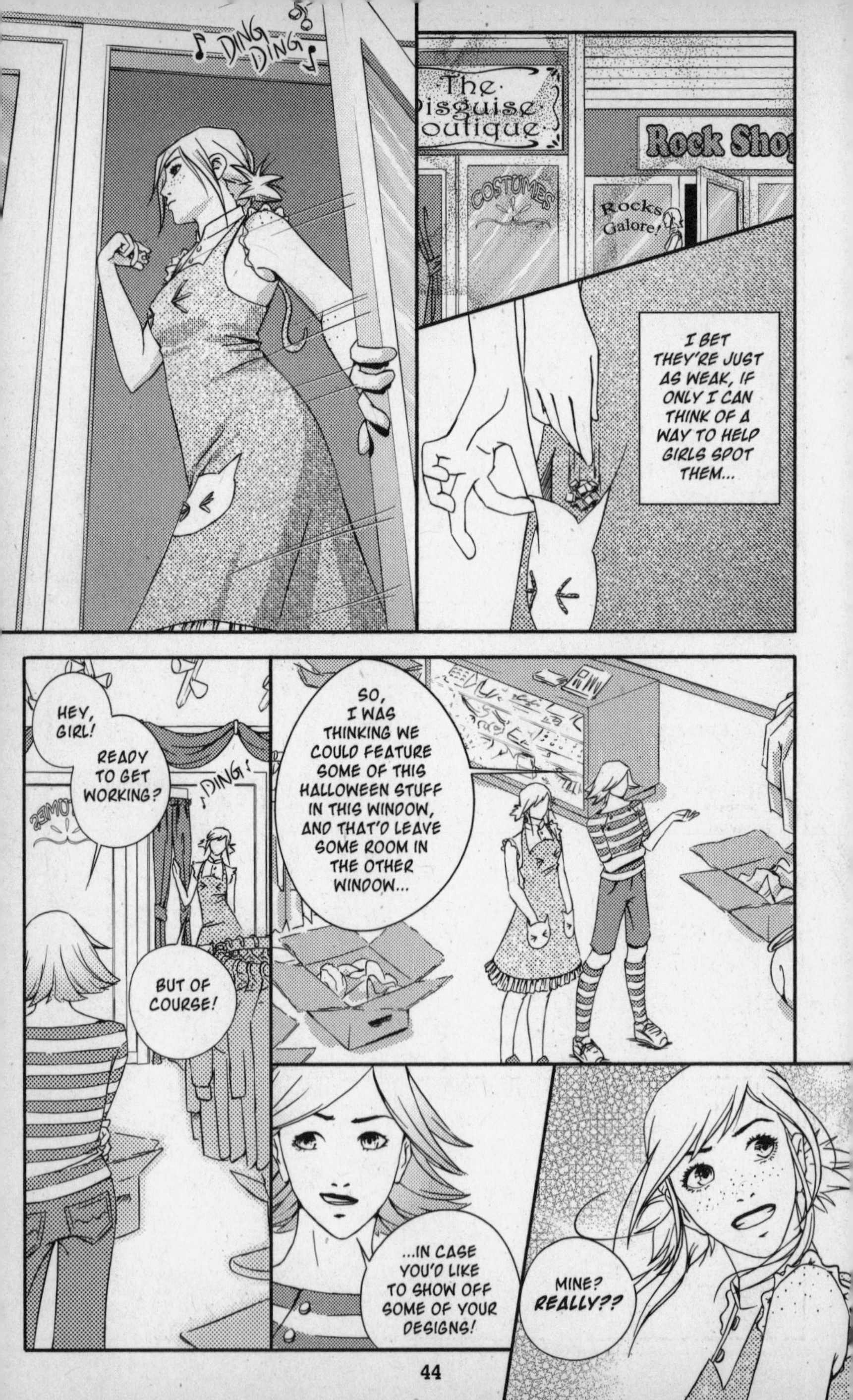
DING DING
The Disguise Boutique
Rock Shop
COSTUMES
Rocks Galore!
I BET THEY'RE JUST AS WEAK, IF ONLY I CAN THINK OF A WAY TO HELP GIRLS SPOT THEM...
HEY, GIRL!
READY TO GET WORKING?
DING!
BUT OF COURSE!
SO, I WAS THINKING WE COULD FEATURE SOME OF THIS HALLOWEEN STUFF IN THIS WINDOW, AND THAT'D LEAVE SOME ROOM IN THE OTHER WINDOW...
...IN CASE YOU'D LIKE TO SHOW OFF SOME OF YOUR DESIGNS!
MINE? **REALLY??**

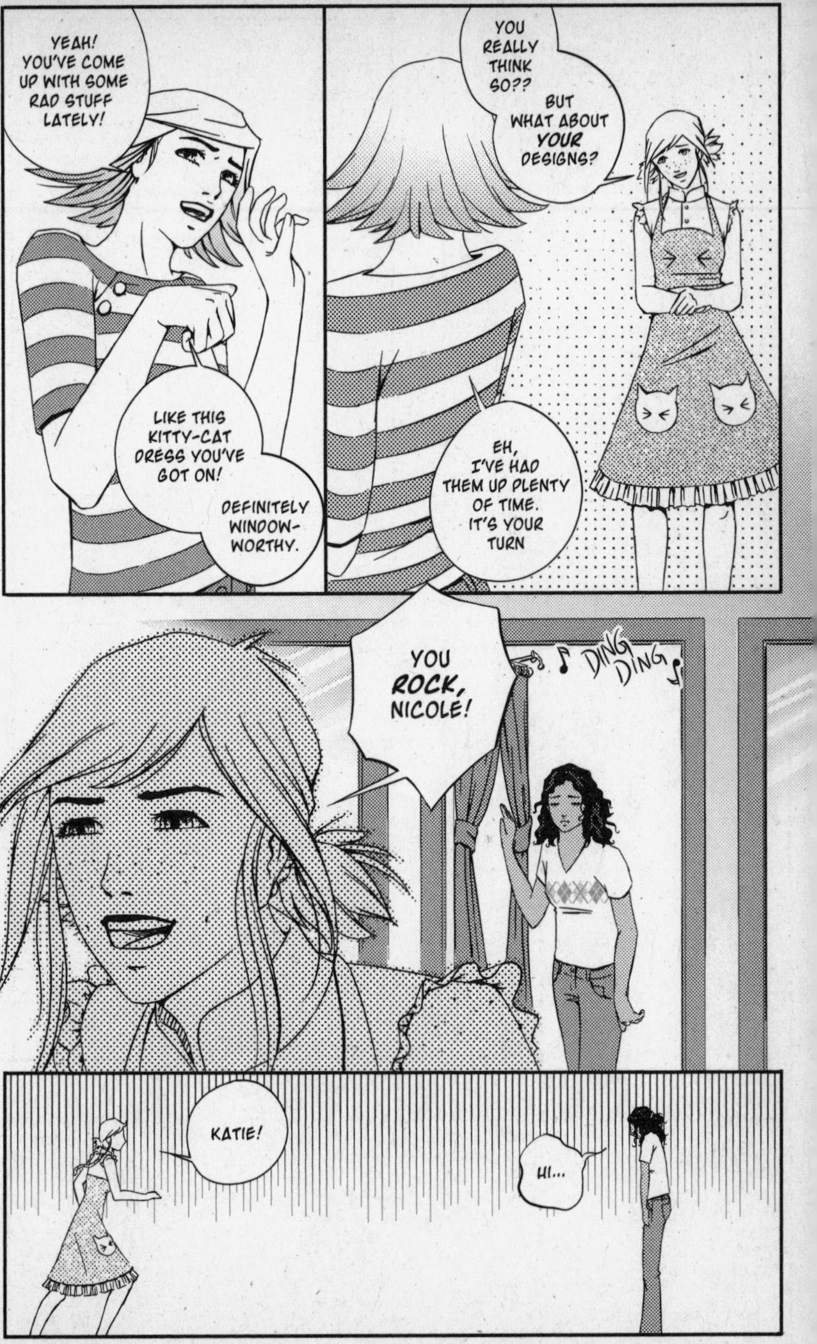
YEAH! YOU'VE COME UP WITH SOME RAD STUFF LATELY!
LIKE THIS KITTY-CAT DRESS YOU'VE GOT ON!
DEFINITELY WINDOW-WORTHY.
YOU REALLY THINK SO??
BUT WHAT ABOUT YOUR DESIGNS?
EH, I'VE HAD THEM UP PLENTY OF TIME. IT'S YOUR TURN
YOU ROCK, NICOLE!
DING DING
KATIE!
HI...

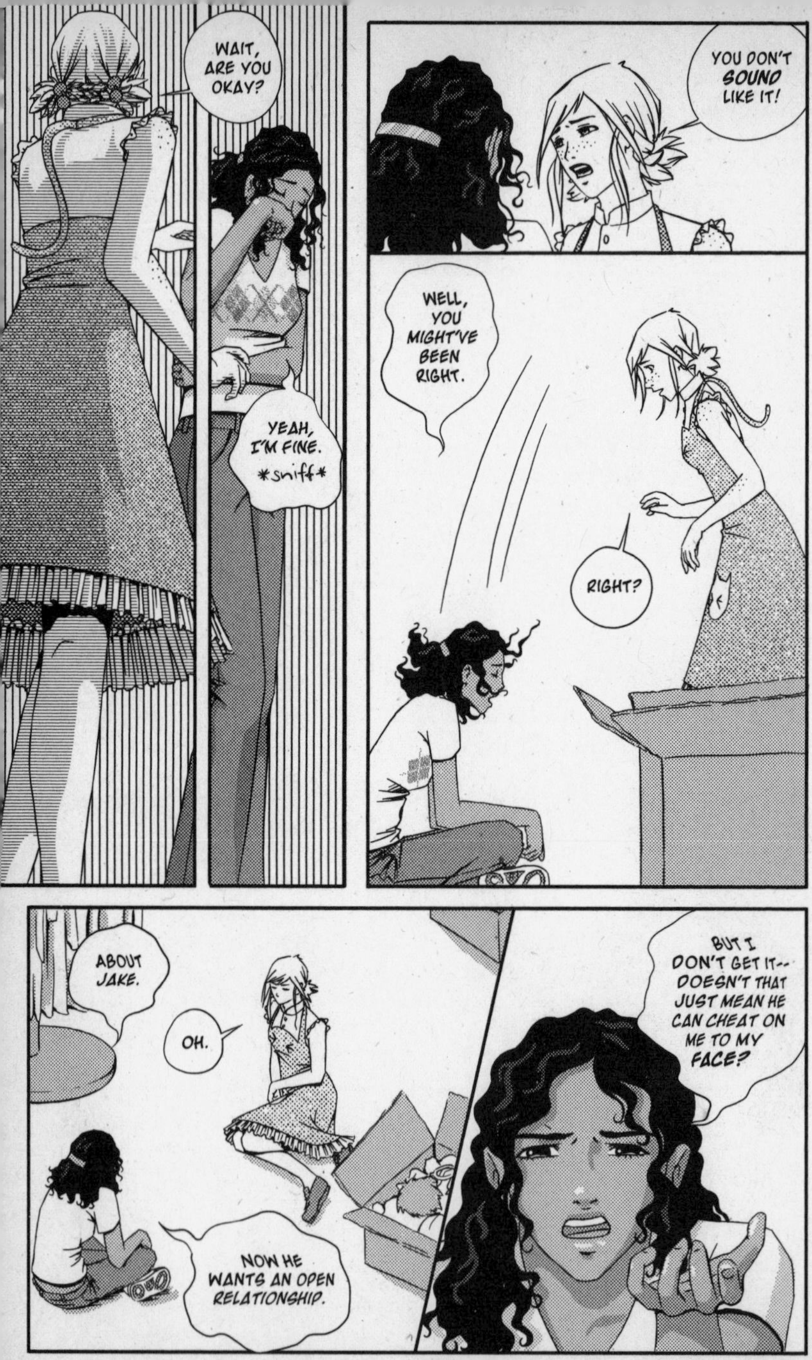
WAIT, ARE YOU OKAY?
YEAH, I'M FINE. *sniff*
YOU DON'T SOUND LIKE IT!
WELL, YOU MIGHT'VE BEEN RIGHT.
RIGHT?
ABOUT JAKE.
OH.
NOW HE WANTS AN OPEN RELATIONSHIP.
BUT I DON'T GET IT-- DOESN'T THAT JUST MEAN HE CAN CHEAT ON ME TO MY FACE?

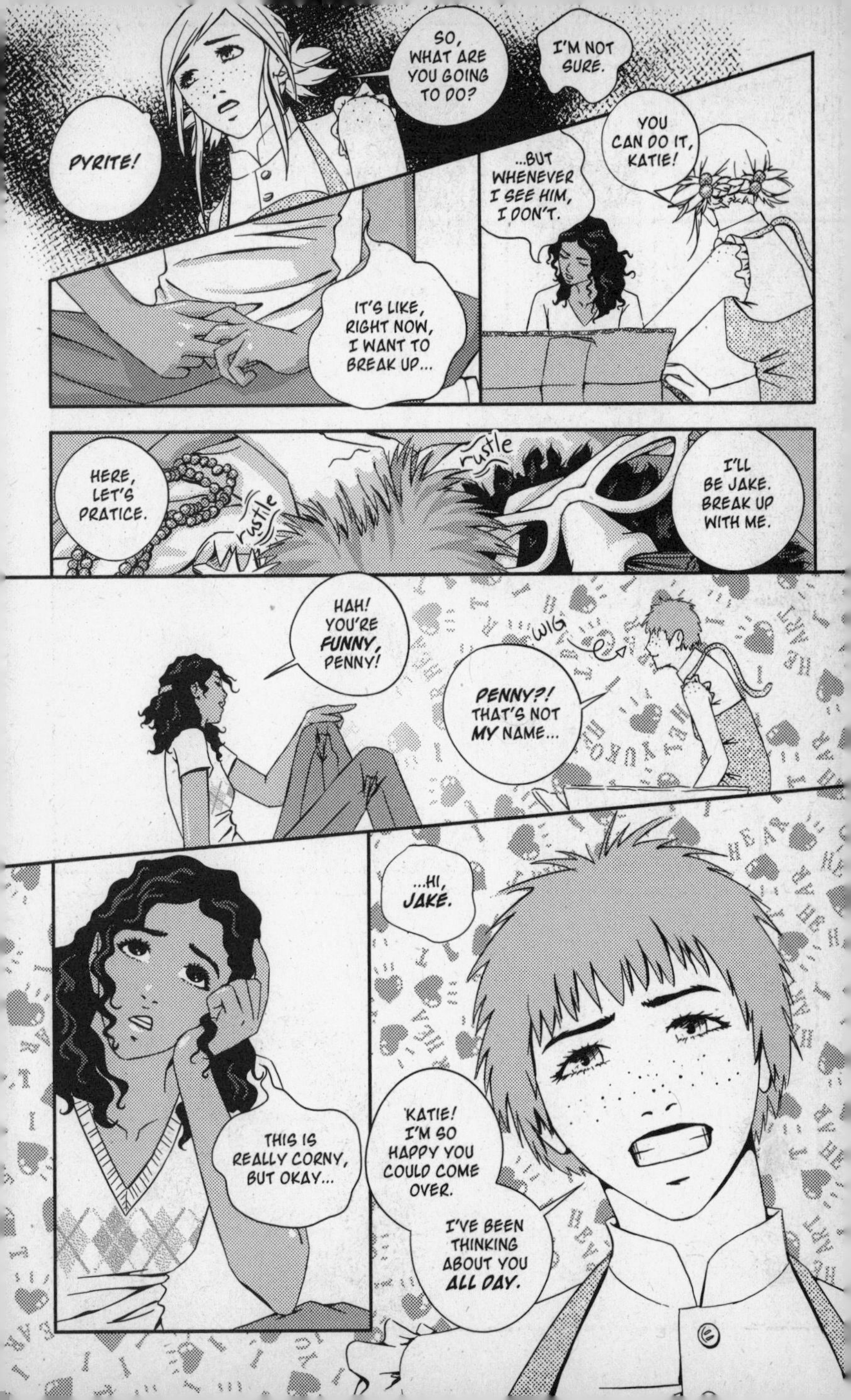
SO, WHAT ARE YOU GOING TO DO?
I'M NOT SURE.
PYRITE!
IT'S LIKE, RIGHT NOW, I WANT TO BREAK UP...
...BUT WHENEVER I SEE HIM, I DON'T.
YOU CAN DO IT, KATIE!
HERE, LET'S PRATICE.
rustle
rustle
I'LL BE JAKE. BREAK UP WITH ME.
HAH! YOU'RE FUNNY, PENNY!
WIG
PENNY?! THAT'S NOT MY NAME...
THIS IS REALLY CORNY, BUT OKAY...
...HI, JAKE.
KATIE! I'M SO HAPPY YOU COULD COME OVER.
I'VE BEEN THINKING ABOUT YOU ALL DAY.

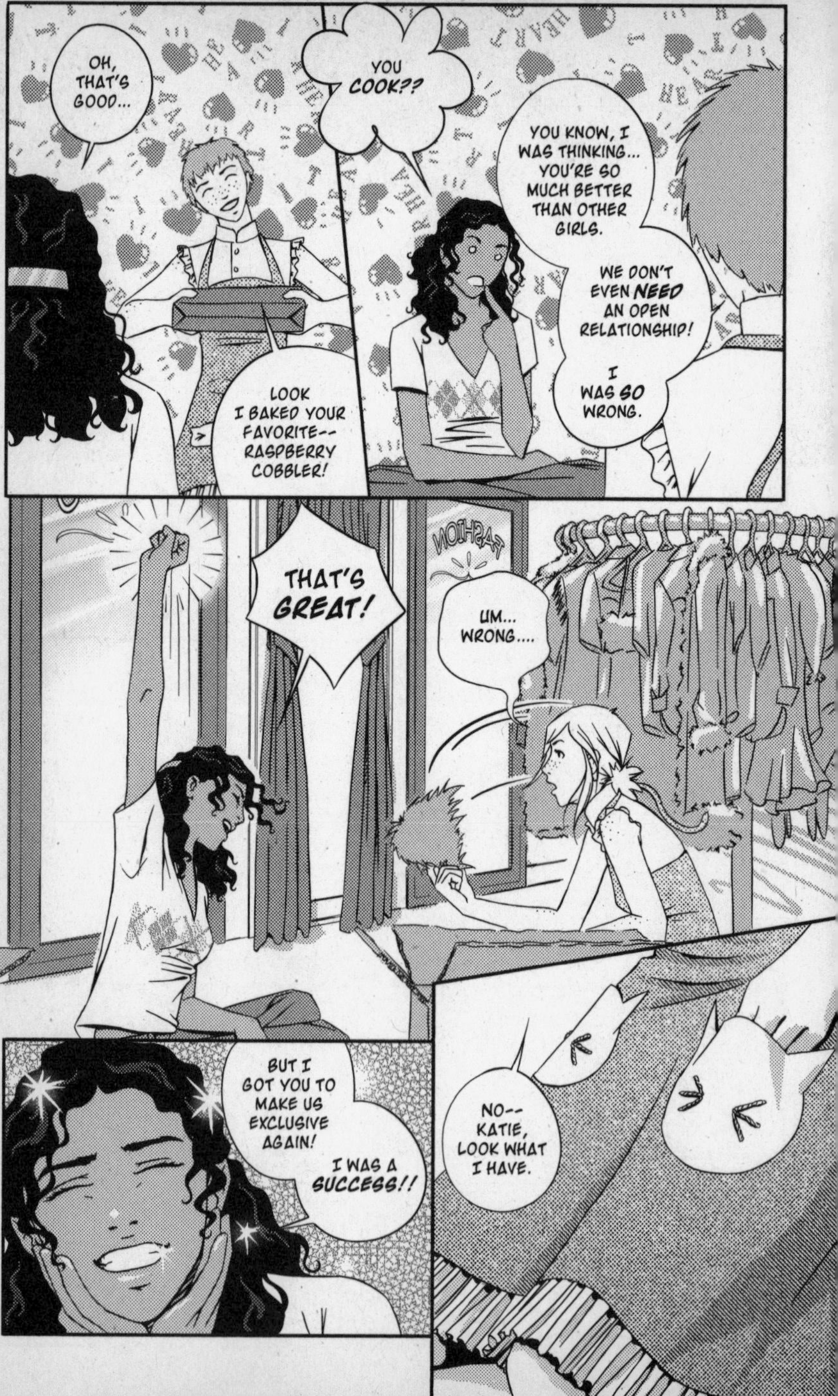
OH, THAT'S GOOD...
LOOK I BAKED YOUR FAVORITE-- RASPBERRY COBBLER!
YOU COOK??
YOU KNOW, I WAS THINKING... YOU'RE SO MUCH BETTER THAN OTHER GIRLS.
WE DON'T EVEN NEED AN OPEN RELATIONSHIP!
I WAS SO WRONG.
THAT'S GREAT!
UM... WRONG....
BUT I GOT YOU TO MAKE US EXCLUSIVE AGAIN!
I WAS A SUCCESS!!
NO-- KATIE, LOOK WHAT I HAVE.

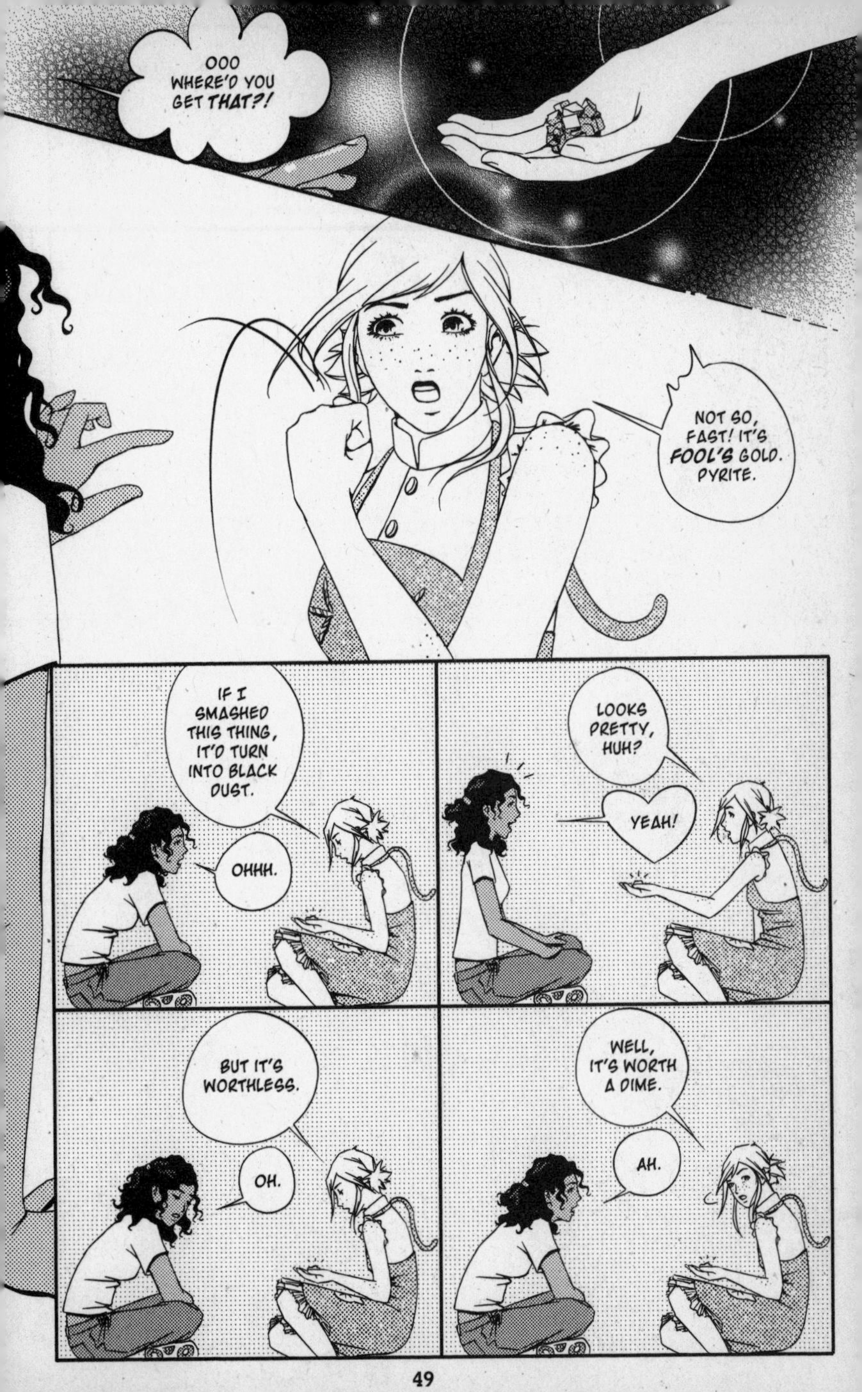
OOO WHERE'D YOU GET ***THAT?!***
NOT SO, FAST! IT'S ***FOOL'S*** GOLD. PYRITE.
IF I SMASHED THIS THING, IT'D TURN INTO BLACK DUST.
OHHH.
LOOKS PRETTY, HUH?
YEAH!
BUT IT'S WORTHLESS.
OH.
WELL, IT'S WORTH A DIME.
AH.

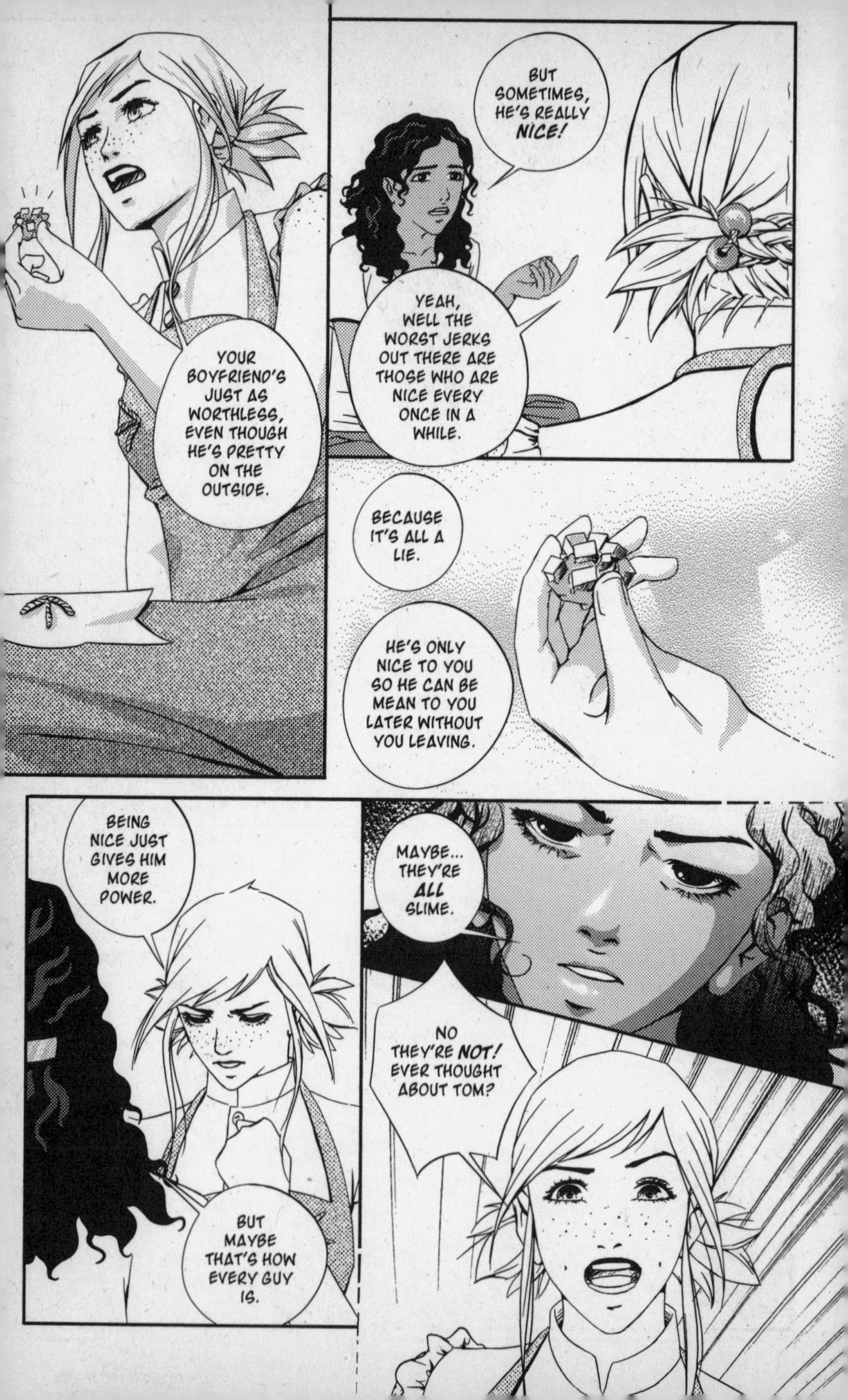
YOUR BOYFRIEND'S JUST AS WORTHLESS, EVEN THOUGH HE'S PRETTY ON THE OUTSIDE.
BUT SOMETIMES, HE'S REALLY ***NICE!***
YEAH, WELL THE WORST JERKS OUT THERE ARE THOSE WHO ARE NICE EVERY ONCE IN A WHILE.
BECAUSE IT'S ALL A LIE.
HE'S ONLY NICE TO YOU SO HE CAN BE MEAN TO YOU LATER WITHOUT YOU LEAVING.
BEING NICE JUST GIVES HIM MORE POWER.
BUT MAYBE THAT'S HOW EVERY GUY IS.
MAYBE... THEY'RE ***ALL*** SLIME.
NO THEY'RE ***NOT!*** EVER THOUGHT ABOUT TOM?

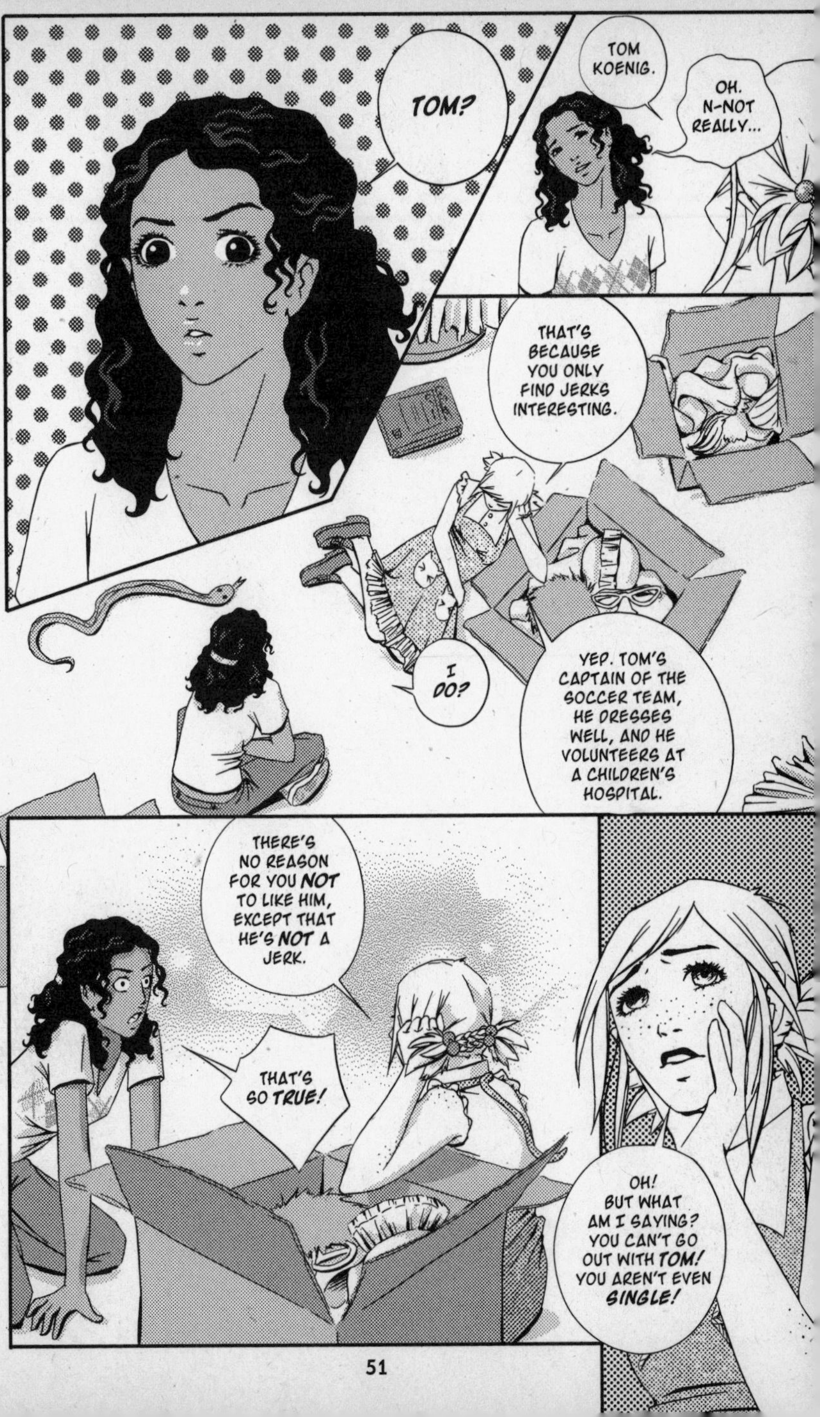
TOM?
TOM KOENIG.
OH. N-NOT REALLY...
THAT'S BECAUSE YOU ONLY FIND JERKS INTERESTING.
I DO?
YEP. TOM'S CAPTAIN OF THE SOCCER TEAM, HE DRESSES WELL, AND HE VOLUNTEERS AT A CHILDREN'S HOSPITAL.
THERE'S NO REASON FOR YOU NOT TO LIKE HIM, EXCEPT THAT HE'S NOT A JERK.
THAT'S SO TRUE!
OH! BUT WHAT AM I SAYING? YOU CAN'T GO OUT WITH TOM! YOU AREN'T EVEN SINGLE!

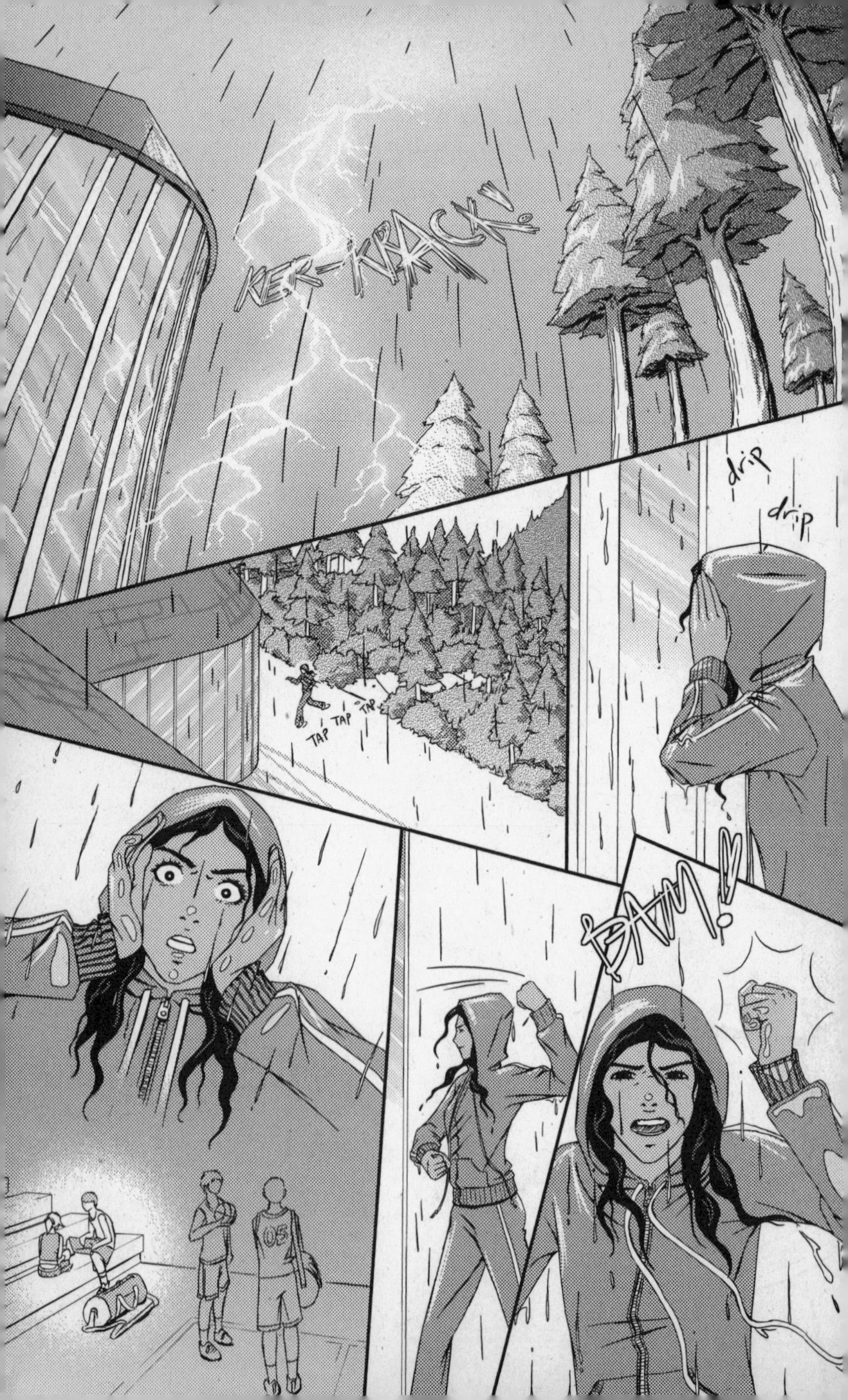
KER-KRACK!
TAP TAP TAP
drip
drip
BAM!!

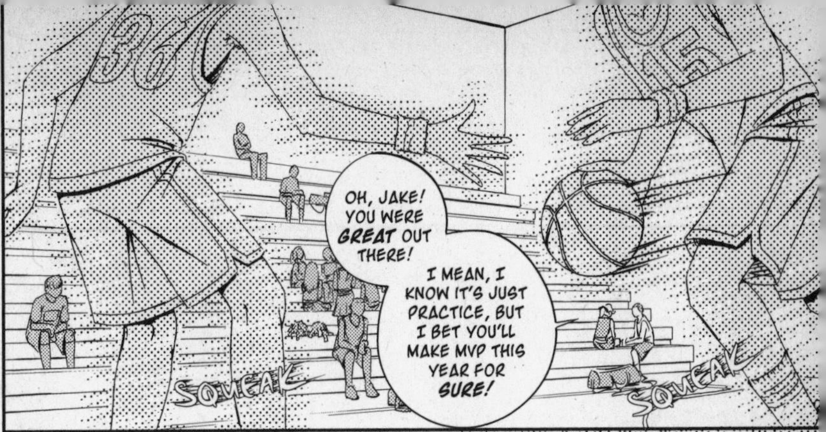
OH, JAKE! YOU WERE **GREAT** OUT THERE!
I MEAN, I KNOW IT'S JUST PRACTICE, BUT I BET YOU'LL MAKE MVP THIS YEAR FOR **SURE!**
SQUEAK
SQUEAK

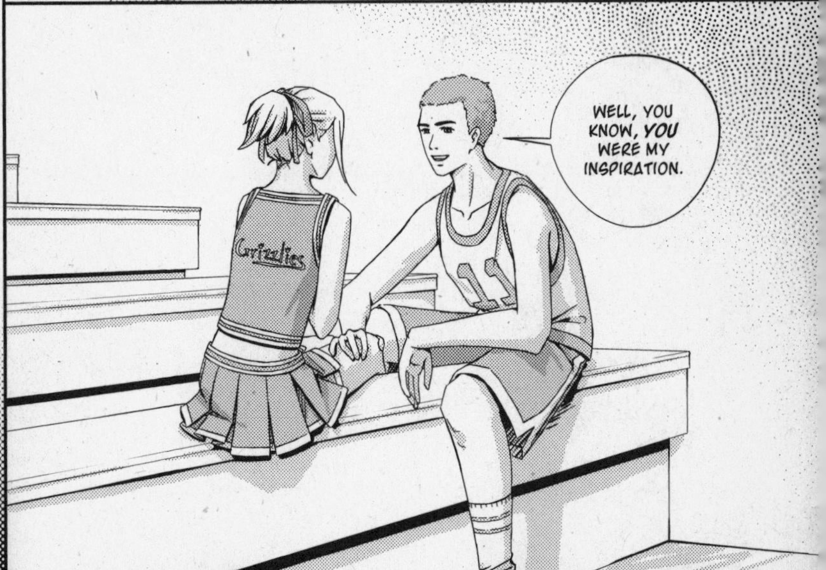
Grizzlies
WELL, YOU KNOW, ***YOU*** WERE MY INSPIRATION.

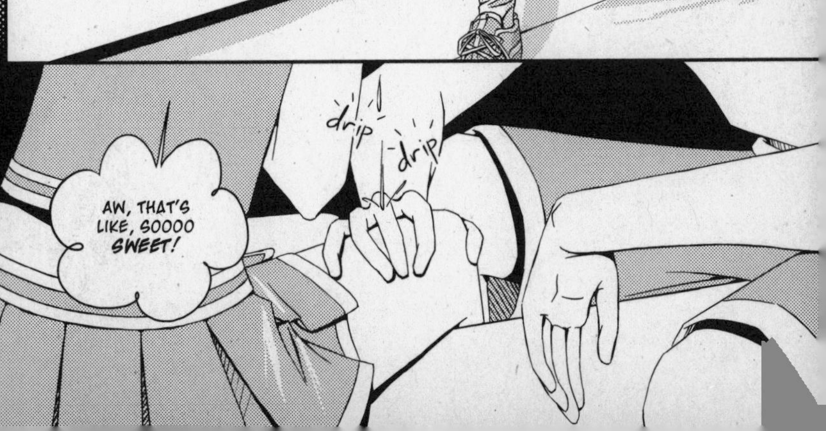
drip
drip
AW, THAT'S LIKE, SOOOO **SWEET!**

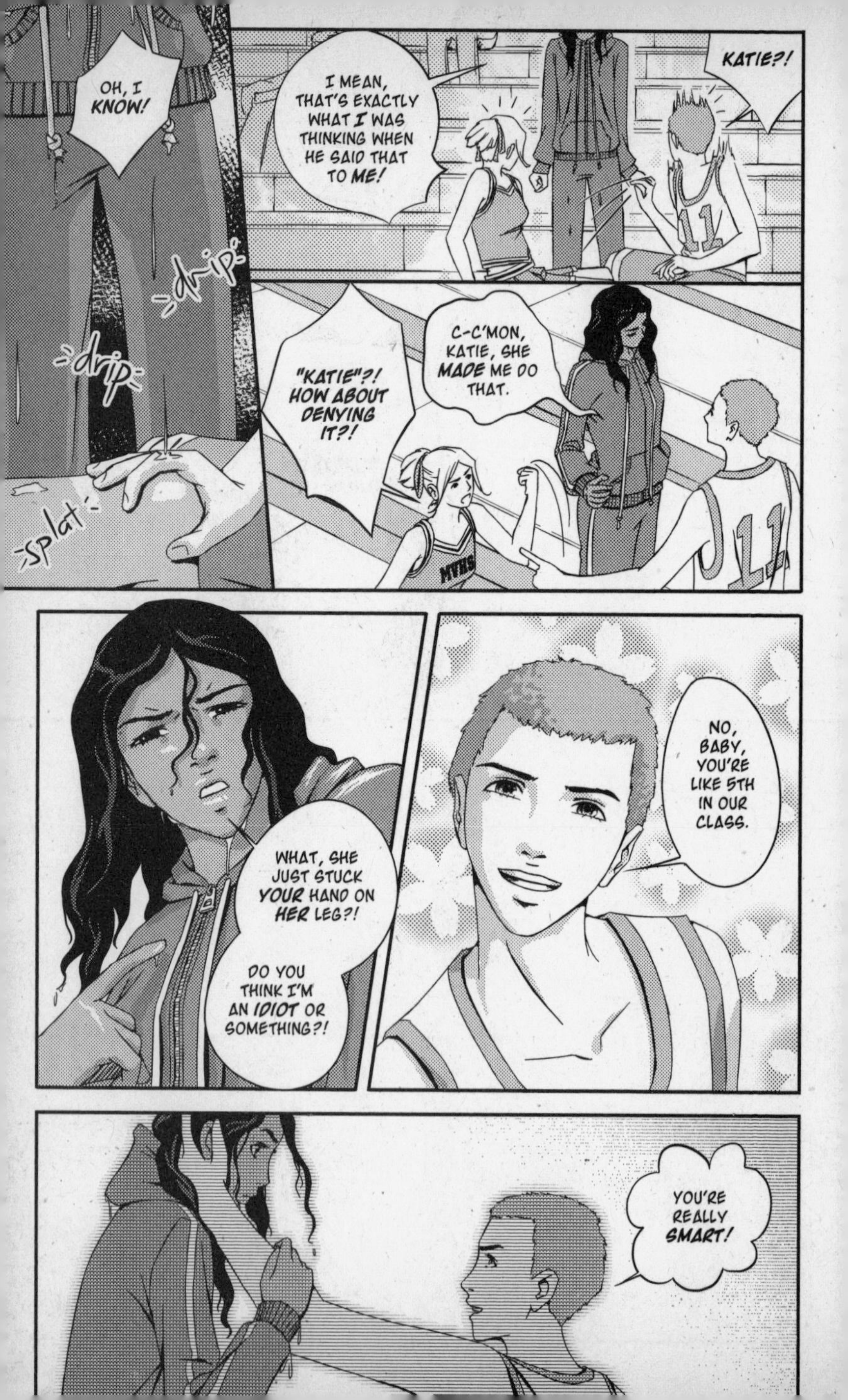
OH, I KNOW!
-drip-
-drip-
-splat-
I MEAN, THAT'S EXACTLY WHAT I WAS THINKING WHEN HE SAID THAT TO ME!
KATIE?!
"KATIE"?! HOW ABOUT DENYING IT?!
C-C'MON, KATIE, SHE MADE ME DO THAT.
MVHS
11
WHAT, SHE JUST STUCK YOUR HAND ON HER LEG?!
DO YOU THINK I'M AN IDIOT OR SOMETHING?!
NO, BABY, YOU'RE LIKE 5TH IN OUR CLASS.
YOU'RE REALLY SMART!

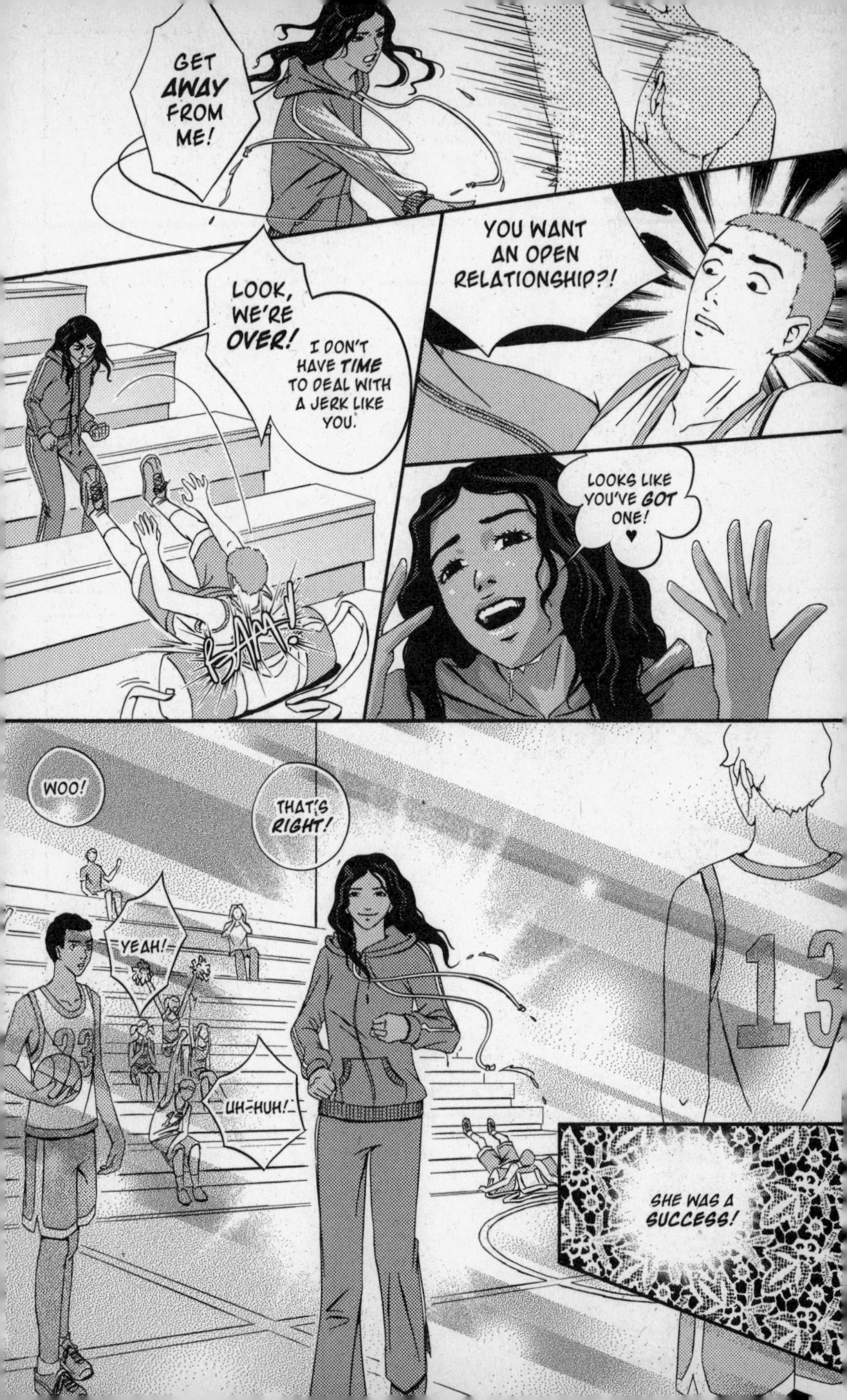
GET AWAY FROM ME!
LOOK, WE'RE OVER! I DON'T HAVE TIME TO DEAL WITH A JERK LIKE YOU.
BAM!
YOU WANT AN OPEN RELATIONSHIP?!
LOOKS LIKE YOU'VE GOT ONE! ♥
WOO!
THAT'S RIGHT!
YEAH!
UH-HUH!
SHE WAS A SUCCESS!

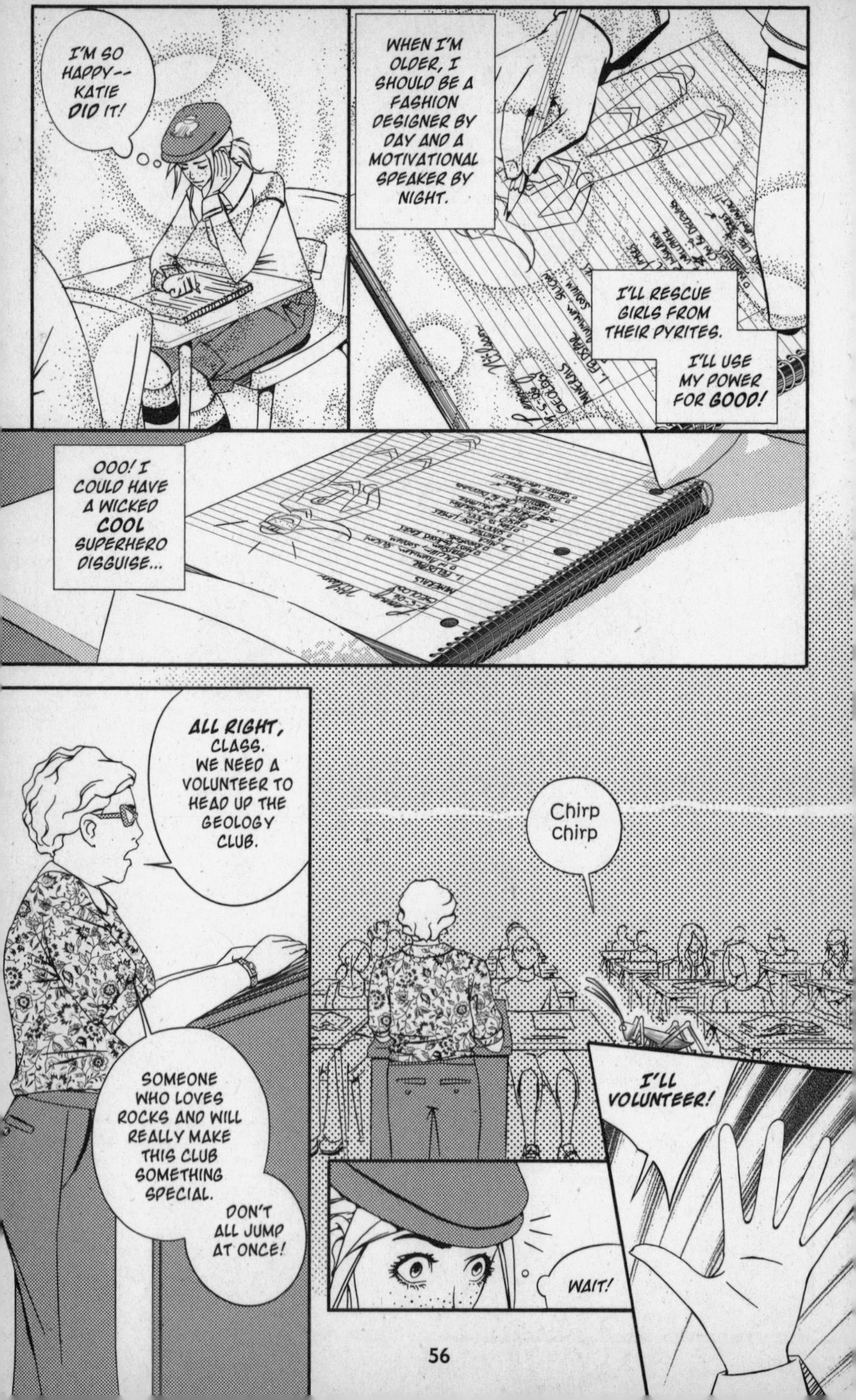
I'M SO HAPPY-- KATIE DID IT!
WHEN I'M OLDER, I SHOULD BE A FASHION DESIGNER BY DAY AND A MOTIVATIONAL SPEAKER BY NIGHT.
I'LL RESCUE GIRLS FROM THEIR PYRITES.
I'LL USE MY POWER FOR GOOD!
OOO! I COULD HAVE A WICKED COOL SUPERHERO DISGUISE...
ALL RIGHT, CLASS. WE NEED A VOLUNTEER TO HEAD UP THE GEOLOGY CLUB.
SOMEONE WHO LOVES ROCKS AND WILL REALLY MAKE THIS CLUB SOMETHING SPECIAL.
DON'T ALL JUMP AT ONCE!
Chirp Chirp
I'LL VOLUNTEER!
WAIT!

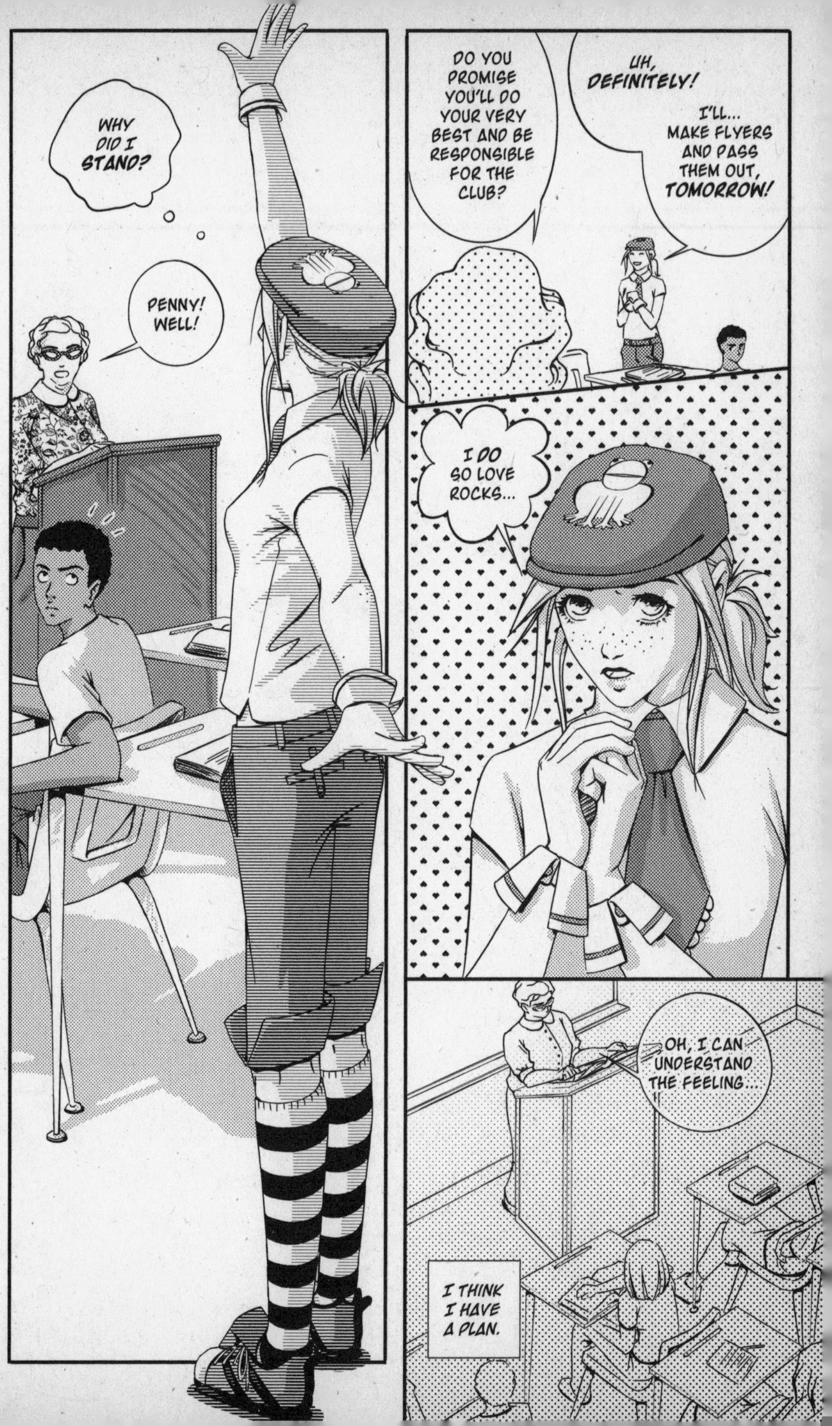
WHY DID I STAND?
PENNY! WELL!
DO YOU PROMISE YOU'LL DO YOUR VERY BEST AND BE RESPONSIBLE FOR THE CLUB?
UH, DEFINITELY!
I'LL... MAKE FLYERS AND PASS THEM OUT, TOMORROW!
I DO SO LOVE ROCKS...
OH, I CAN UNDERSTAND THE FEELING...
I THINK I HAVE A PLAN.

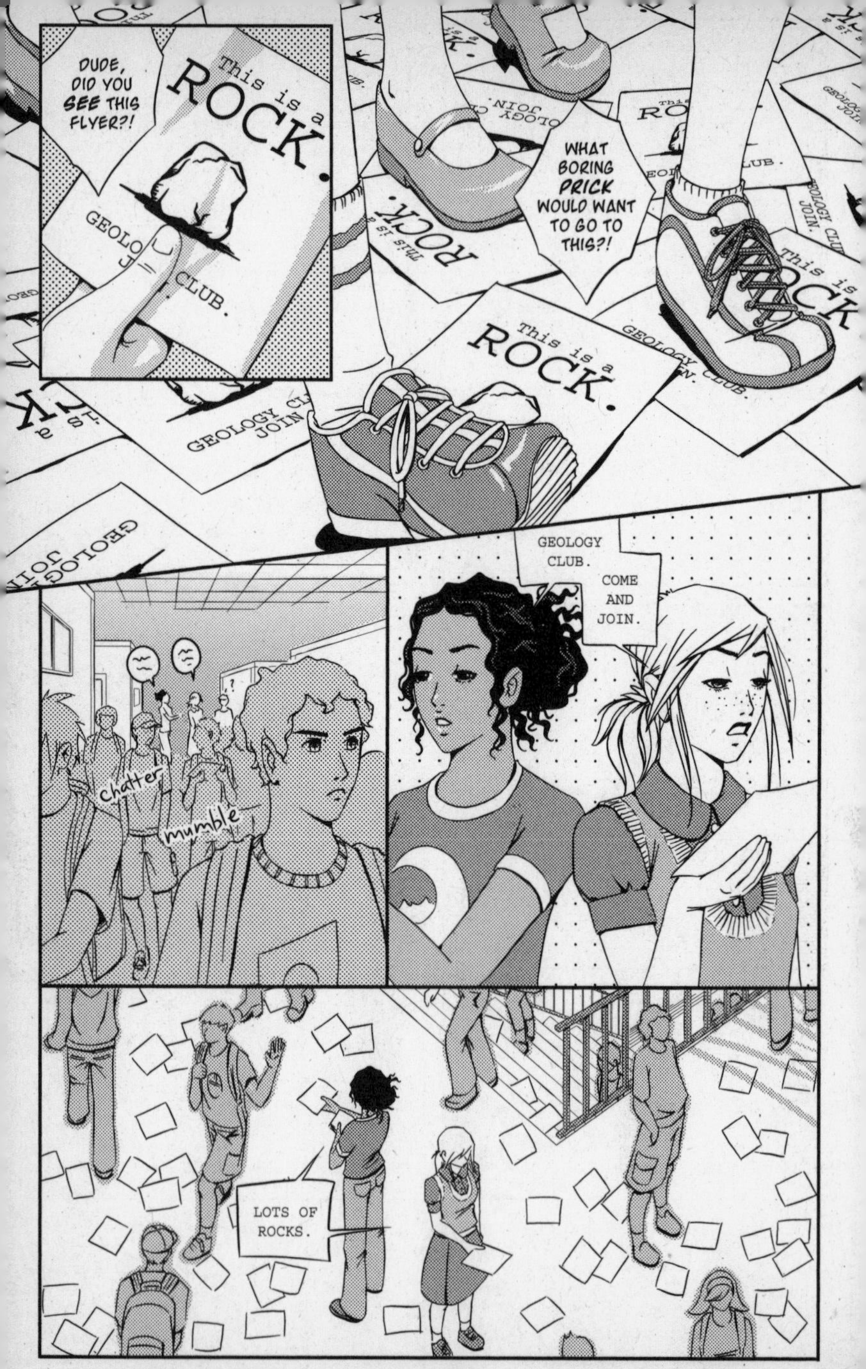
DUDE, DID YOU SEE THIS FLYER?!
This is a ROCK. GEOLOGY CLUB.
WHAT BORING PRICK WOULD WANT TO GO TO THIS?!
This is a ROCK.
chatter
mumble
GEOLOGY CLUB.
COME AND JOIN.
LOTS OF ROCKS.

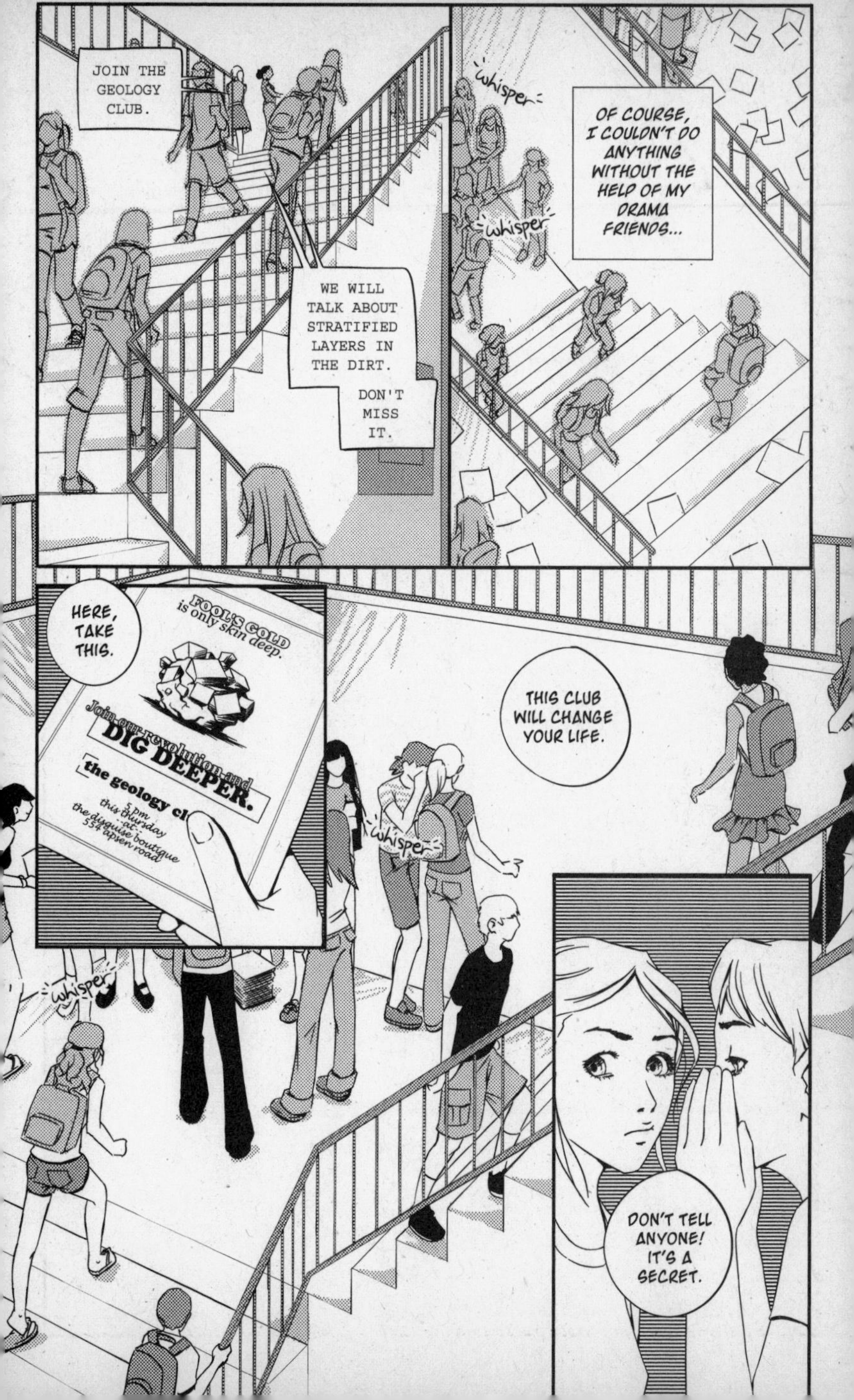
JOIN THE GEOLOGY CLUB.
WE WILL TALK ABOUT STRATIFIED LAYERS IN THE DIRT.
DON'T MISS IT.
whisper
OF COURSE, I COULDN'T DO ANYTHING WITHOUT THE HELP OF MY DRAMA FRIENDS...
whisper
HERE, TAKE THIS.
FOOL'S GOLD is only skin deep.
Join our revolution and DIG DEEPER.
the geology cl
5 pm
this thursday
-at-
the disguise boutique
554 apsen road
THIS CLUB WILL CHANGE YOUR LIFE.
whisper
whisper
DON'T TELL ANYONE! IT'S A SECRET.

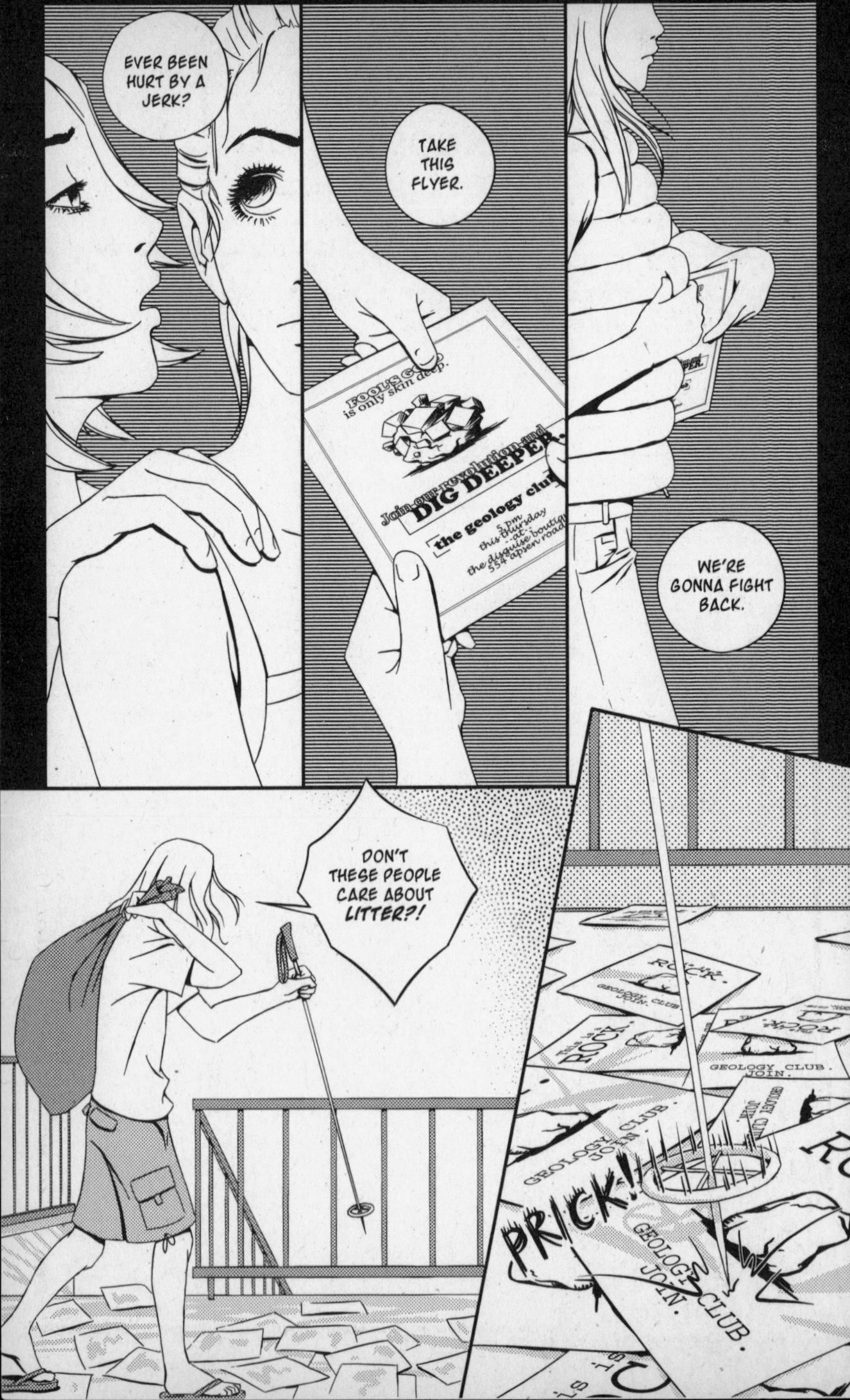
EVER BEEN HURT BY A JERK?
TAKE THIS FLYER.
is only skin deep.
Join our revolution and
DIG DEEPER.
the geology club
5 pm
this thursday
-at-
554 apsen road
WE'RE GONNA FIGHT BACK.
DON'T THESE PEOPLE CARE ABOUT *LITTER?!*
ROCK.
GEOLOGY CLUB.
JOIN.
PRICK!

Chapter 3:
The Geology Club

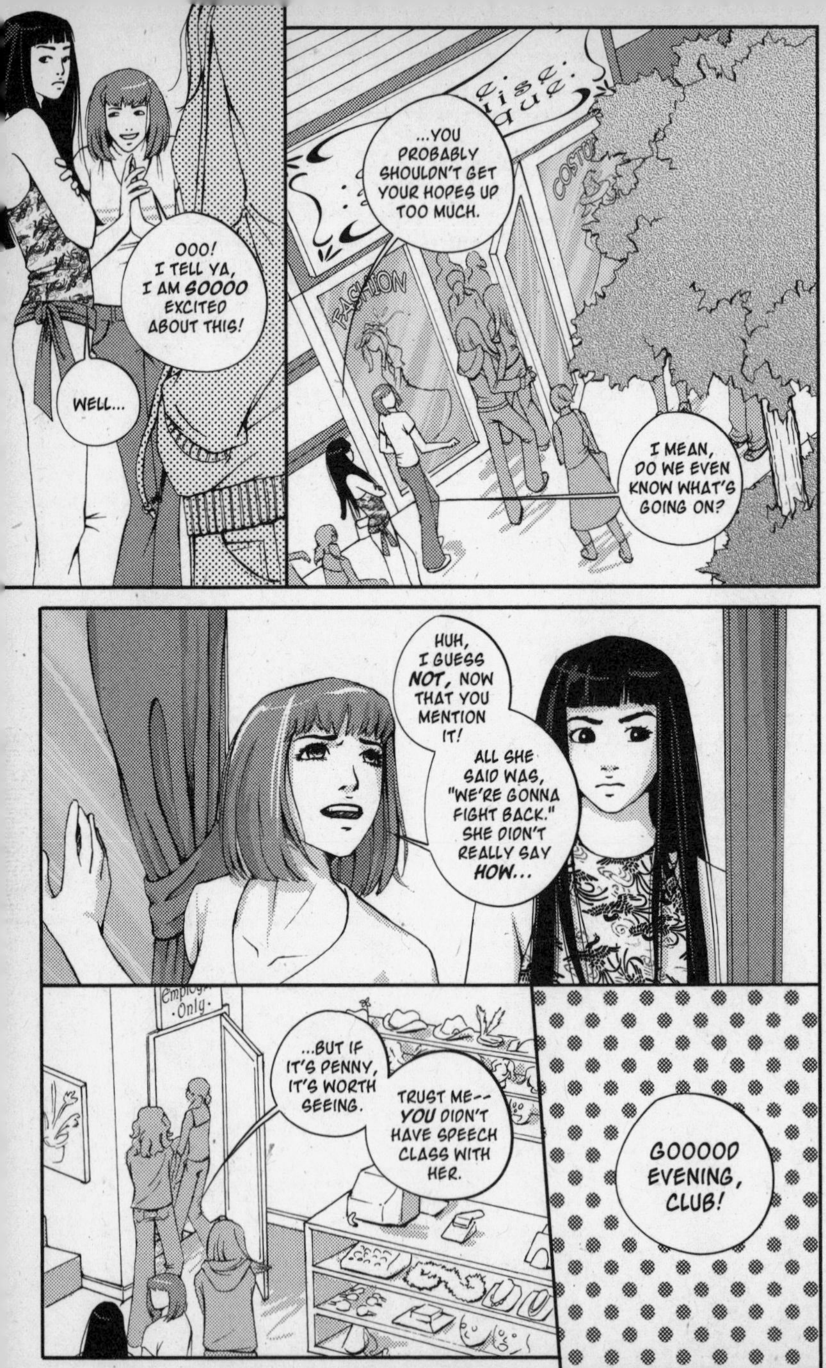
OOO! I TELL YA, I AM SOOOO EXCITED ABOUT THIS!
WELL...
...YOU PROBABLY SHOULDN'T GET YOUR HOPES UP TOO MUCH.
FASHION
I MEAN, DO WE EVEN KNOW WHAT'S GOING ON?
HUH, I GUESS NOT, NOW THAT YOU MENTION IT!
ALL SHE SAID WAS, "WE'RE GONNA FIGHT BACK." SHE DIDN'T REALLY SAY HOW...
...BUT IF IT'S PENNY, IT'S WORTH SEEING.
TRUST ME--YOU DIDN'T HAVE SPEECH CLASS WITH HER.
GOOOOD EVENING, CLUB!

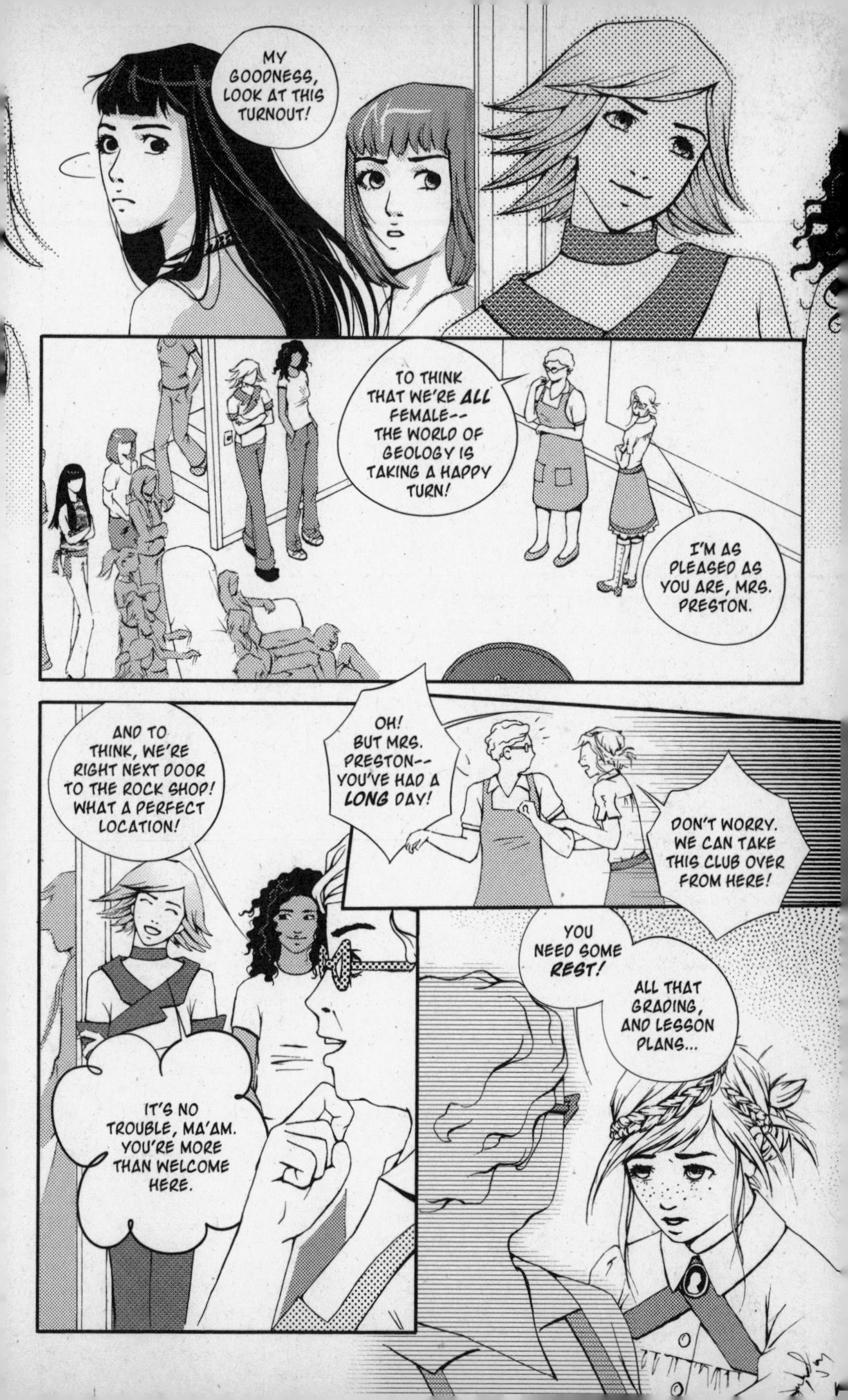
MY GOODNESS, LOOK AT THIS TURNOUT!
TO THINK THAT WE'RE ALL FEMALE-- THE WORLD OF GEOLOGY IS TAKING A HAPPY TURN!
I'M AS PLEASED AS YOU ARE, MRS. PRESTON.
AND TO THINK, WE'RE RIGHT NEXT DOOR TO THE ROCK SHOP! WHAT A PERFECT LOCATION!
IT'S NO TROUBLE, MA'AM. YOU'RE MORE THAN WELCOME HERE.
OH! BUT MRS. PRESTON-- YOU'VE HAD A LONG DAY!
DON'T WORRY. WE CAN TAKE THIS CLUB OVER FROM HERE!
YOU NEED SOME REST!
ALL THAT GRADING, AND LESSON PLANS...

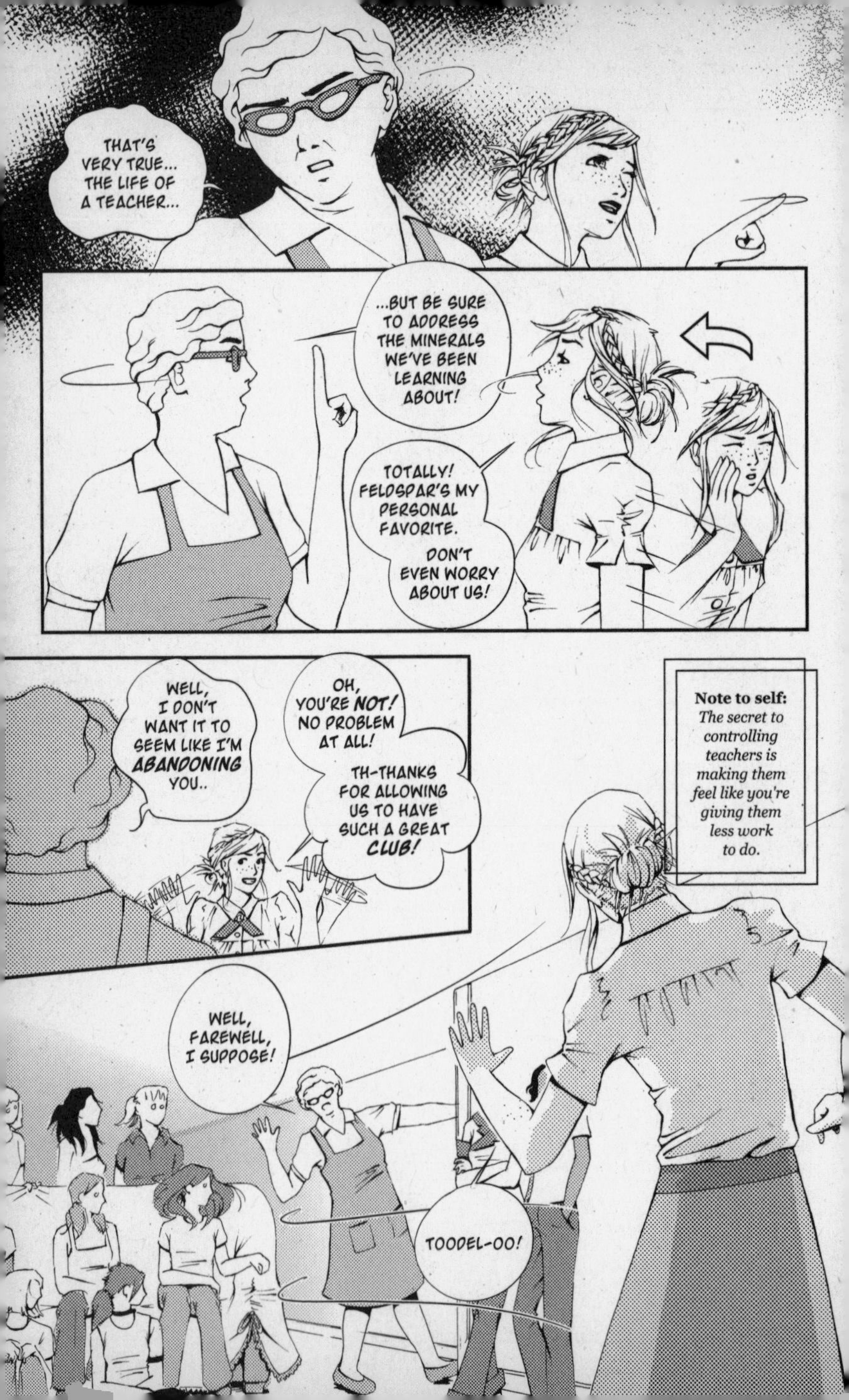
THAT'S VERY TRUE... THE LIFE OF A TEACHER...
...BUT BE SURE TO ADDRESS THE MINERALS WE'VE BEEN LEARNING ABOUT!
TOTALLY! FELDSPAR'S MY PERSONAL FAVORITE.
DON'T EVEN WORRY ABOUT US!
WELL, I DON'T WANT IT TO SEEM LIKE I'M ABANDONING YOU..
OH, YOU'RE NOT! NO PROBLEM AT ALL!
TH-THANKS FOR ALLOWING US TO HAVE SUCH A GREAT CLUB!
Note to self: The secret to controlling teachers is making them feel like you're giving them less work to do.
WELL, FAREWELL, I SUPPOSE!
TOODEL-OO!

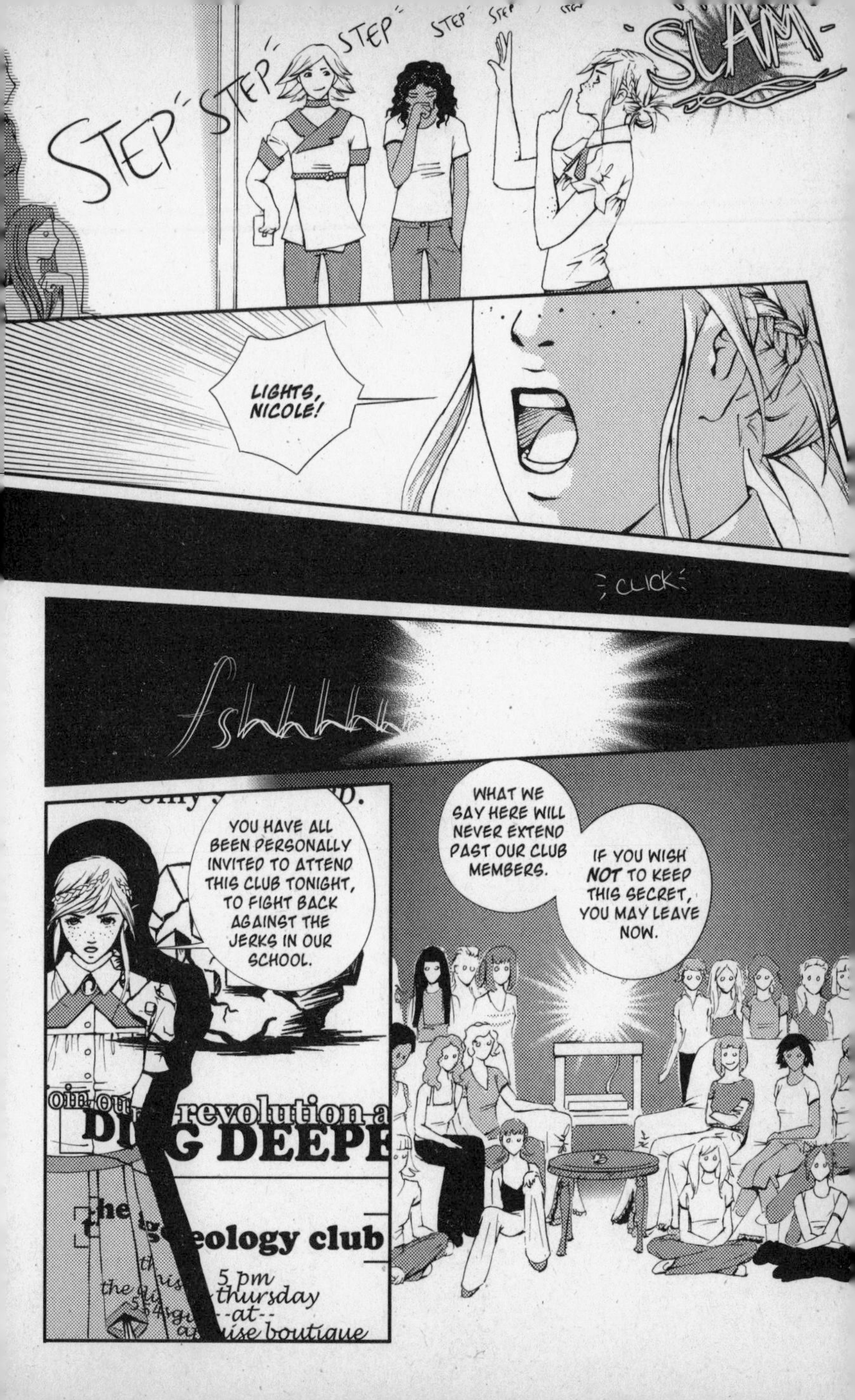

STEP
STEP
STEP
STEP
STEP
-SLAM-
LIGHTS, NICOLE!
CLICK
fshhhhhh
YOU HAVE ALL BEEN PERSONALLY INVITED TO ATTEND THIS CLUB TONIGHT, TO FIGHT BACK AGAINST THE JERKS IN OUR SCHOOL.
WHAT WE SAY HERE WILL NEVER EXTEND PAST OUR CLUB MEMBERS.
IF YOU WISH NOT TO KEEP THIS SECRET, YOU MAY LEAVE NOW.
revolution
G DEEPE
eology club
5 pm
thursday
--at--
boutique

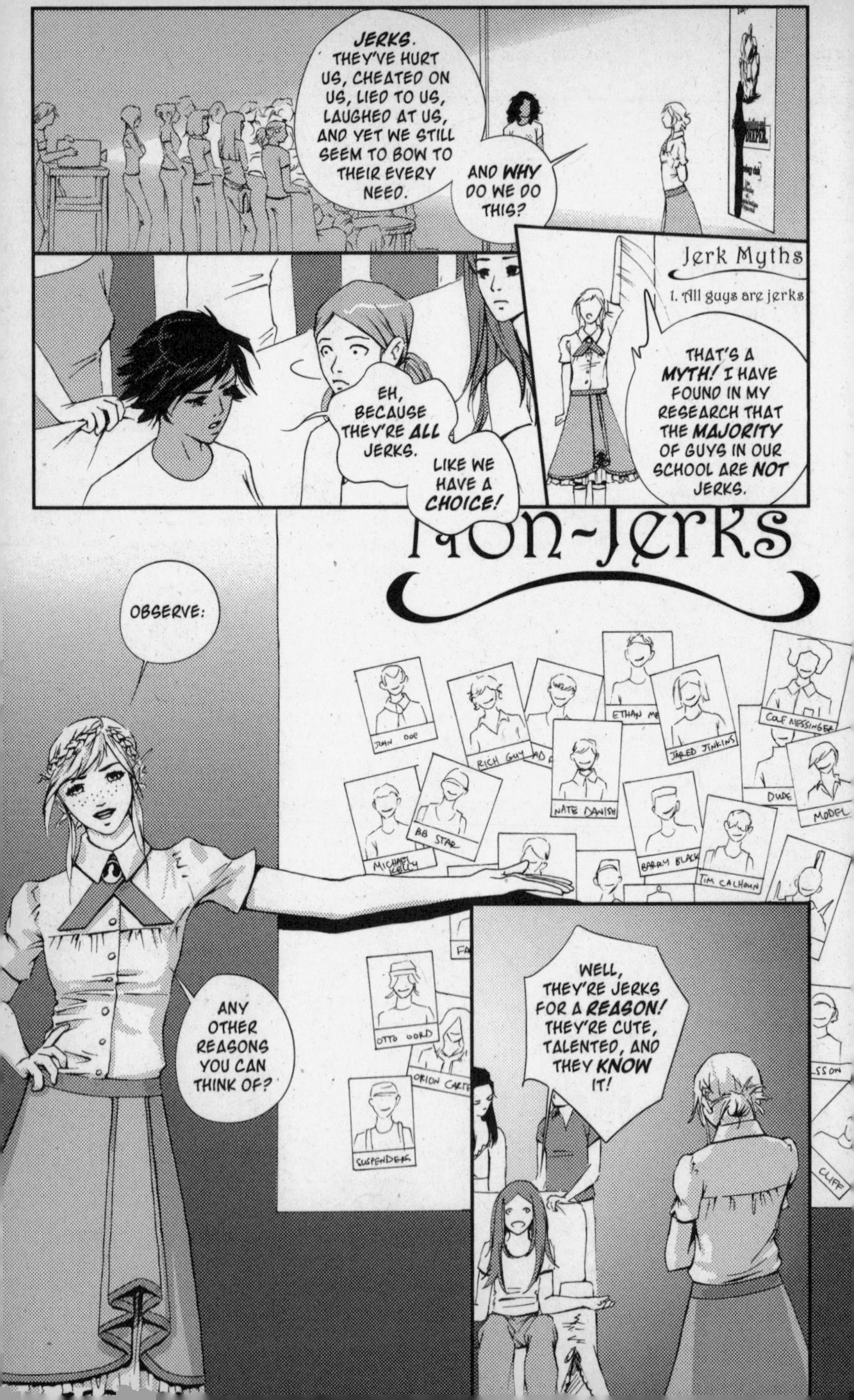
JERKS. THEY'VE HURT US, CHEATED ON US, LIED TO US, LAUGHED AT US, AND YET WE STILL SEEM TO BOW TO THEIR EVERY NEED.
AND WHY DO WE DO THIS?
EH, BECAUSE THEY'RE ALL JERKS.
LIKE WE HAVE A CHOICE!
Jerk Myths
1. All guys are jerks
THAT'S A MYTH! I HAVE FOUND IN MY RESEARCH THAT THE MAJORITY OF GUYS IN OUR SCHOOL ARE NOT JERKS.
OBSERVE:
Non-Jerks
JOHN DOE
RICH GUY
ETHAN M
JARED JINKINS
COLE MESSINGER
NATE DANISH
DUDE
MODEL
BB STAR
MICHAEL KELLY
BARRY BLACK
TIM CALHOUN
OTTO GORD
SUSPENDERS
CLIFF
ANY OTHER REASONS YOU CAN THINK OF?
WELL, THEY'RE JERKS FOR A REASON! THEY'RE CUTE, TALENTED, AND THEY KNOW IT!

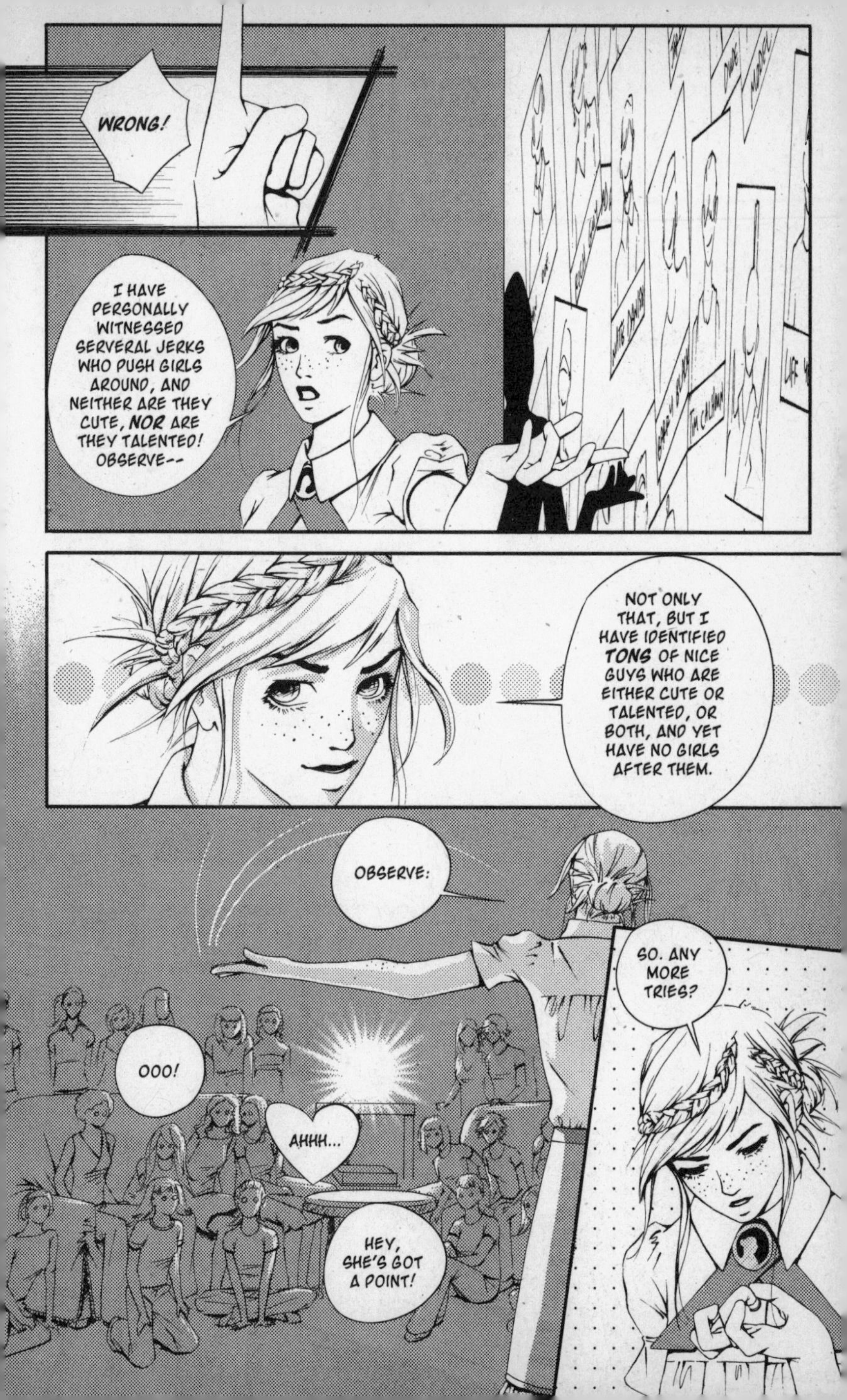
WRONG!
I HAVE PERSONALLY WITNESSED SERVERAL JERKS WHO PUSH GIRLS AROUND, AND NEITHER ARE THEY CUTE, NOR ARE THEY TALENTED! OBSERVE--
NOT ONLY THAT, BUT I HAVE IDENTIFIED TONS OF NICE GUYS WHO ARE EITHER CUTE OR TALENTED, OR BOTH, AND YET HAVE NO GIRLS AFTER THEM.
OBSERVE:
OOO!
AHHH...
HEY, SHE'S GOT A POINT!
SO. ANY MORE TRIES?

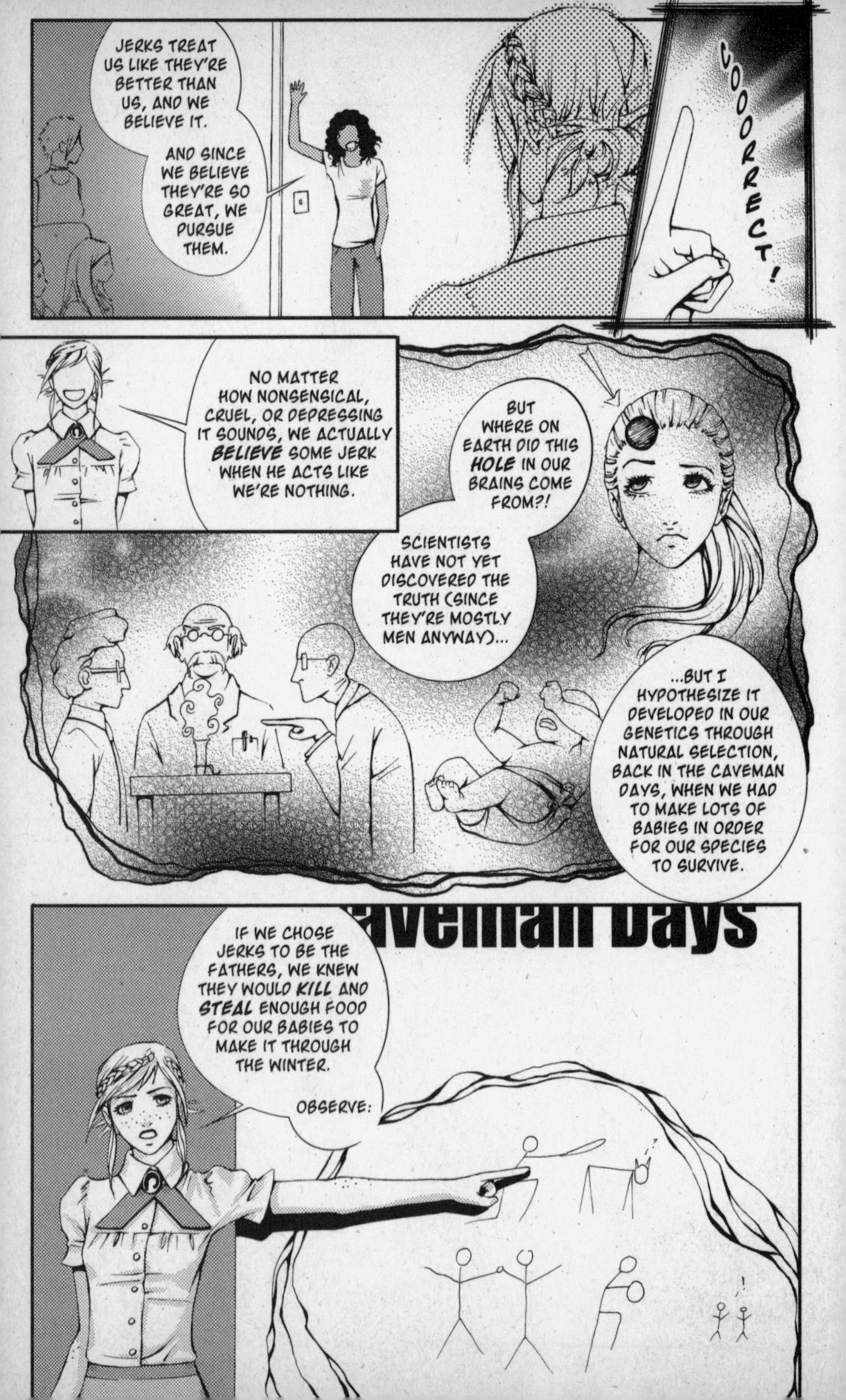
JERKS TREAT US LIKE THEY'RE BETTER THAN US, AND WE BELIEVE IT.
AND SINCE WE BELIEVE THEY'RE SO GREAT, WE PURSUE THEM.
COOOORRECT!
NO MATTER HOW NONSENSICAL, CRUEL, OR DEPRESSING IT SOUNDS, WE ACTUALLY BELIEVE SOME JERK WHEN HE ACTS LIKE WE'RE NOTHING.
BUT WHERE ON EARTH DID THIS HOLE IN OUR BRAINS COME FROM?!
SCIENTISTS HAVE NOT YET DISCOVERED THE TRUTH (SINCE THEY'RE MOSTLY MEN ANYWAY)...
...BUT I HYPOTHESIZE IT DEVELOPED IN OUR GENETICS THROUGH NATURAL SELECTION, BACK IN THE CAVEMAN DAYS, WHEN WE HAD TO MAKE LOTS OF BABIES IN ORDER FOR OUR SPECIES TO SURVIVE.
aveman Days
IF WE CHOSE JERKS TO BE THE FATHERS, WE KNEW THEY WOULD KILL AND STEAL ENOUGH FOOD FOR OUR BABIES TO MAKE IT THROUGH THE WINTER.
OBSERVE:

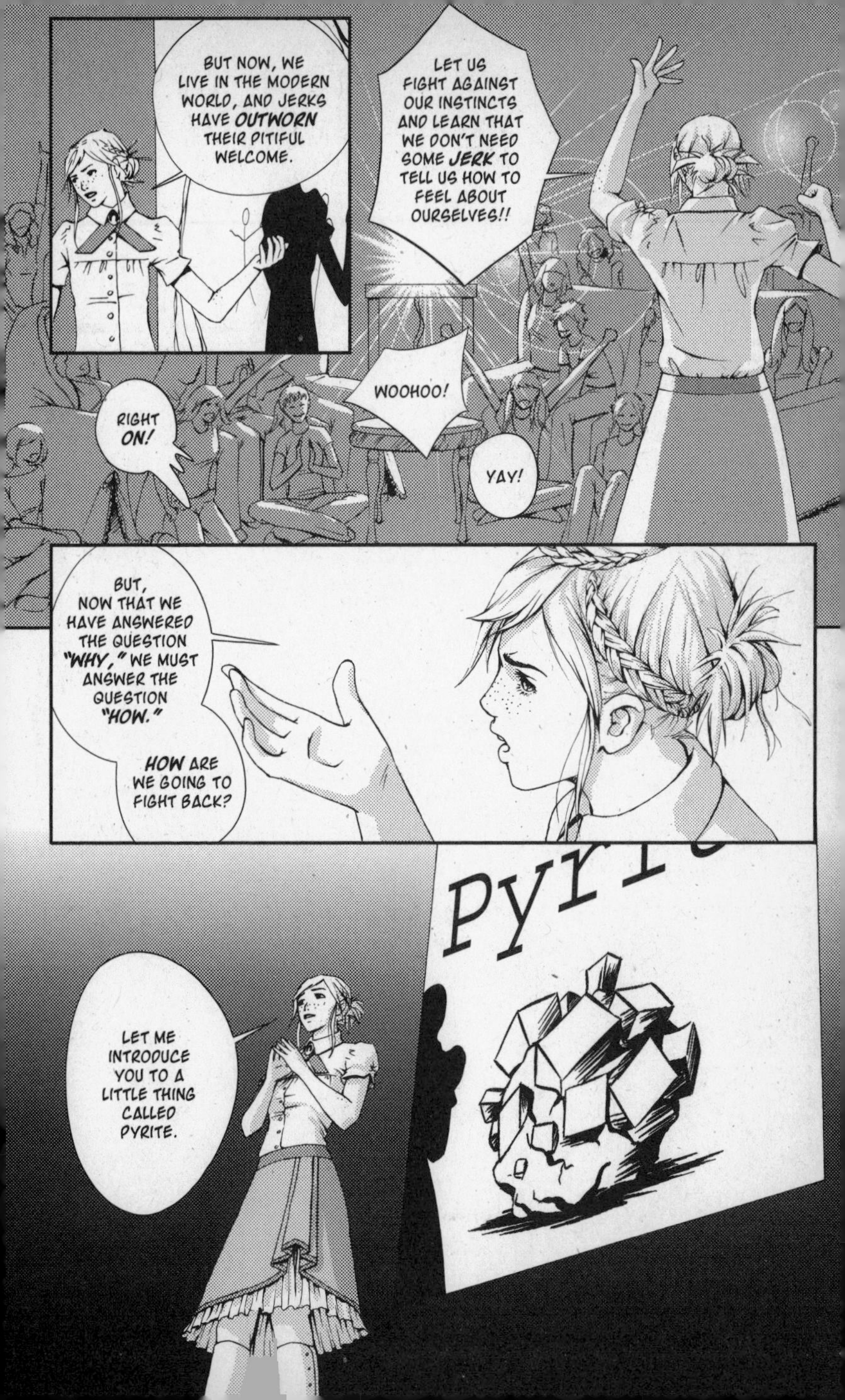
BUT NOW, WE LIVE IN THE MODERN WORLD, AND JERKS HAVE **OUTWORN** THEIR PITIFUL WELCOME.
LET US FIGHT AGAINST OUR INSTINCTS AND LEARN THAT WE DON'T NEED SOME **JERK** TO TELL US HOW TO FEEL ABOUT OURSELVES!!
RIGHT **ON!**
WOOHOO!
YAY!
BUT, NOW THAT WE HAVE ANSWERED THE QUESTION **"WHY,"** WE MUST ANSWER THE QUESTION **"HOW."**
HOW ARE WE GOING TO FIGHT BACK?
LET ME INTRODUCE YOU TO A LITTLE THING CALLED PYRITE.
Pyrite

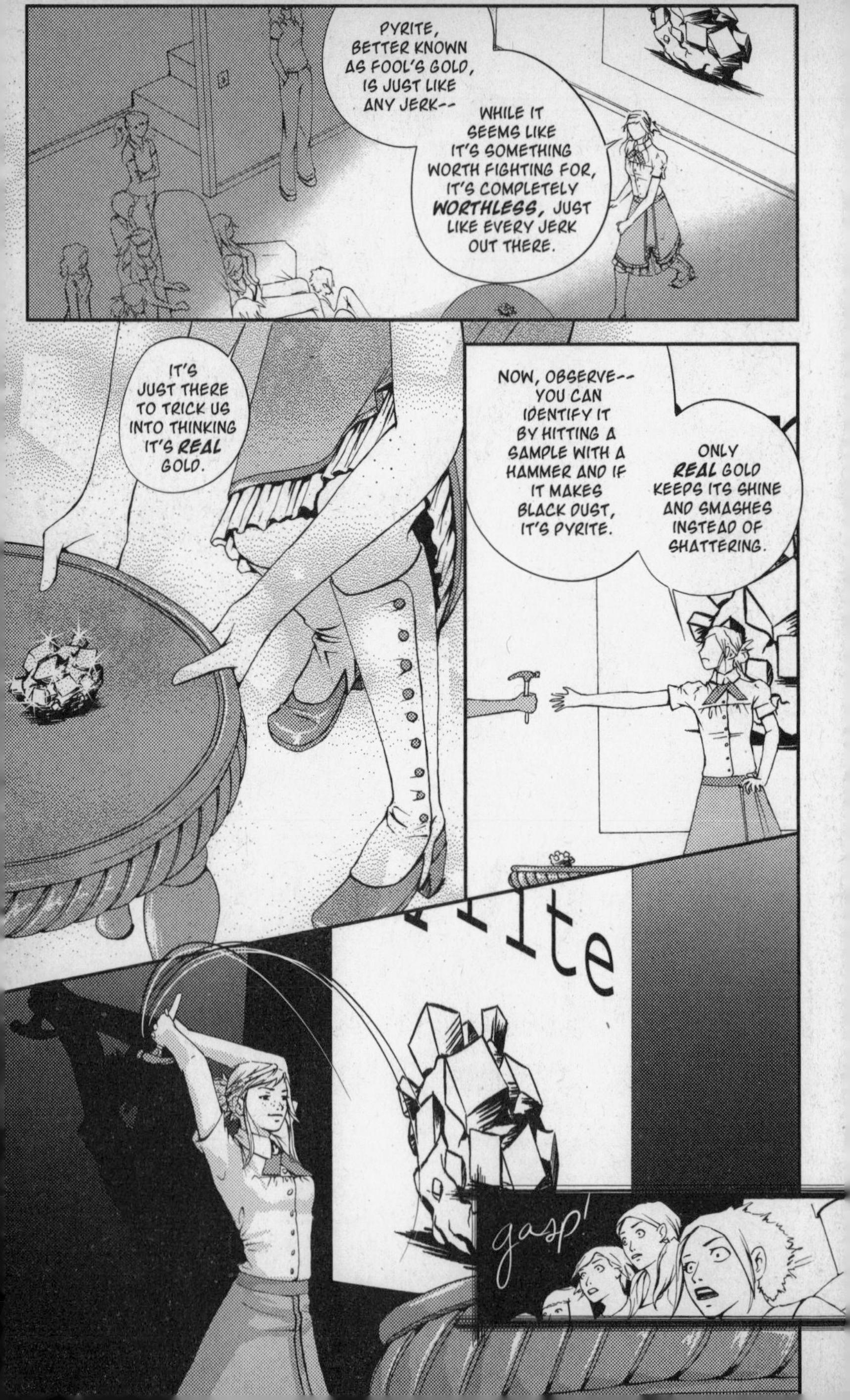
PYRITE, BETTER KNOWN AS FOOL'S GOLD, IS JUST LIKE ANY JERK--
WHILE IT SEEMS LIKE IT'S SOMETHING WORTH FIGHTING FOR, IT'S COMPLETELY WORTHLESS, JUST LIKE EVERY JERK OUT THERE.
IT'S JUST THERE TO TRICK US INTO THINKING IT'S REAL GOLD.
NOW, OBSERVE--YOU CAN IDENTIFY IT BY HITTING A SAMPLE WITH A HAMMER AND IF IT MAKES BLACK DUST, IT'S PYRITE.
ONLY REAL GOLD KEEPS ITS SHINE AND SMASHES INSTEAD OF SHATTERING.
gasp!

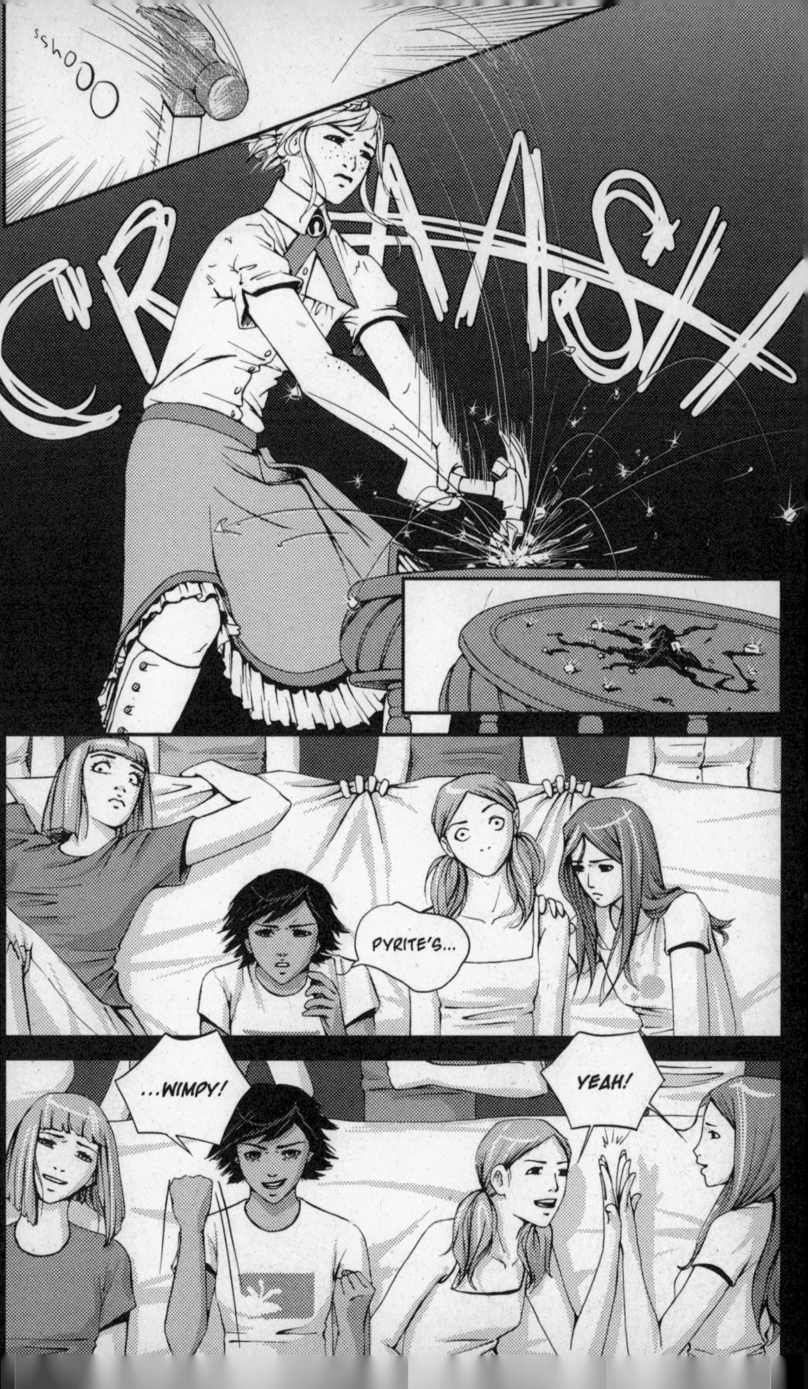
sshOOO
CRASH
PYRITE'S...
...WIMPY!
YEAH!

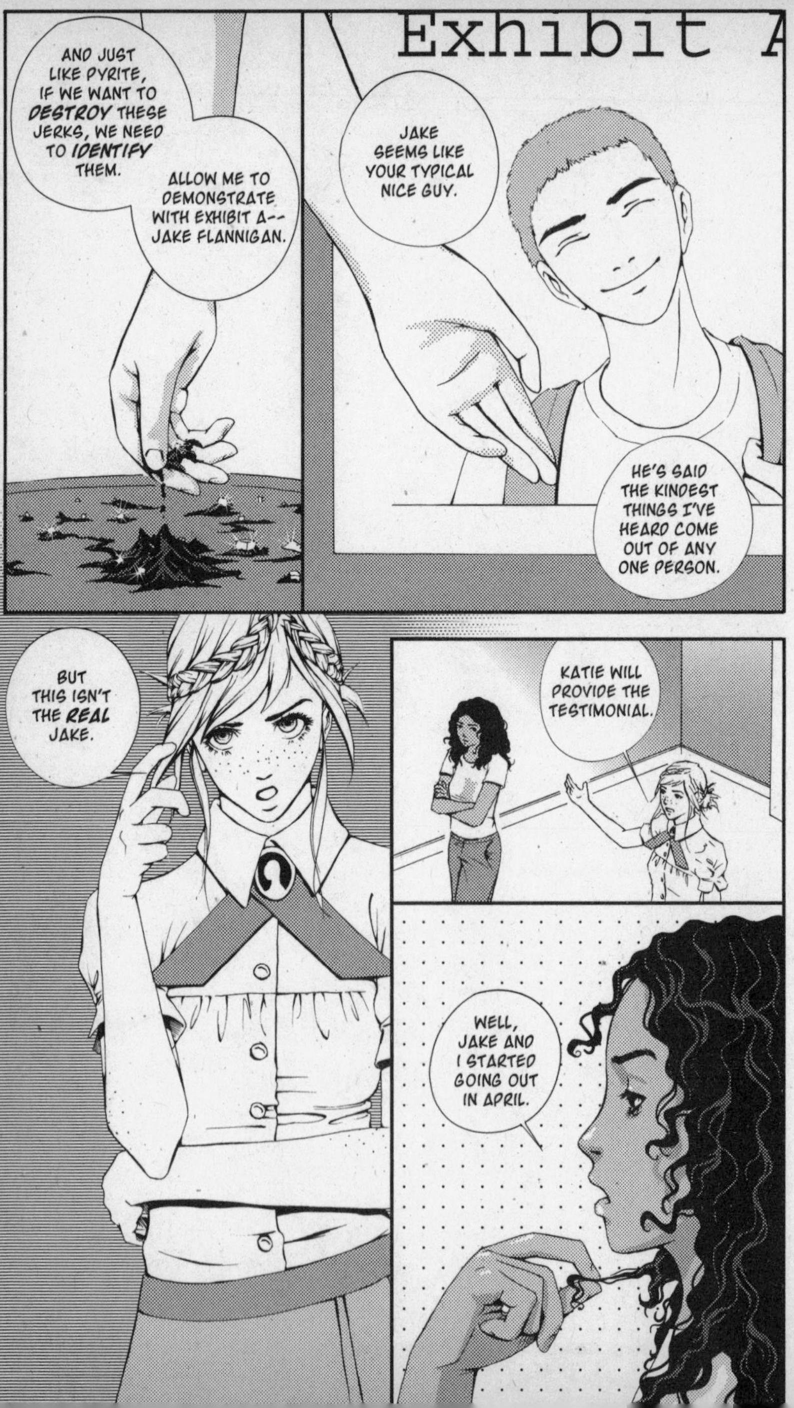
Exhibit A
AND JUST LIKE PYRITE, IF WE WANT TO DESTROY THESE JERKS, WE NEED TO IDENTIFY THEM.
ALLOW ME TO DEMONSTRATE WITH EXHIBIT A-- JAKE FLANNIGAN.
JAKE SEEMS LIKE YOUR TYPICAL NICE GUY.
HE'S SAID THE KINDEST THINGS I'VE HEARD COME OUT OF ANY ONE PERSON.
BUT THIS ISN'T THE REAL JAKE.
KATIE WILL PROVIDE THE TESTIMONIAL.
WELL, JAKE AND I STARTED GOING OUT IN APRIL.

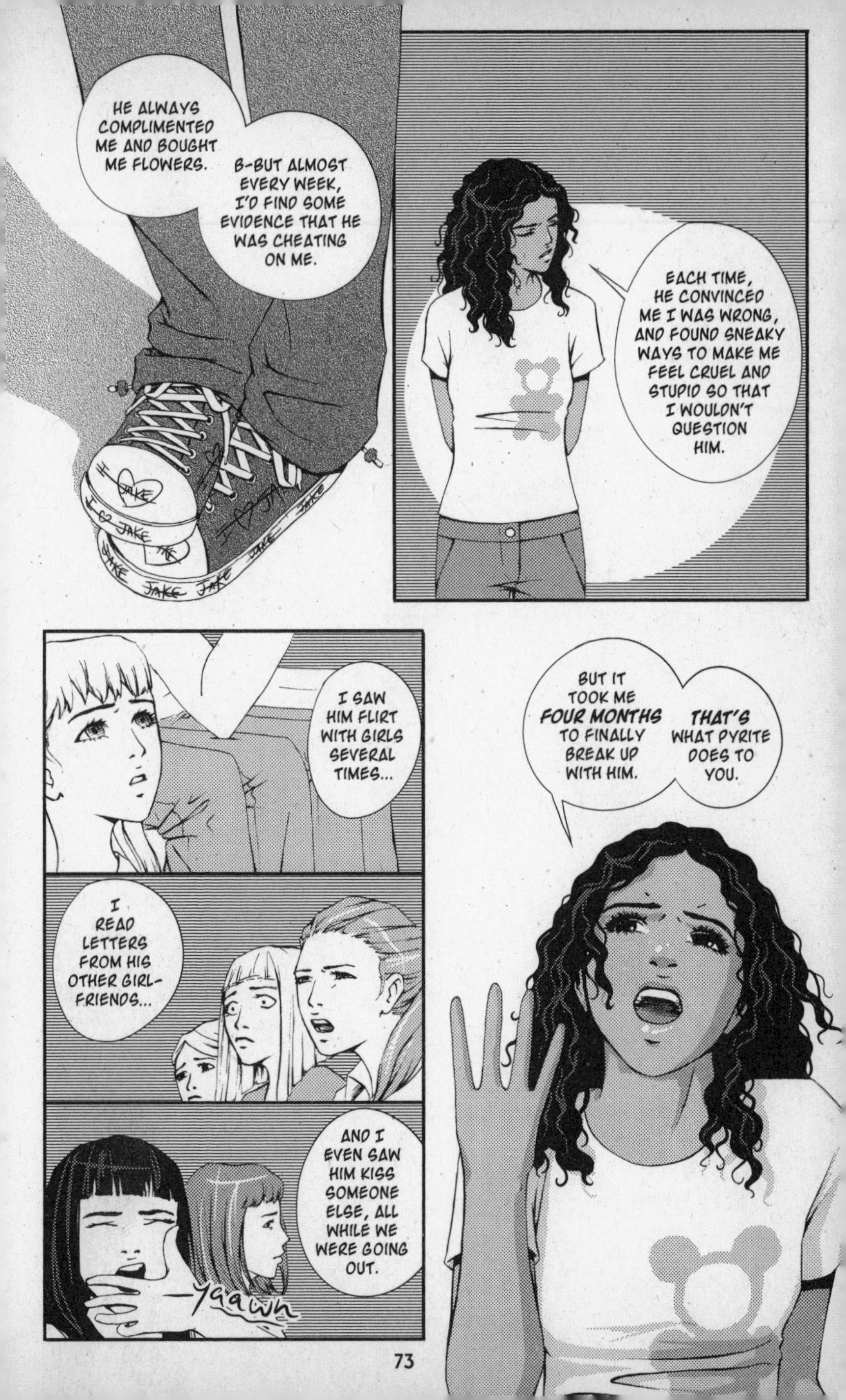
HE ALWAYS COMPLIMENTED ME AND BOUGHT ME FLOWERS.
B-BUT ALMOST EVERY WEEK, I'D FIND SOME EVIDENCE THAT HE WAS CHEATING ON ME.
EACH TIME, HE CONVINCED ME I WAS WRONG, AND FOUND SNEAKY WAYS TO MAKE ME FEEL CRUEL AND STUPID SO THAT I WOULDN'T QUESTION HIM.
I SAW HIM FLIRT WITH GIRLS SEVERAL TIMES...
I READ LETTERS FROM HIS OTHER GIRL-FRIENDS...
AND I EVEN SAW HIM KISS SOMEONE ELSE, ALL WHILE WE WERE GOING OUT.
yaawn
BUT IT TOOK ME **FOUR MONTHS** TO FINALLY BREAK UP WITH HIM.
THAT'S WHAT PYRITE DOES TO YOU.

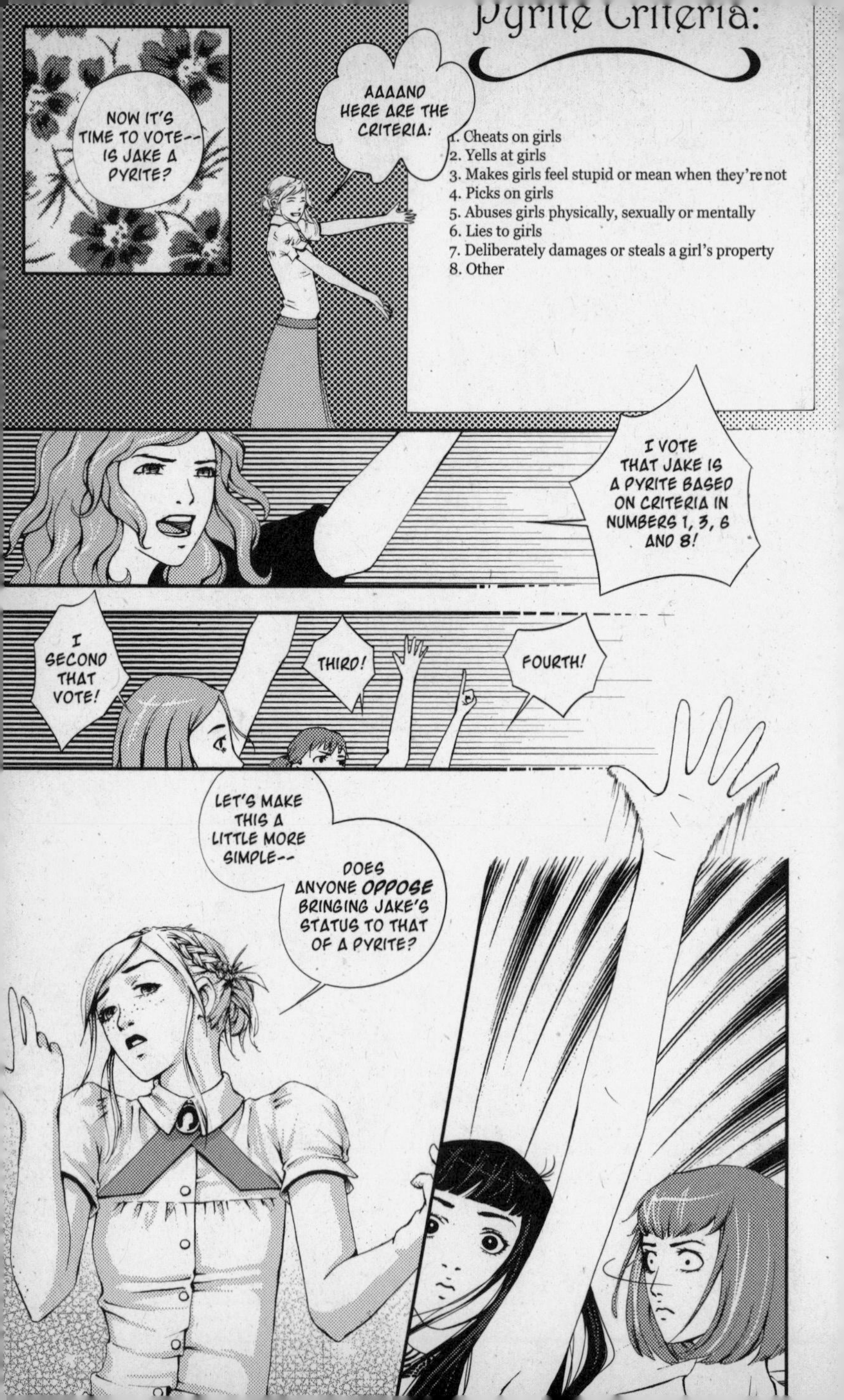
NOW IT'S TIME TO VOTE--IS JAKE A PYRITE?
AAAAND HERE ARE THE CRITERIA:
Pyrite Criteria:
1. Cheats on girls
2. Yells at girls
3. Makes girls feel stupid or mean when they're not
4. Picks on girls
5. Abuses girls physically, sexually or mentally
6. Lies to girls
7. Deliberately damages or steals a girl's property
8. Other
I VOTE THAT JAKE IS A PYRITE BASED ON CRITERIA IN NUMBERS 1, 3, 6 AND 8!
I SECOND THAT VOTE!
THIRD!
FOURTH!
LET'S MAKE THIS A LITTLE MORE SIMPLE--
DOES ANYONE OPPOSE BRINGING JAKE'S STATUS TO THAT OF A PYRITE?

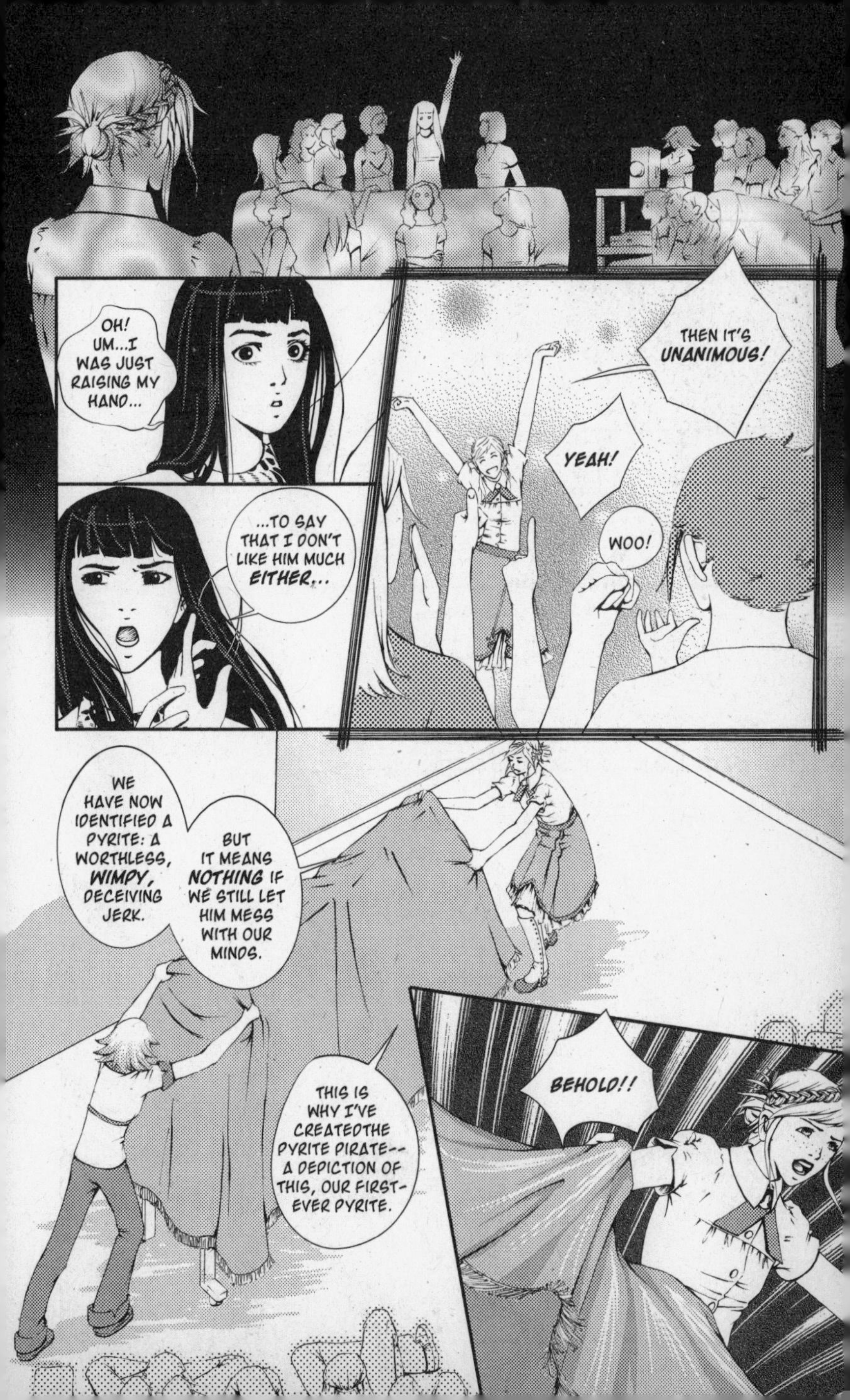
OH! UM...I WAS JUST RAISING MY HAND...
THEN IT'S UNANIMOUS!
YEAH!
...TO SAY THAT I DON'T LIKE HIM MUCH EITHER...
WOO!
WE HAVE NOW IDENTIFIED A PYRITE: A WORTHLESS, WIMPY, DECEIVING JERK.
BUT IT MEANS NOTHING IF WE STILL LET HIM MESS WITH OUR MINDS.
THIS IS WHY I'VE CREATEDTHE PYRITE PIRATE--A DEPICTION OF THIS, OUR FIRST-EVER PYRITE.
BEHOLD!!

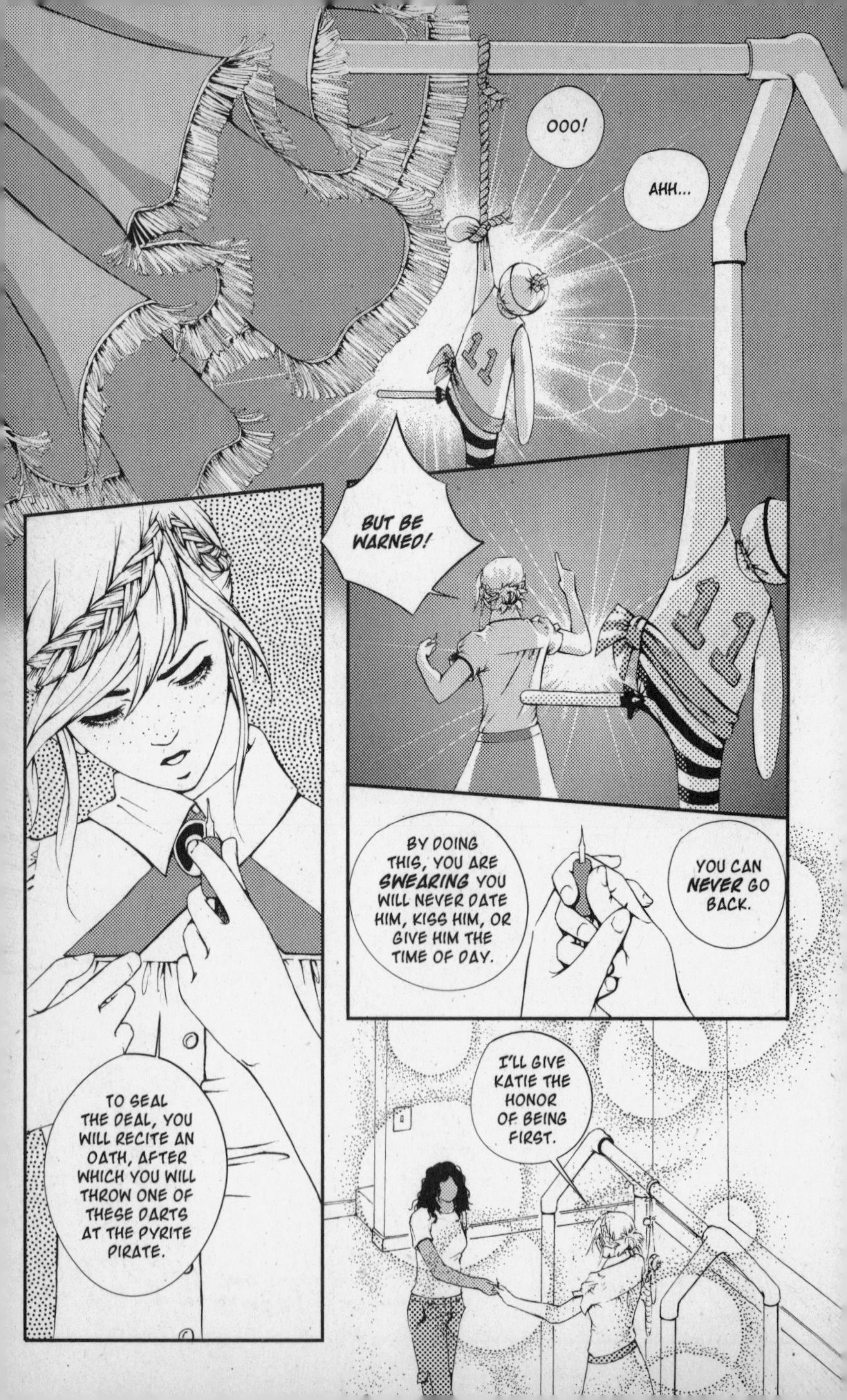

OOO!
AHH...
TO SEAL THE DEAL, YOU WILL RECITE AN OATH, AFTER WHICH YOU WILL THROW ONE OF THESE DARTS AT THE PYRITE PIRATE.
BUT BE WARNED!
BY DOING THIS, YOU ARE **SWEARING** YOU WILL NEVER DATE HIM, KISS HIM, OR GIVE HIM THE TIME OF DAY.
YOU CAN **NEVER** GO BACK.
I'LL GIVE KATIE THE HONOR OF BEING FIRST.

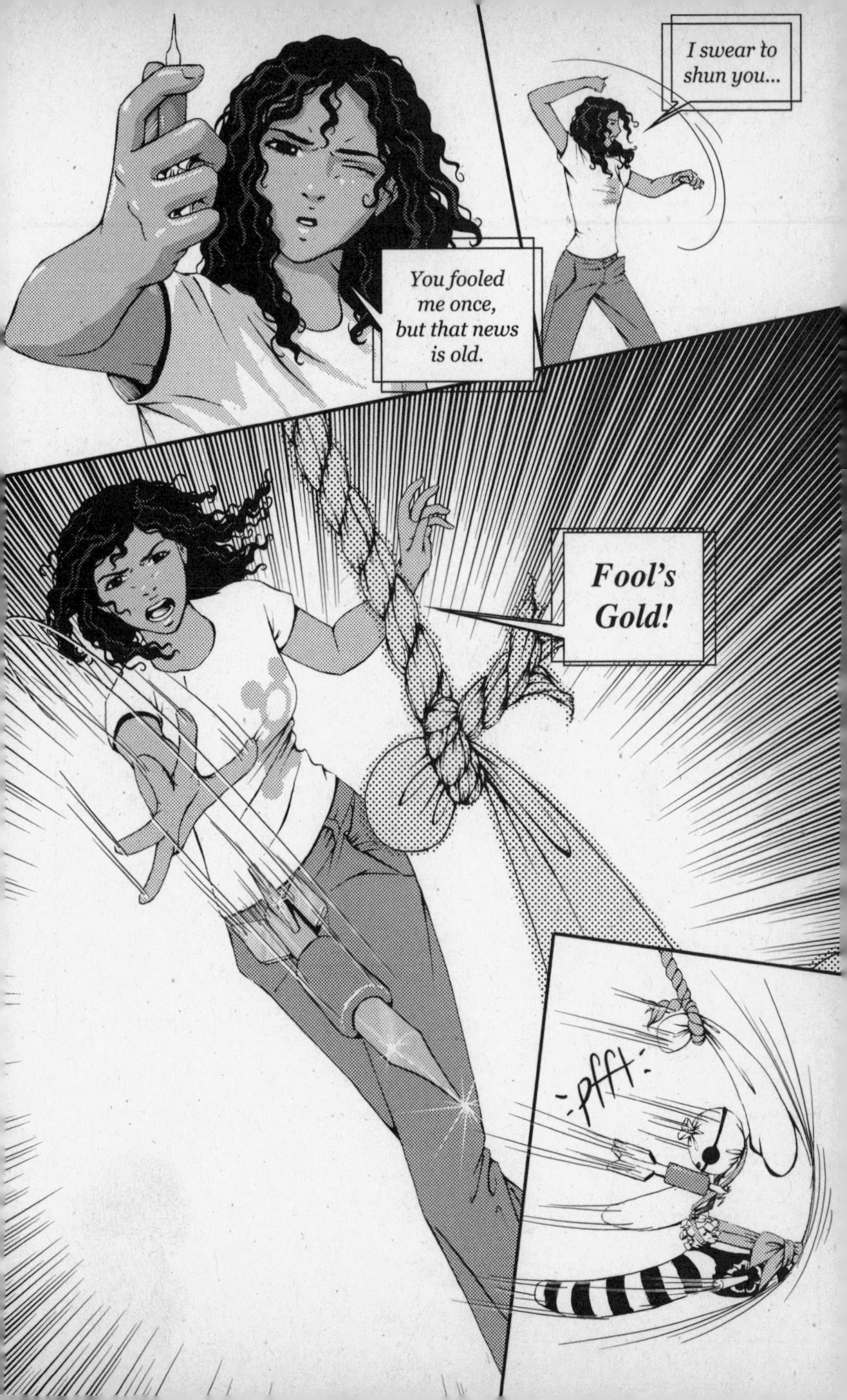
You fooled me once, but that news is old.
I swear to shun you...
Fool's Gold!
-pfft-

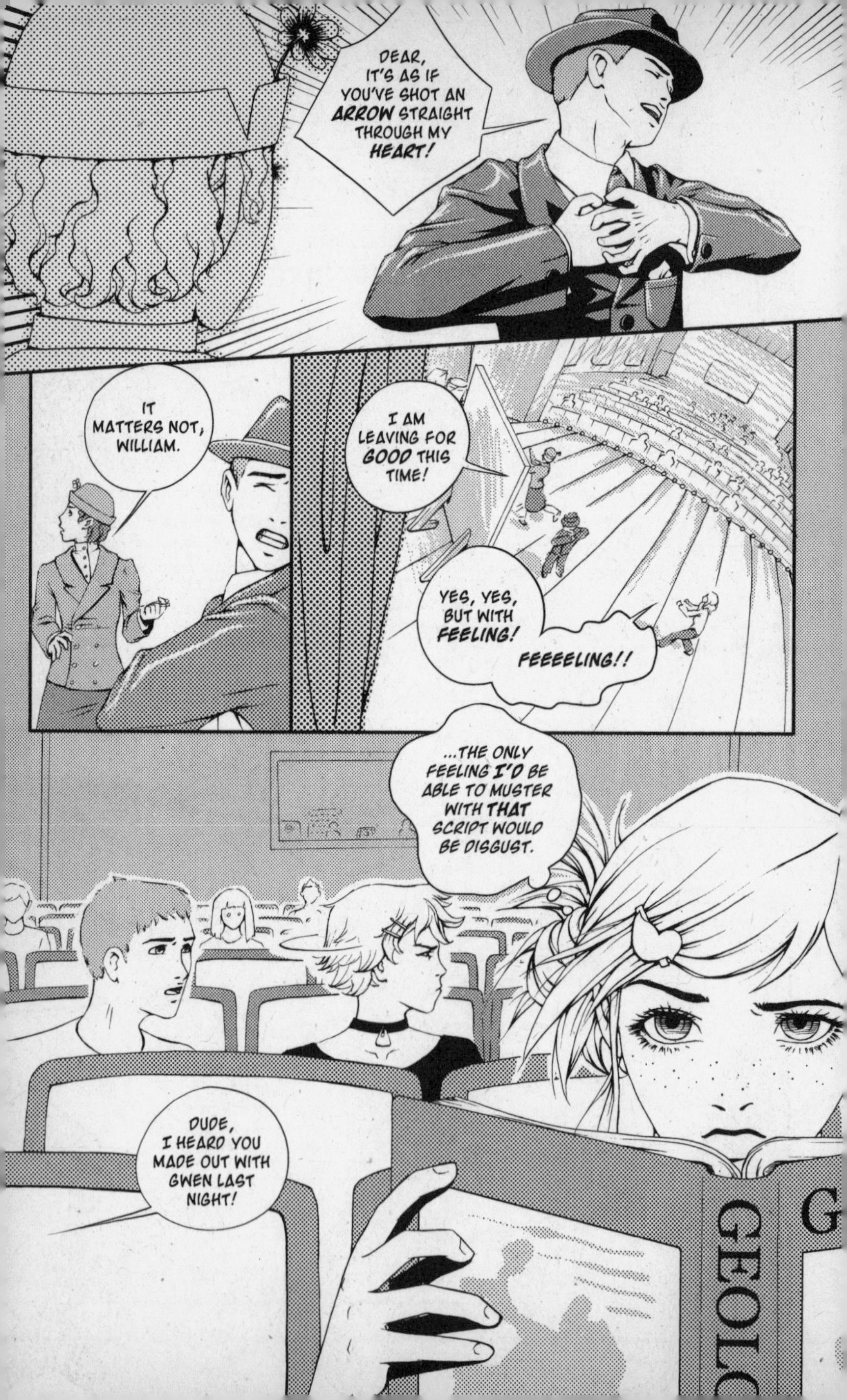
DEAR, IT'S AS IF YOU'VE SHOT AN ARROW STRAIGHT THROUGH MY HEART!
IT MATTERS NOT, WILLIAM.
I AM LEAVING FOR GOOD THIS TIME!
YES, YES, BUT WITH FEELING!
FEEEELING!!
...THE ONLY FEELING I'D BE ABLE TO MUSTER WITH THAT SCRIPT WOULD BE DISGUST.
DUDE, I HEARD YOU MADE OUT WITH GWEN LAST NIGHT!
GEOLO
G

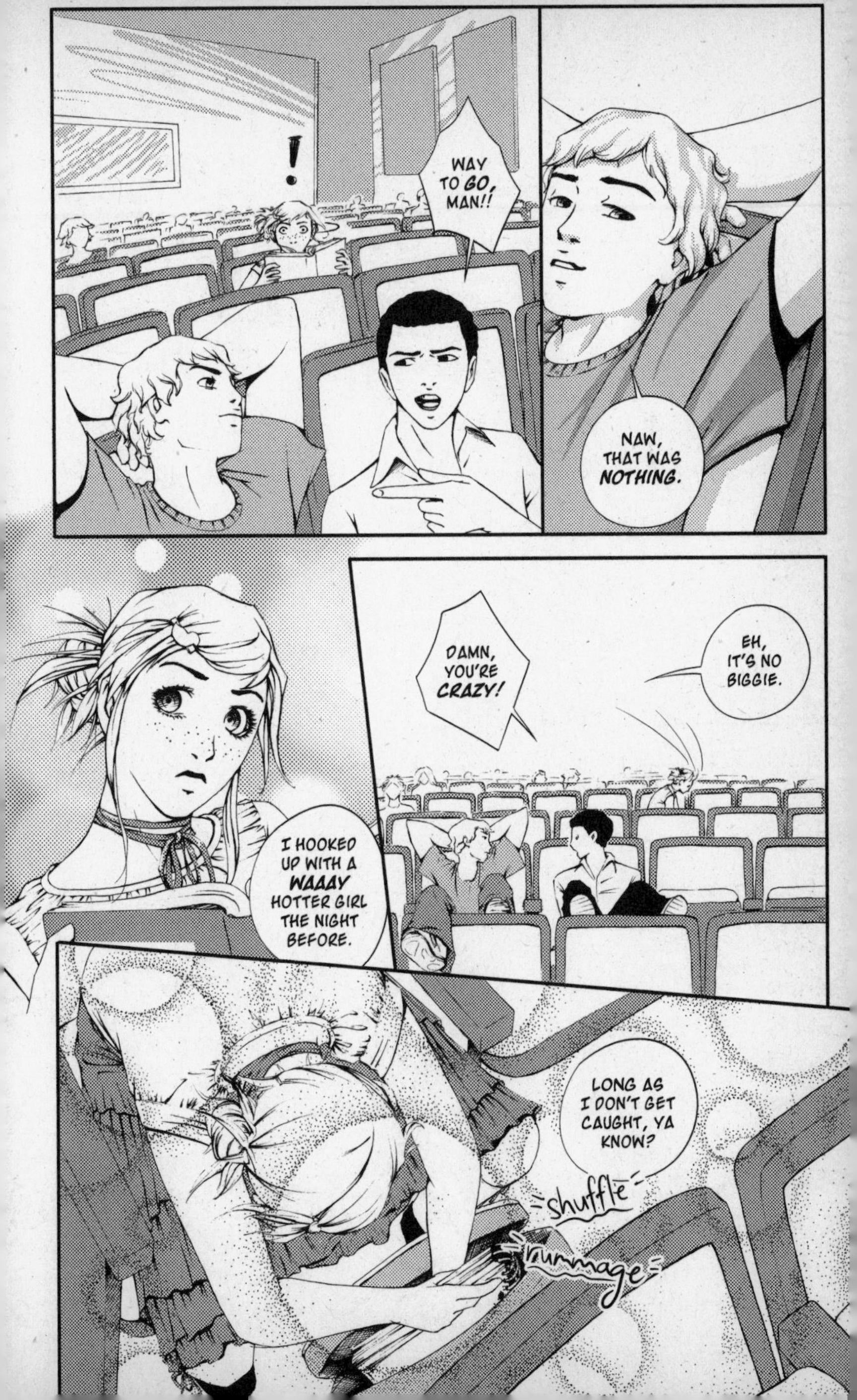
!
WAY TO GO, MAN!!
NAW, THAT WAS NOTHING.
I HOOKED UP WITH A WAAAY HOTTER GIRL THE NIGHT BEFORE.
DAMN, YOU'RE CRAZY!
EH, IT'S NO BIGGIE.
LONG AS I DON'T GET CAUGHT, YA KNOW?
shuffle
rummage

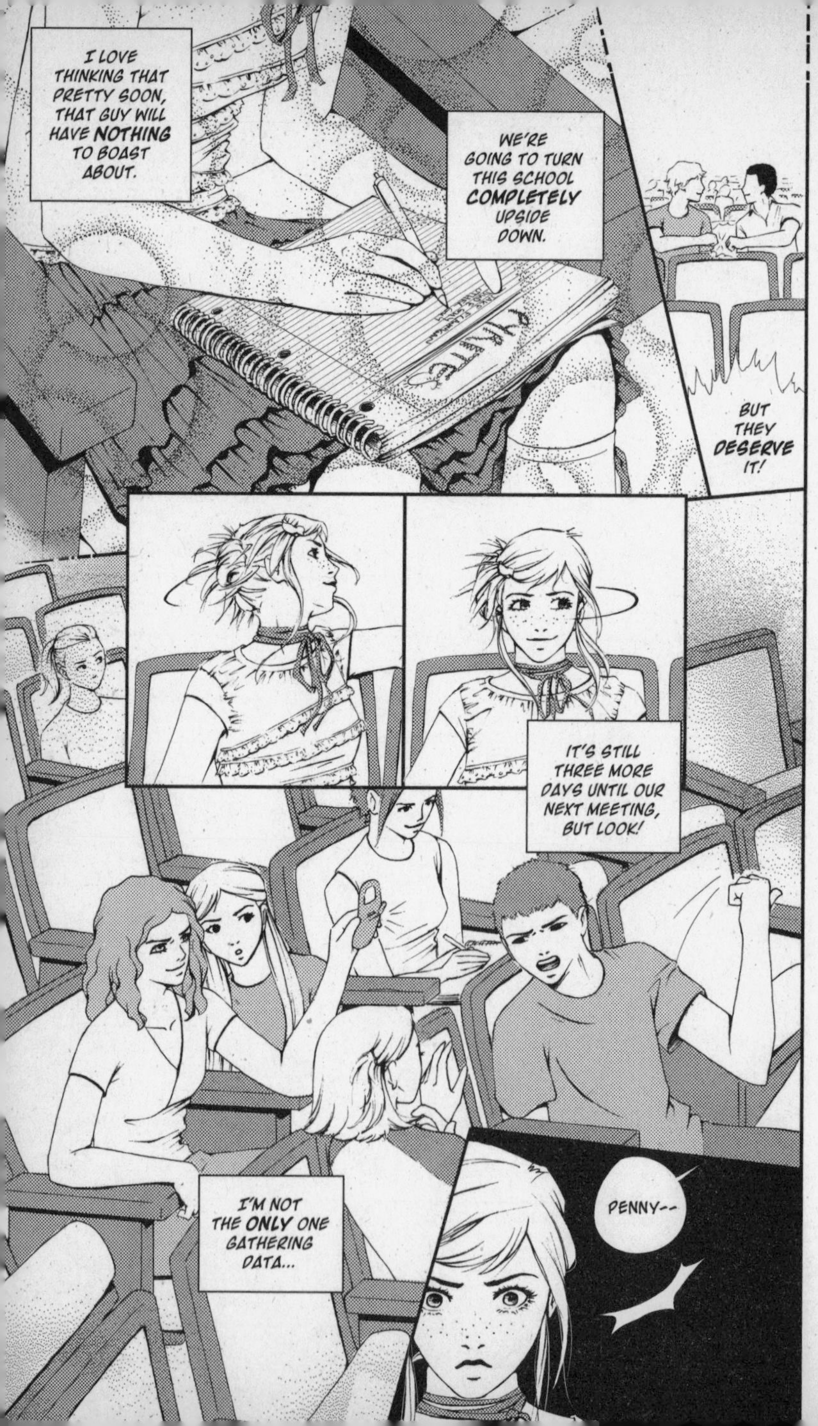
I LOVE THINKING THAT PRETTY SOON, THAT GUY WILL HAVE NOTHING TO BOAST ABOUT.
WE'RE GOING TO TURN THIS SCHOOL COMPLETELY UPSIDE DOWN.
BUT THEY DESERVE IT!
IT'S STILL THREE MORE DAYS UNTIL OUR NEXT MEETING, BUT LOOK!
I'M NOT THE ONLY ONE GATHERING DATA...
PENNY--

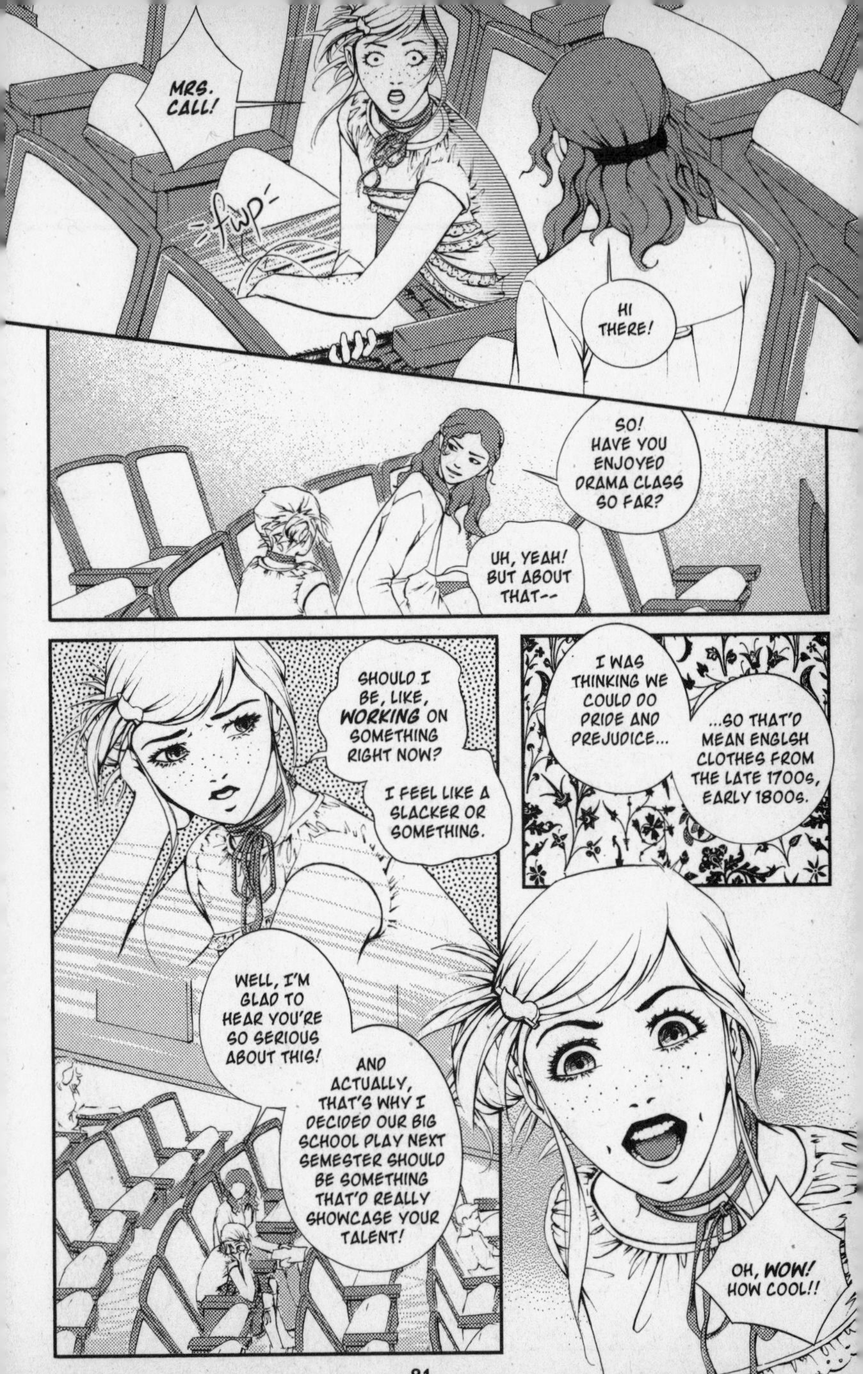
MRS. CALL!
fwp
HI THERE!
SO! HAVE YOU ENJOYED DRAMA CLASS SO FAR?
UH, YEAH! BUT ABOUT THAT--
SHOULD I BE, LIKE, **WORKING** ON SOMETHING RIGHT NOW?
I FEEL LIKE A SLACKER OR SOMETHING.
WELL, I'M GLAD TO HEAR YOU'RE SO SERIOUS ABOUT THIS!
AND ACTUALLY, THAT'S WHY I DECIDED OUR BIG SCHOOL PLAY NEXT SEMESTER SHOULD BE SOMETHING THAT'D REALLY SHOWCASE YOUR TALENT!
I WAS THINKING WE COULD DO PRIDE AND PREJUDICE...
...SO THAT'D MEAN ENGLSH CLOTHES FROM THE LATE 1700s, EARLY 1800s.
OH, **WOW!** HOW COOL!!

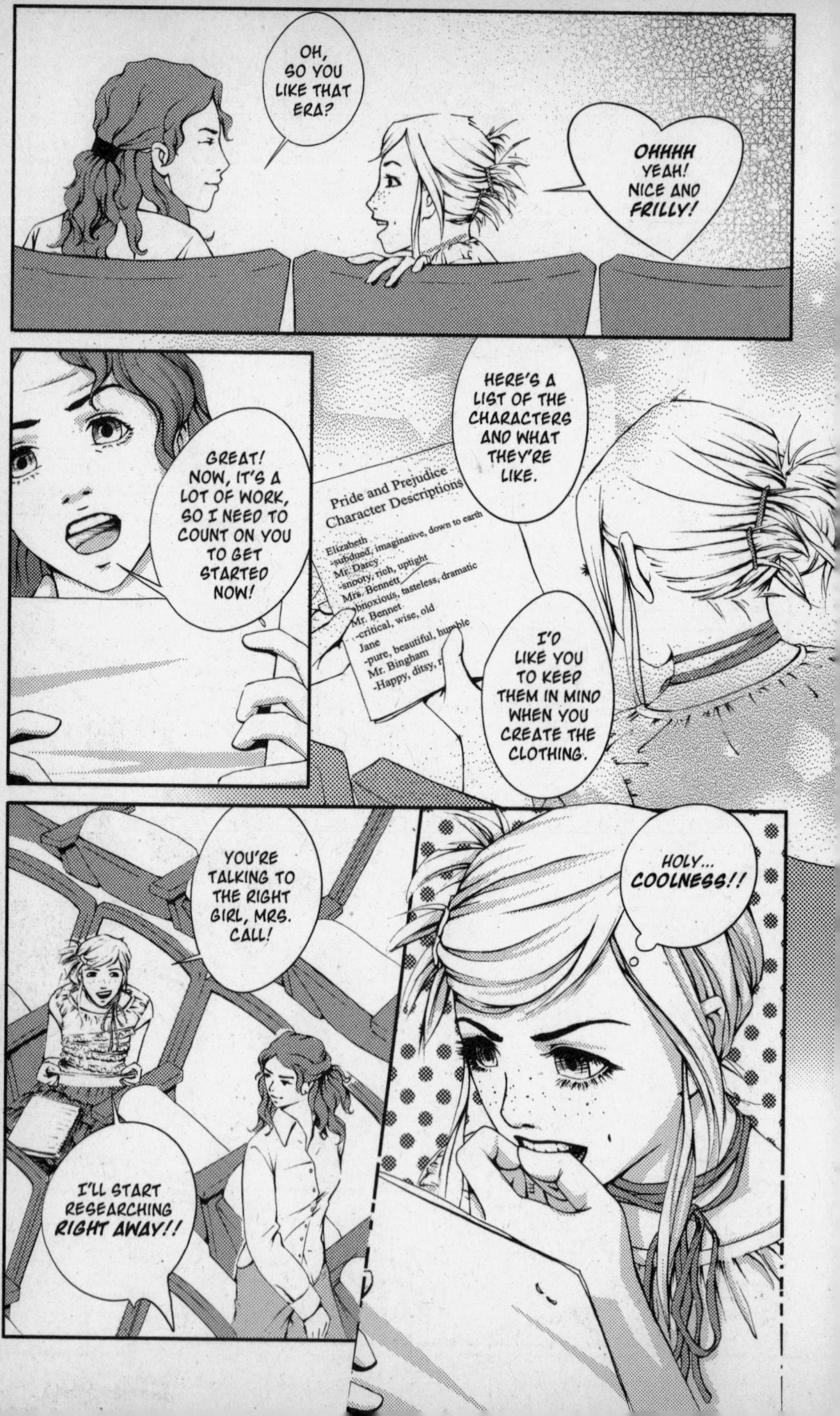
OH, SO YOU LIKE THAT ERA?
OHHHH YEAH! NICE AND FRILLY!
GREAT! NOW, IT'S A LOT OF WORK, SO I NEED TO COUNT ON YOU TO GET STARTED NOW!
HERE'S A LIST OF THE CHARACTERS AND WHAT THEY'RE LIKE.
Pride and Prejudice
Character Descriptions
Elizabeth
-subdued, imaginative, down to earth
Mr. Darcy
-snooty, rich, uptight
Mrs. Bennett
bnoxious, tasteless, dramatic
Mr. Bennet
-critical, wise, old
Jane
-pure, beautiful, humble
Mr. Bingham
-Happy, ditsy,
I'D LIKE YOU TO KEEP THEM IN MIND WHEN YOU CREATE THE CLOTHING.
YOU'RE TALKING TO THE RIGHT GIRL, MRS. CALL!
I'LL START RESEARCHING RIGHT AWAY!!
HOLY... COOLNESS!!

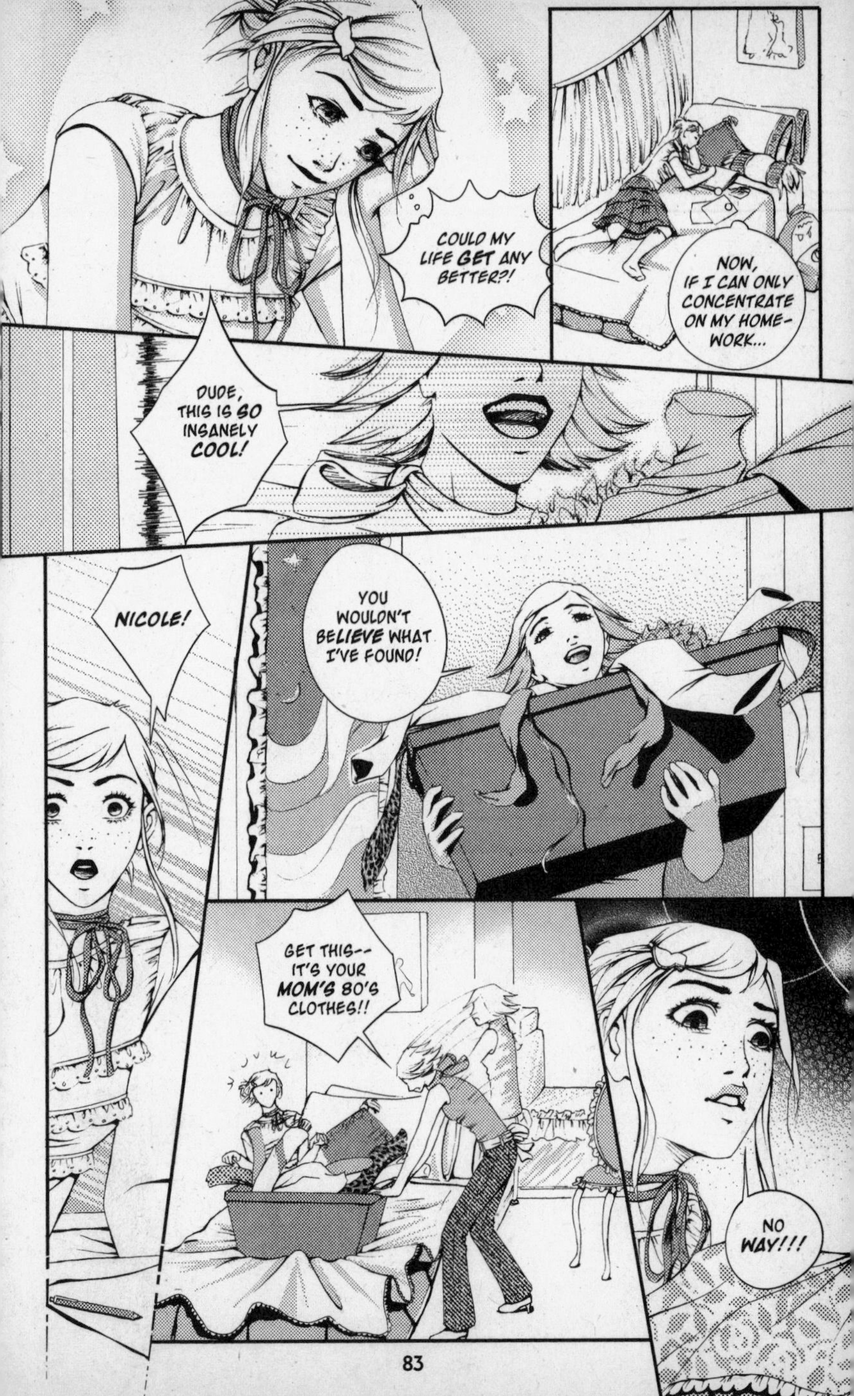
COULD MY LIFE **GET** ANY BETTER?!
NOW, IF I CAN ONLY CONCENTRATE ON MY HOMEWORK...
DUDE, THIS IS **SO** INSANELY **COOL!**
NICOLE!
YOU WOULDN'T BE**LIEVE** WHAT I'VE FOUND!
GET THIS-- IT'S YOUR **MOM'S** 80'S CLOTHES!!
NO **WAY!!!**

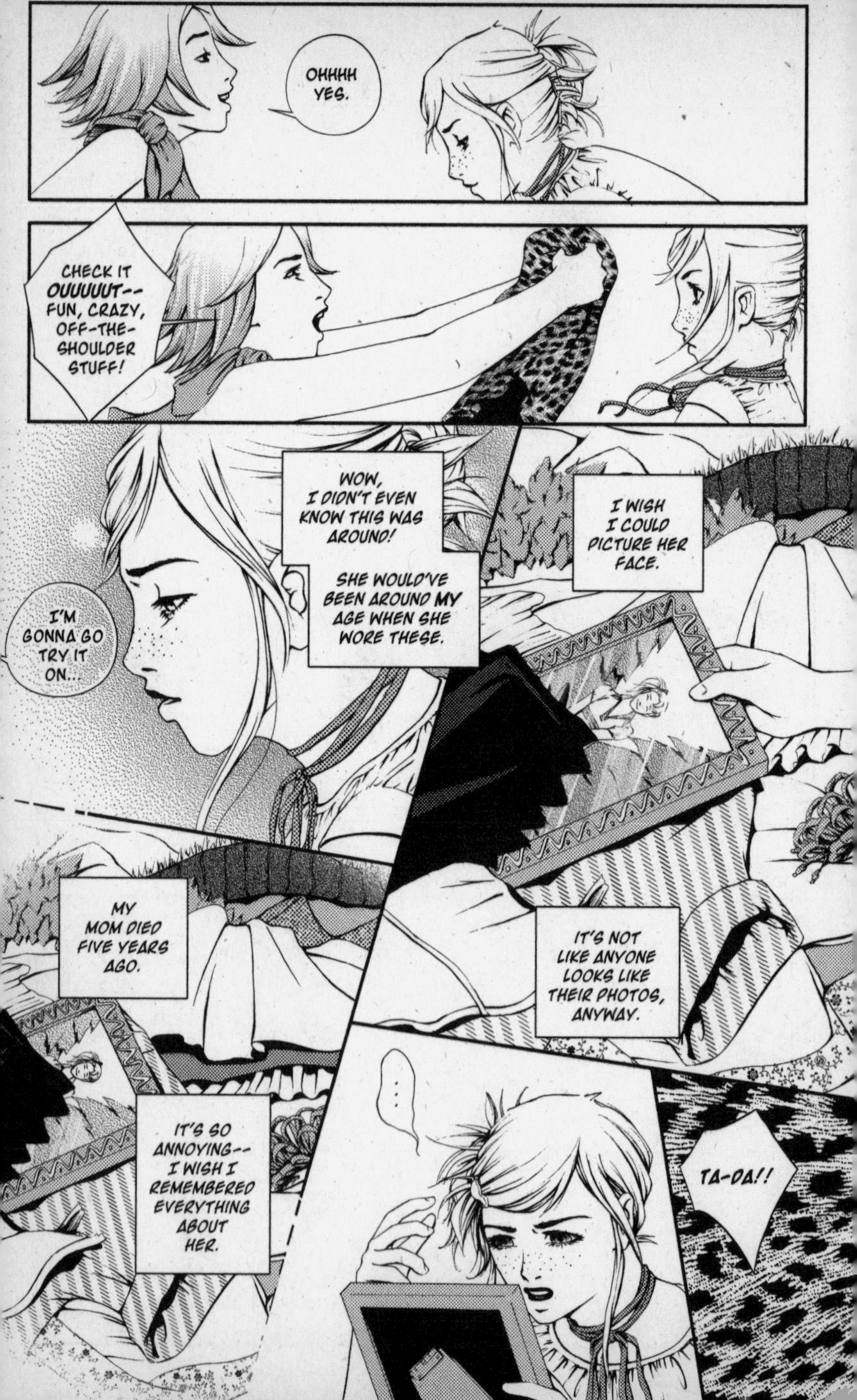
OHHHH YES.
CHECK IT OUUUUUT--FUN, CRAZY, OFF-THE-SHOULDER STUFF!
I'M GONNA GO TRY IT ON...
WOW, I DIDN'T EVEN KNOW THIS WAS AROUND!
SHE WOULD'VE BEEN AROUND MY AGE WHEN SHE WORE THESE.
I WISH I COULD PICTURE HER FACE.
MY MOM DIED FIVE YEARS AGO.
IT'S NOT LIKE ANYONE LOOKS LIKE THEIR PHOTOS, ANYWAY.
IT'S SO ANNOYING--I WISH I REMEMBERED EVERYTHING ABOUT HER.
...
TA-DA!!

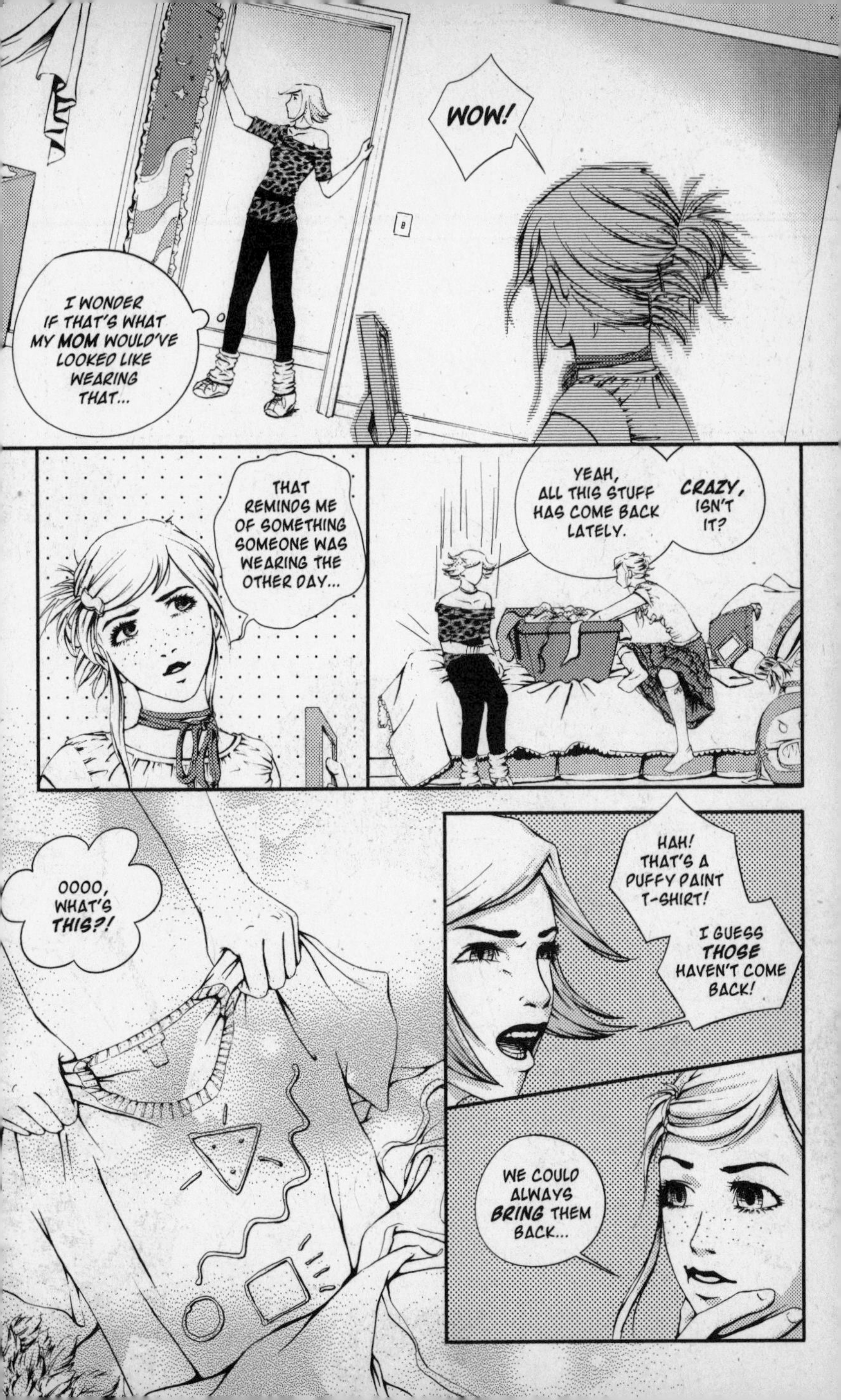
WOW!
I WONDER IF THAT'S WHAT MY MOM WOULD'VE LOOKED LIKE WEARING THAT...
THAT REMINDS ME OF SOMETHING SOMEONE WAS WEARING THE OTHER DAY...
YEAH, ALL THIS STUFF HAS COME BACK LATELY.
CRAZY, ISN'T IT?
OOOO, WHAT'S THIS?!
HAH! THAT'S A PUFFY PAINT T-SHIRT!
I GUESS THOSE HAVEN'T COME BACK!
WE COULD ALWAYS BRING THEM BACK...

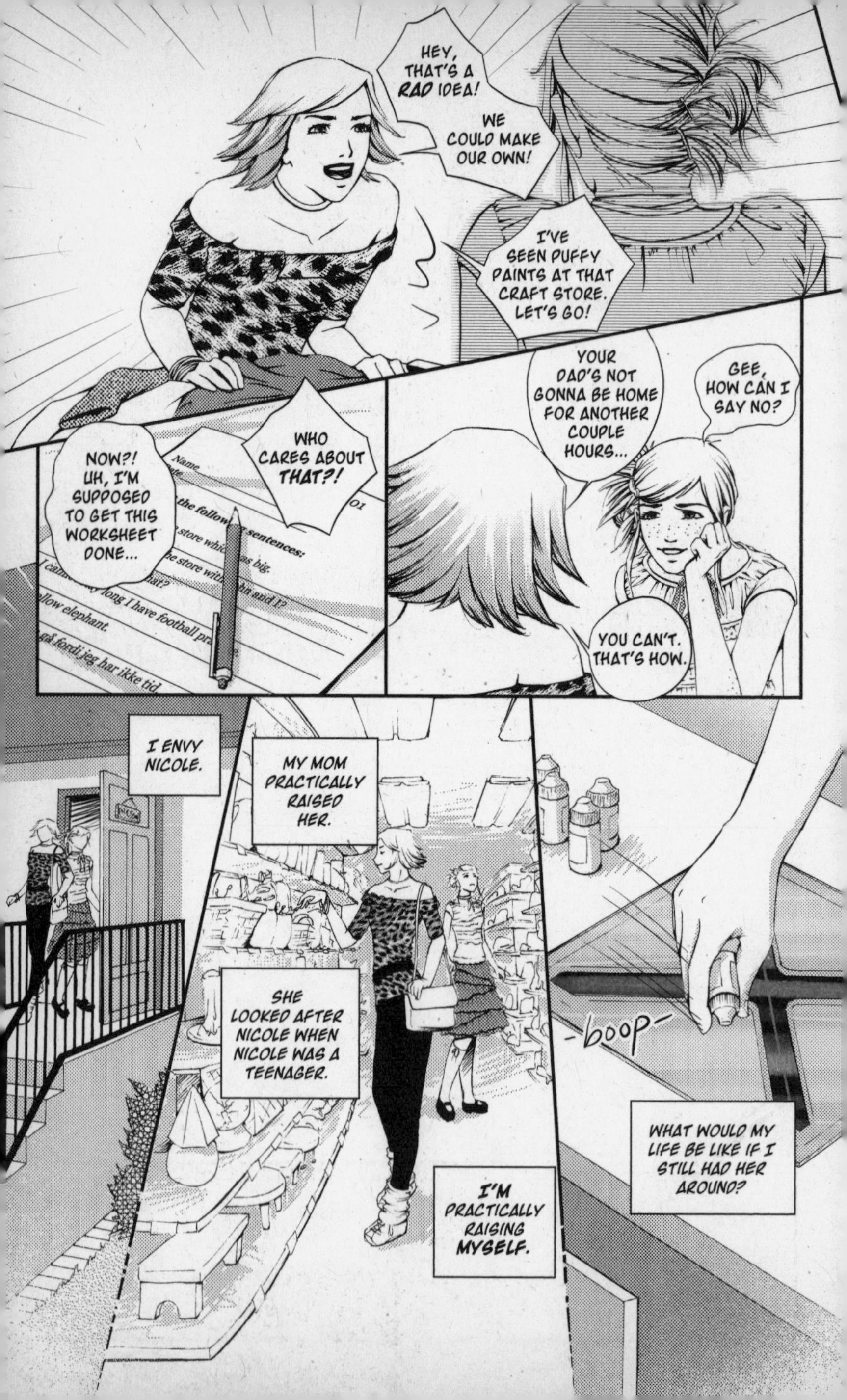
HEY, THAT'S A RAD IDEA!
WE COULD MAKE OUR OWN!
I'VE SEEN PUFFY PAINTS AT THAT CRAFT STORE. LET'S GO!
NOW?! UH, I'M SUPPOSED TO GET THIS WORKSHEET DONE...
WHO CARES ABOUT THAT?!
YOUR DAD'S NOT GONNA BE HOME FOR ANOTHER COUPLE HOURS...
GEE, HOW CAN I SAY NO?
YOU CAN'T. THAT'S HOW.
I ENVY NICOLE.
MY MOM PRACTICALLY RAISED HER.
SHE LOOKED AFTER NICOLE WHEN NICOLE WAS A TEENAGER.
I'M PRACTICALLY RAISING MYSELF.
-boop-
WHAT WOULD MY LIFE BE LIKE IF I STILL HAD HER AROUND?

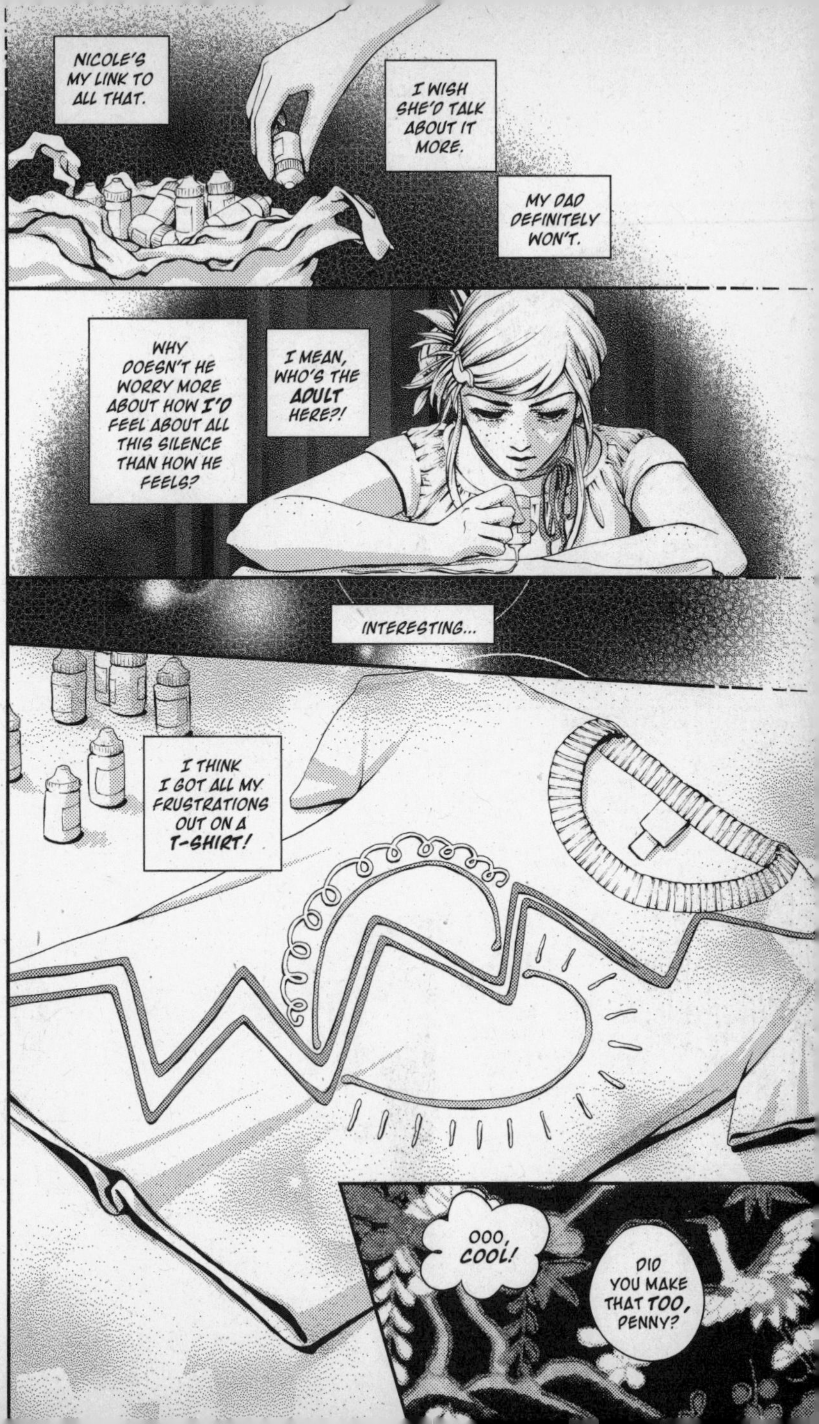
NICOLE'S MY LINK TO ALL THAT.
I WISH SHE'D TALK ABOUT IT MORE.
MY DAD DEFINITELY WON'T.
WHY DOESN'T HE WORRY MORE ABOUT HOW I'D FEEL ABOUT ALL THIS SILENCE THAN HOW HE FEELS?
I MEAN, WHO'S THE ADULT HERE?!
INTERESTING...
I THINK I GOT ALL MY FRUSTRATIONS OUT ON A T-SHIRT!
OOO, COOL!
DID YOU MAKE THAT TOO, PENNY?

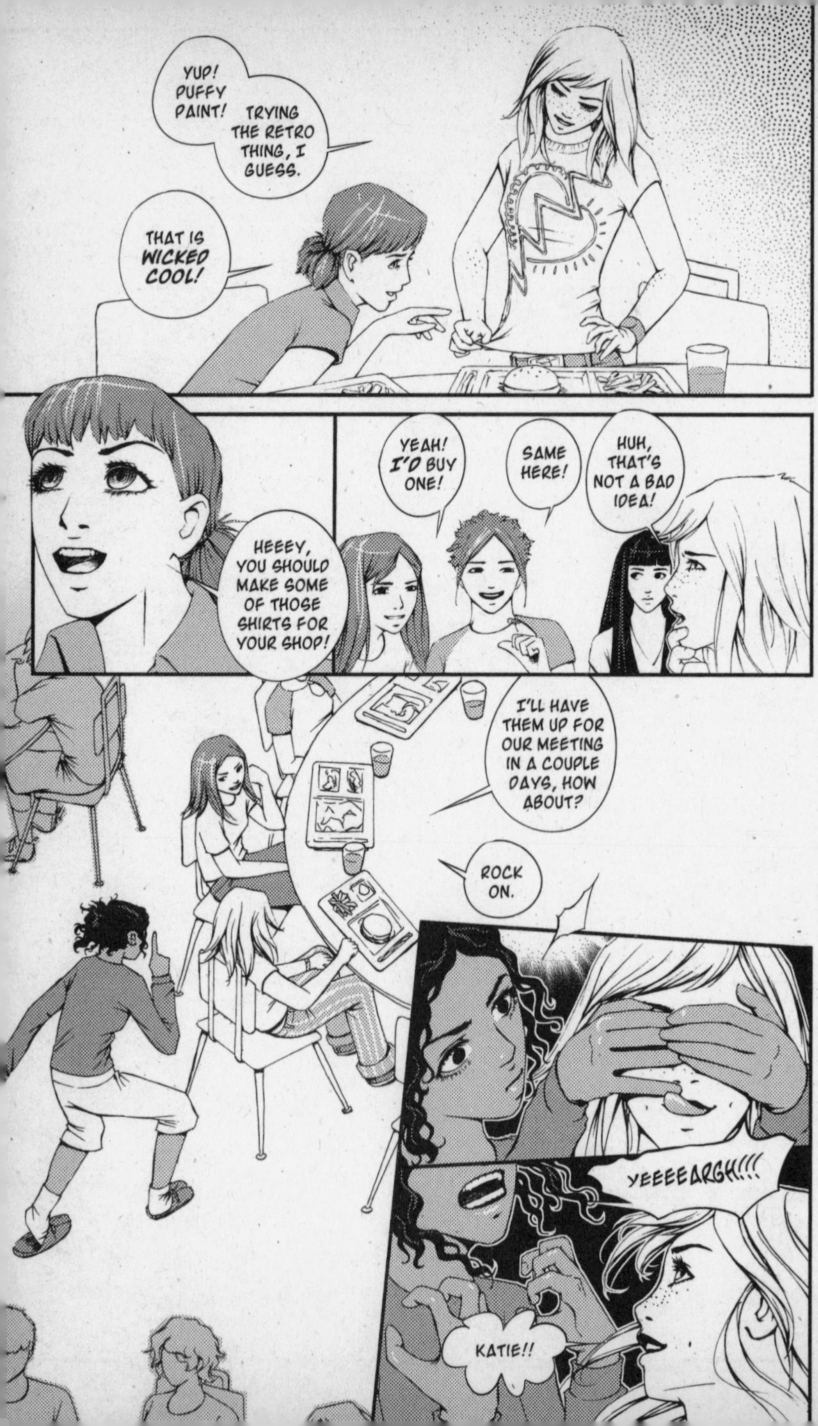

YUP! PUFFY PAINT! TRYING THE RETRO THING, I GUESS.
THAT IS WICKED COOL!
HEEEY, YOU SHOULD MAKE SOME OF THOSE SHIRTS FOR YOUR SHOP!
YEAH! I'D BUY ONE!
SAME HERE!
HUH, THAT'S NOT A BAD IDEA!
I'LL HAVE THEM UP FOR OUR MEETING IN A COUPLE DAYS, HOW ABOUT?
ROCK ON.
YEEEEARGH!!!
KATIE!!

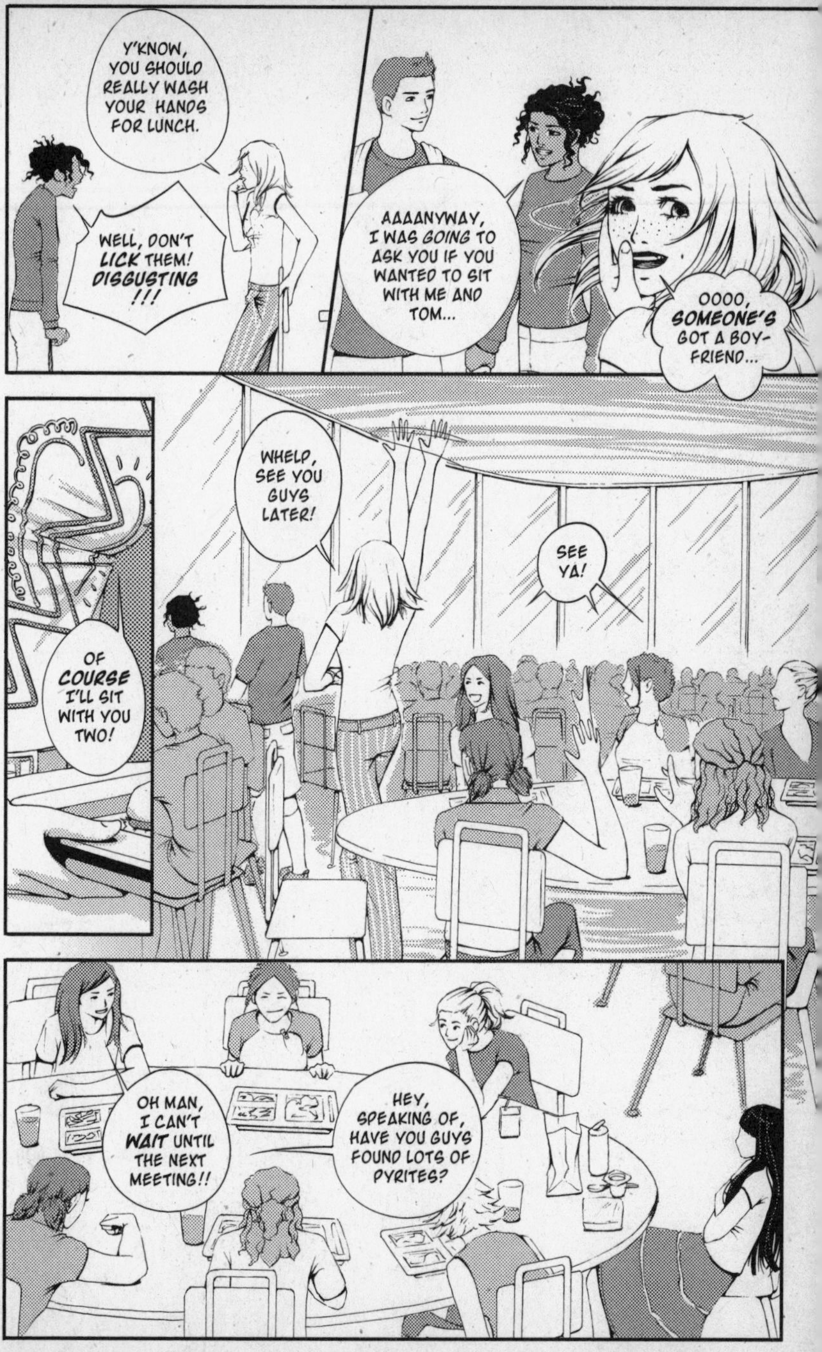

Y'KNOW, YOU SHOULD REALLY WASH YOUR HANDS FOR LUNCH.
WELL, DON'T LICK THEM! DISGUSTING!!!
AAAANYWAY, I WAS GOING TO ASK YOU IF YOU WANTED TO SIT WITH ME AND TOM...
OOOO, SOMEONE'S GOT A BOY-FRIEND...
OF COURSE I'LL SIT WITH YOU TWO!
WHELP, SEE YOU GUYS LATER!
SEE YA!
OH MAN, I CAN'T WAIT UNTIL THE NEXT MEETING!!
HEY, SPEAKING OF, HAVE YOU GUYS FOUND LOTS OF PYRITES?

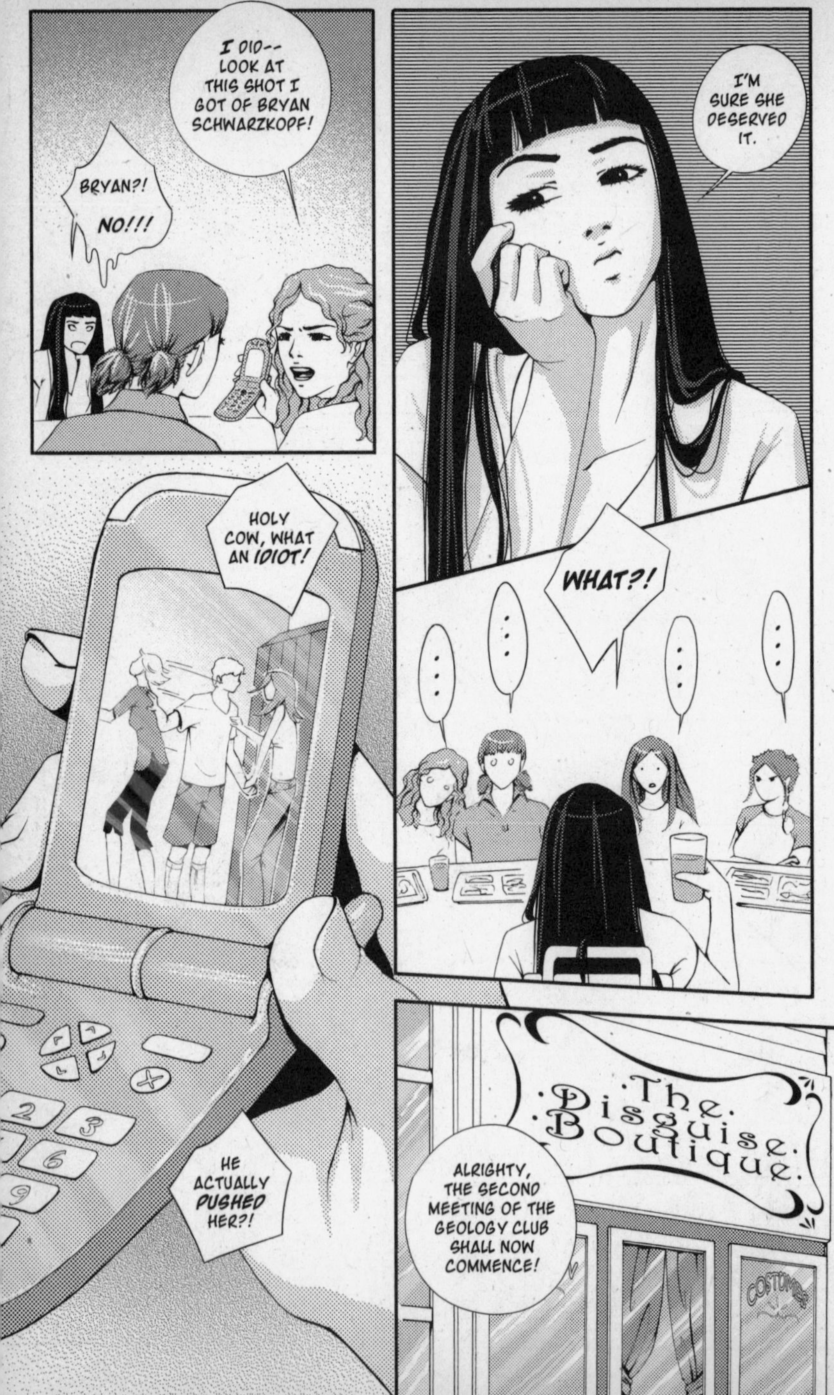
I DID-- LOOK AT THIS SHOT I GOT OF BRYAN SCHWARZKOPF!
BRYAN?! NO!!!
I'M SURE SHE DESERVED IT.
HOLY COW, WHAT AN *IDIOT*!
HE ACTUALLY **PUSHED** HER?!
WHAT?!
The Disguise Boutique
ALRIGHTY, THE SECOND MEETING OF THE GEOLOGY CLUB SHALL NOW COMMENCE!

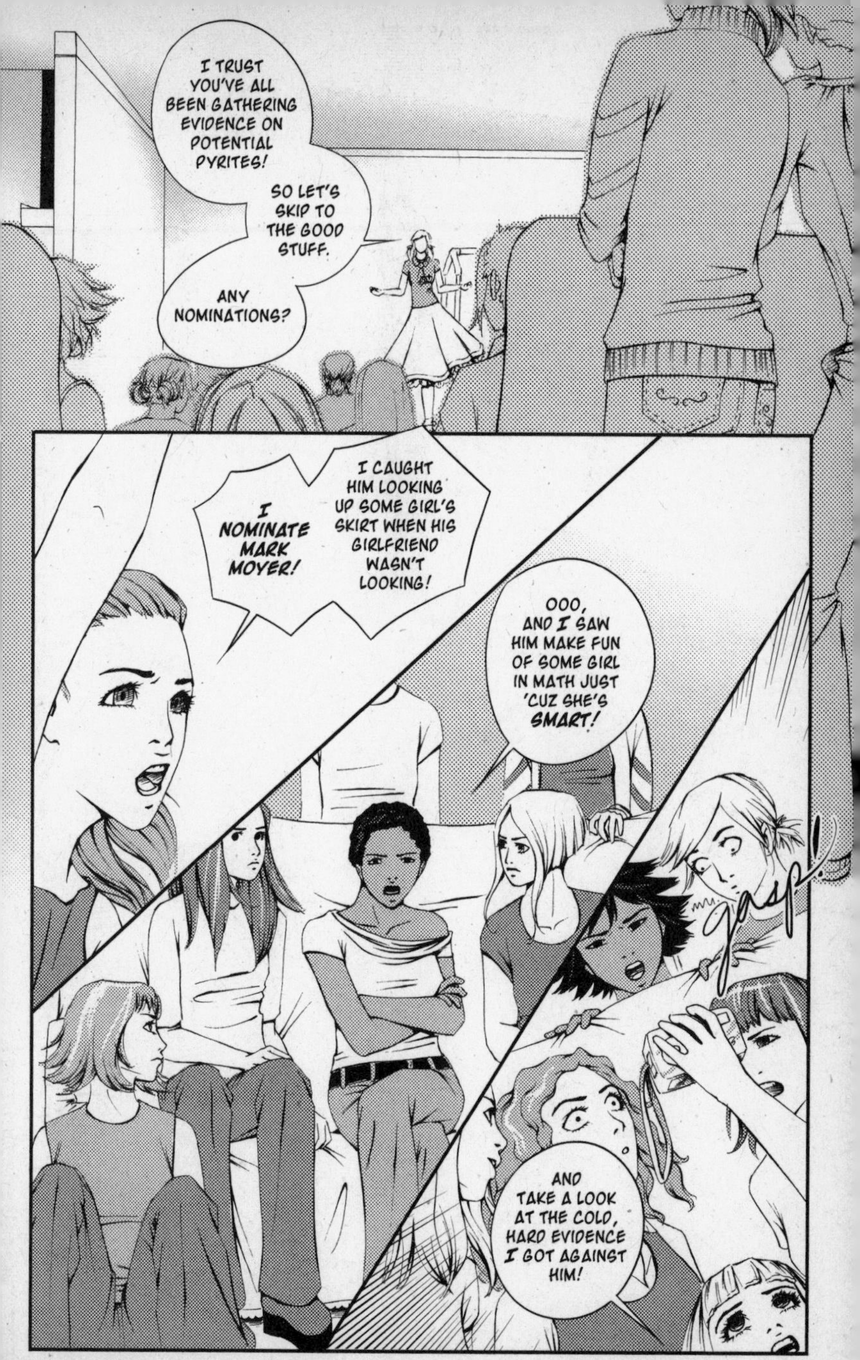
I TRUST YOU'VE ALL BEEN GATHERING EVIDENCE ON POTENTIAL PYRITES!
SO LET'S SKIP TO THE GOOD STUFF.
ANY NOMINATIONS?
I NOMINATE MARK MOYER!
I CAUGHT HIM LOOKING UP SOME GIRL'S SKIRT WHEN HIS GIRLFRIEND WASN'T LOOKING!
OOO, AND I SAW HIM MAKE FUN OF SOME GIRL IN MATH JUST 'CUZ SHE'S SMART!
gasp!
AND TAKE A LOOK AT THE COLD, HARD EVIDENCE I GOT AGAINST HIM!

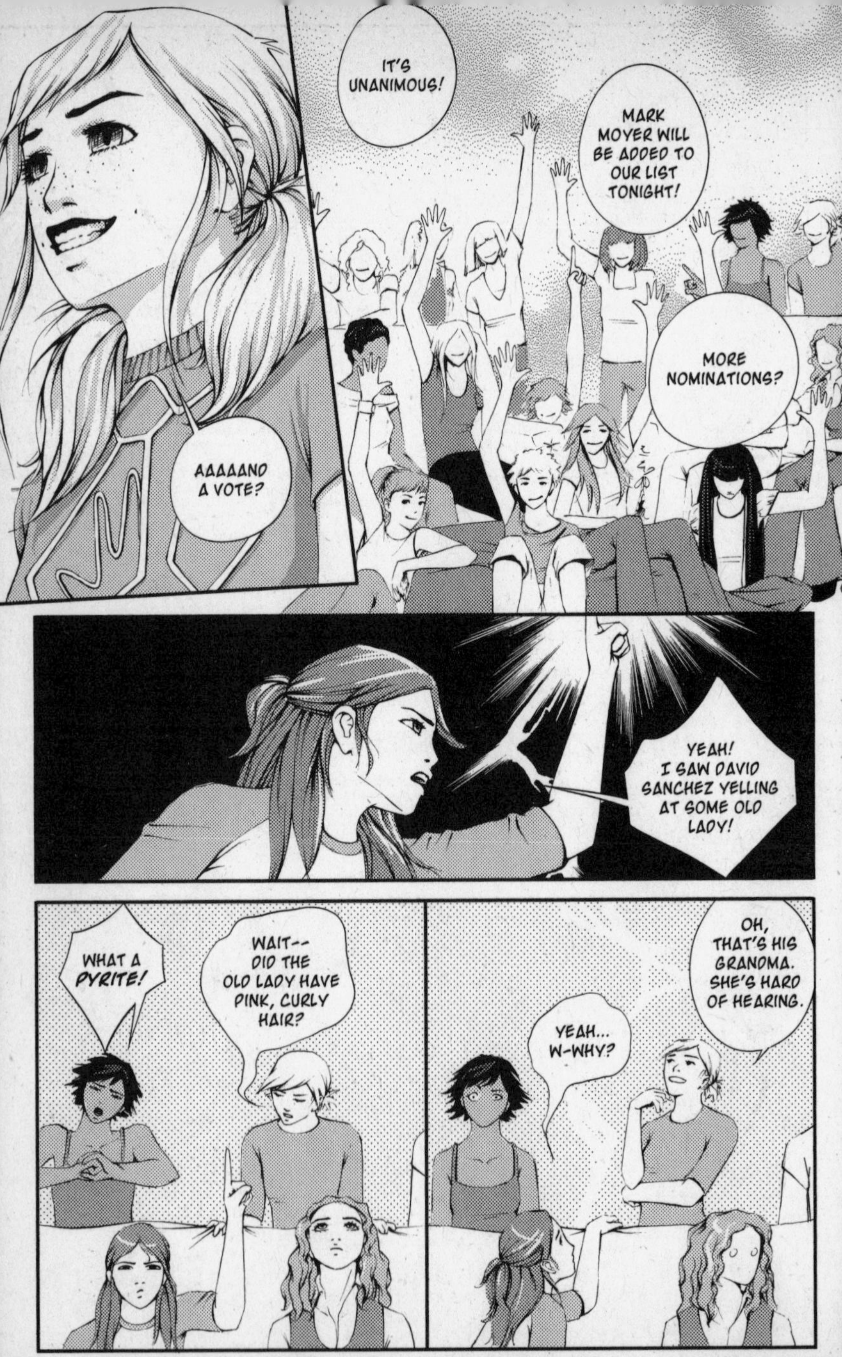
AAAAAND A VOTE?
IT'S UNANIMOUS!
MARK MOYER WILL BE ADDED TO OUR LIST TONIGHT!
MORE NOMINATIONS?
YEAH! I SAW DAVID SANCHEZ YELLING AT SOME OLD LADY!
WHAT A PYRITE!
WAIT-- DID THE OLD LADY HAVE PINK, CURLY HAIR?
YEAH... W-WHY?
OH, THAT'S HIS GRANDMA. SHE'S HARD OF HEARING.

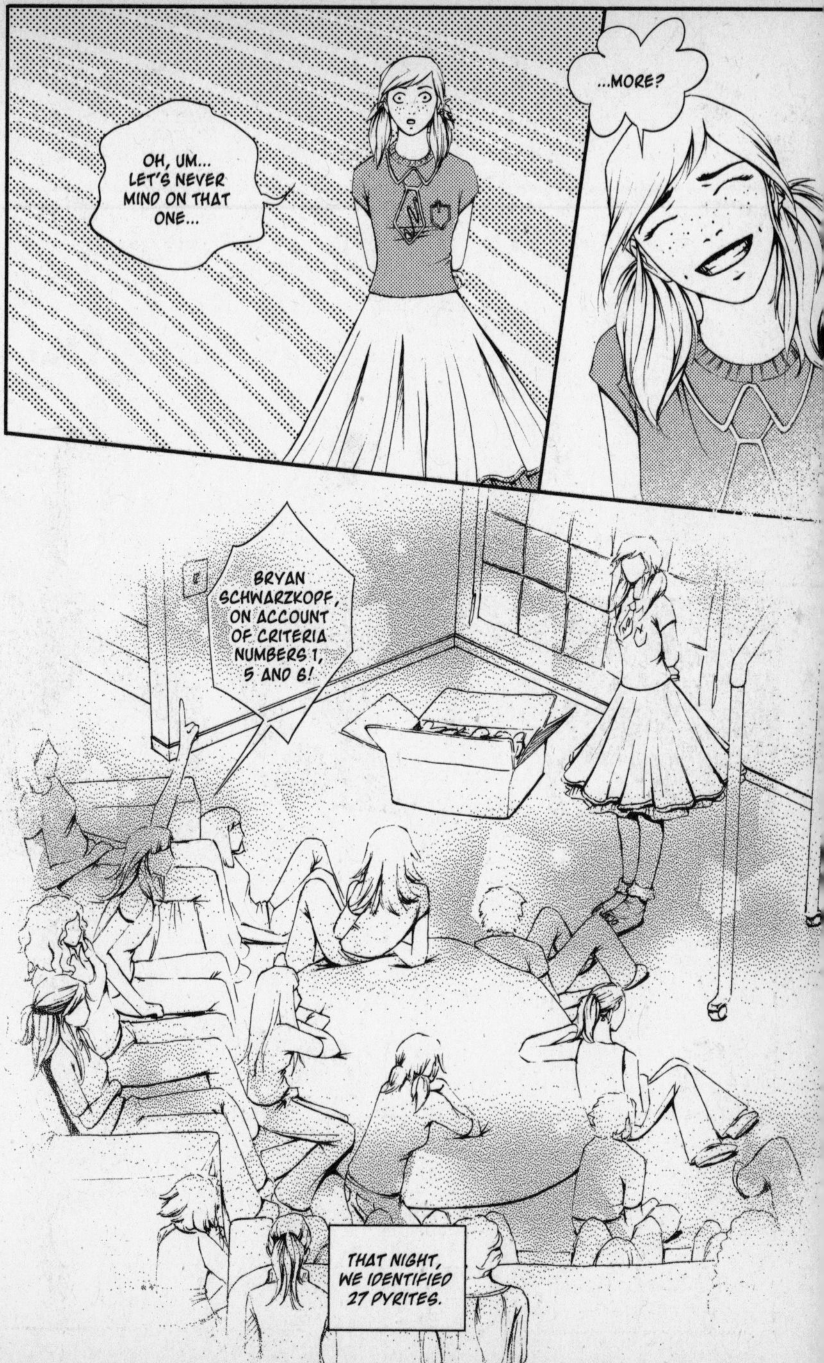
OH, UM... LET'S NEVER MIND ON THAT ONE...
...MORE?
BRYAN SCHWARZKOPF, ON ACCOUNT OF CRITERIA NUMBERS 1, 5 AND 6!
THAT NIGHT, WE IDENTIFIED 27 PYRITES.

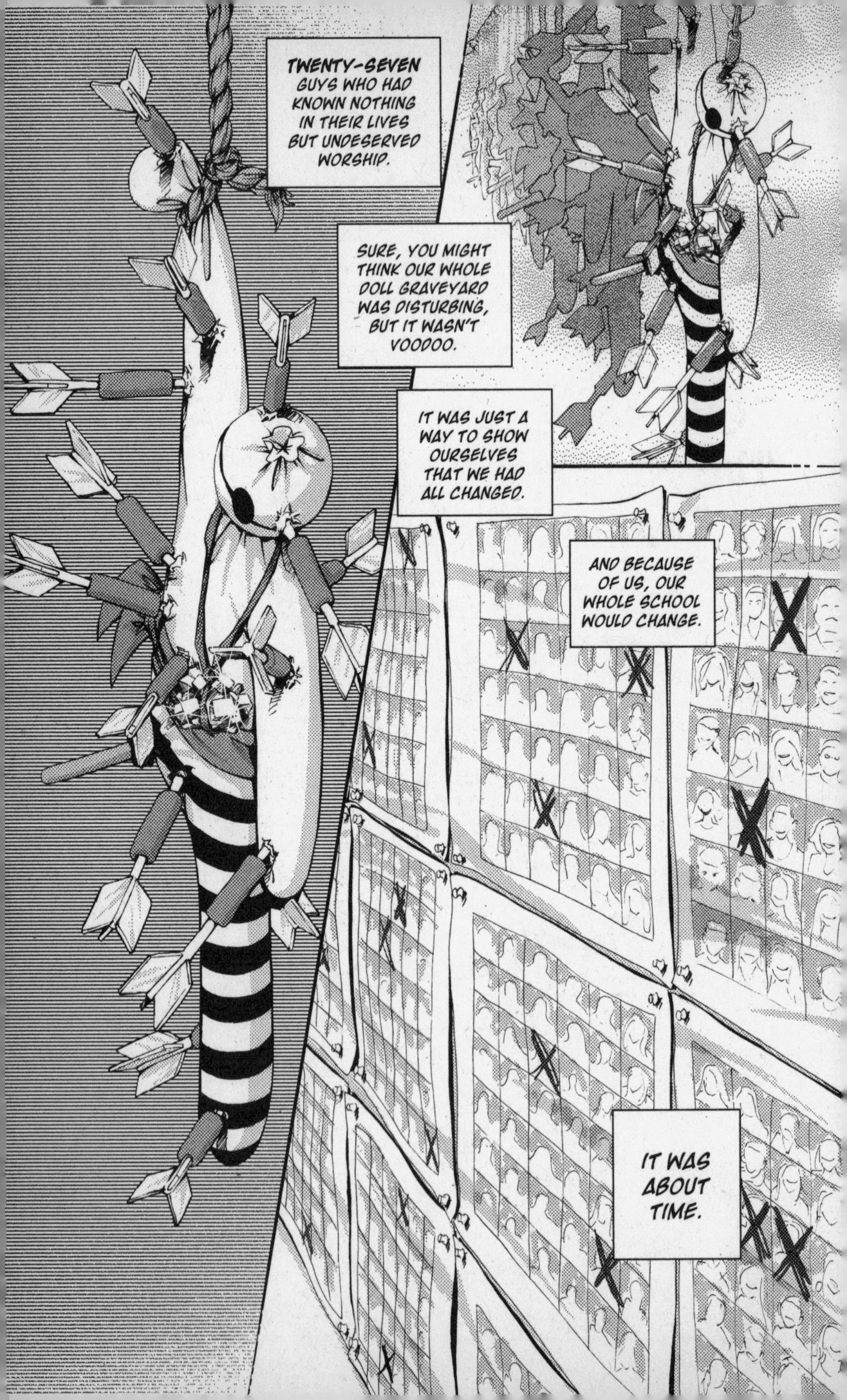
TWENTY-SEVEN GUYS WHO HAD KNOWN NOTHING IN THEIR LIVES BUT UNDESERVED WORSHIP.
SURE, YOU MIGHT THINK OUR WHOLE DOLL GRAVEYARD WAS DISTURBING, BUT IT WASN'T VOODOO.
IT WAS JUST A WAY TO SHOW OURSELVES THAT WE HAD ALL CHANGED.
AND BECAUSE OF US, OUR WHOLE SCHOOL WOULD CHANGE.
IT WAS ABOUT TIME.

Chapter 4: The Midnight Tagger

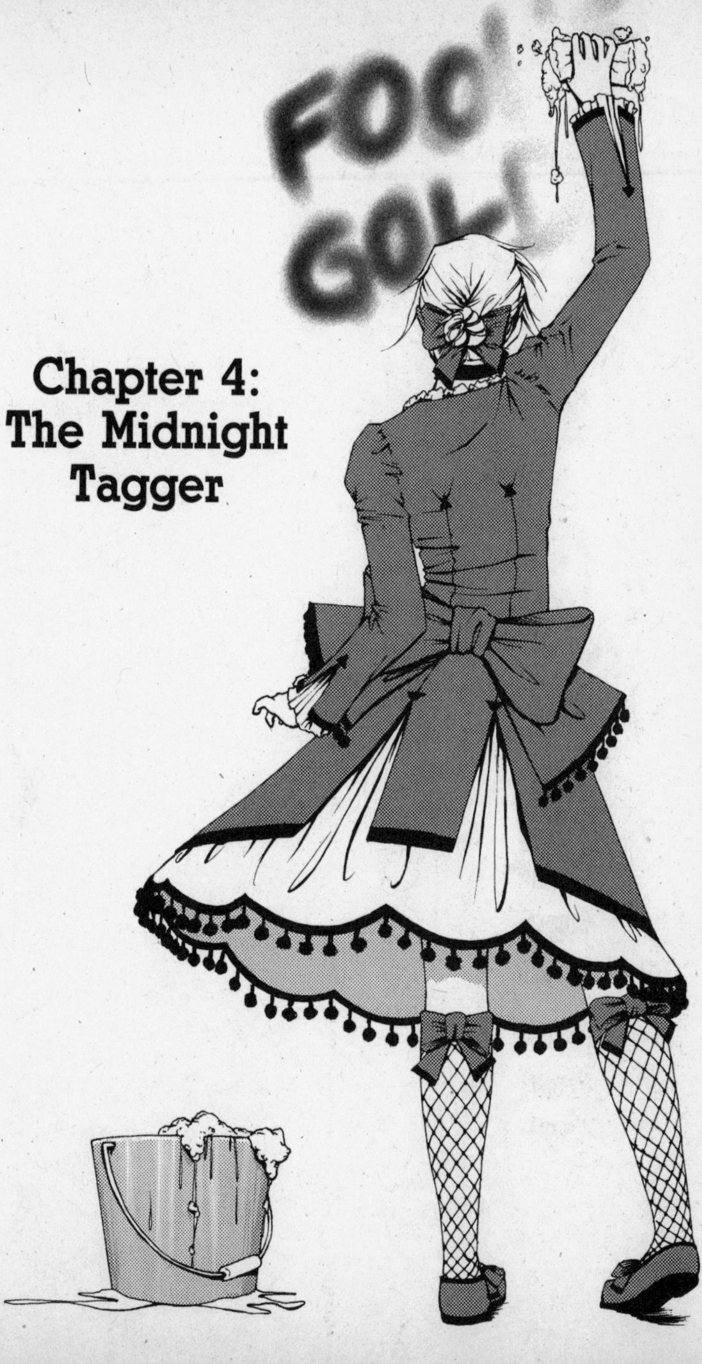

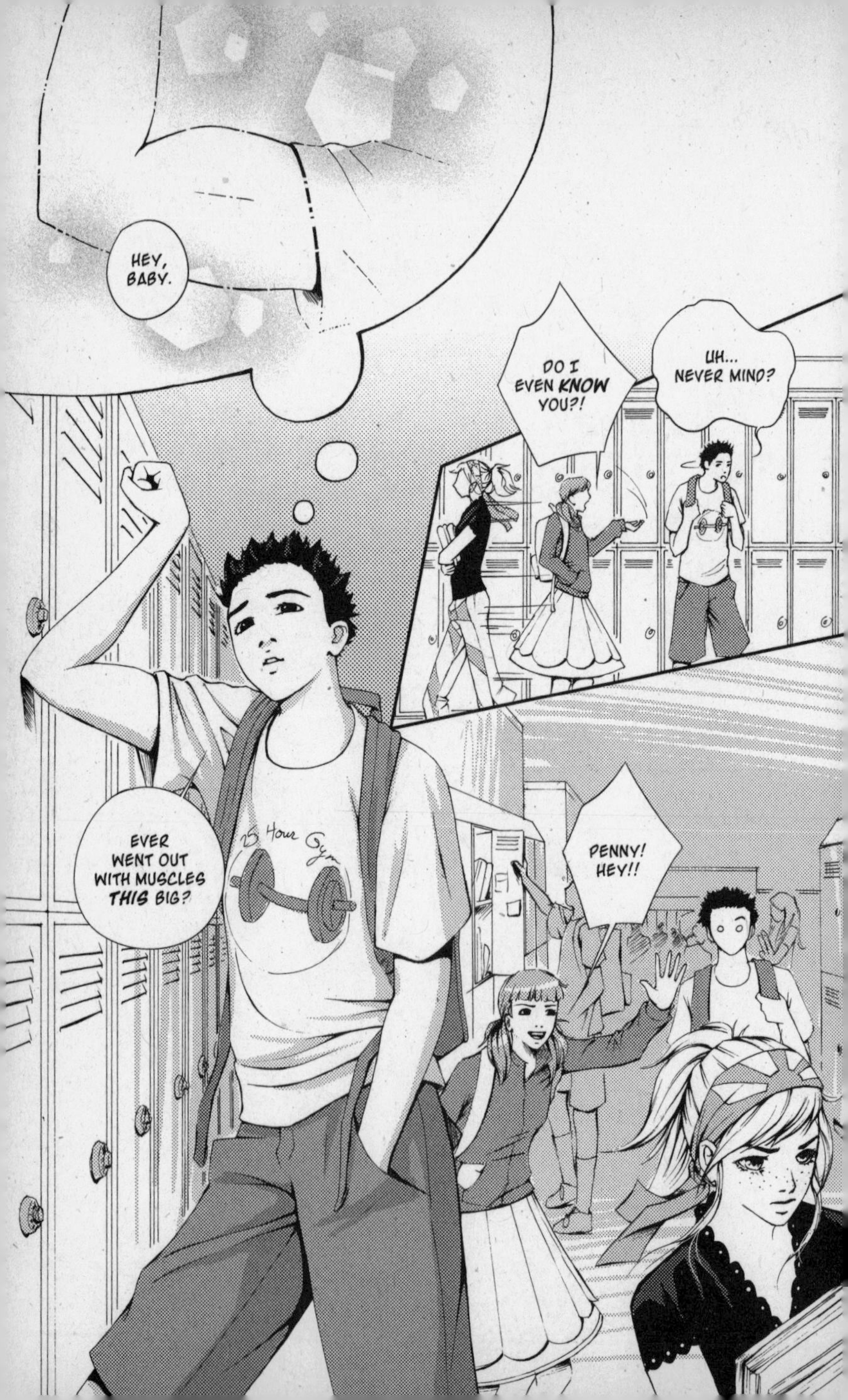
HEY, BABY.
25 Hour Gym
EVER WENT OUT WITH MUSCLES THIS BIG?
DO I EVEN KNOW YOU?!
UH... NEVER MIND?
PENNY! HEY!!

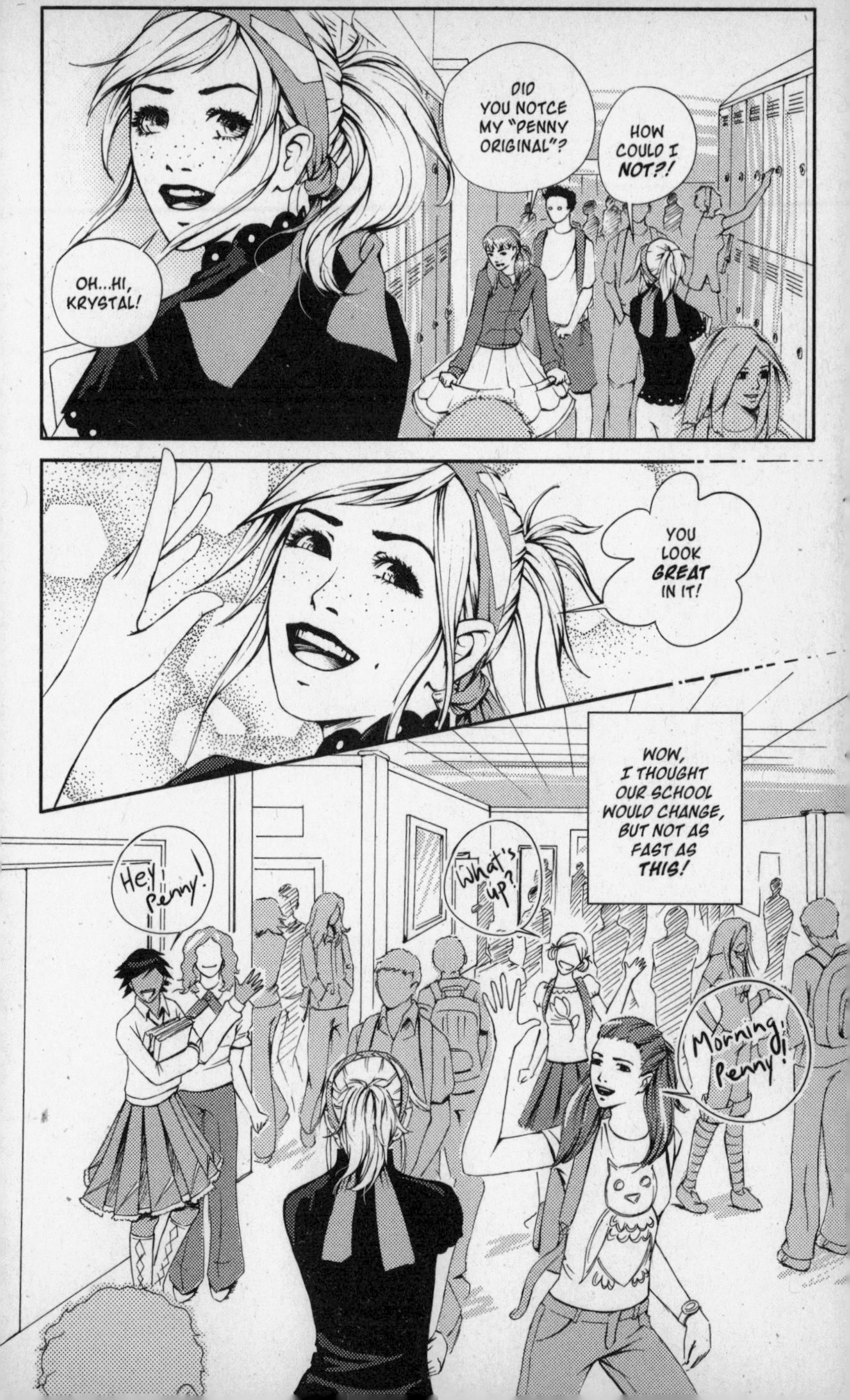
OH...HI, KRYSTAL!
DID YOU NOTCE MY "PENNY ORIGINAL"?
HOW COULD I NOT?!
YOU LOOK GREAT IN IT!
WOW, I THOUGHT OUR SCHOOL WOULD CHANGE, BUT NOT AS FAST AS THIS!
Hey Penny!
What's up?
Morning, Penny!

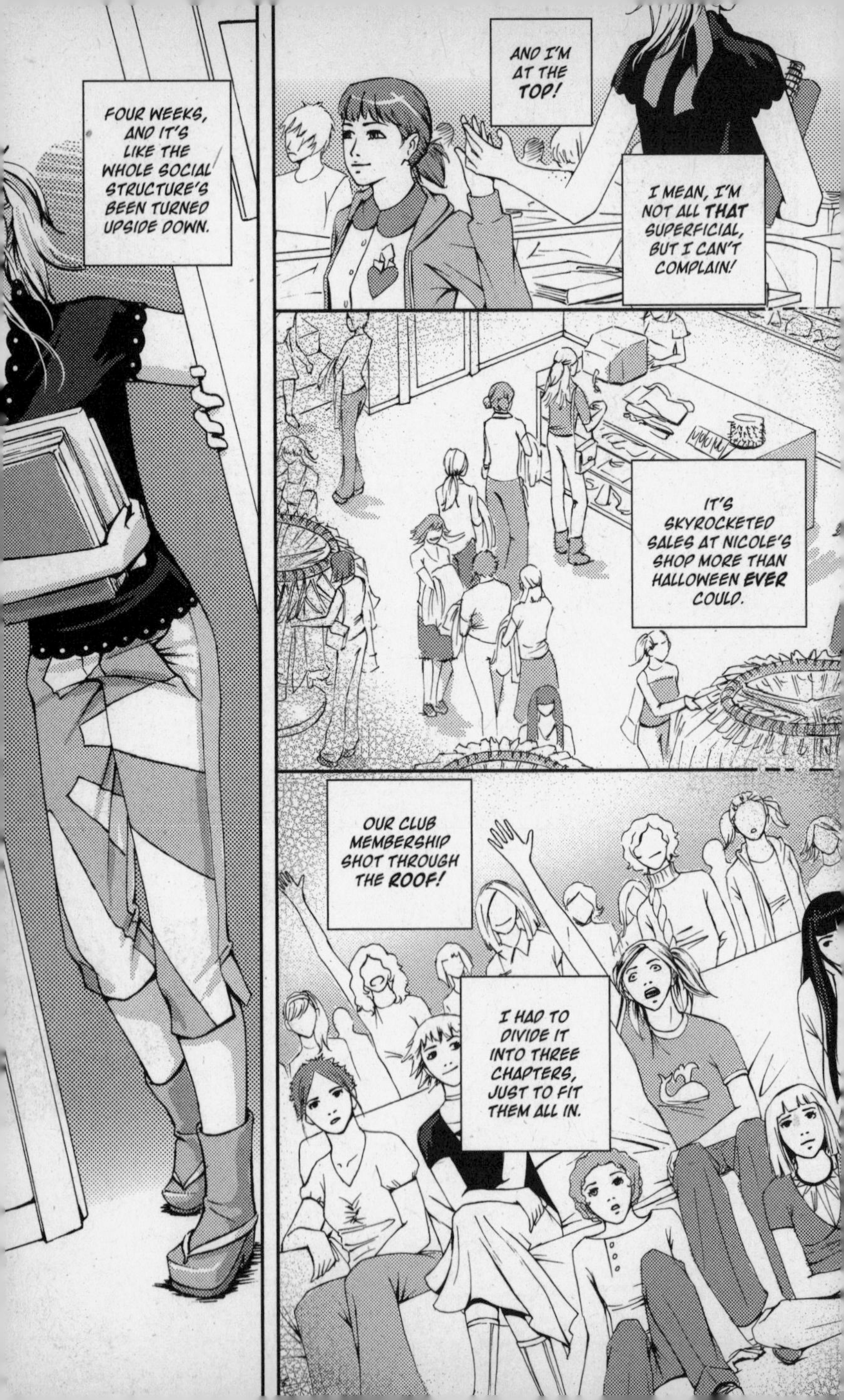
FOUR WEEKS, AND IT'S LIKE THE WHOLE SOCIAL STRUCTURE'S BEEN TURNED UPSIDE DOWN.
AND I'M AT THE TOP!
I MEAN, I'M NOT ALL THAT SUPERFICIAL, BUT I CAN'T COMPLAIN!
IT'S SKYROCKETED SALES AT NICOLE'S SHOP MORE THAN HALLOWEEN EVER COULD.
OUR CLUB MEMBERSHIP SHOT THROUGH THE ROOF!
I HAD TO DIVIDE IT INTO THREE CHAPTERS, JUST TO FIT THEM ALL IN.

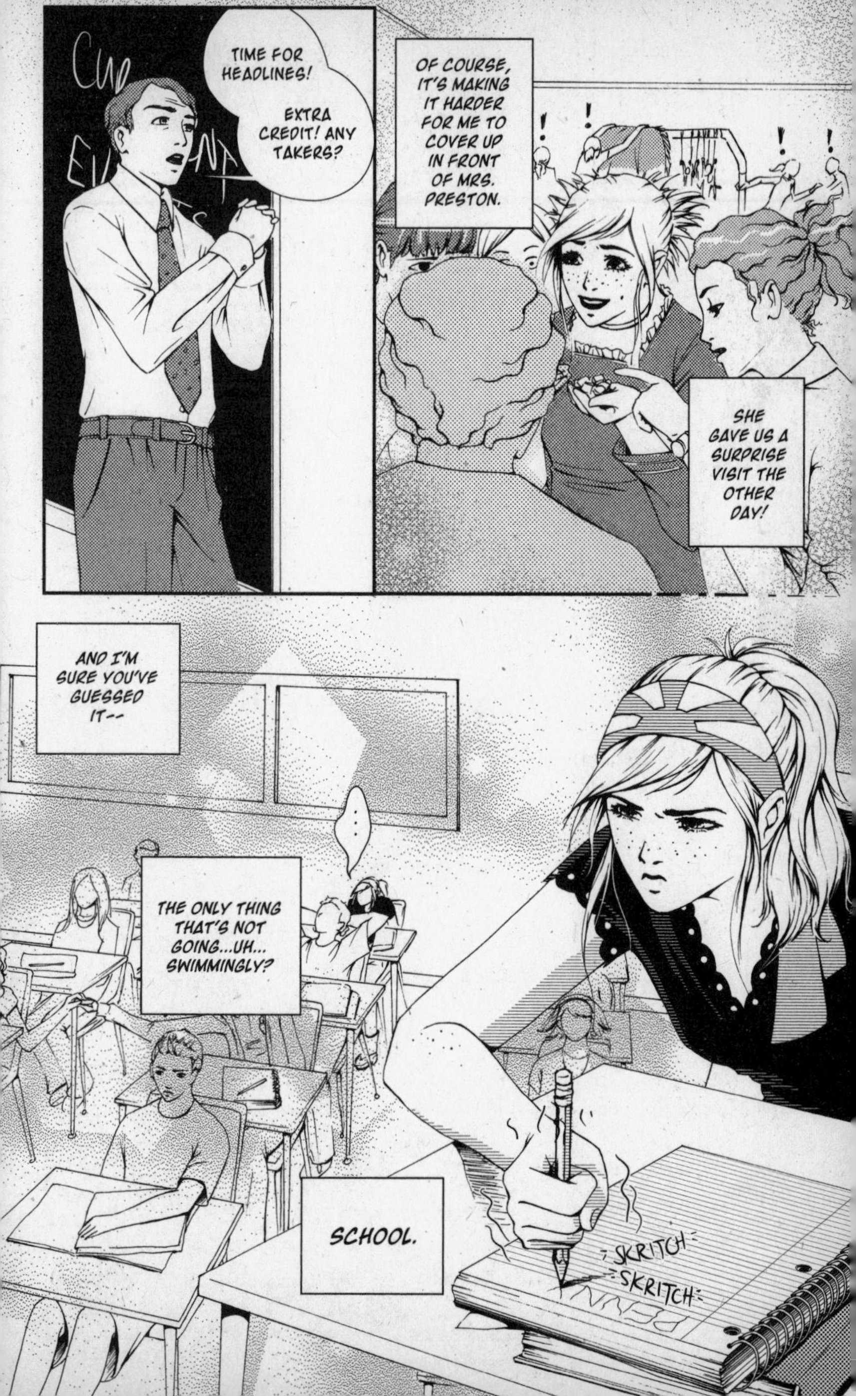
TIME FOR HEADLINES!
EXTRA CREDIT! ANY TAKERS?
OF COURSE, IT'S MAKING IT HARDER FOR ME TO COVER UP IN FRONT OF MRS. PRESTON.
SHE GAVE US A SURPRISE VISIT THE OTHER DAY!
AND I'M SURE YOU'VE GUESSED IT--
...
THE ONLY THING THAT'S NOT GOING...UH... SWIMMINGLY?
SCHOOL.
SKRITCH
SKRITCH

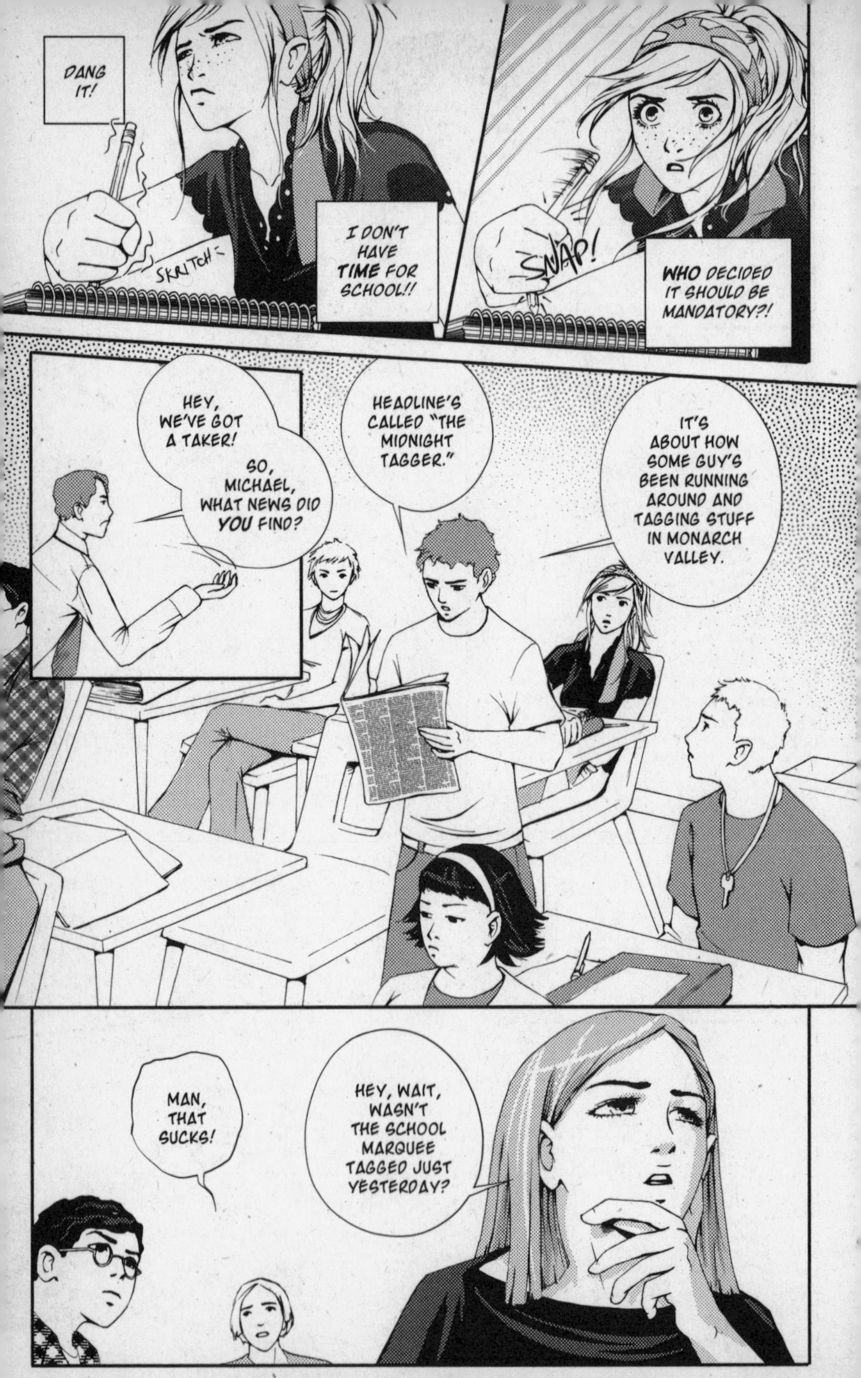
DANG IT!
SKRITCH
I DON'T HAVE TIME FOR SCHOOL!!
SNAP!
WHO DECIDED IT SHOULD BE MANDATORY?!
HEY, WE'VE GOT A TAKER!
SO, MICHAEL, WHAT NEWS DID YOU FIND?
HEADLINE'S CALLED "THE MIDNIGHT TAGGER."
IT'S ABOUT HOW SOME GUY'S BEEN RUNNING AROUND AND TAGGING STUFF IN MONARCH VALLEY.
MAN, THAT SUCKS!
HEY, WAIT, WASN'T THE SCHOOL MARQUEE TAGGED JUST YESTERDAY?

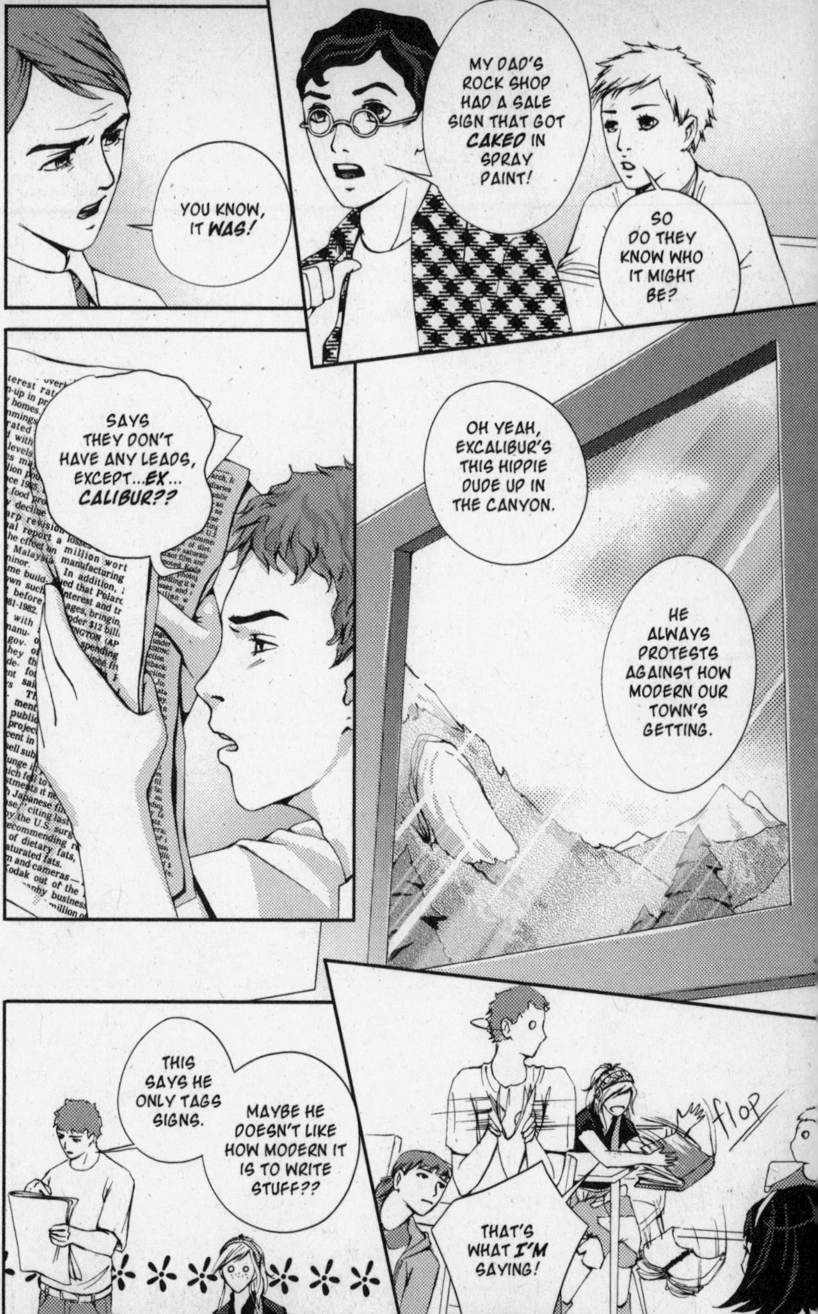
YOU KNOW, IT WAS!
MY DAD'S ROCK SHOP HAD A SALE SIGN THAT GOT CAKED IN SPRAY PAINT!
SO DO THEY KNOW WHO IT MIGHT BE?
SAYS THEY DON'T HAVE ANY LEADS, EXCEPT...EX... CALIBUR??
OH YEAH, EXCALIBUR'S THIS HIPPIE DUDE UP IN THE CANYON.
HE ALWAYS PROTESTS AGAINST HOW MODERN OUR TOWN'S GETTING.
THIS SAYS HE ONLY TAGS SIGNS.
MAYBE HE DOESN'T LIKE HOW MODERN IT IS TO WRITE STUFF??
flop
THAT'S WHAT I'M SAYING!

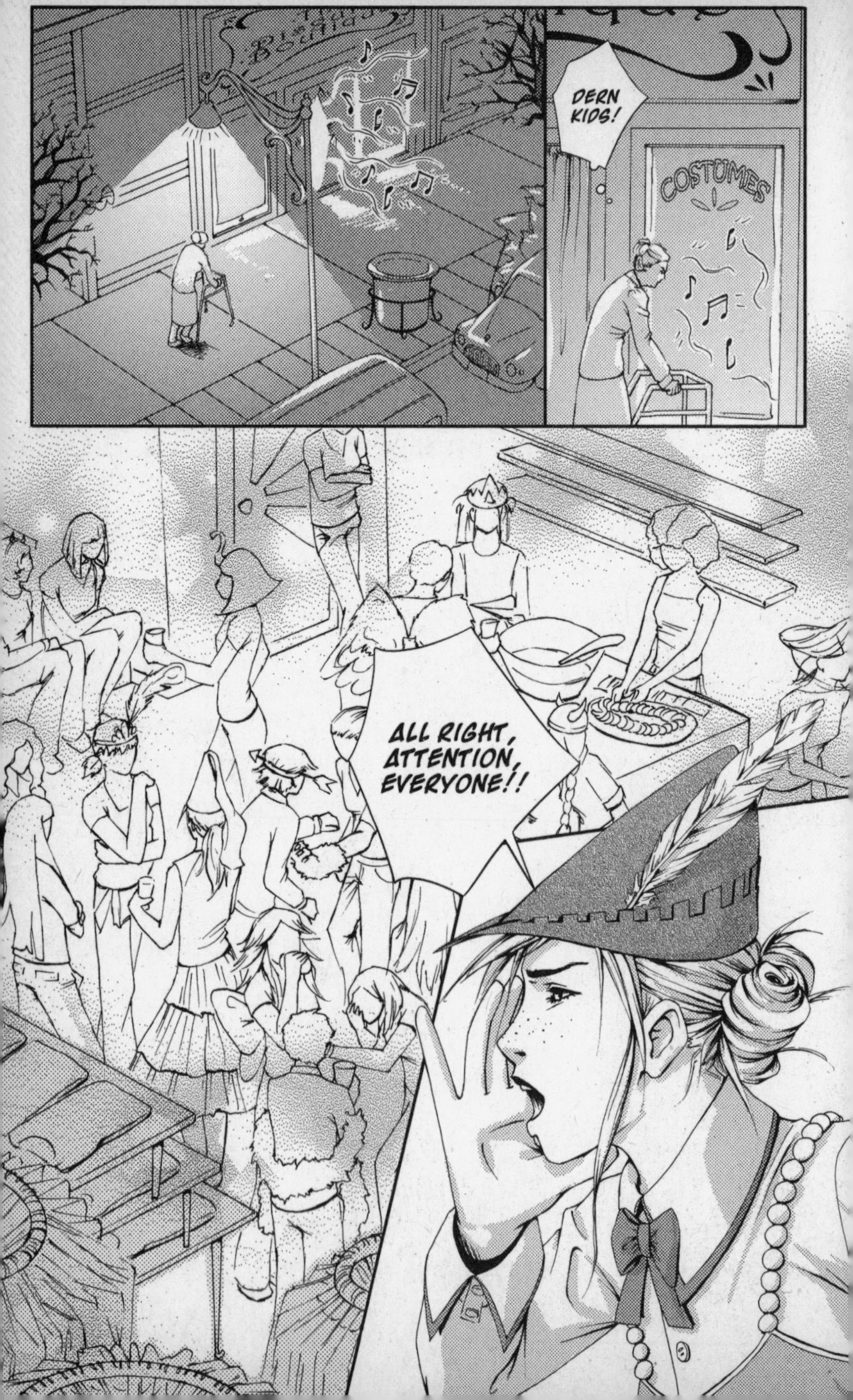
DERN KIDS!
COSTUMES
ALL RIGHT, ATTENTION, EVERYONE!!

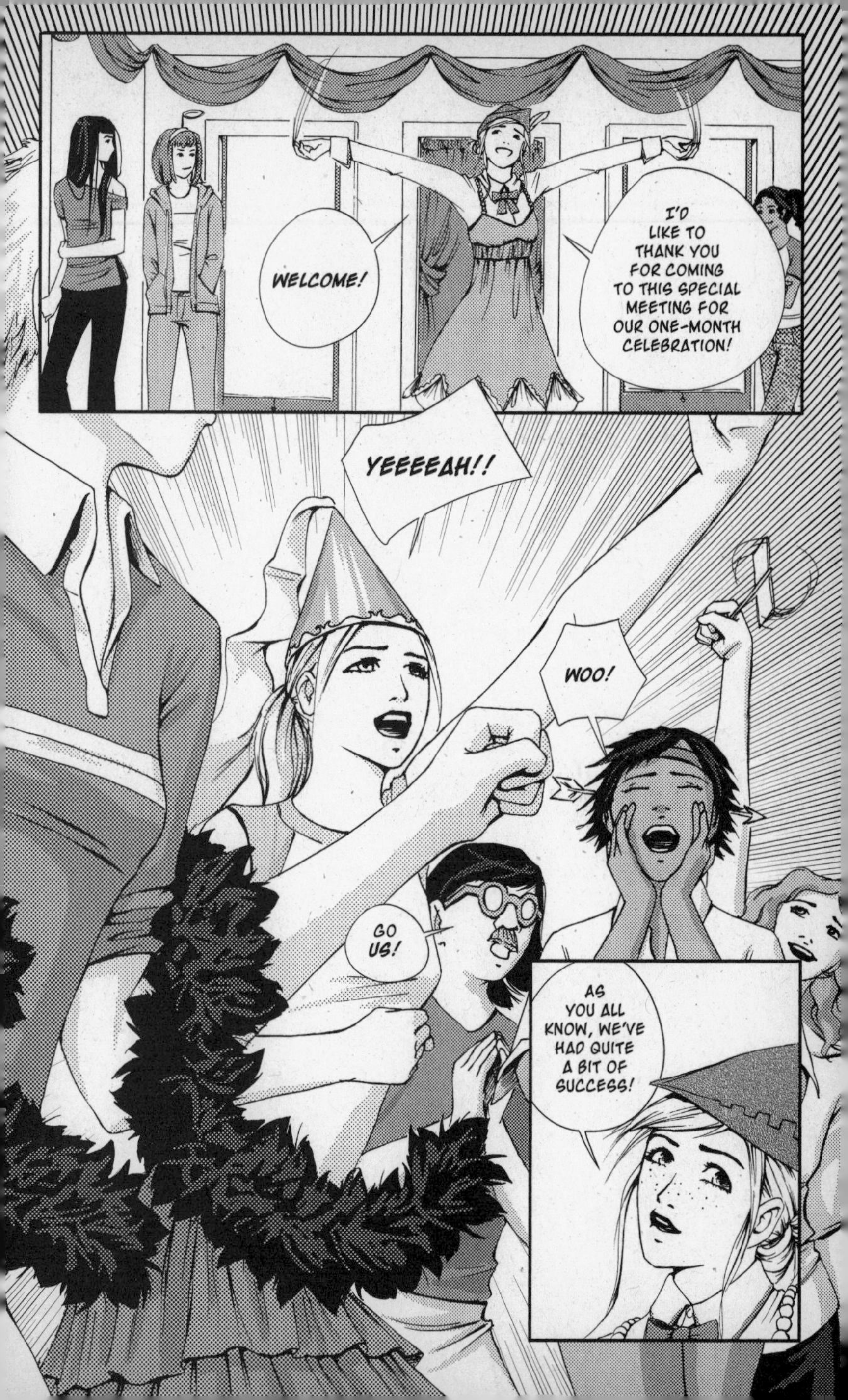
WELCOME!
I'D LIKE TO THANK YOU FOR COMING TO THIS SPECIAL MEETING FOR OUR ONE-MONTH CELEBRATION!
YEEEEAH!!
WOO!
GO US!
AS YOU ALL KNOW, WE'VE HAD QUITE A BIT OF SUCCESS!

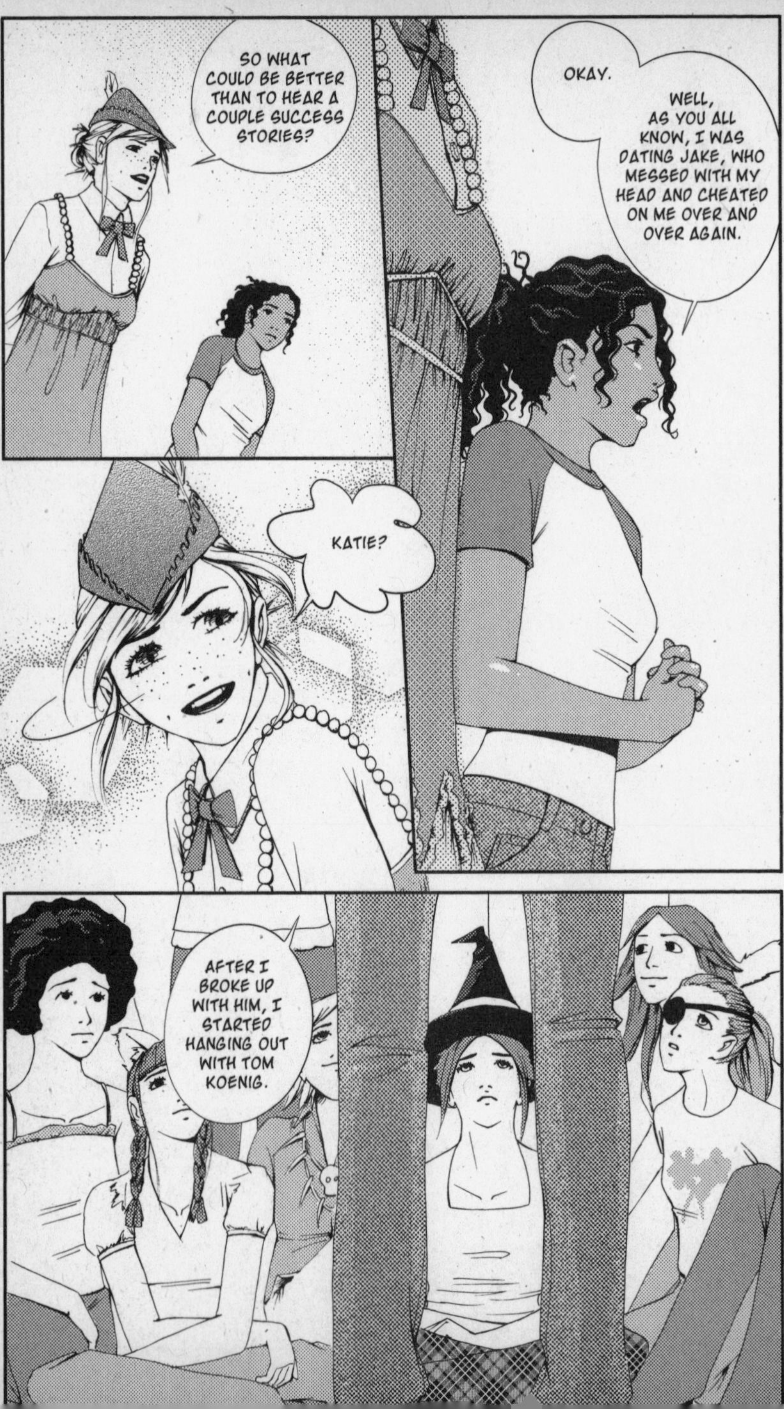
SO WHAT COULD BE BETTER THAN TO HEAR A COUPLE SUCCESS STORIES?
KATIE?
OKAY.
WELL, AS YOU ALL KNOW, I WAS DATING JAKE, WHO MESSED WITH MY HEAD AND CHEATED ON ME OVER AND OVER AGAIN.
AFTER I BROKE UP WITH HIM, I STARTED HANGING OUT WITH TOM KOENIG.

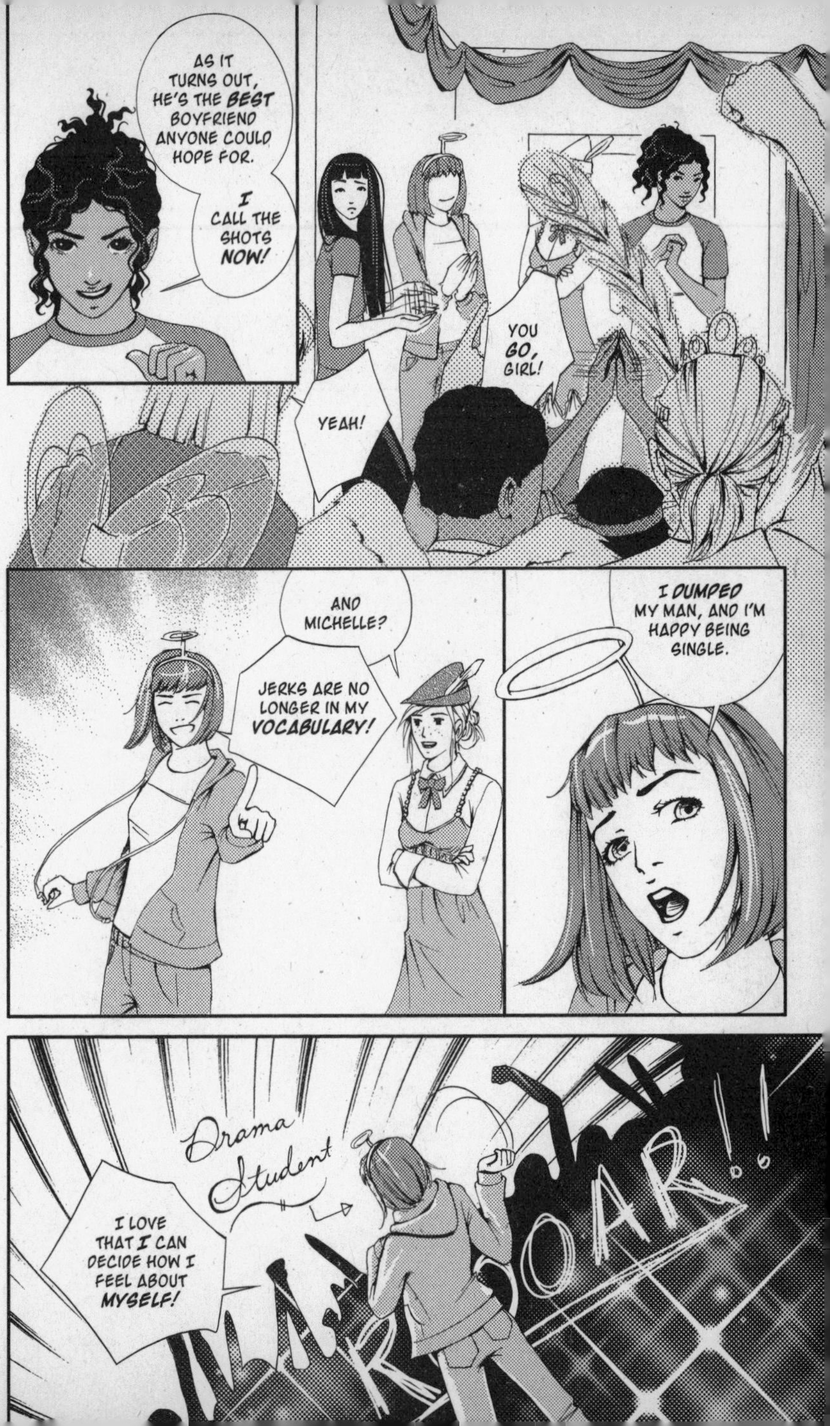
AS IT TURNS OUT, HE'S THE **BEST** BOYFRIEND ANYONE COULD HOPE FOR.
I CALL THE SHOTS **NOW!**
YOU **GO,** GIRL!
YEAH!
AND MICHELLE?
JERKS ARE NO LONGER IN MY **VOCABULARY!**
I **DUMPED** MY MAN, AND I'M HAPPY BEING SINGLE.
Drama Student
I LOVE THAT **I** CAN DECIDE HOW I FEEL ABOUT **MYSELF!**
ROAR!!

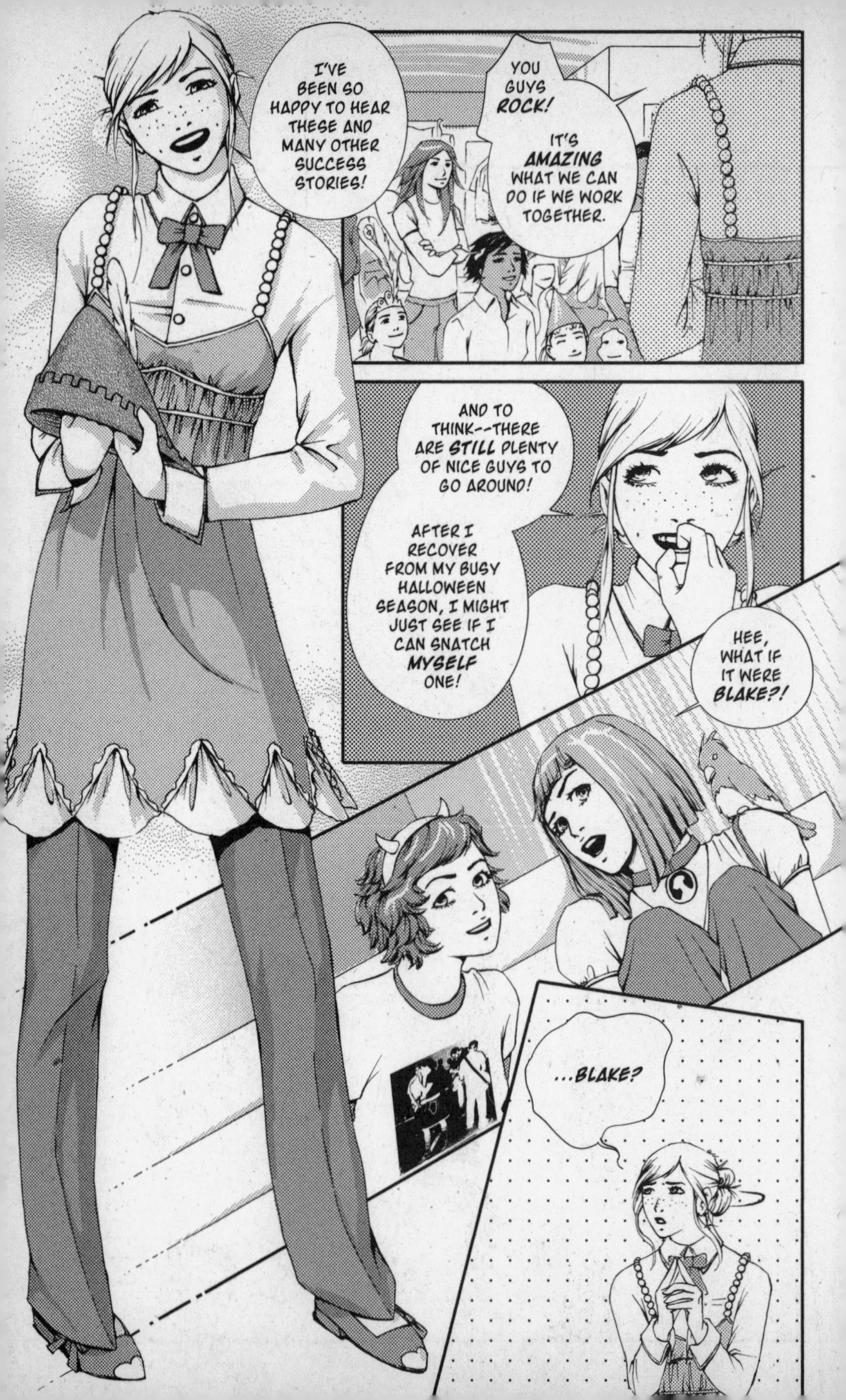
I'VE BEEN SO HAPPY TO HEAR THESE AND MANY OTHER SUCCESS STORIES!
YOU GUYS **ROCK!**
IT'S **AMAZING** WHAT WE CAN DO IF WE WORK TOGETHER.
AND TO THINK--THERE ARE **STILL** PLENTY OF NICE GUYS TO GO AROUND!
AFTER I RECOVER FROM MY BUSY HALLOWEEN SEASON, I MIGHT JUST SEE IF I CAN SNATCH **MYSELF** ONE!
HEE, WHAT IF IT WERE **BLAKE?!**
...**BLAKE?**

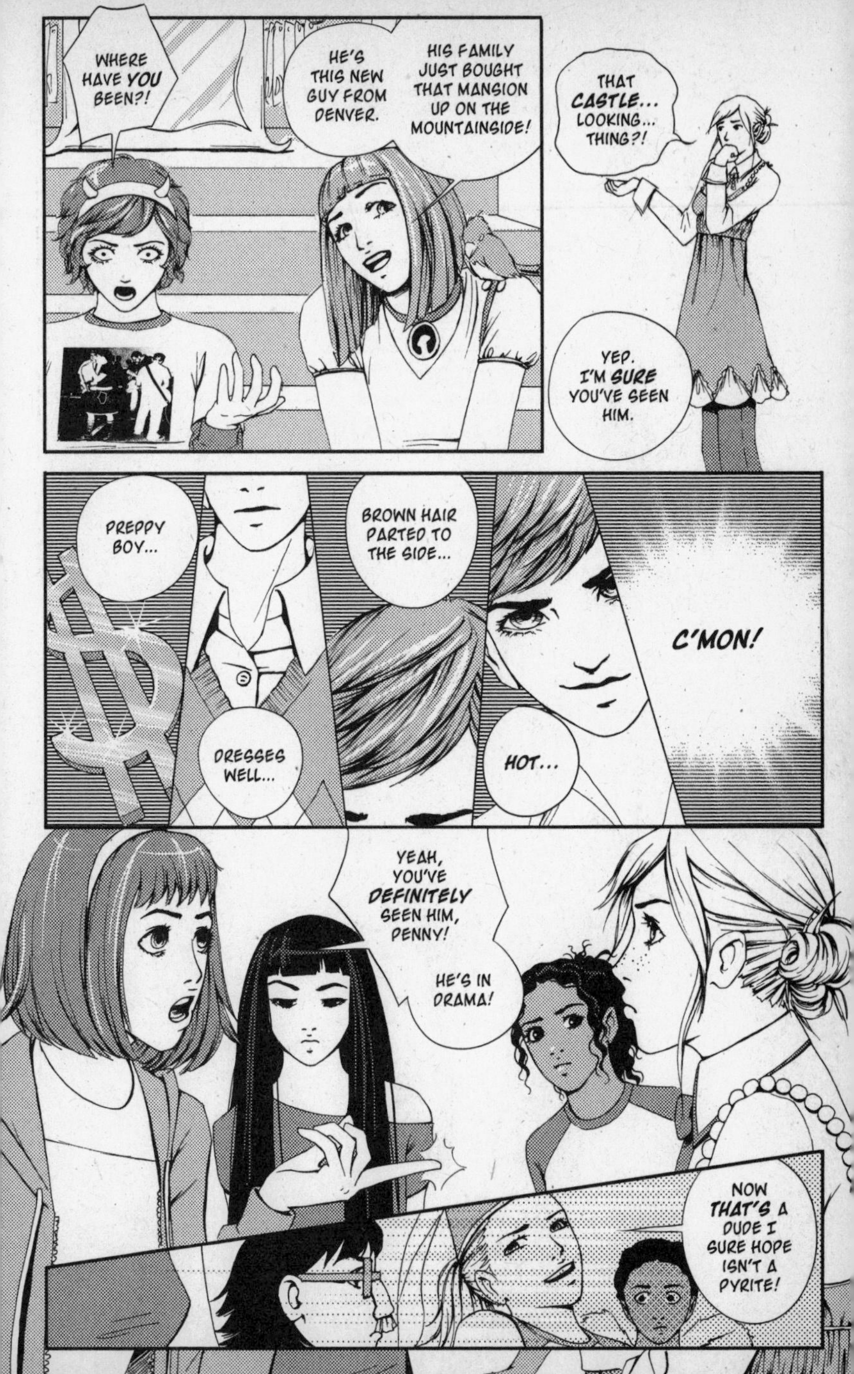
WHERE HAVE YOU BEEN?!
HE'S THIS NEW GUY FROM DENVER.
HIS FAMILY JUST BOUGHT THAT MANSION UP ON THE MOUNTAINSIDE!
THAT CASTLE... LOOKING... THING?!
YEP. I'M SURE YOU'VE SEEN HIM.
PREPPY BOY...
DRESSES WELL...
BROWN HAIR PARTED TO THE SIDE...
HOT...
C'MON!
YEAH, YOU'VE DEFINITELY SEEN HIM, PENNY!
HE'S IN DRAMA!
NOW THAT'S A DUDE I SURE HOPE ISN'T A PYRITE!

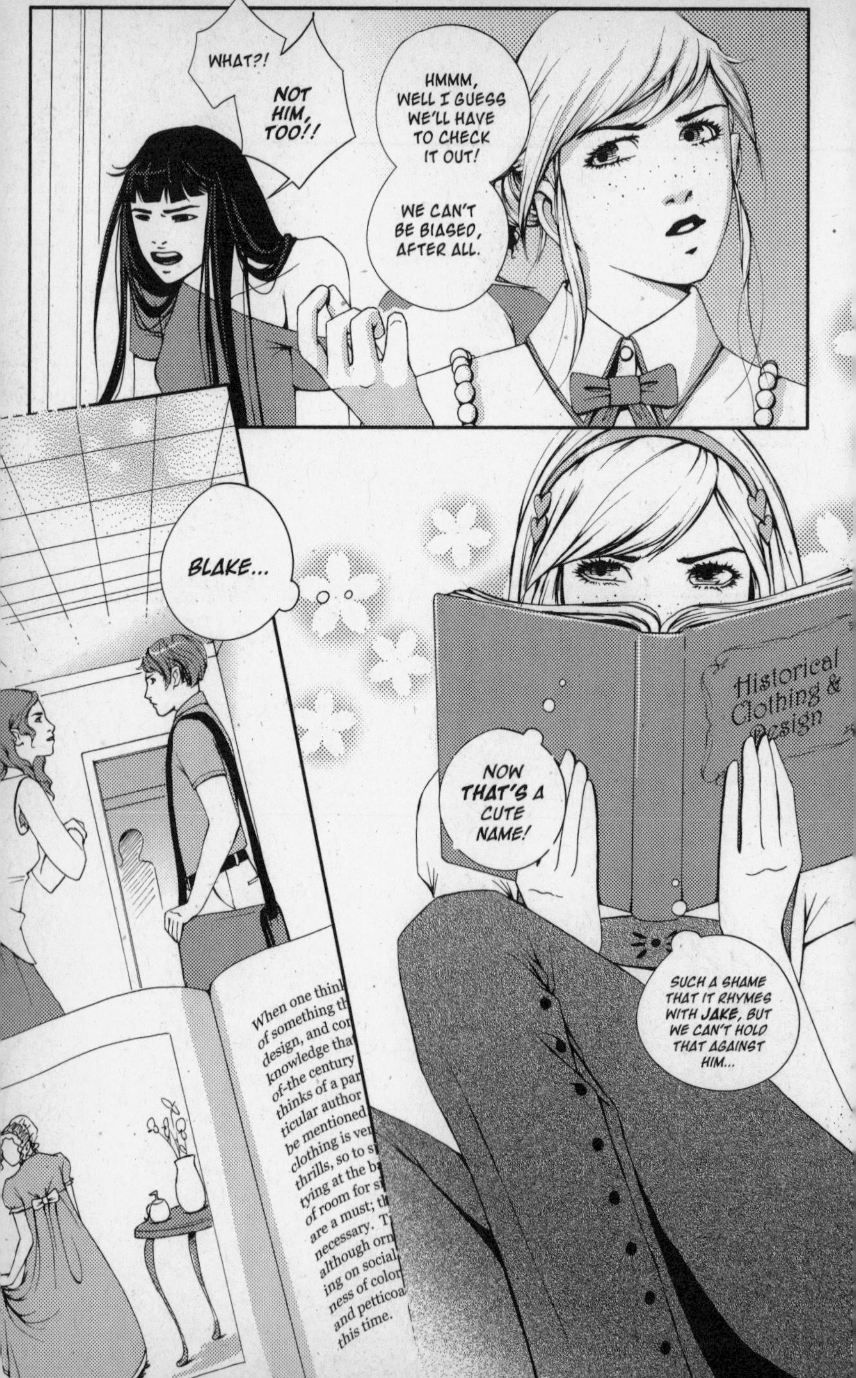
WHAT?!
NOT HIM, TOO!!
HMMM, WELL I GUESS WE'LL HAVE TO CHECK IT OUT!
WE CAN'T BE BIASED, AFTER ALL.
BLAKE...
Historical Clothing & Design
NOW THAT'S A CUTE NAME!
SUCH A SHAME THAT IT RHYMES WITH JAKE, BUT WE CAN'T HOLD THAT AGAINST HIM...
When one think
of something th
design, and co
knowledge tha
of-the century
thinks of a par
ticular author
be mentioned
clothing is ver
thrills, so to s
tying at the b
of room for s
are a must; t
necessary. T
although orn
ing on social
ness of colo
and petticoa
this time.

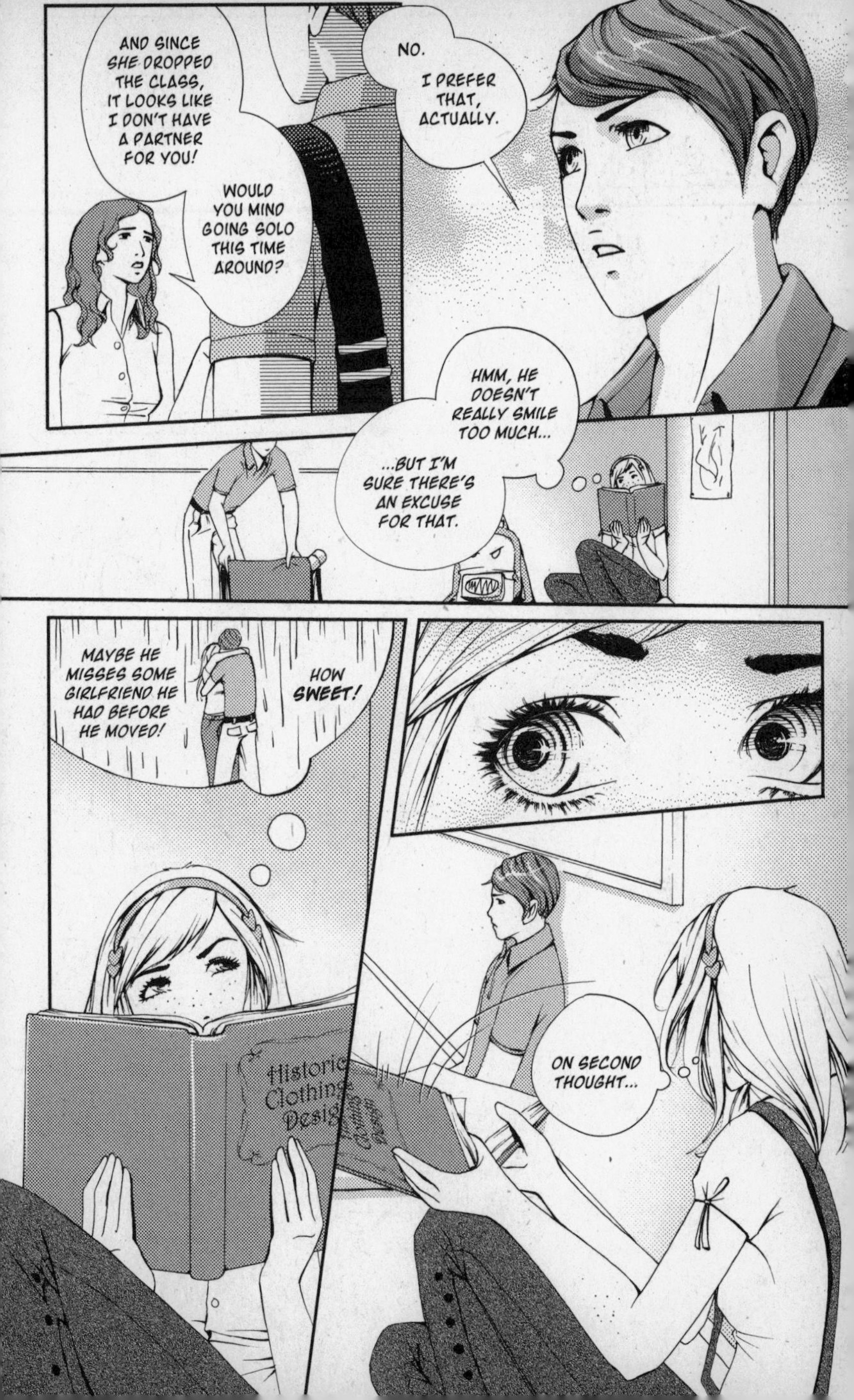
AND SINCE SHE DROPPED THE CLASS, IT LOOKS LIKE I DON'T HAVE A PARTNER FOR YOU!
WOULD YOU MIND GOING SOLO THIS TIME AROUND?
NO.
I PREFER THAT, ACTUALLY.
HMM, HE DOESN'T REALLY SMILE TOO MUCH...
...BUT I'M SURE THERE'S AN EXCUSE FOR THAT.
MAYBE HE MISSES SOME GIRLFRIEND HE HAD BEFORE HE MOVED!
HOW SWEET!
Historic Clothing Design
ON SECOND THOUGHT...

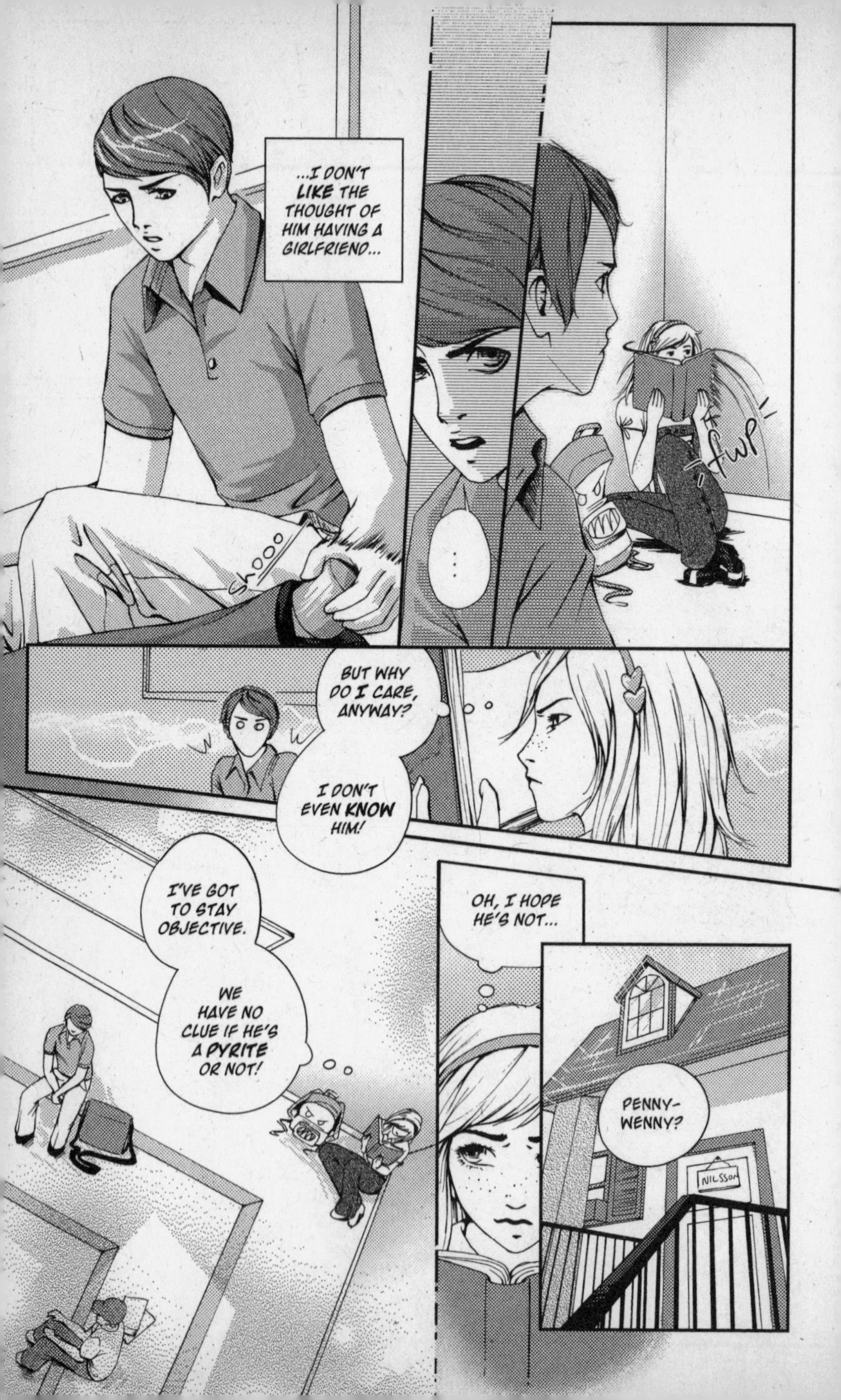
...I DON'T LIKE THE THOUGHT OF HIM HAVING A GIRLFRIEND...
SHOOO
...
FWP
BUT WHY DO I CARE, ANYWAY?
I DON'T EVEN KNOW HIM!
I'VE GOT TO STAY OBJECTIVE.
WE HAVE NO CLUE IF HE'S A PYRITE OR NOT!
OH, I HOPE HE'S NOT...
PENNY-WENNY?
NILSSON

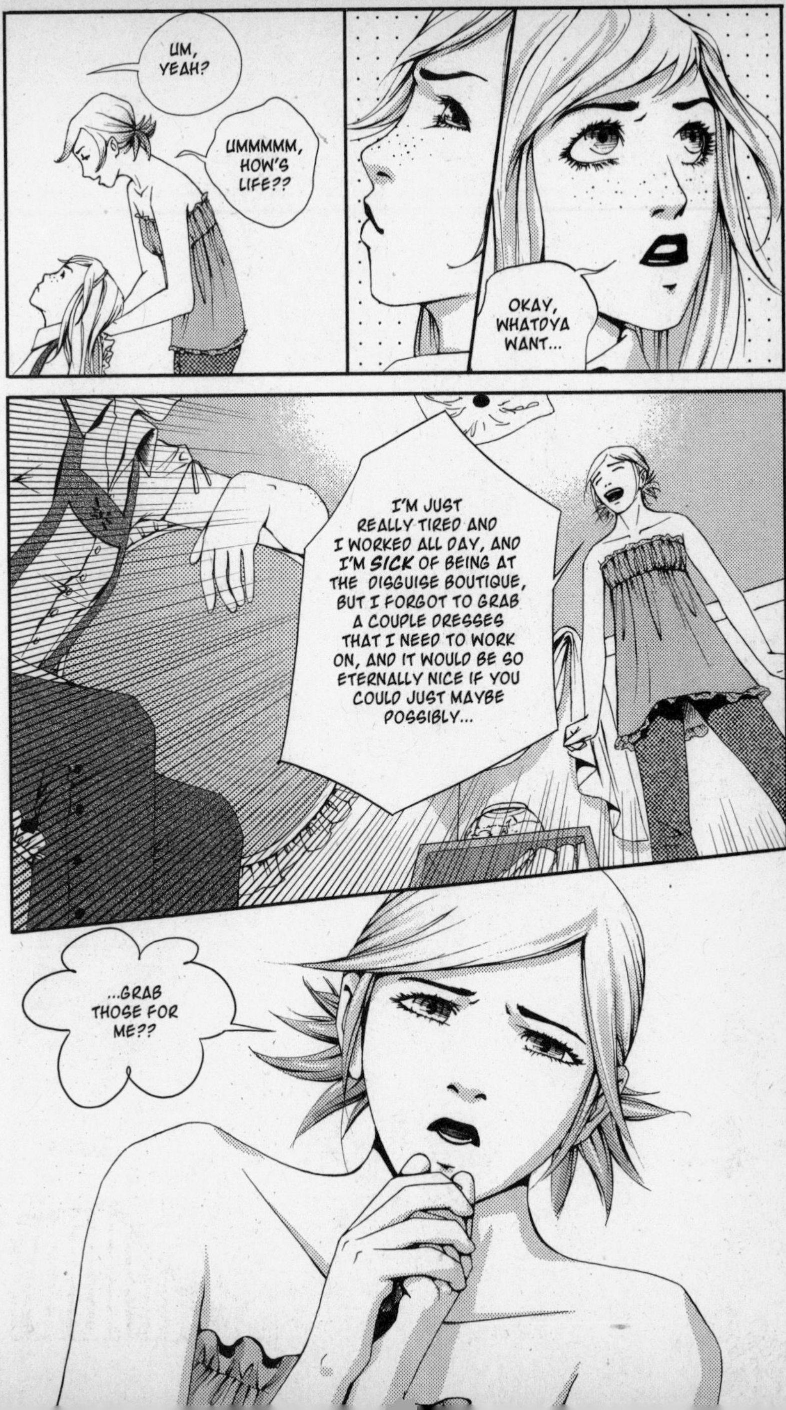
UM, YEAH?
UMMMMM, HOW'S LIFE??
OKAY, WHATDYA WANT...
I'M JUST REALLY TIRED AND I WORKED ALL DAY, AND I'M SICK OF BEING AT THE DISGUISE BOUTIQUE, BUT I FORGOT TO GRAB A COUPLE DRESSES THAT I NEED TO WORK ON, AND IT WOULD BE SO ETERNALLY NICE IF YOU COULD JUST MAYBE POSSIBLY...
...GRAB THOSE FOR ME??

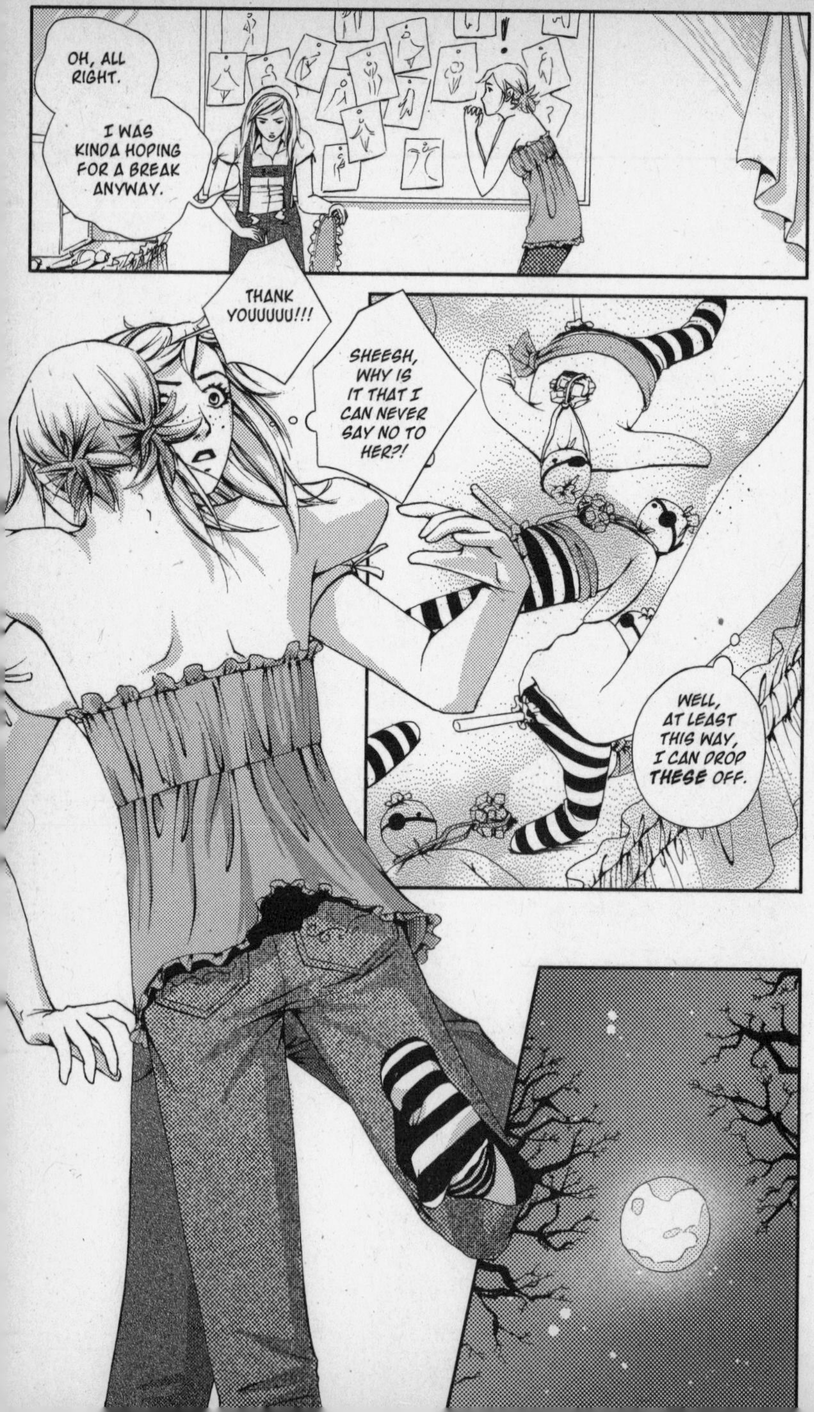
OH, ALL RIGHT.
I WAS KINDA HOPING FOR A BREAK ANYWAY.
THANK YOUUUUU!!!
SHEESH, WHY IS IT THAT I CAN NEVER SAY NO TO HER?!
WELL, AT LEAST THIS WAY, I CAN DROP THESE OFF.

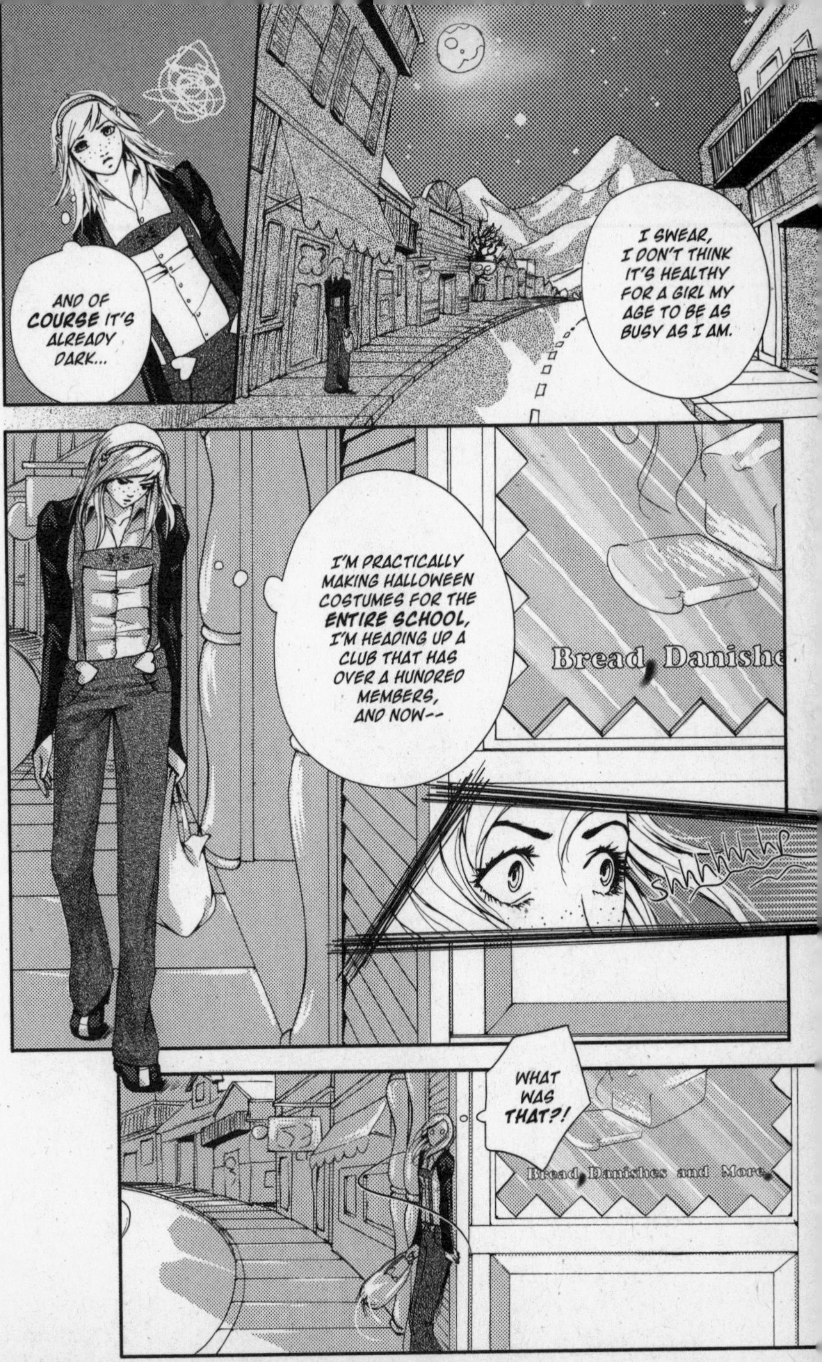
AND OF COURSE IT'S ALREADY DARK...
I SWEAR, I DON'T THINK IT'S HEALTHY FOR A GIRL MY AGE TO BE AS BUSY AS I AM.
I'M PRACTICALLY MAKING HALLOWEEN COSTUMES FOR THE ENTIRE SCHOOL, I'M HEADING UP A CLUB THAT HAS OVER A HUNDRED MEMBERS, AND NOW--
Bread, Danishe
WHAT WAS THAT?!
Bread, Danishes and More.

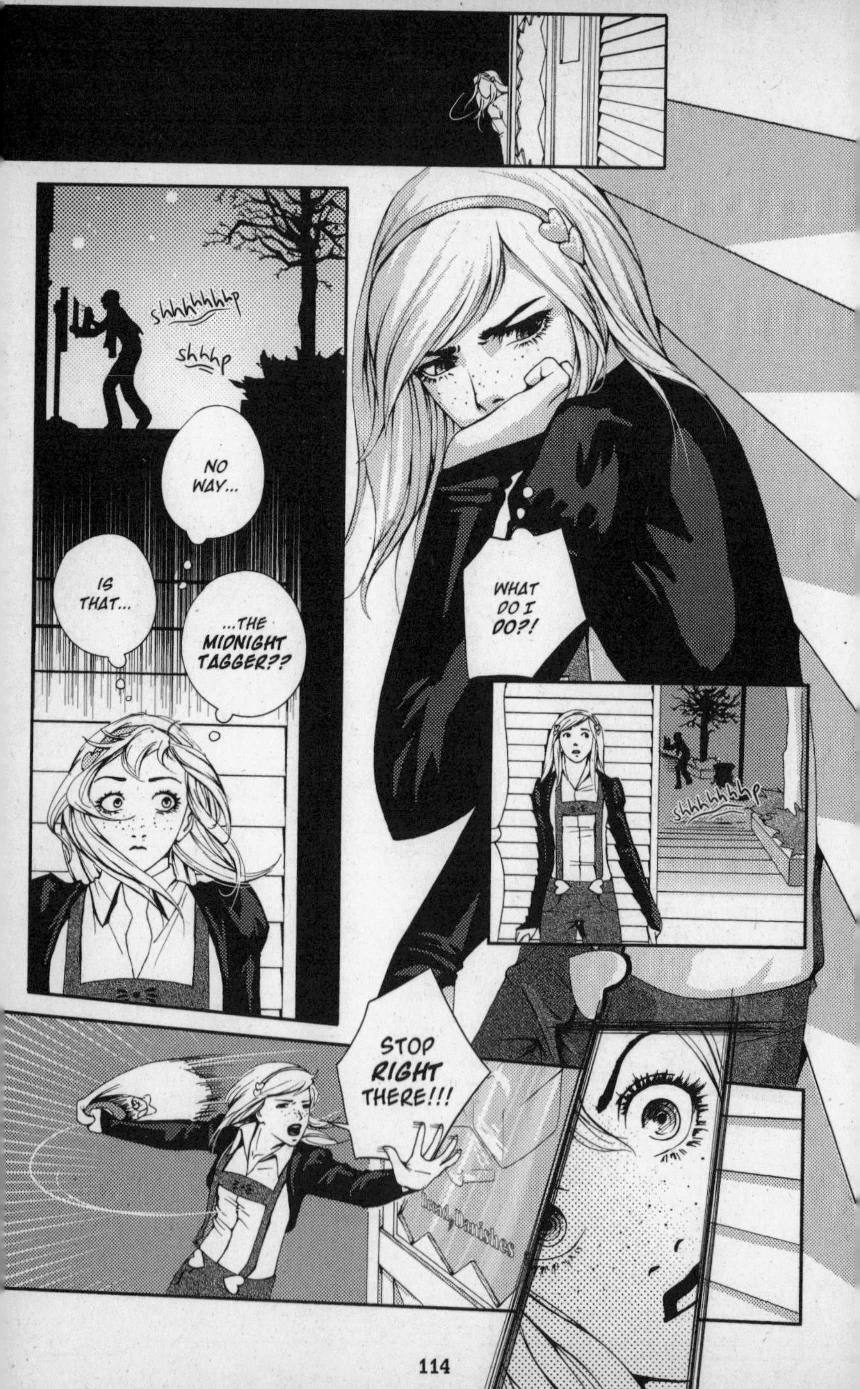
shhhhhhp
shhhp
NO WAY...
IS THAT...
...THE MIDNIGHT TAGGER??
WHAT DO I DO?!
shhhhhhp
STOP RIGHT THERE!!!
Bread Danishes

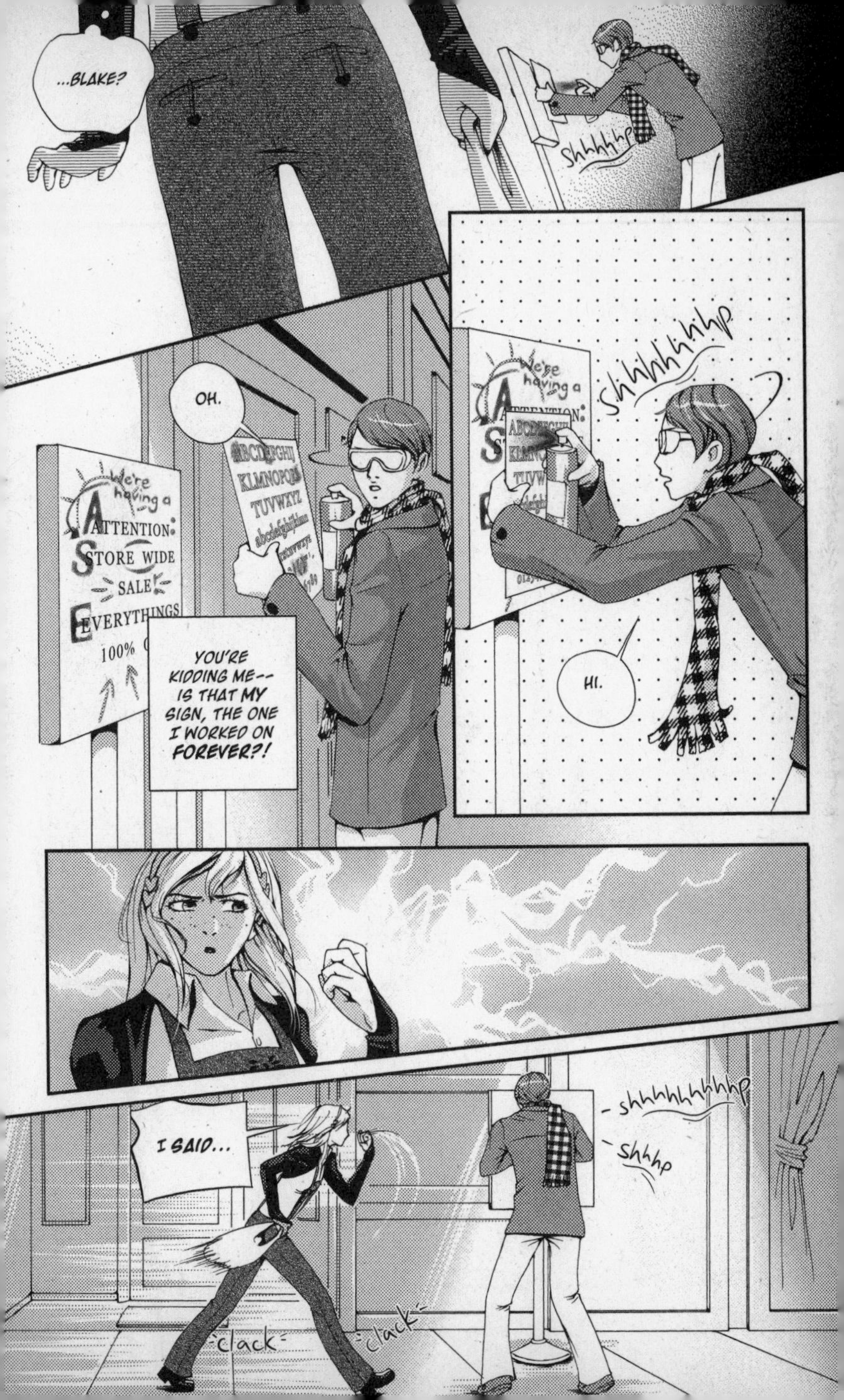
...BLAKE?
Shhhhhp
OH.
We're having a
ATTENTION:
STORE WIDE
SALE!
EVERYTHINGS
100%
YOU'RE KIDDING ME-- IS THAT MY SIGN, THE ONE I WORKED ON FOREVER?!
Shhhhhhhp
HI.
I SAID...
-shhhhhhhhhp
-Shhhp
-clack-
-clack-

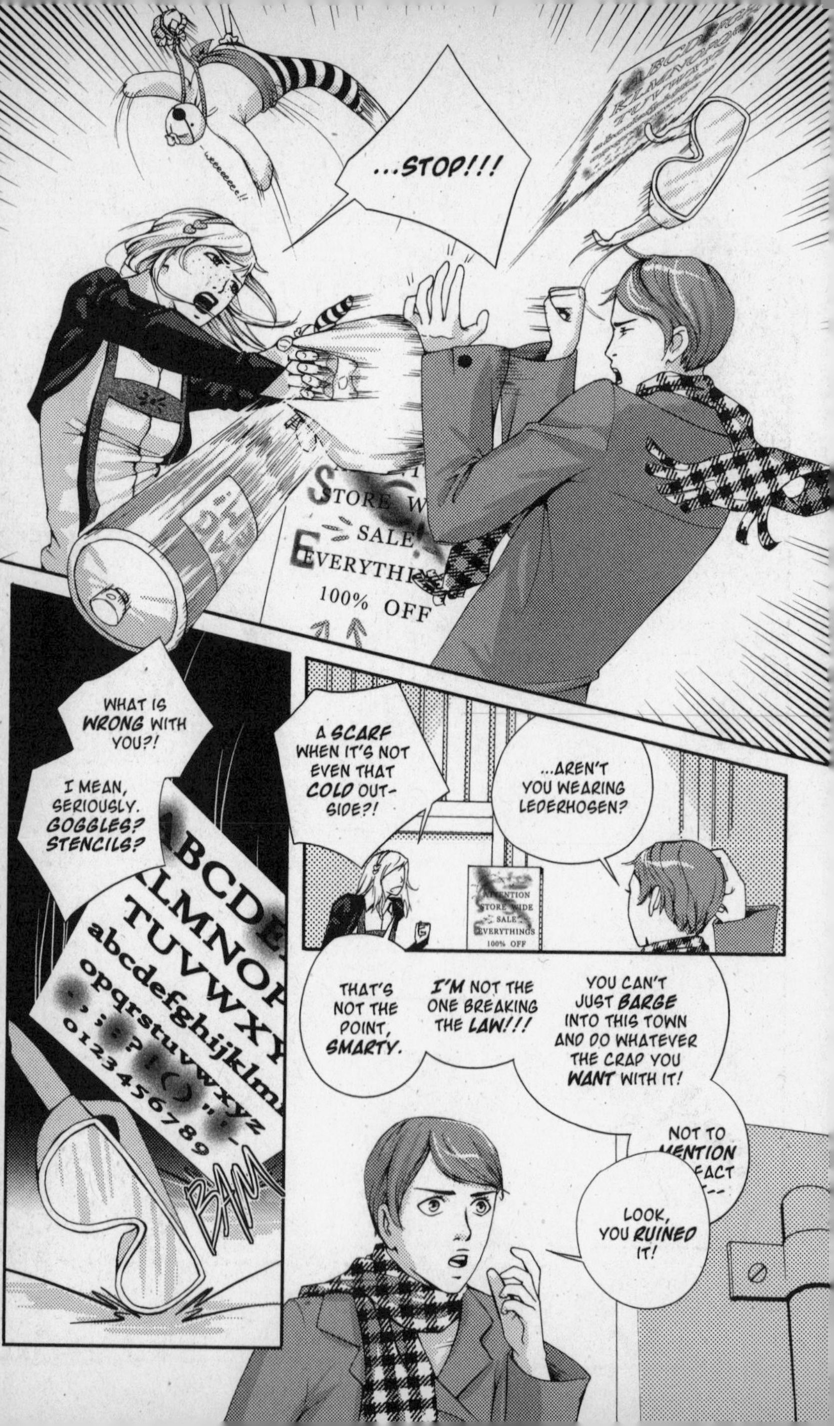

—weeeeeeee!!
...STOP!!!
STORE
SALE
100% OFF
WHAT IS WRONG WITH YOU?!
I MEAN, SERIOUSLY. GOGGLES? STENCILS?
BAM
A SCARF WHEN IT'S NOT EVEN THAT COLD OUT-SIDE?!
...AREN'T YOU WEARING LEDERHOSEN?
ATTENTION STORE WIDE SALE EVERYTHINGS 100% OFF
THAT'S NOT THE POINT, SMARTY.
I'M NOT THE ONE BREAKING THE LAW!!!
YOU CAN'T JUST BARGE INTO THIS TOWN AND DO WHATEVER THE CRAP YOU WANT WITH IT!
NOT TO
LOOK, YOU RUINED IT!

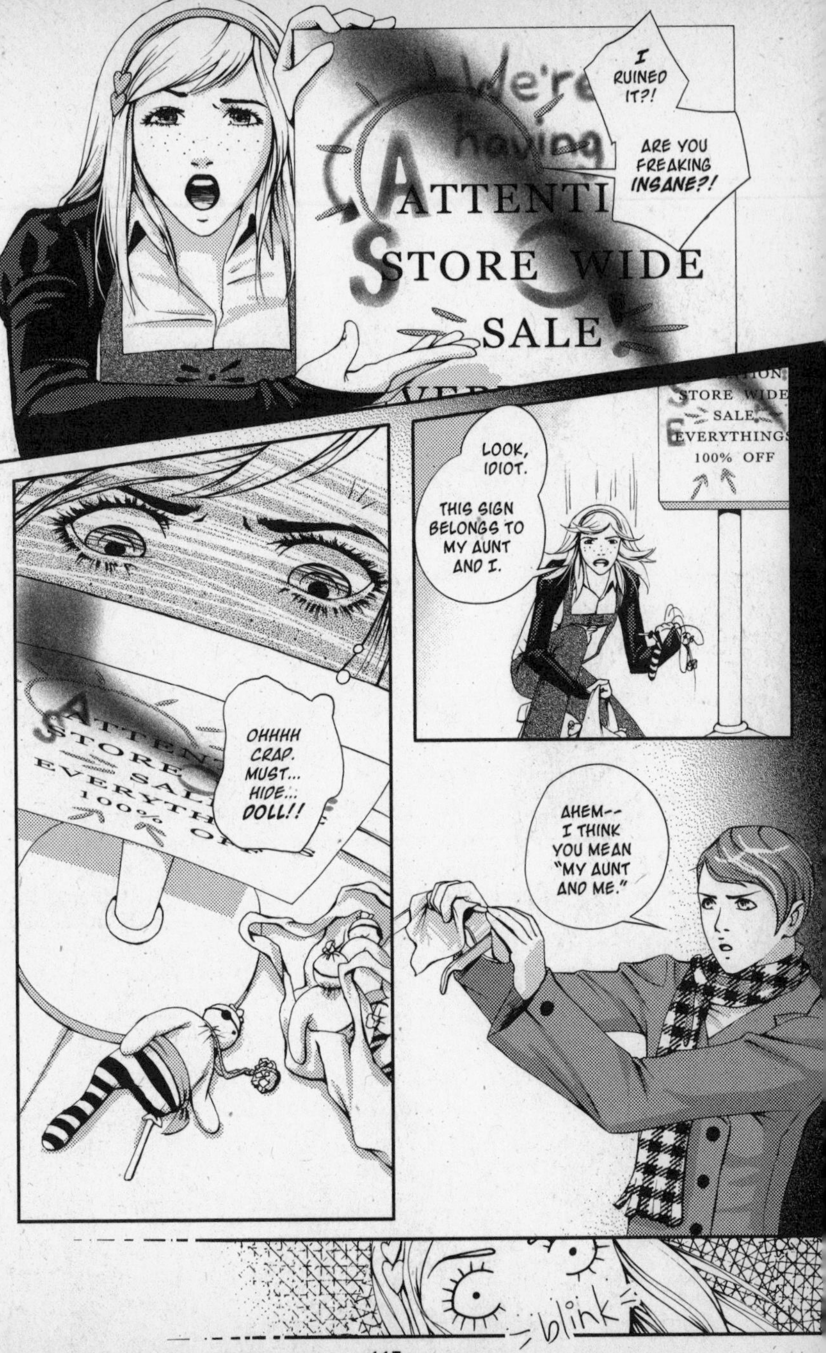
ATTENTI
STORE WIDE
SALE
I RUINED IT?!
ARE YOU FREAKING INSANE?!
OHHHH CRAP. MUST... HIDE... DOLL!!
STORE WIDE SALE EVERYTHINGS 100% OFF
LOOK, IDIOT.
THIS SIGN BELONGS TO MY AUNT AND I.
AHEM-- I THINK YOU MEAN "MY AUNT AND ME."
blink

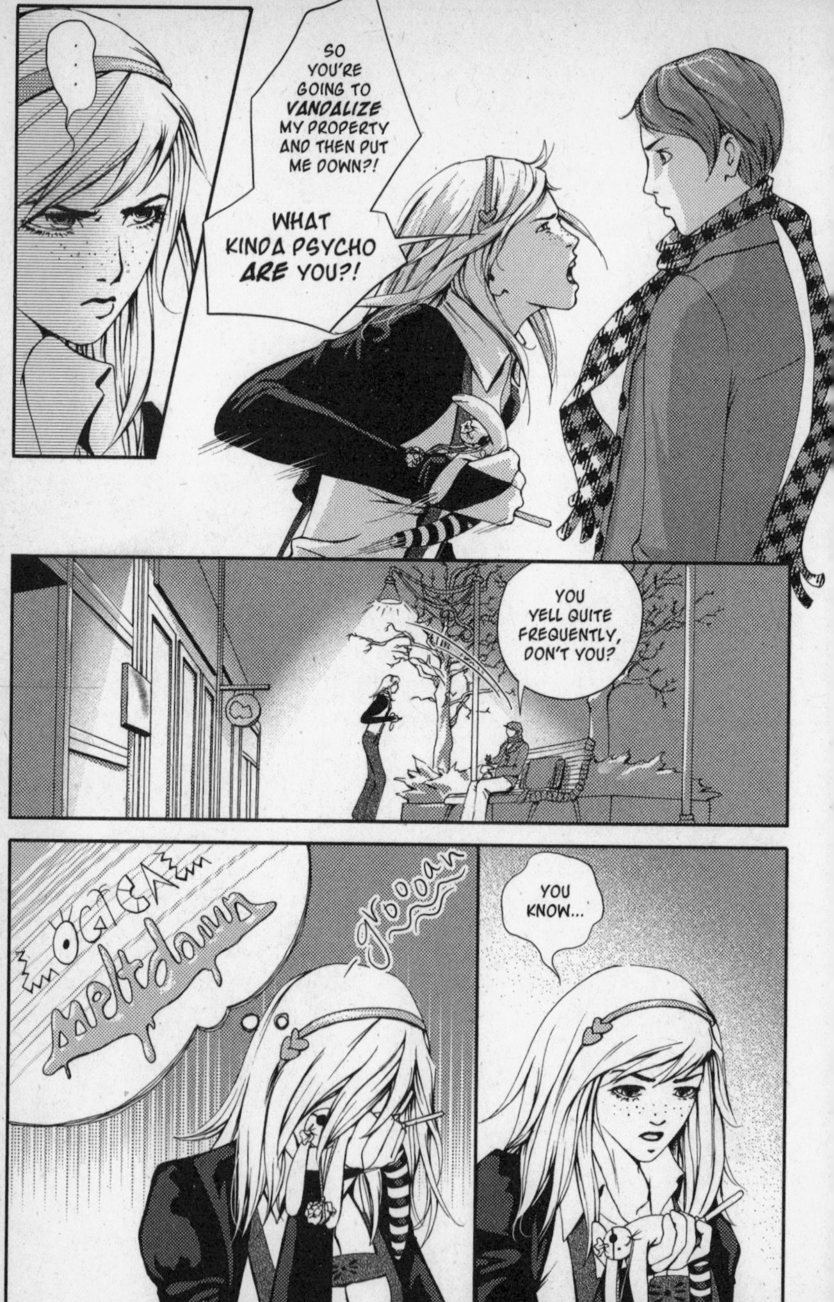
SO YOU'RE GOING TO VANDALIZE MY PROPERTY AND THEN PUT ME DOWN?!
WHAT KINDA PSYCHO ARE YOU?!
YOU YELL QUITE FREQUENTLY, DON'T YOU?
meltdown
grooan
YOU KNOW...

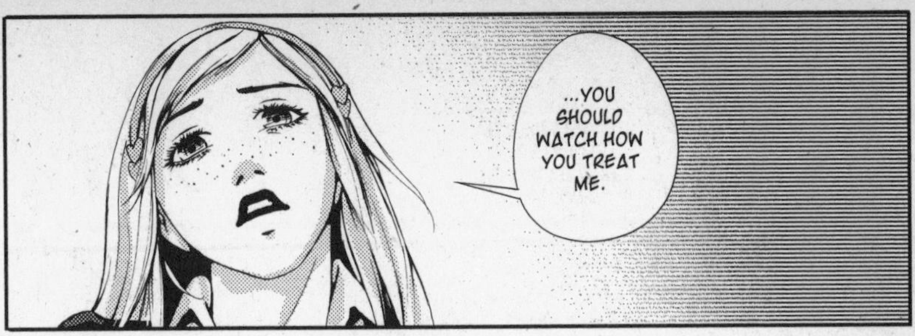
...YOU SHOULD WATCH HOW YOU TREAT ME.

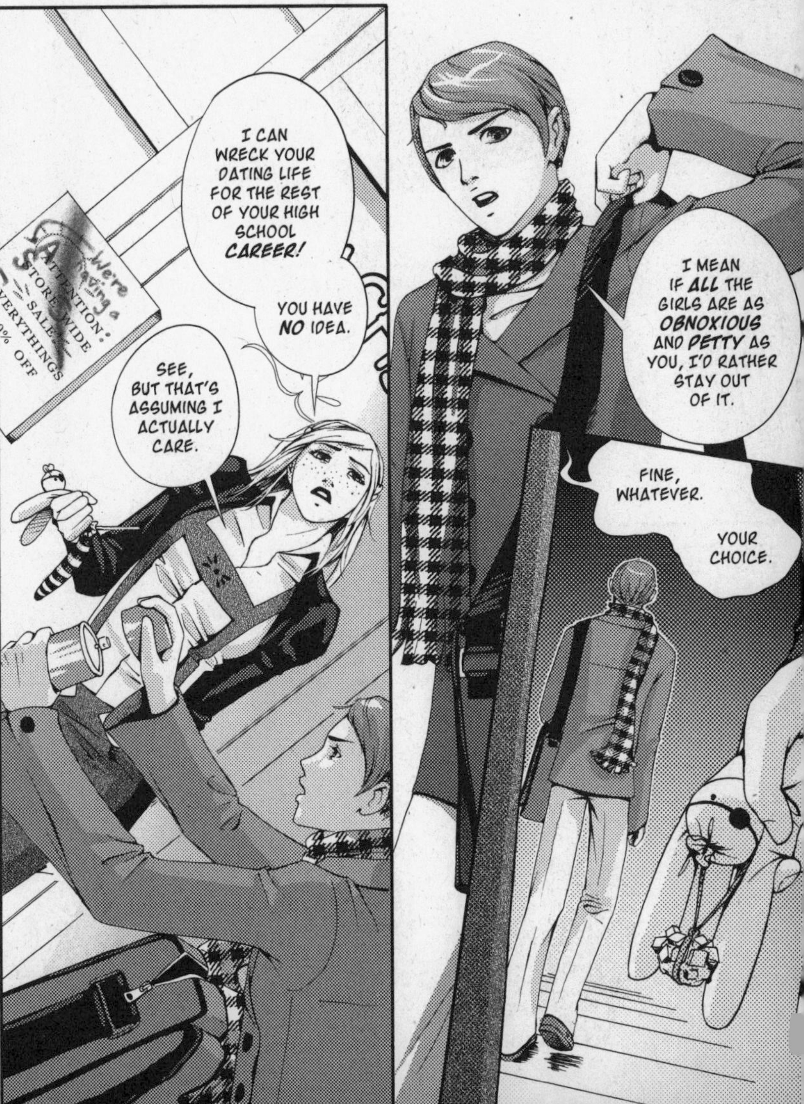
ATTENTION:
STORE WIDE
SALE
I CAN WRECK YOUR DATING LIFE FOR THE REST OF YOUR HIGH SCHOOL **CAREER!**
YOU HAVE **NO** IDEA.
SEE, BUT THAT'S ASSUMING I ACTUALLY CARE.
I MEAN IF **ALL** THE GIRLS ARE AS **OBNOXIOUS** AND **PETTY** AS YOU, I'D RATHER STAY OUT OF IT.
FINE, WHATEVER.
YOUR CHOICE.

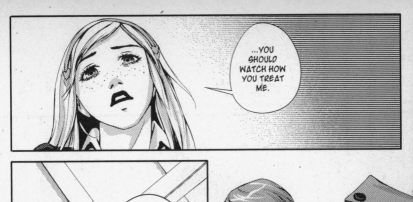

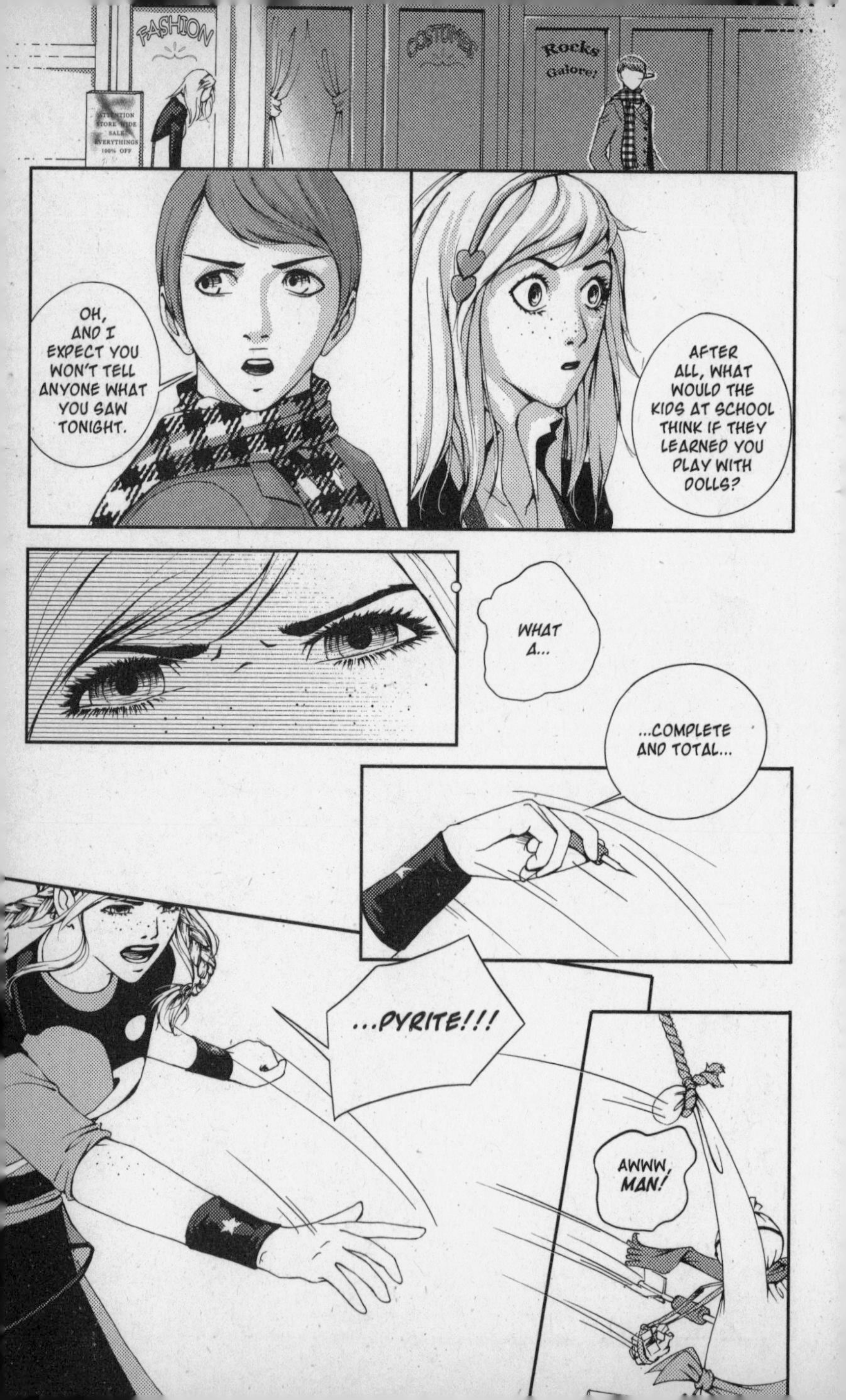
FASHION
COSTUMES
Rocks Galore!
ATTENTION STORE WIDE SALE EVERYTHINGS 100% OFF
OH, AND I EXPECT YOU WON'T TELL ANYONE WHAT YOU SAW TONIGHT.
AFTER ALL, WHAT WOULD THE KIDS AT SCHOOL THINK IF THEY LEARNED YOU PLAY WITH DOLLS?
WHAT A...
...COMPLETE AND TOTAL...
...PYRITE!!!
AWWW, MAN!

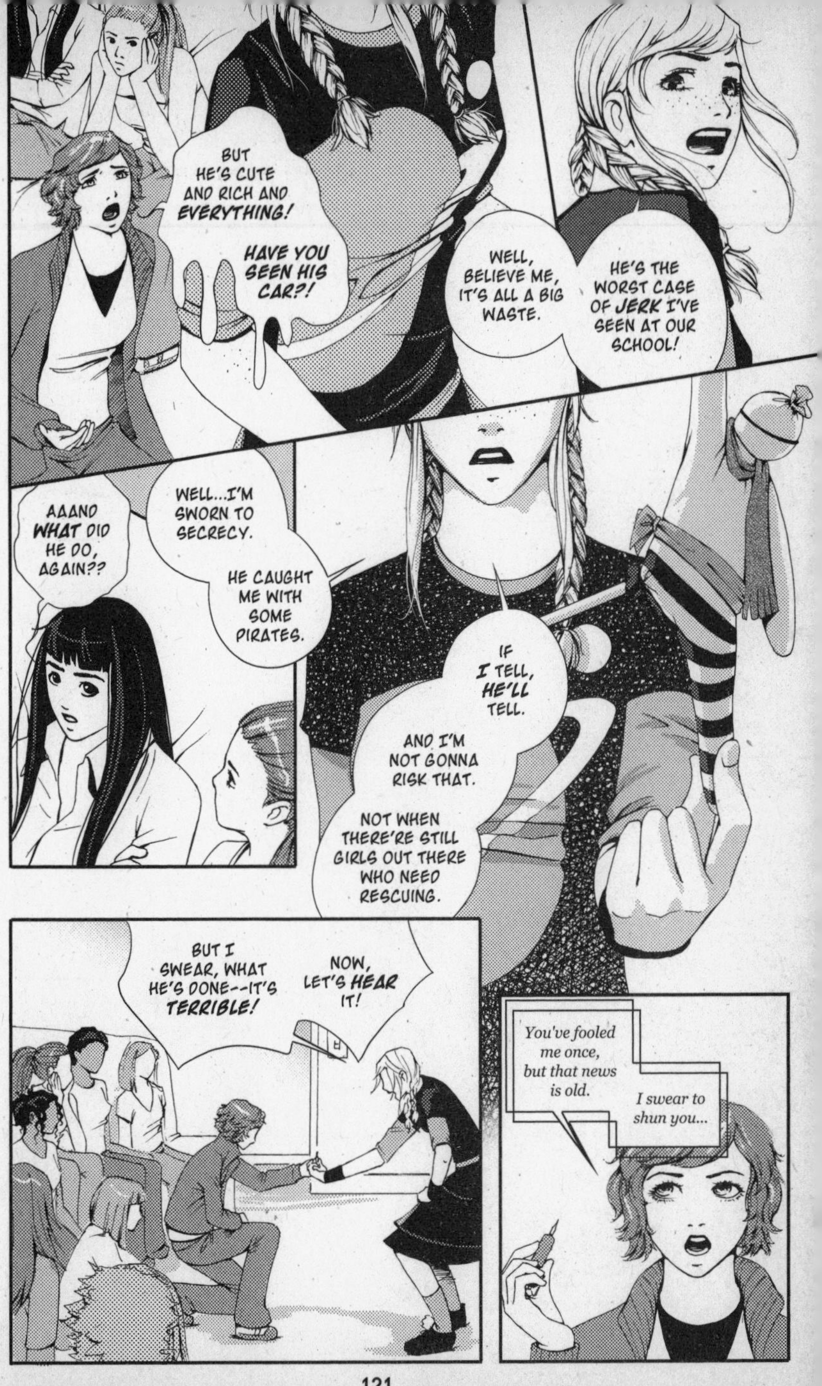
BUT HE'S CUTE AND RICH AND EVERYTHING!
HAVE YOU SEEN HIS CAR?!
WELL, BELIEVE ME, IT'S ALL A BIG WASTE.
HE'S THE WORST CASE OF JERK I'VE SEEN AT OUR SCHOOL!
AAAND WHAT DID HE DO, AGAIN??
WELL...I'M SWORN TO SECRECY.
HE CAUGHT ME WITH SOME PIRATES.
IF I TELL, HE'LL TELL.
AND I'M NOT GONNA RISK THAT.
NOT WHEN THERE'RE STILL GIRLS OUT THERE WHO NEED RESCUING.
BUT I SWEAR, WHAT HE'S DONE--IT'S TERRIBLE!
NOW, LET'S HEAR IT!
You've fooled me once, but that news is old.
I swear to shun you...

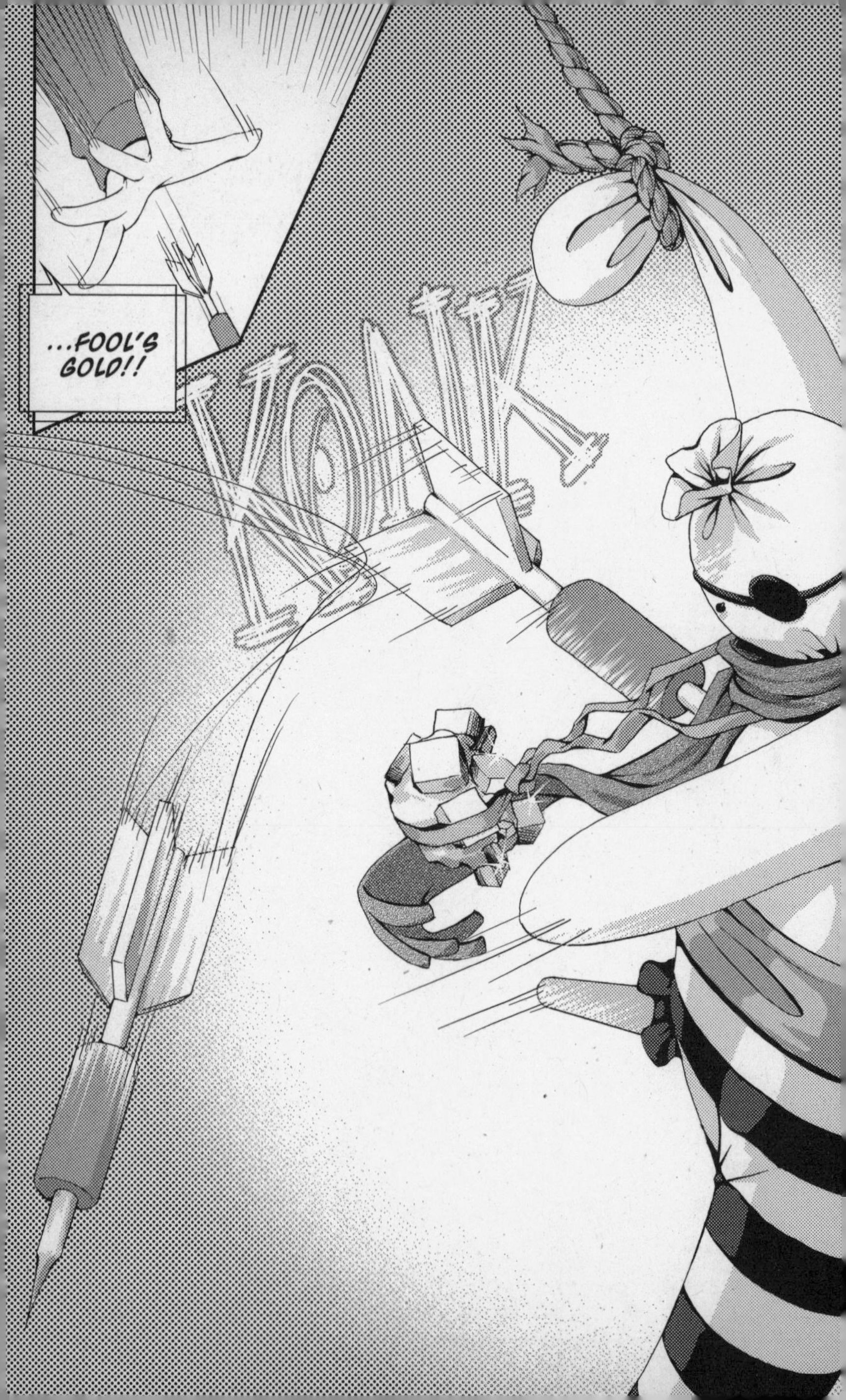
...FOOL'S GOLD!!
KONK

Chapter 5: Halloween

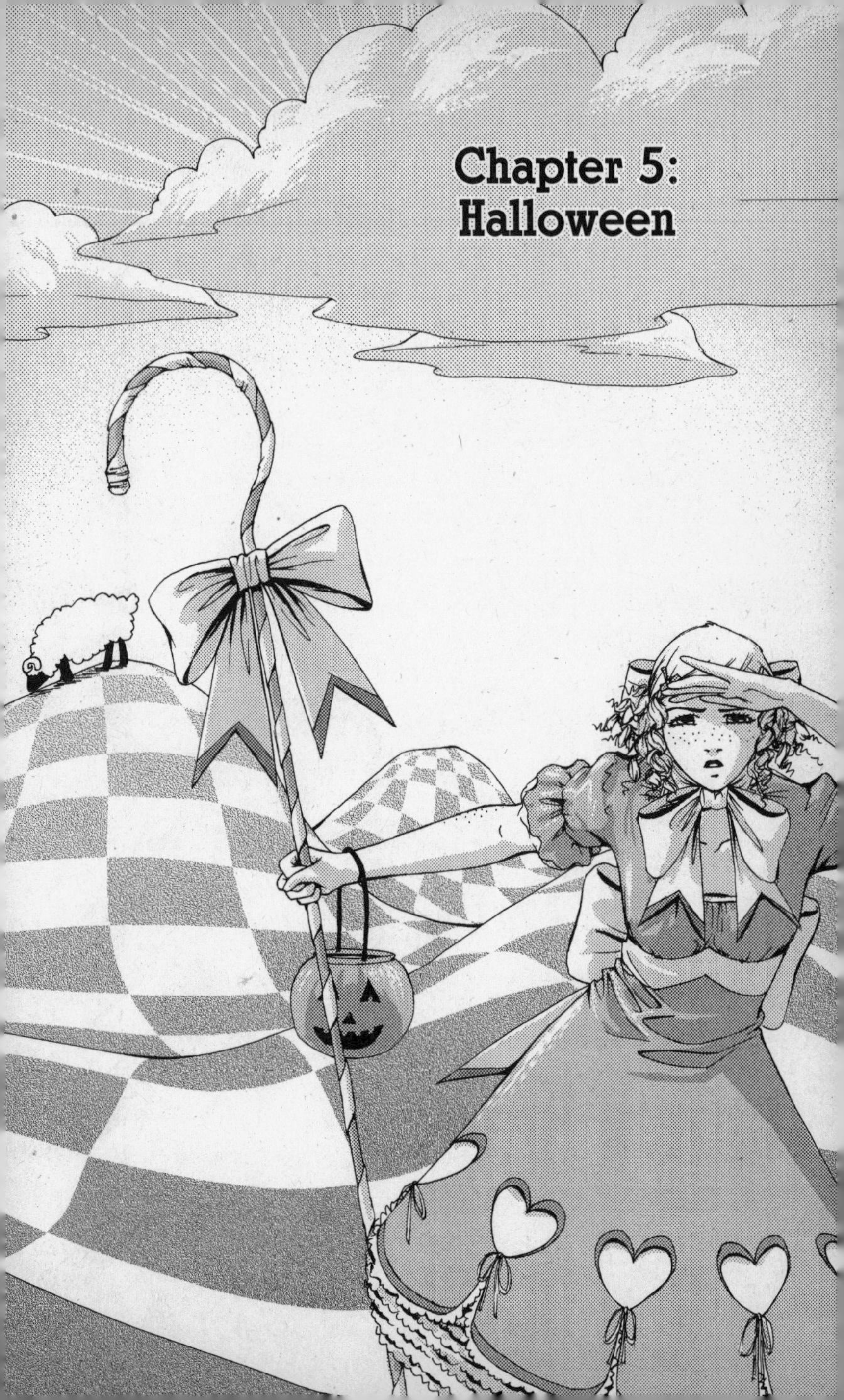

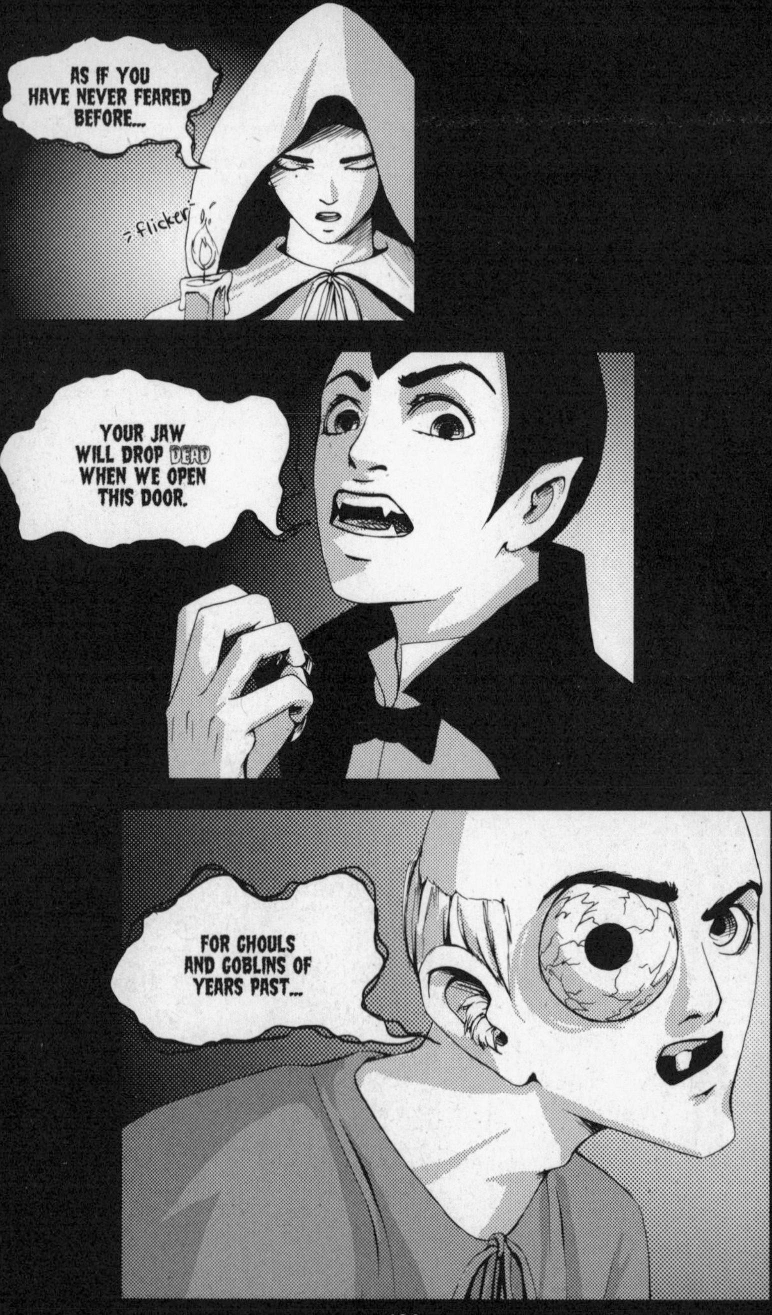
AS IF YOU HAVE NEVER FEARED BEFORE...
flicker
YOUR JAW WILL DROP DEAD WHEN WE OPEN THIS DOOR.
FOR GHOULS AND GOBLINS OF YEARS PAST...

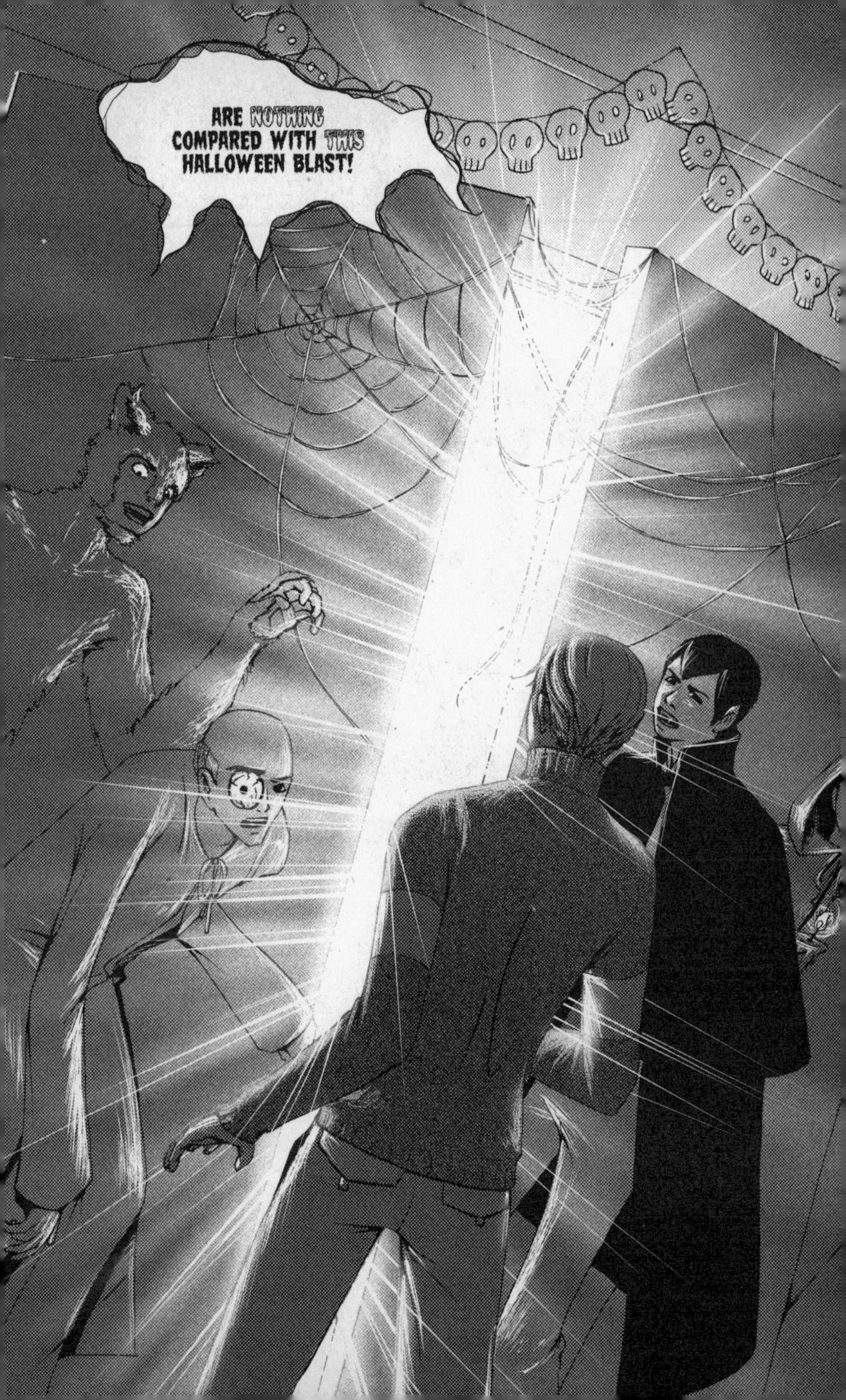
ARE NOTHING COMPARED WITH THIS HALLOWEEN BLAST!

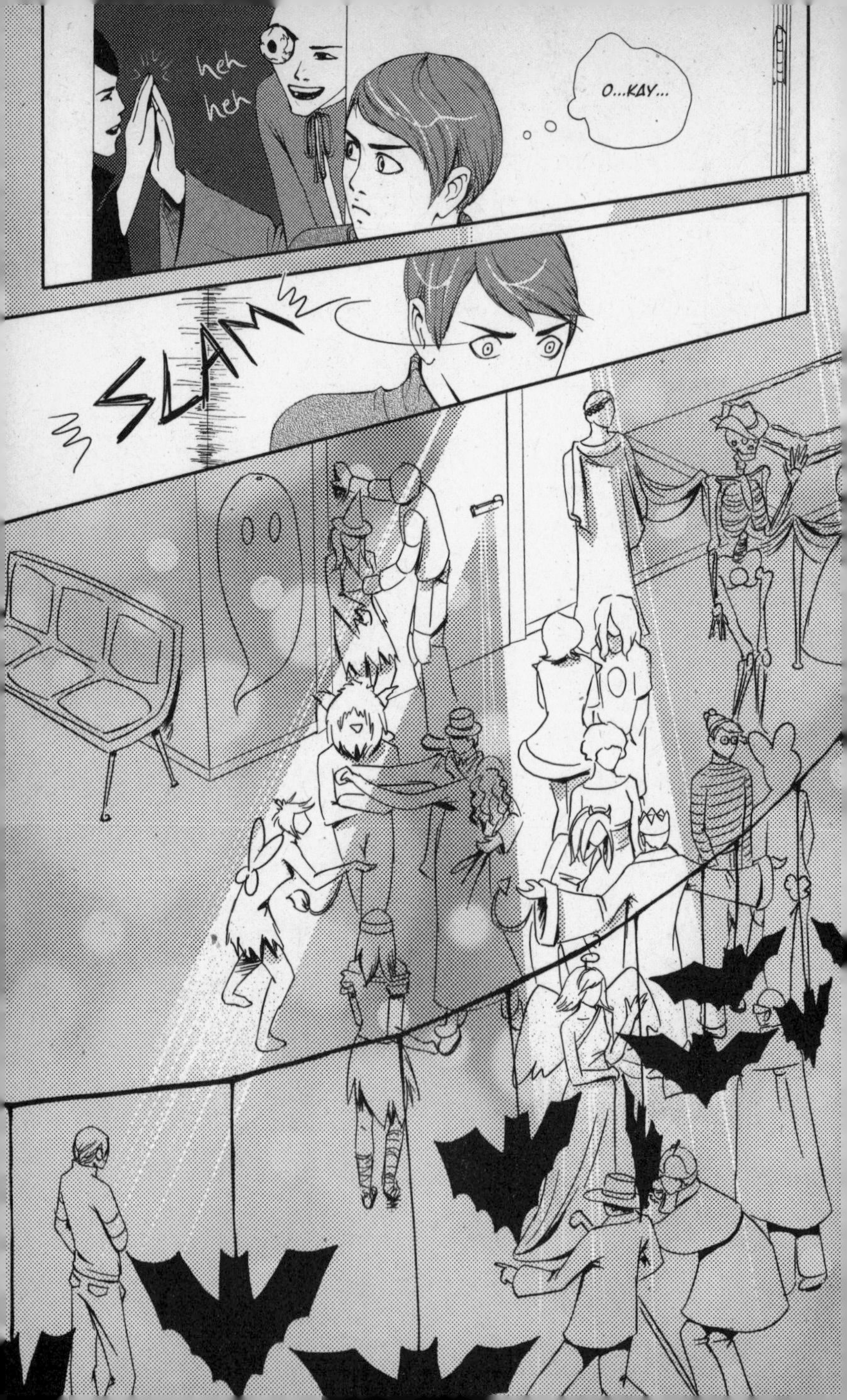
heh
heh
O...KAY...
SLAM

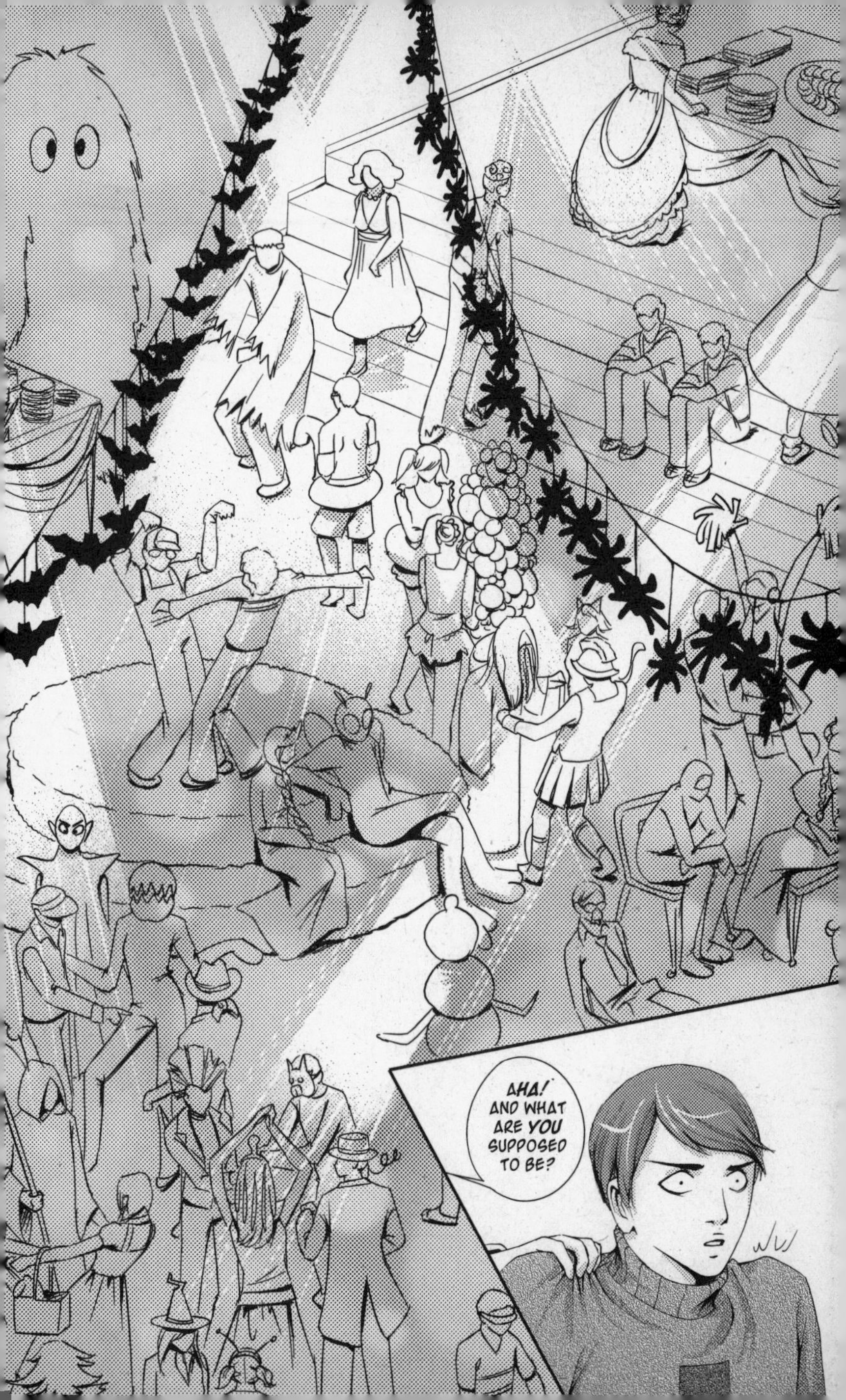
AHA! AND WHAT ARE YOU SUPPOSED TO BE?

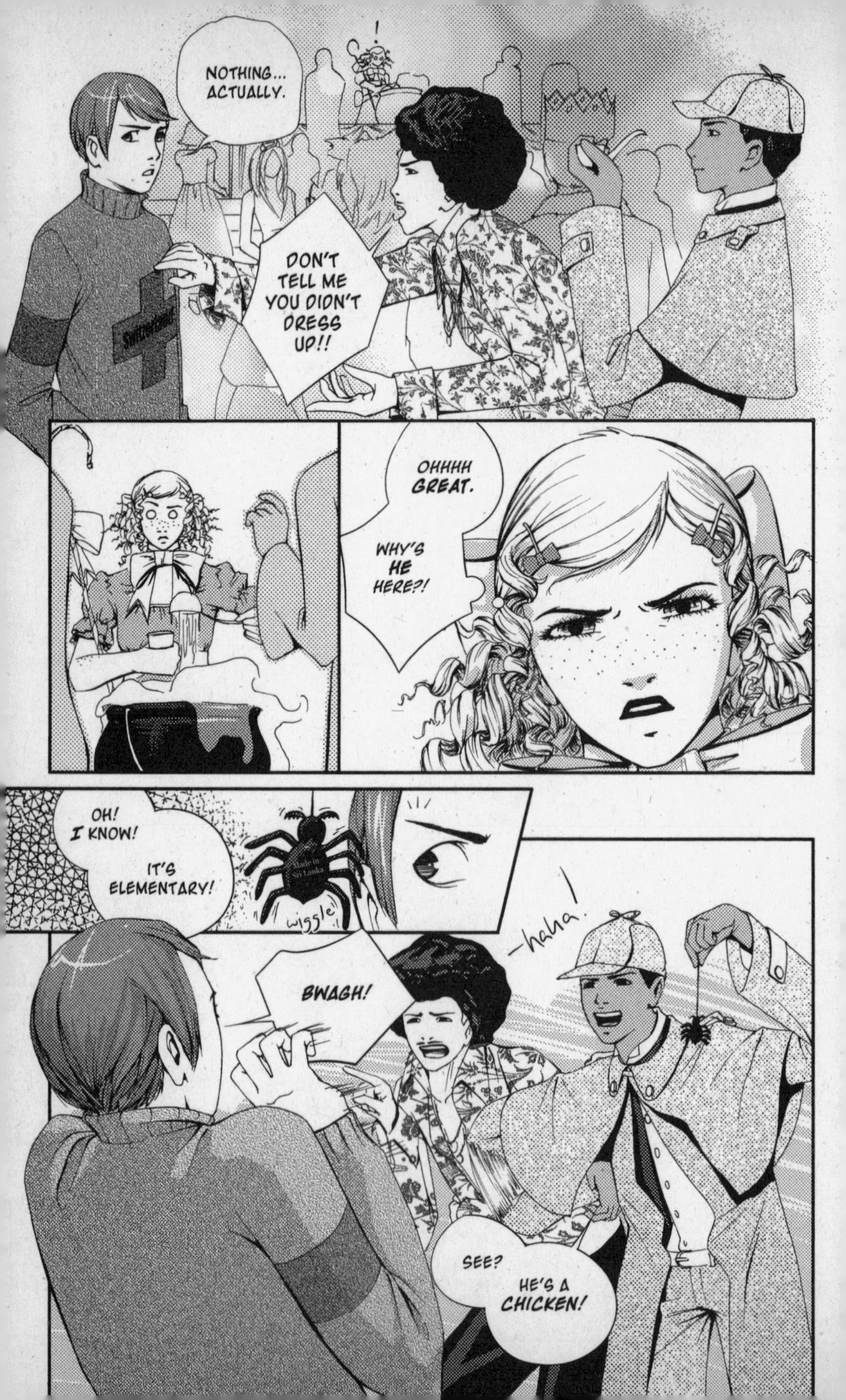
!
NOTHING... ACTUALLY.
DON'T TELL ME YOU DIDN'T DRESS UP!!
OHHHH GREAT.
WHY'S HE HERE?!
OH! I KNOW!
IT'S ELEMENTARY!
Made in Sri Lanka
wiggle
BWAGH!
-haha!
SEE?
HE'S A CHICKEN!

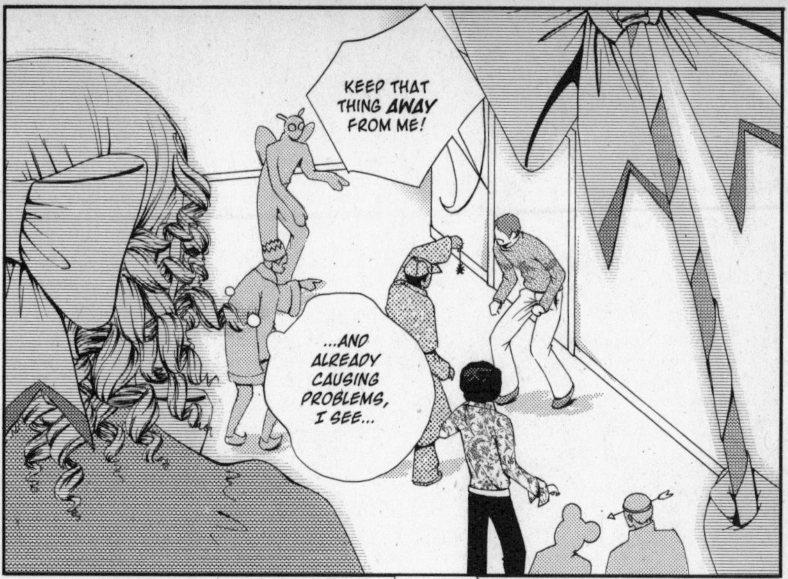
KEEP THAT THING **AWAY** FROM ME!
...AND ALREADY CAUSING PROBLEMS, I SEE...

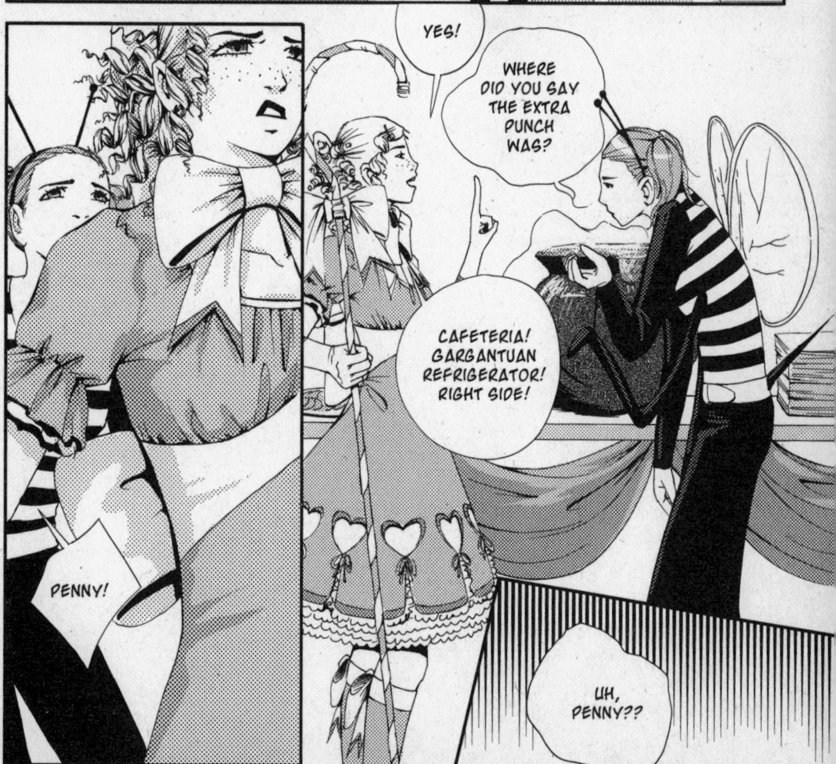
PENNY!
YES!
WHERE DID YOU SAY THE EXTRA PUNCH WAS?
CAFETERIA! GARGANTUAN REFRIGERATOR! RIGHT SIDE!
UH, PENNY??

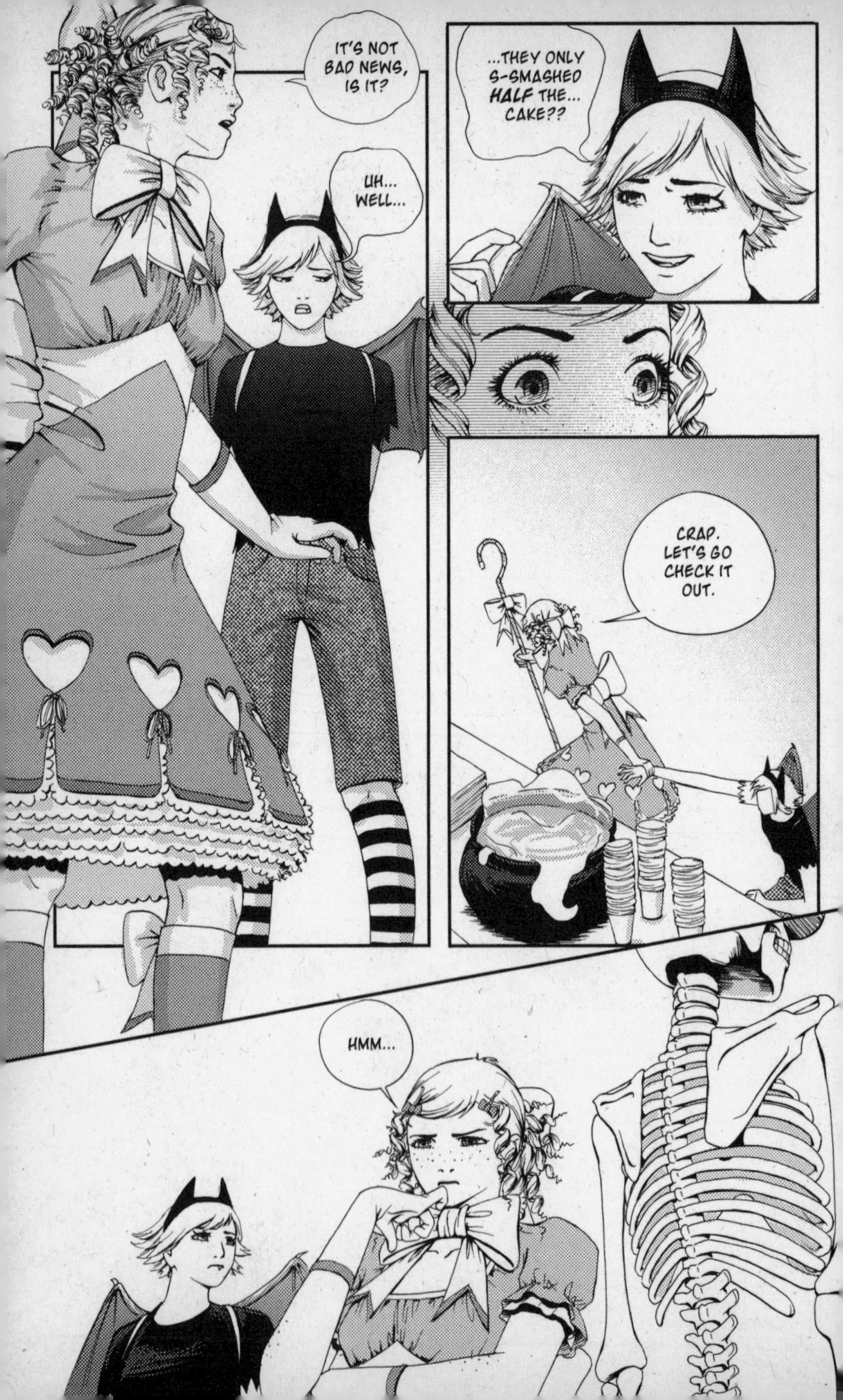
IT'S NOT BAD NEWS, IS IT?
UH... WELL...
...THEY ONLY S-SMASHED **HALF** THE... CAKE??
CRAP. LET'S GO CHECK IT OUT.
HMM...

AFTER ALL THAT WORK, TOO...

I KNOW. I'M *REALLY* SORRY!!

OOO, WAIT!

I'VE GOT IT!

SORRY, MAN, NOTHING PERSONAL.

SNNNNAP!

...AND *VOILA!*

HOLY COW, PENNY!

YOU, LIKE, KNOW HOW TO SOLVE *EVERY* PROBLEM!

HEH. I TRY!

PENNY! CAN I TALK TO YOU??

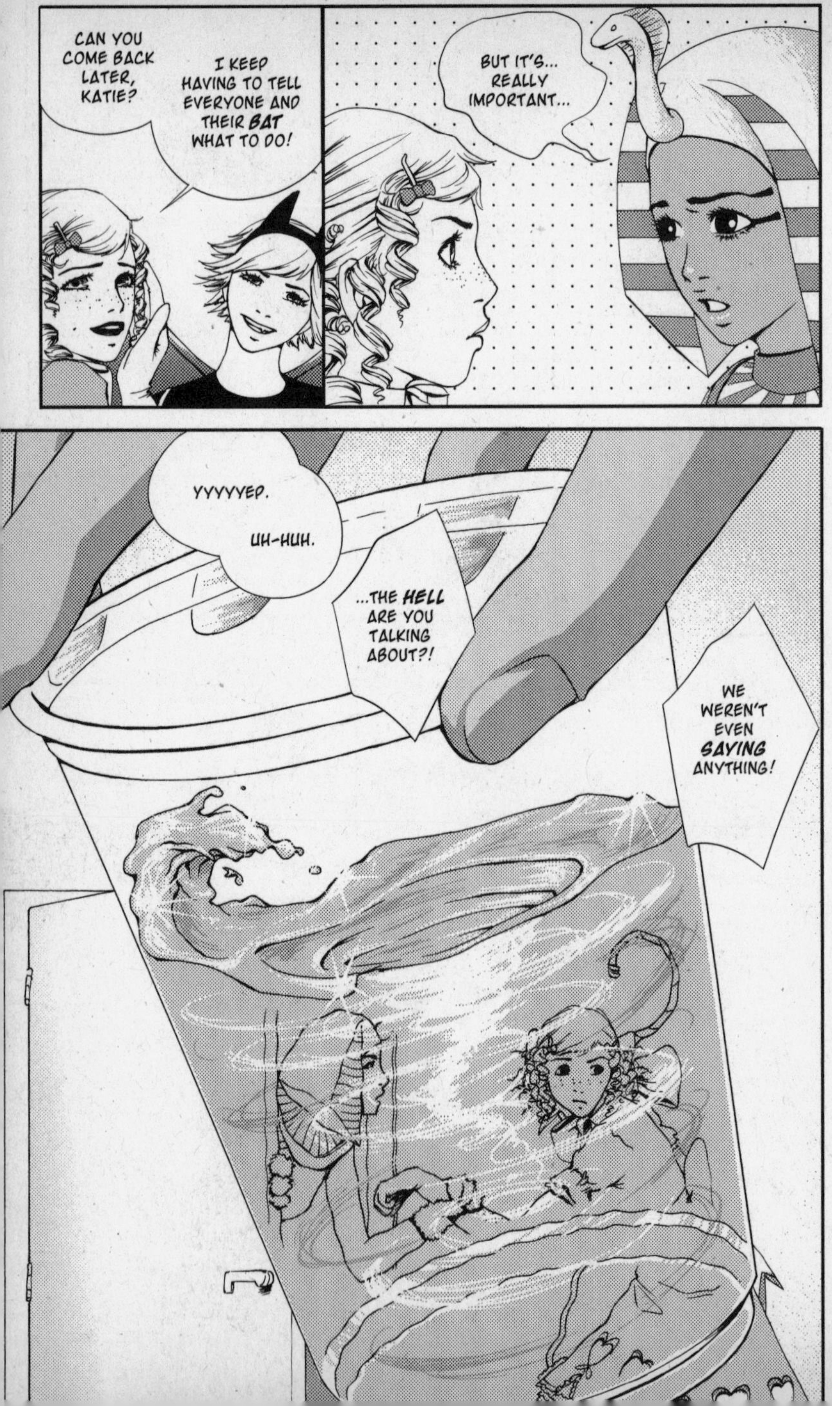
CAN YOU COME BACK LATER, KATIE?
I KEEP HAVING TO TELL EVERYONE AND THEIR BAT WHAT TO DO!
BUT IT'S... REALLY IMPORTANT...
YYYYYEP.
UH-HUH.
...THE HELL ARE YOU TALKING ABOUT?!
WE WEREN'T EVEN SAYING ANYTHING!

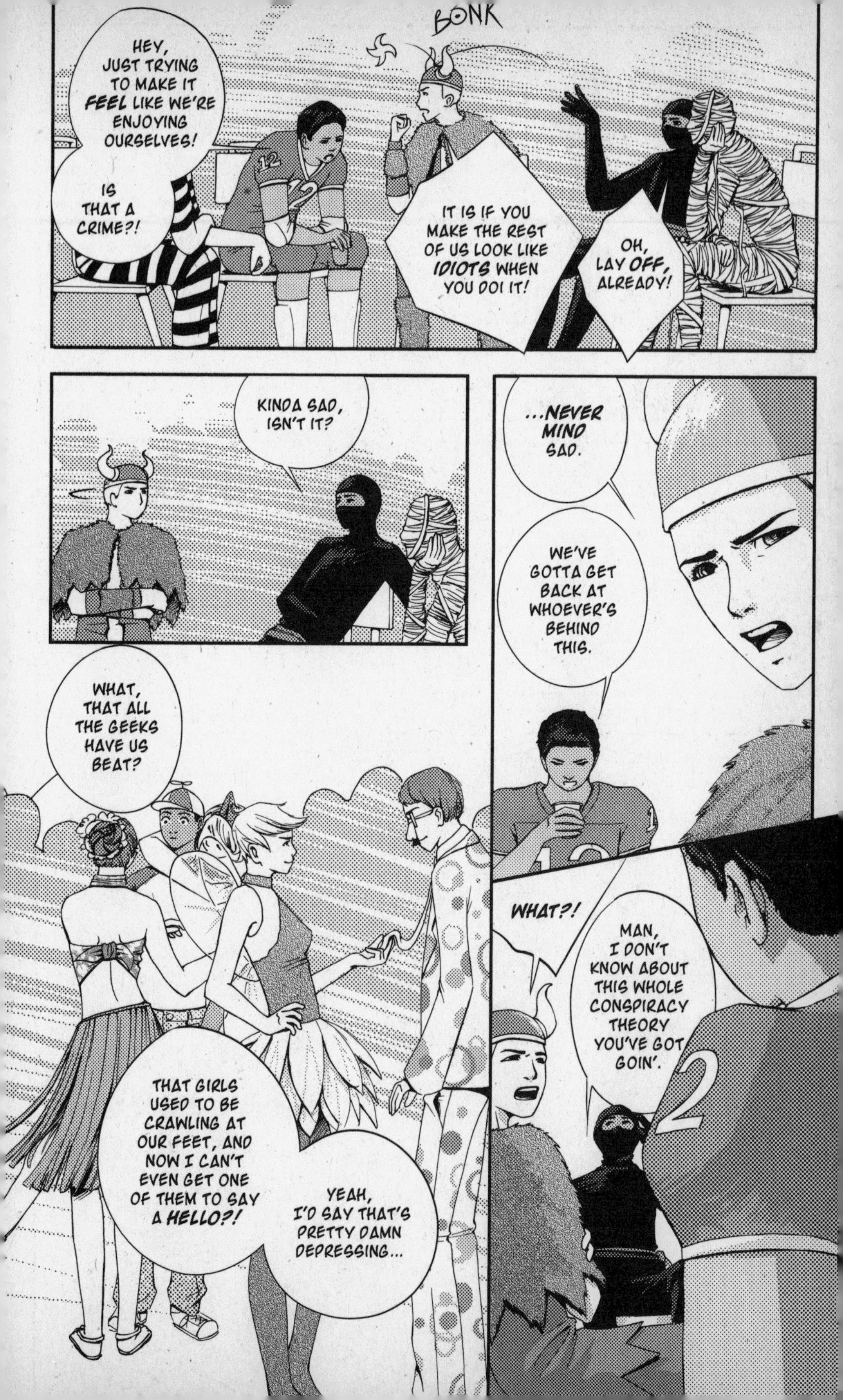
HEY, JUST TRYING TO MAKE IT FEEL LIKE WE'RE ENJOYING OURSELVES!
IS THAT A CRIME?!
BONK
IT IS IF YOU MAKE THE REST OF US LOOK LIKE IDIOTS WHEN YOU DOI IT!
OH, LAY OFF, ALREADY!
KINDA SAD, ISN'T IT?
WHAT, THAT ALL THE GEEKS HAVE US BEAT?
THAT GIRLS USED TO BE CRAWLING AT OUR FEET, AND NOW I CAN'T EVEN GET ONE OF THEM TO SAY A HELLO?!
YEAH, I'D SAY THAT'S PRETTY DAMN DEPRESSING...
...NEVER MIND SAD.
WE'VE GOTTA GET BACK AT WHOEVER'S BEHIND THIS.
WHAT?!
MAN, I DON'T KNOW ABOUT THIS WHOLE CONSPIRACY THEORY YOU'VE GOT GOIN'.

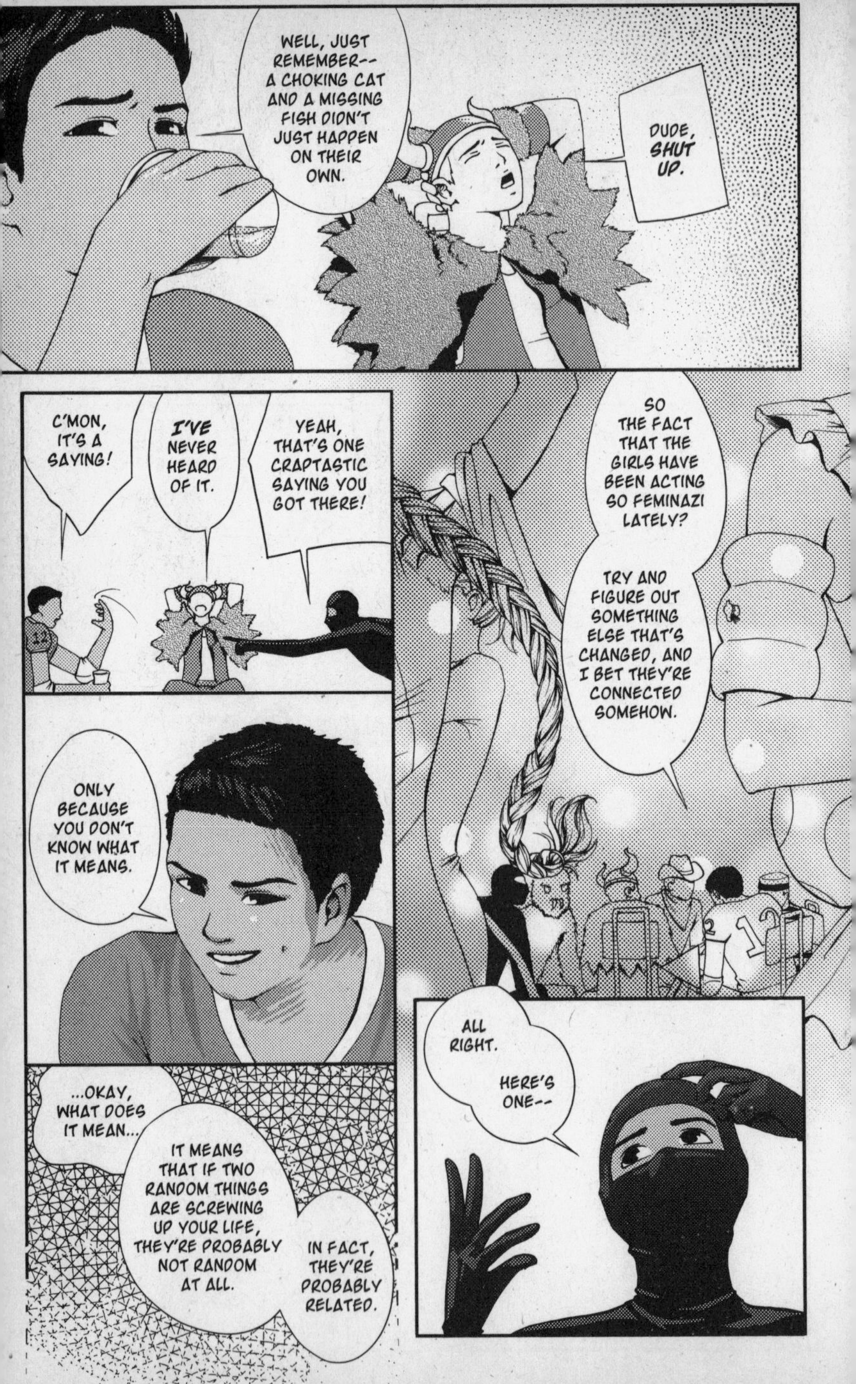
WELL, JUST REMEMBER-- A CHOKING CAT AND A MISSING FISH DIDN'T JUST HAPPEN ON THEIR OWN.
DUDE, SHUT UP.
C'MON, IT'S A SAYING!
I'VE NEVER HEARD OF IT.
YEAH, THAT'S ONE CRAPTASTIC SAYING YOU GOT THERE!
ONLY BECAUSE YOU DON'T KNOW WHAT IT MEANS.
...OKAY, WHAT DOES IT MEAN...
IT MEANS THAT IF TWO RANDOM THINGS ARE SCREWING UP YOUR LIFE, THEY'RE PROBABLY NOT RANDOM AT ALL.
IN FACT, THEY'RE PROBABLY RELATED.
SO THE FACT THAT THE GIRLS HAVE BEEN ACTING SO FEMINAZI LATELY?
TRY AND FIGURE OUT SOMETHING ELSE THAT'S CHANGED, AND I BET THEY'RE CONNECTED SOMEHOW.
ALL RIGHT.
HERE'S ONE--

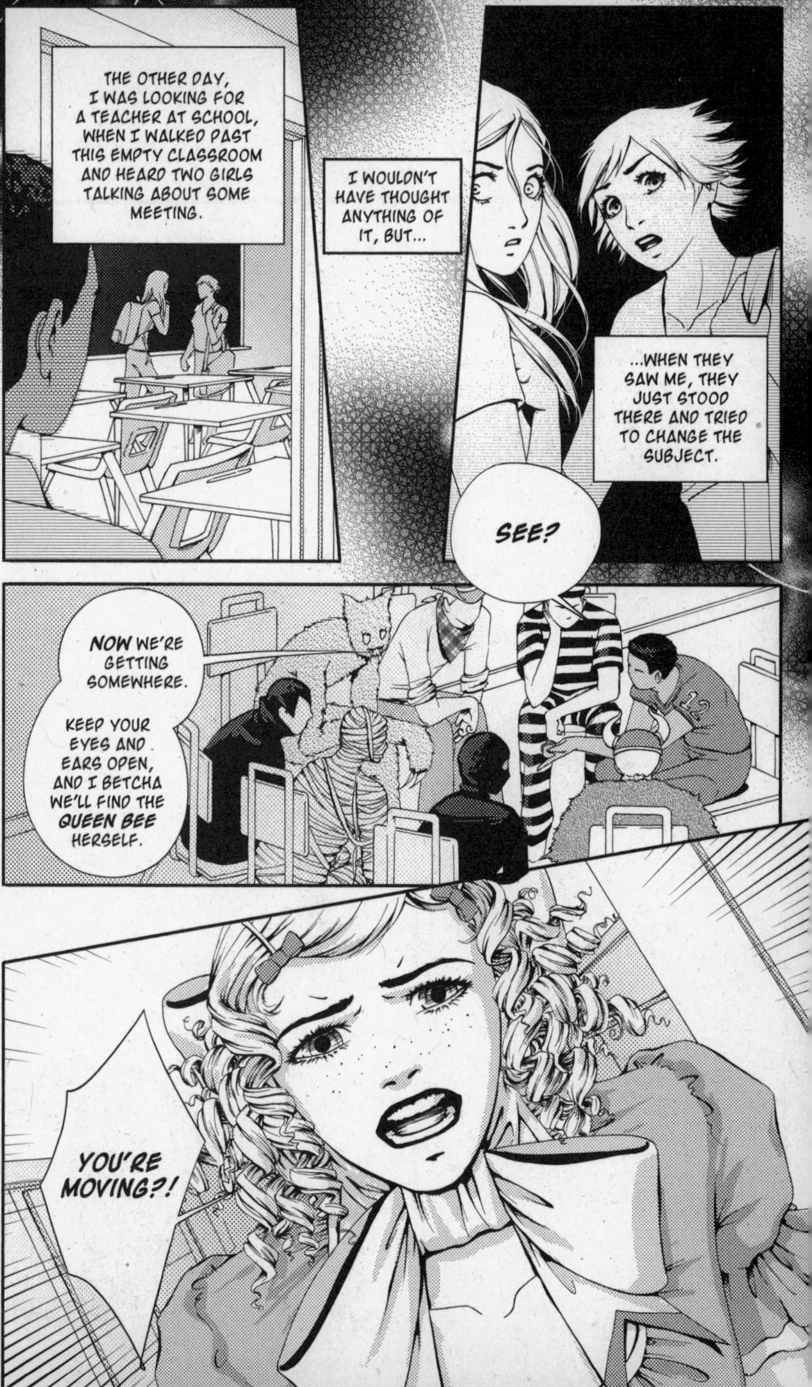
THE OTHER DAY, I WAS LOOKING FOR A TEACHER AT SCHOOL, WHEN I WALKED PAST THIS EMPTY CLASSROOM AND HEARD TWO GIRLS TALKING ABOUT SOME MEETING.
I WOULDN'T HAVE THOUGHT ANYTHING OF IT, BUT...
...WHEN THEY SAW ME, THEY JUST STOOD THERE AND TRIED TO CHANGE THE SUBJECT.
SEE?
NOW WE'RE GETTING SOMEWHERE.
KEEP YOUR EYES AND EARS OPEN, AND I BETCHA WE'LL FIND THE QUEEN BEE HERSELF.
12
YOU'RE MOVING?!

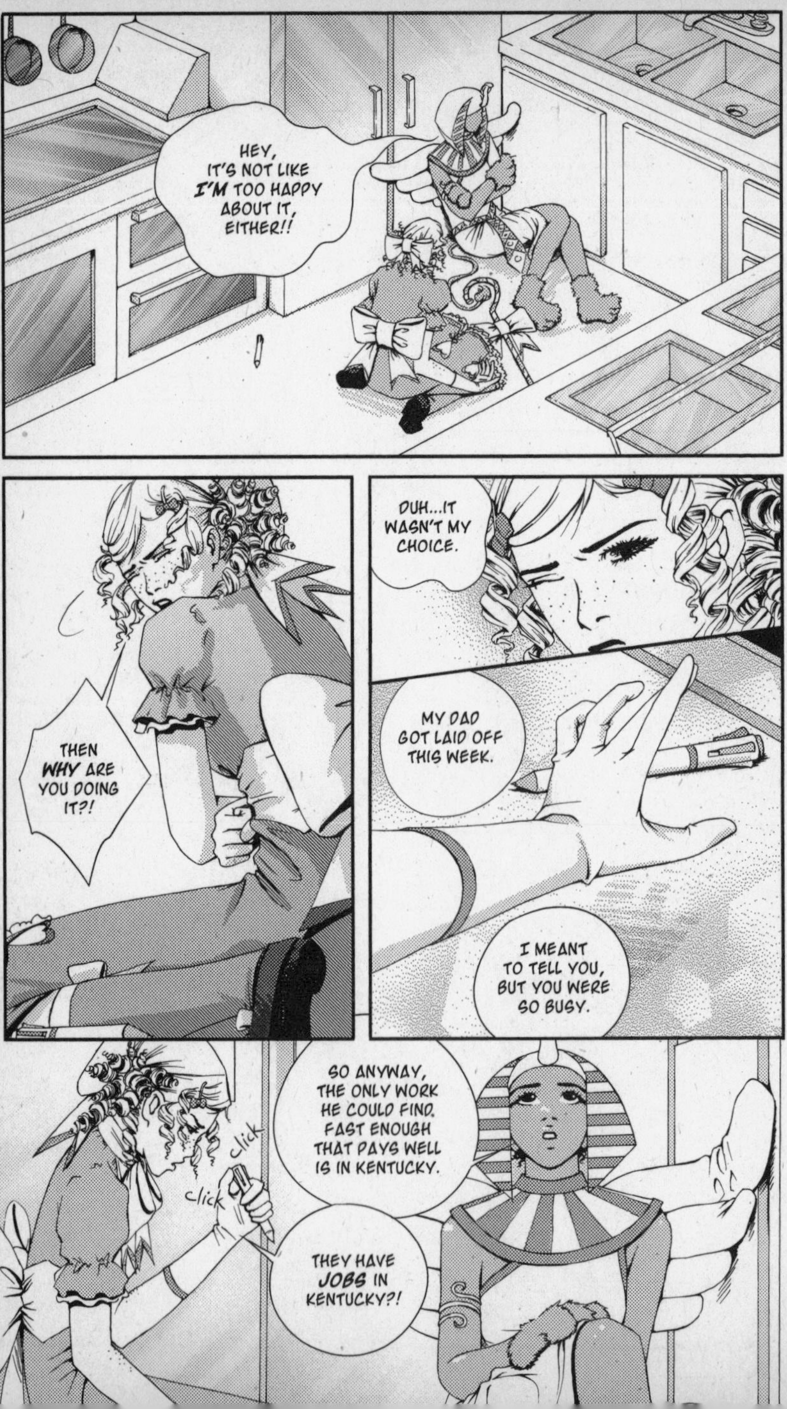
HEY, IT'S NOT LIKE I'M TOO HAPPY ABOUT IT, EITHER!!
THEN WHY ARE YOU DOING IT?!
DUH...IT WASN'T MY CHOICE.
MY DAD GOT LAID OFF THIS WEEK.
I MEANT TO TELL YOU, BUT YOU WERE SO BUSY.
click
click
SO ANYWAY, THE ONLY WORK HE COULD FIND. FAST ENOUGH THAT PAYS WELL IS IN KENTUCKY.
THEY HAVE JOBS IN KENTUCKY?!

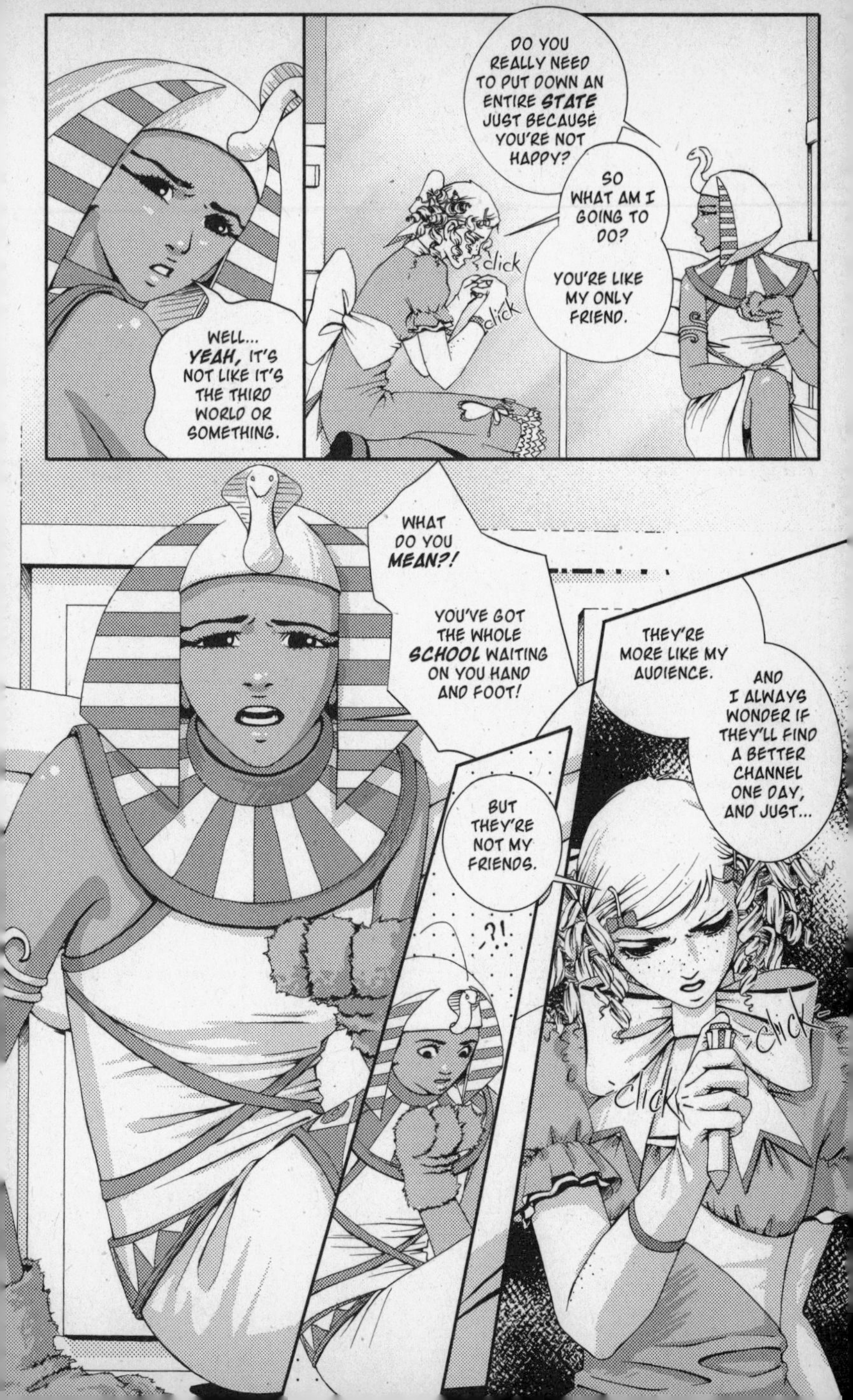
WELL... **YEAH,** IT'S NOT LIKE IT'S THE THIRD WORLD OR SOMETHING.
DO YOU REALLY NEED TO PUT DOWN AN ENTIRE **STATE** JUST BECAUSE YOU'RE NOT HAPPY?
SO WHAT AM I GOING TO DO?
YOU'RE LIKE MY ONLY FRIEND.
click
click
WHAT DO YOU **MEAN?!**
YOU'VE GOT THE WHOLE **SCHOOL** WAITING ON YOU HAND AND FOOT!
BUT THEY'RE NOT MY FRIENDS.
,?!
THEY'RE MORE LIKE MY AUDIENCE.
AND I ALWAYS WONDER IF THEY'LL FIND A BETTER CHANNEL ONE DAY, AND JUST...
click
click

...SWITCH.

-click-

WOW, THAT'S...

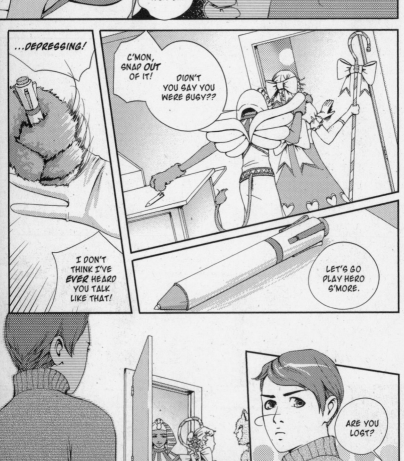

...DEPRESSING!

C'MON, SNAP OUT OF IT!

DIDN'T YOU SAY YOU WERE BUSY??

I DON'T THINK I'VE *EVER* HEARD YOU TALK LIKE THAT!

LET'S GO PLAY HERO S'MORE.

ARE YOU LOST?

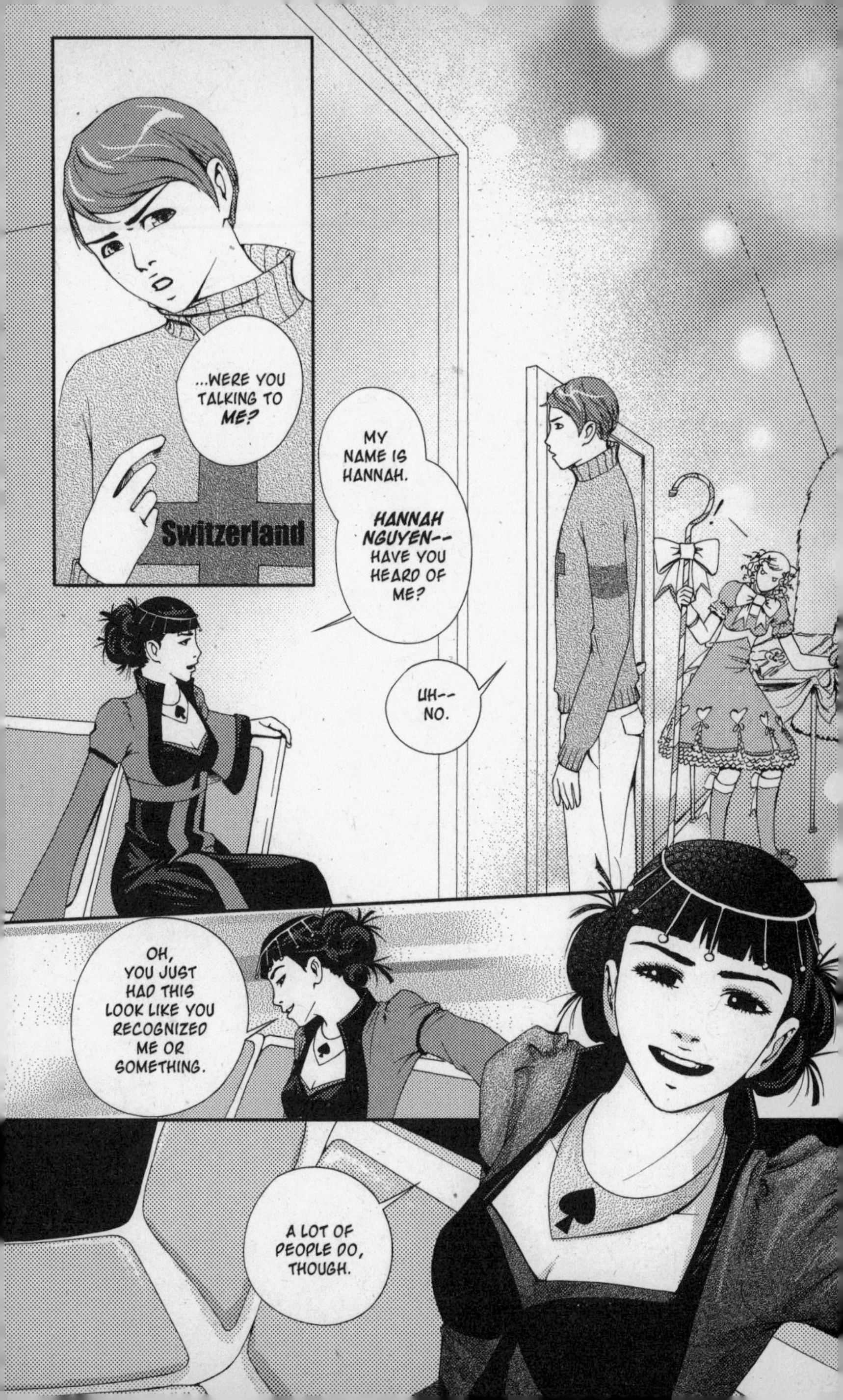
...WERE YOU TALKING TO ME?
Switzerland
MY NAME IS HANNAH.
HANNAH NGUYEN-- HAVE YOU HEARD OF ME?
UH-- NO.
OH, YOU JUST HAD THIS LOOK LIKE YOU RECOGNIZED ME OR SOMETHING.
A LOT OF PEOPLE DO, THOUGH.

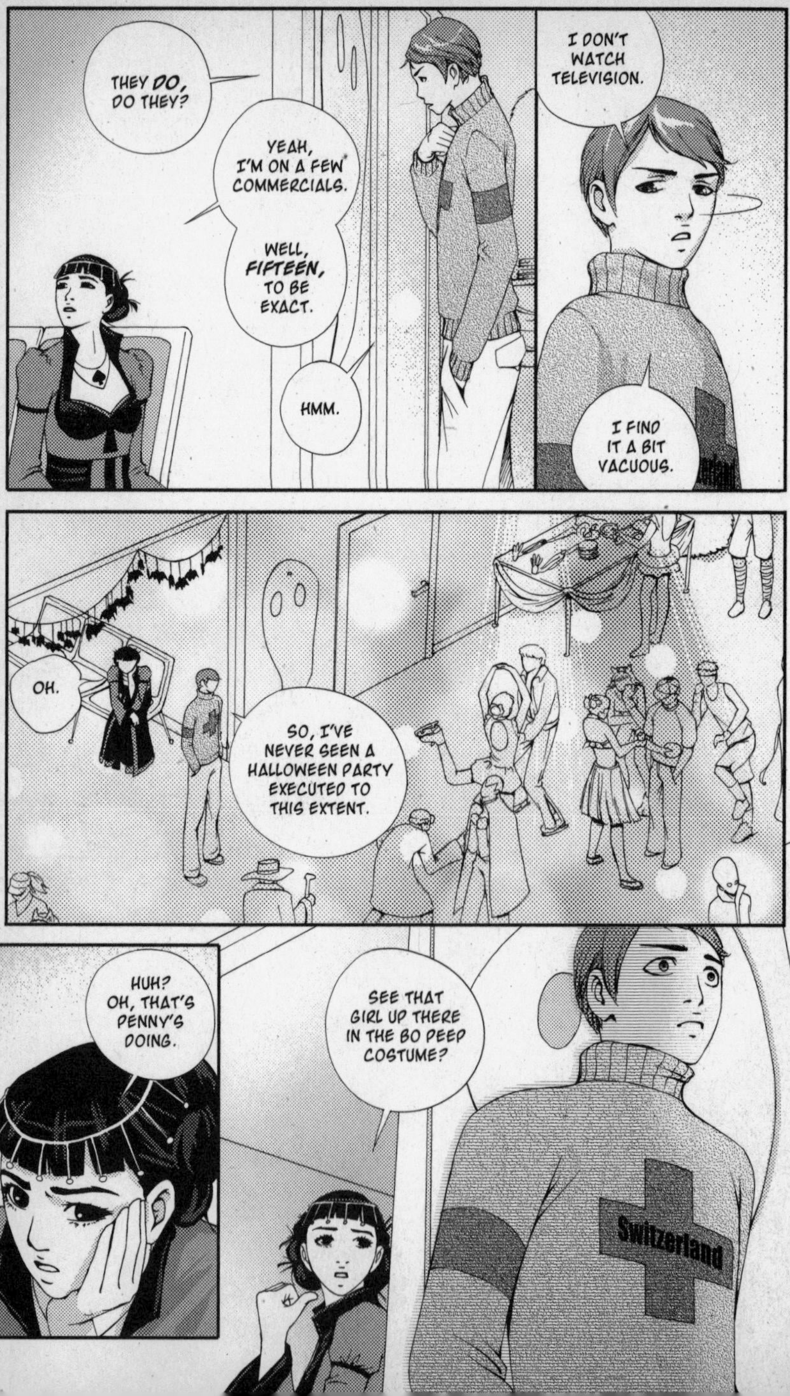
THEY *DO*, DO THEY?
YEAH, I'M ON A FEW COMMERCIALS.
WELL, *FIFTEEN*, TO BE EXACT.
HMM.
I DON'T WATCH TELEVISION.
I FIND IT A BIT VACUOUS.
OH.
SO, I'VE NEVER SEEN A HALLOWEEN PARTY EXECUTED TO THIS EXTENT.
HUH? OH, THAT'S PENNY'S DOING.
SEE THAT GIRL UP THERE IN THE BO PEEP COSTUME?
Switzerland

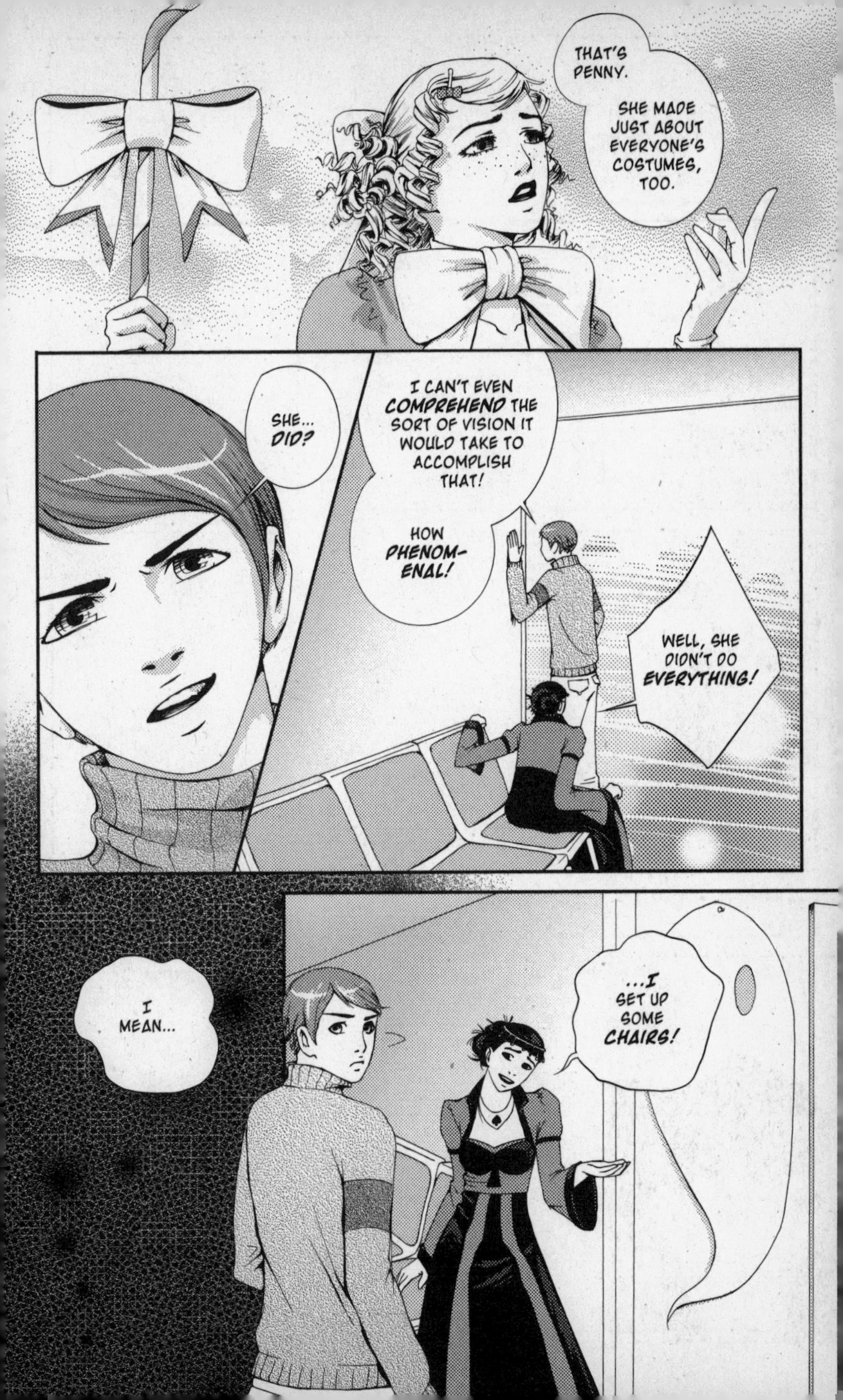
THAT'S PENNY.
SHE MADE JUST ABOUT EVERYONE'S COSTUMES, TOO.
SHE... DID?
I CAN'T EVEN COMPREHEND THE SORT OF VISION IT WOULD TAKE TO ACCOMPLISH THAT!
HOW PHENOM-ENAL!
WELL, SHE DIDN'T DO EVERYTHING!
I MEAN...
...I SET UP SOME CHAIRS!

AH. AND THEY'RE BEING PUT TO GOOD USE, I SEE.

A FINE JOB.

BRRRRRING!

THERE'S THE BELL!

YOU KNOW WHAT THAT MEANS.

I'M NEVER GONNA FIND ANOTHER FRIEND LIKE KATIE.

SHE'S THE MOST GENUINE GIRL I KNOW.

TAKE YOUR ESSAYS OUT, PLEASE.

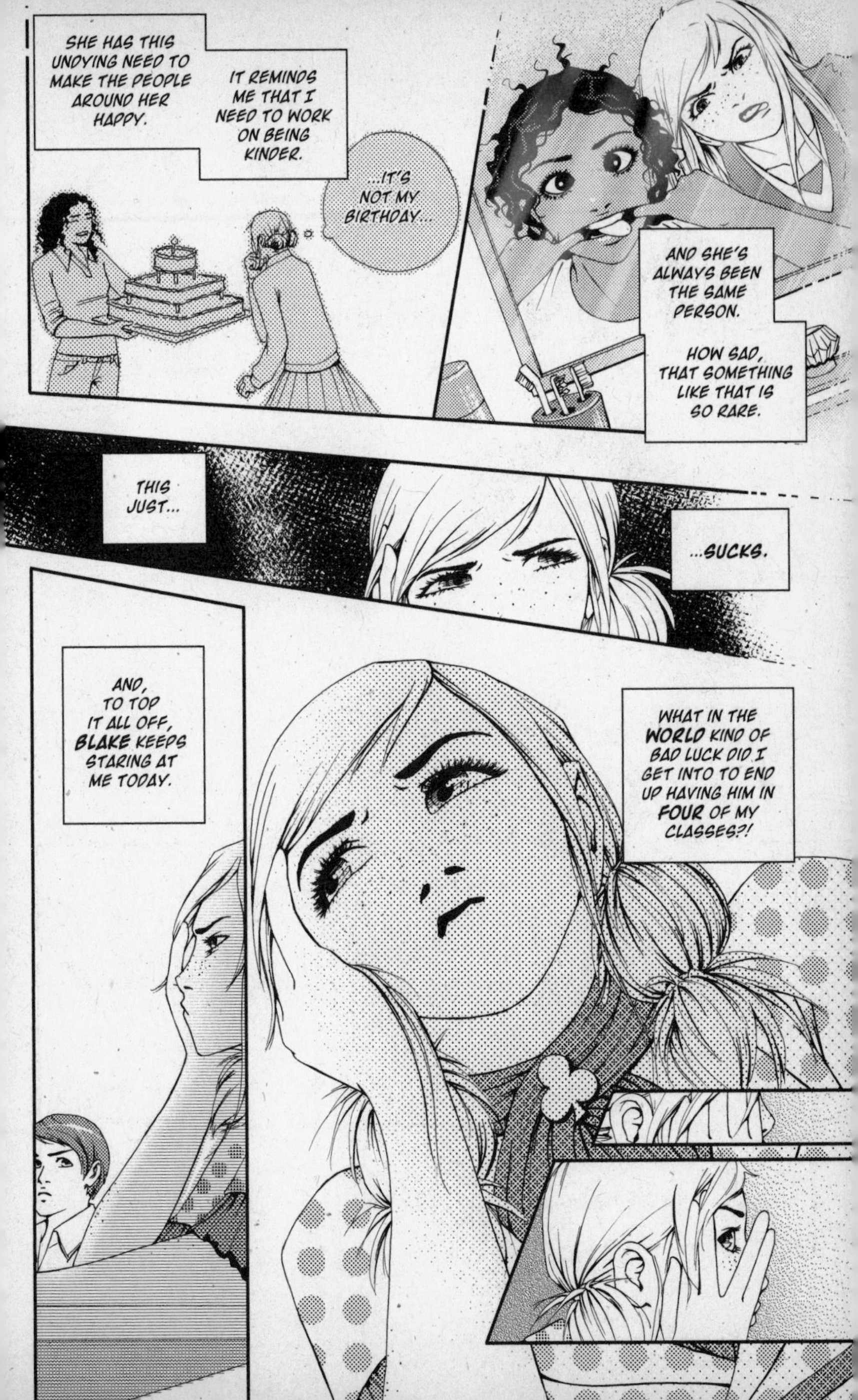
SHE HAS THIS UNDYING NEED TO MAKE THE PEOPLE AROUND HER HAPPY.
IT REMINDS ME THAT I NEED TO WORK ON BEING KINDER.
...IT'S NOT MY BIRTHDAY...
AND SHE'S ALWAYS BEEN THE SAME PERSON.
HOW SAD, THAT SOMETHING LIKE THAT IS SO RARE.
THIS JUST...
...SUCKS.
AND, TO TOP IT ALL OFF, BLAKE KEEPS STARING AT ME TODAY.
WHAT IN THE WORLD KIND OF BAD LUCK DID I GET INTO TO END UP HAVING HIM IN FOUR OF MY CLASSES?!

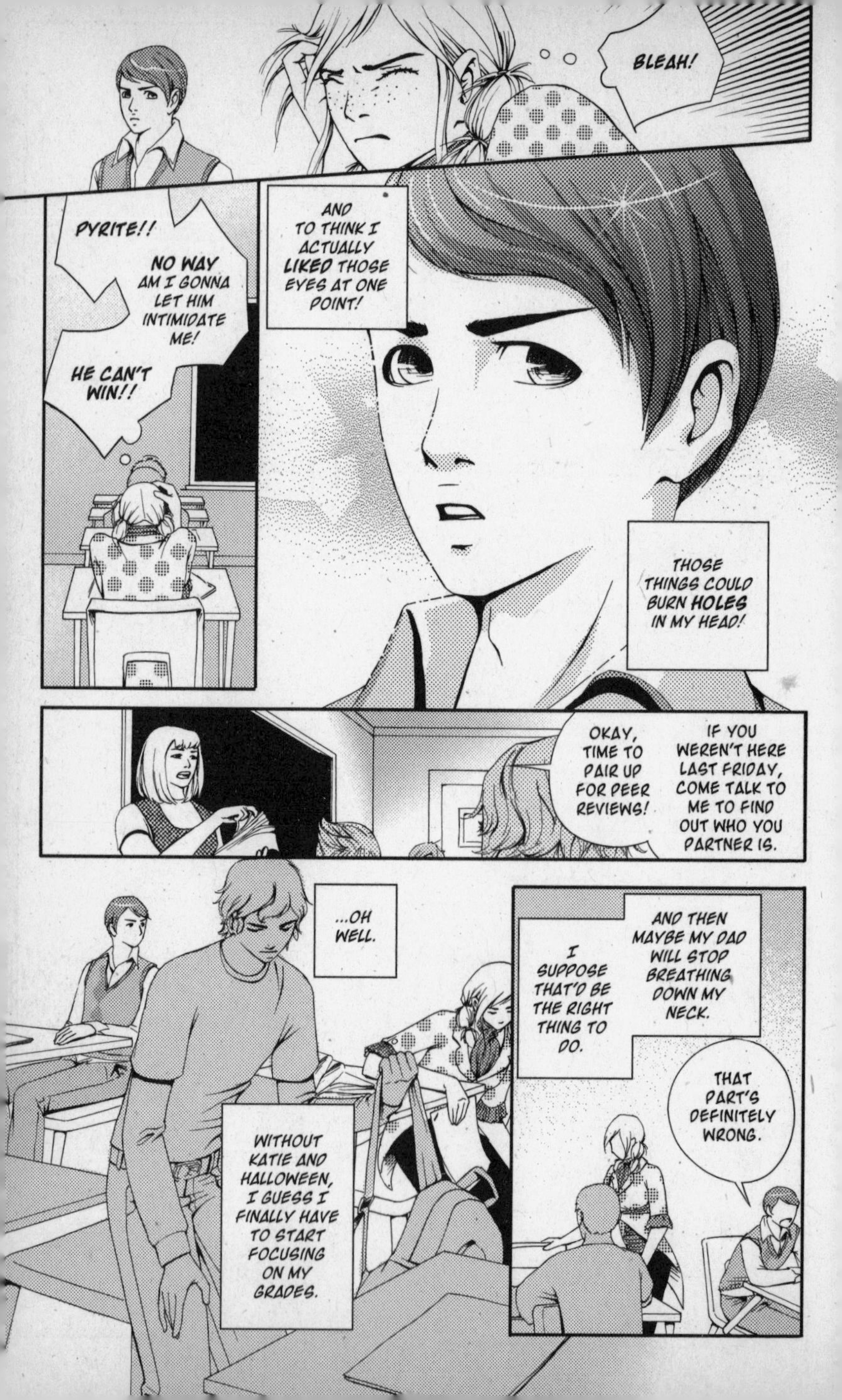

BLEAH!
PYRITE!!
NO WAY AM I GONNA LET HIM INTIMIDATE ME!
HE CAN'T WIN!!
AND TO THINK I ACTUALLY LIKED THOSE EYES AT ONE POINT!
THOSE THINGS COULD BURN HOLES IN MY HEAD!
OKAY, TIME TO PAIR UP FOR PEER REVIEWS!
IF YOU WEREN'T HERE LAST FRIDAY, COME TALK TO ME TO FIND OUT WHO YOU PARTNER IS.
...OH WELL.
WITHOUT KATIE AND HALLOWEEN, I GUESS I FINALLY HAVE TO START FOCUSING ON MY GRADES.
I SUPPOSE THAT'D BE THE RIGHT THING TO DO.
AND THEN MAYBE MY DAD WILL STOP BREATHING DOWN MY NECK.
THAT PART'S DEFINITELY WRONG.

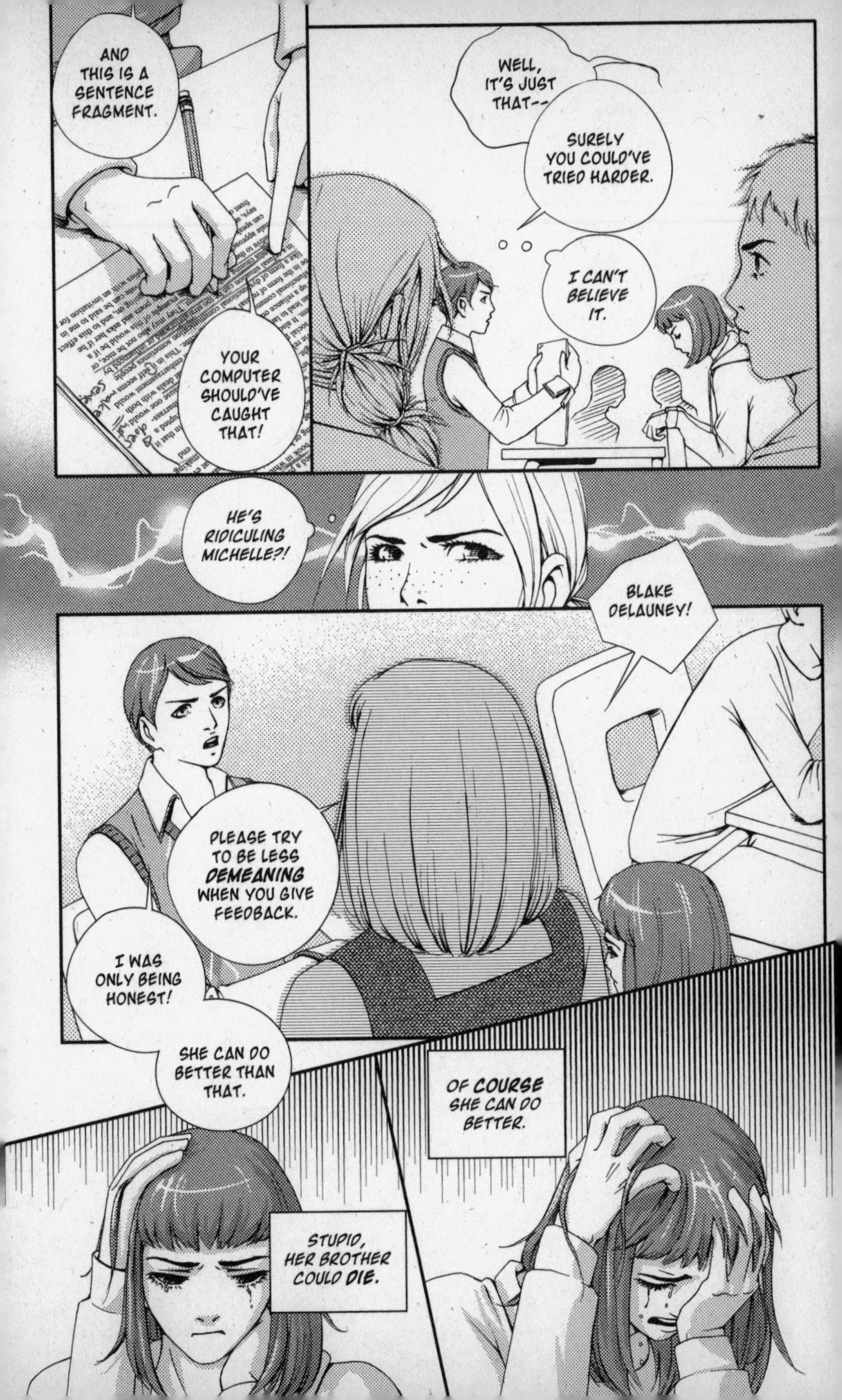
AND THIS IS A SENTENCE FRAGMENT.
YOUR COMPUTER SHOULD'VE CAUGHT THAT!
WELL, IT'S JUST THAT--
SURELY YOU COULD'VE TRIED HARDER.
I CAN'T BELIEVE IT.
HE'S RIDICULING MICHELLE?!
BLAKE DELAUNEY!
PLEASE TRY TO BE LESS **DEMEANING** WHEN YOU GIVE FEEDBACK.
I WAS ONLY BEING HONEST!
SHE CAN DO BETTER THAN THAT.
STUPID, HER BROTHER COULD **DIE**.
OF **COURSE** SHE CAN DO BETTER.

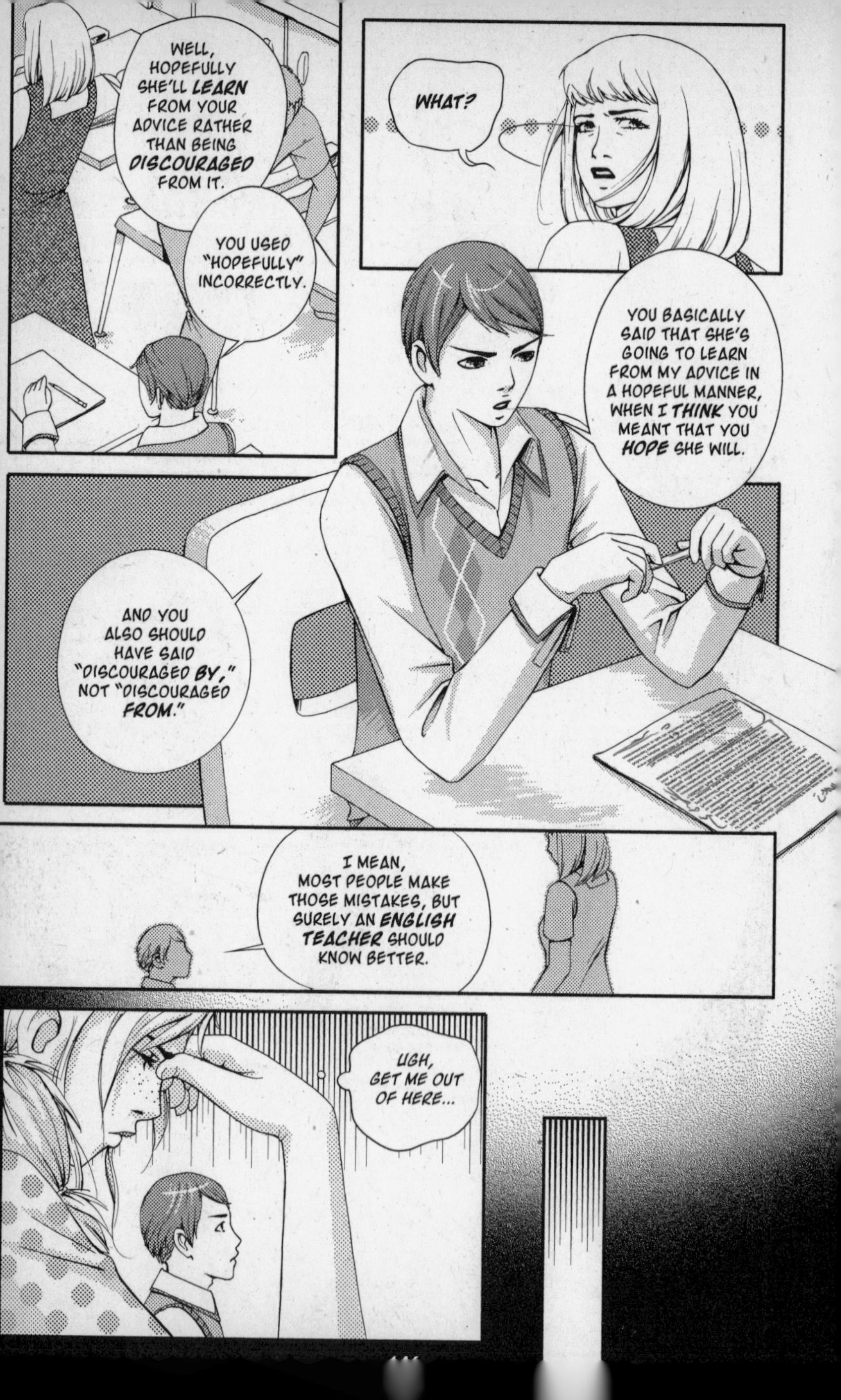

WELL, HOPEFULLY SHE'LL **LEARN** FROM YOUR ADVICE RATHER THAN BEING **DISCOURAGED** FROM IT.
YOU USED "HOPEFULLY" INCORRECTLY.
WHAT?
YOU BASICALLY SAID THAT SHE'S GOING TO LEARN FROM MY ADVICE IN A HOPEFUL MANNER, WHEN I **THINK** YOU MEANT THAT YOU **HOPE** SHE WILL.
AND YOU ALSO SHOULD HAVE SAID "DISCOURAGED **BY**," NOT "DISCOURAGED **FROM**."
I MEAN, MOST PEOPLE MAKE THOSE MISTAKES, BUT SURELY AN **ENGLISH TEACHER** SHOULD KNOW BETTER.
UGH, GET ME OUT OF HERE...

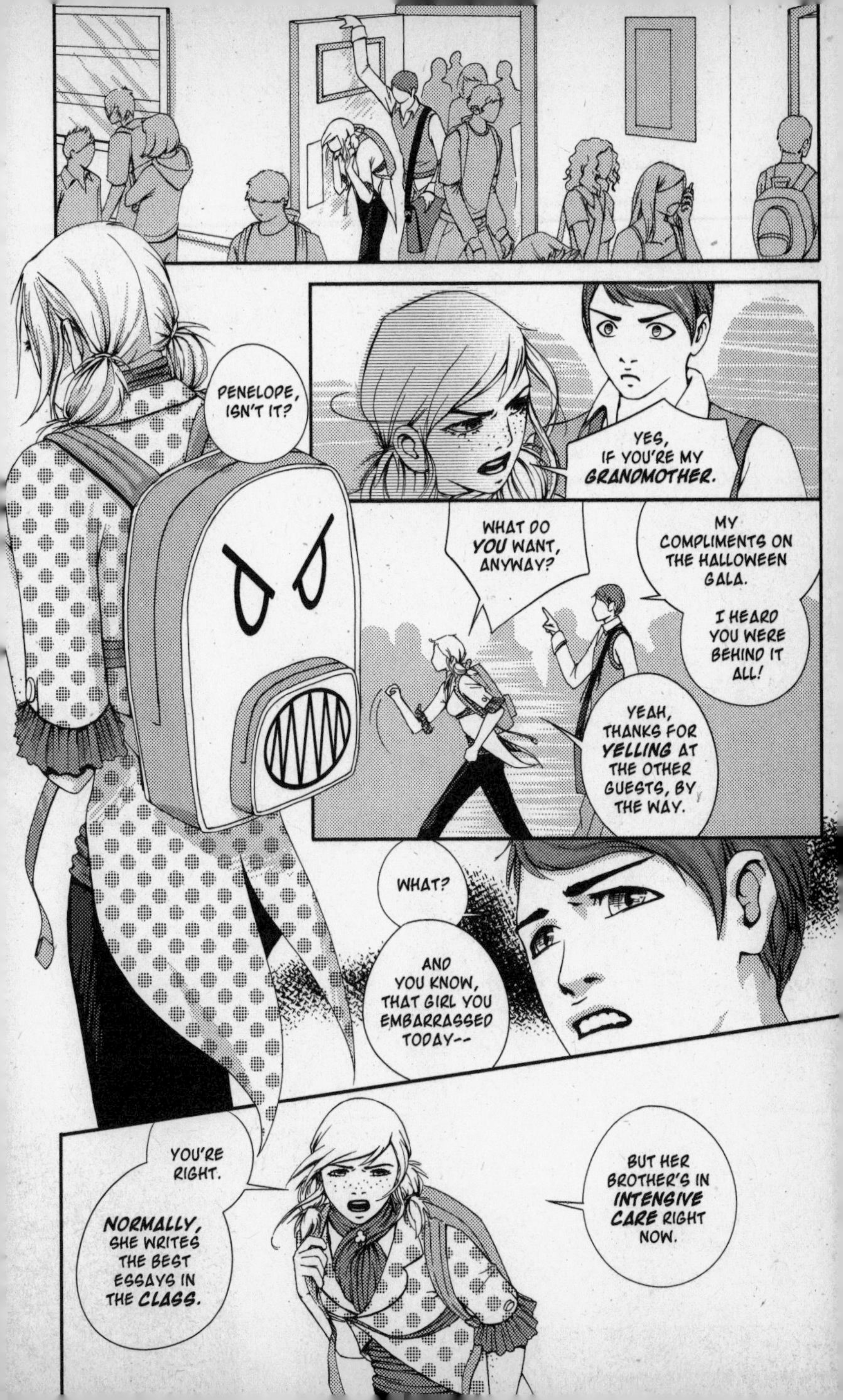
PENELOPE, ISN'T IT?
YES, IF YOU'RE MY GRANDMOTHER.
WHAT DO YOU WANT, ANYWAY?
MY COMPLIMENTS ON THE HALLOWEEN GALA.
I HEARD YOU WERE BEHIND IT ALL!
YEAH, THANKS FOR YELLING AT THE OTHER GUESTS, BY THE WAY.
WHAT?
AND YOU KNOW, THAT GIRL YOU EMBARRASSED TODAY--
YOU'RE RIGHT.
NORMALLY, SHE WRITES THE BEST ESSAYS IN THE CLASS.
BUT HER BROTHER'S IN INTENSIVE CARE RIGHT NOW.

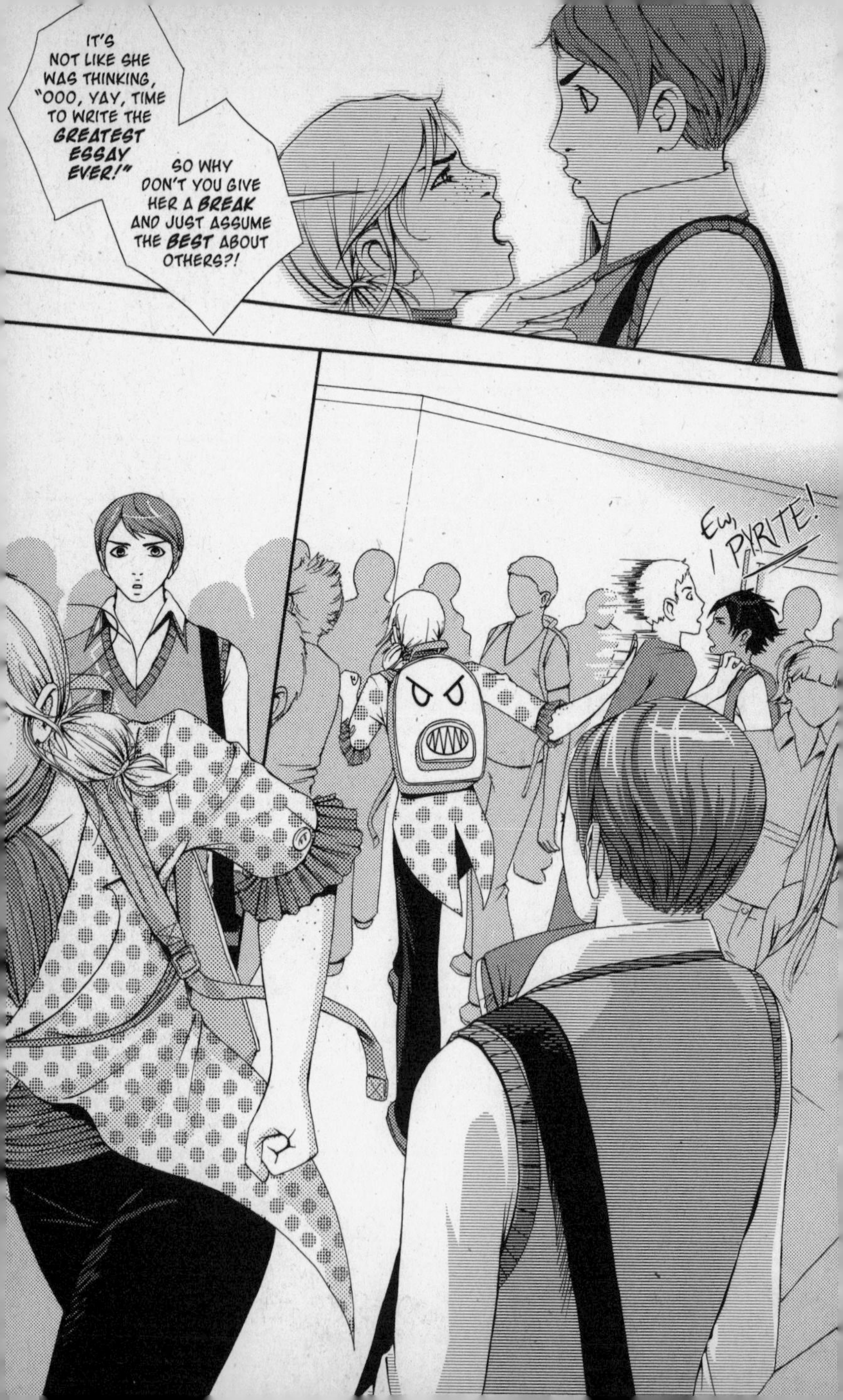
IT'S NOT LIKE SHE WAS THINKING, "OOO, YAY, TIME TO WRITE THE GREATEST ESSAY EVER!"
SO WHY DON'T YOU GIVE HER A BREAK AND JUST ASSUME THE BEST ABOUT OTHERS?!
Ew, PYRITE!

Chapter 6: Hugging Trees

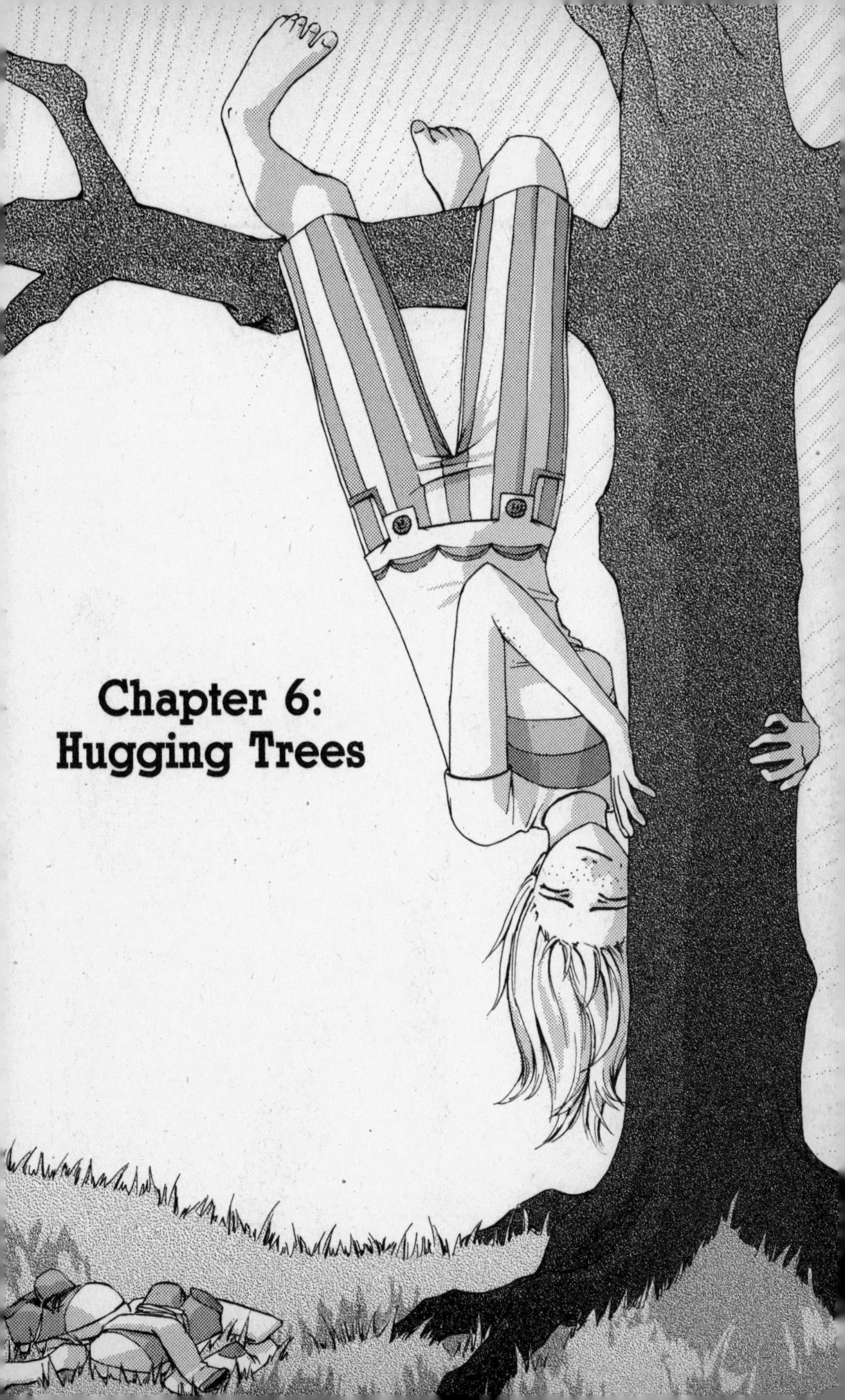

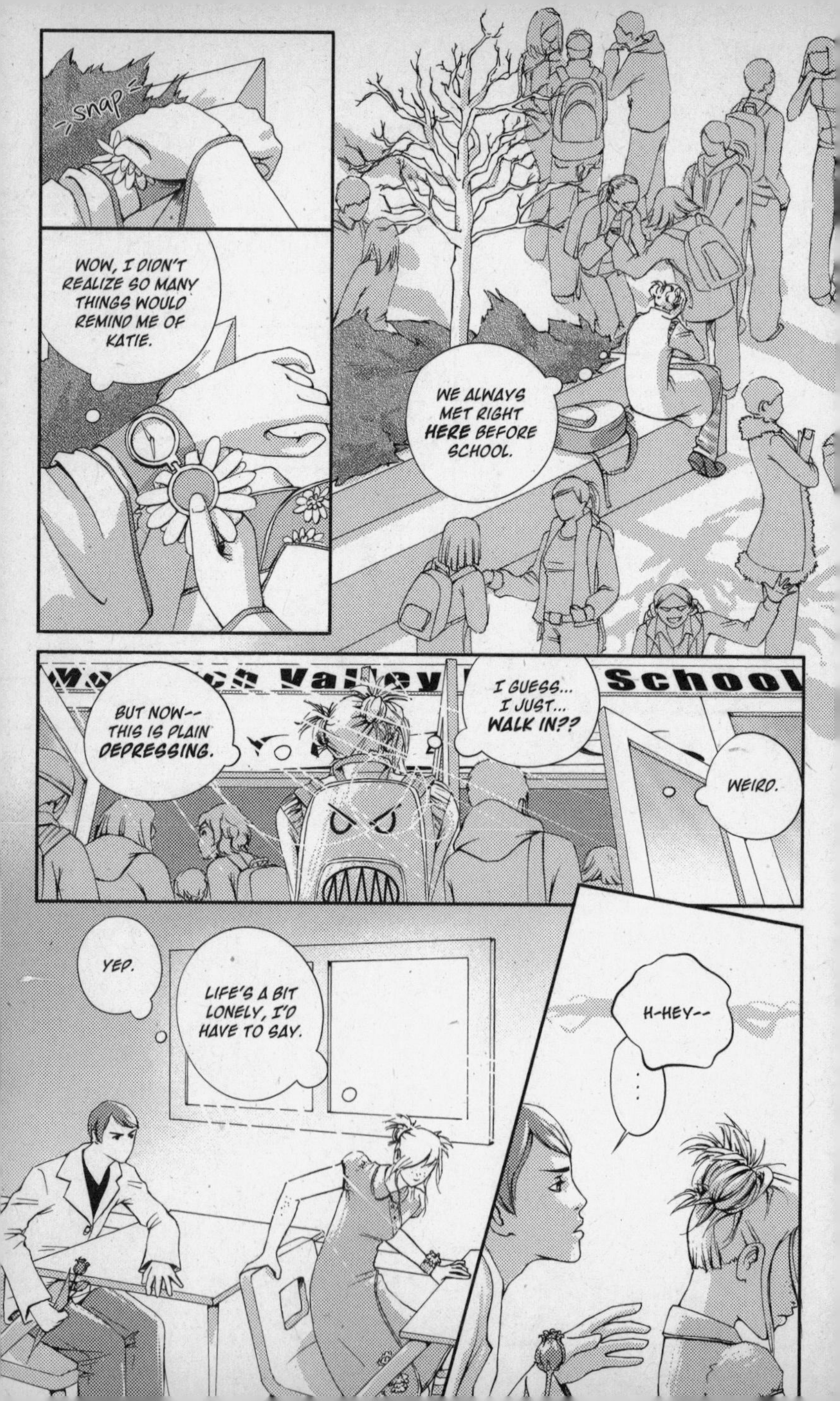
SNAP
WOW, I DIDN'T REALIZE SO MANY THINGS WOULD REMIND ME OF KATIE.
WE ALWAYS MET RIGHT HERE BEFORE SCHOOL.
BUT NOW-- THIS IS PLAIN DEPRESSING.
I GUESS... I JUST... WALK IN??
WEIRD.
YEP.
LIFE'S A BIT LONELY, I'D HAVE TO SAY.
H-HEY--
...

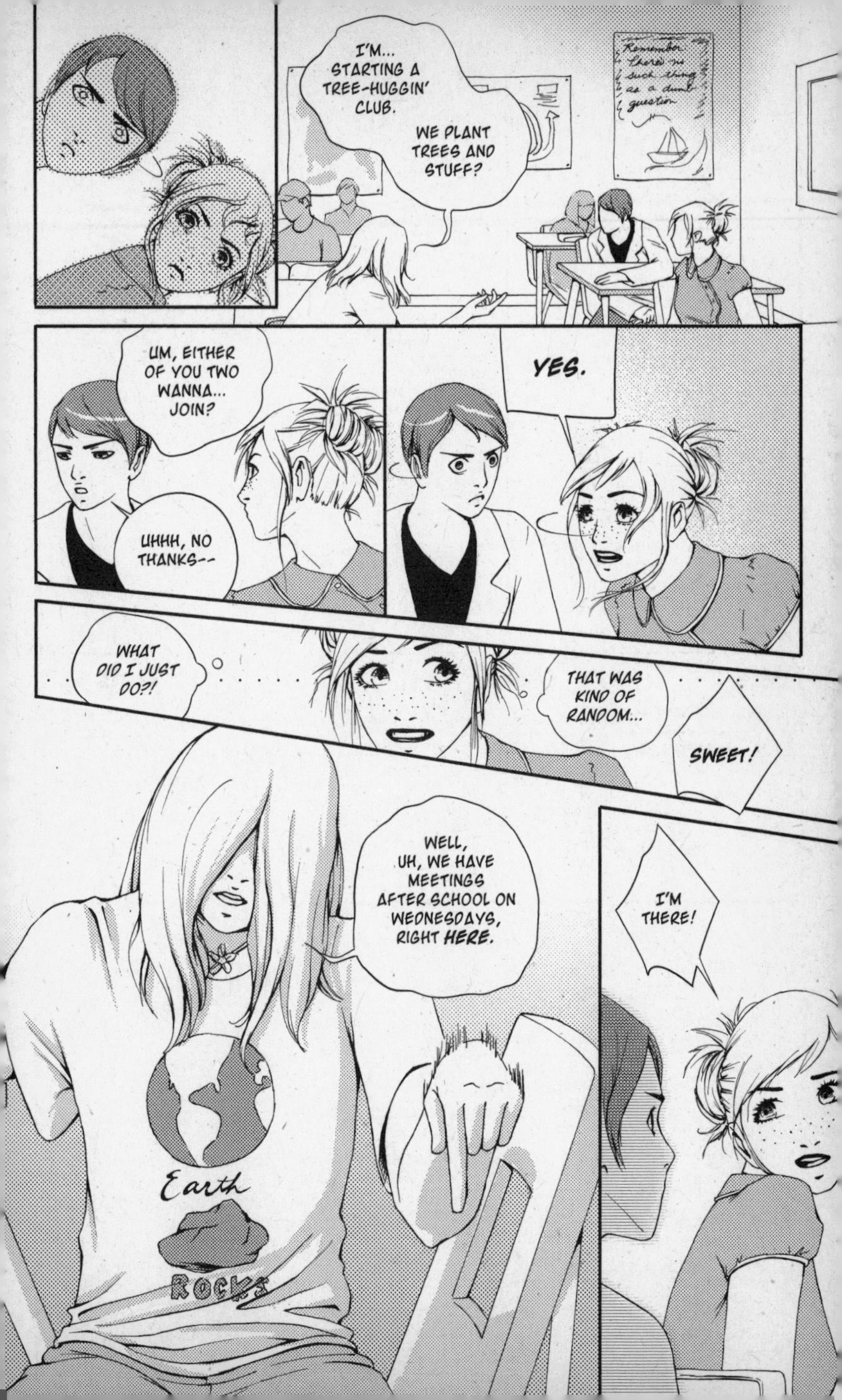
I'M... STARTING A TREE-HUGGIN' CLUB.
WE PLANT TREES AND STUFF?
Remember there is such thing as a dumb question
UM, EITHER OF YOU TWO WANNA... JOIN?
UHHH, NO THANKS--
YES.
WHAT DID I JUST DO?!
THAT WAS KIND OF RANDOM...
SWEET!
WELL, UH, WE HAVE MEETINGS AFTER SCHOOL ON WEDNESDAYS, RIGHT HERE.
Earth ROCKS
I'M THERE!

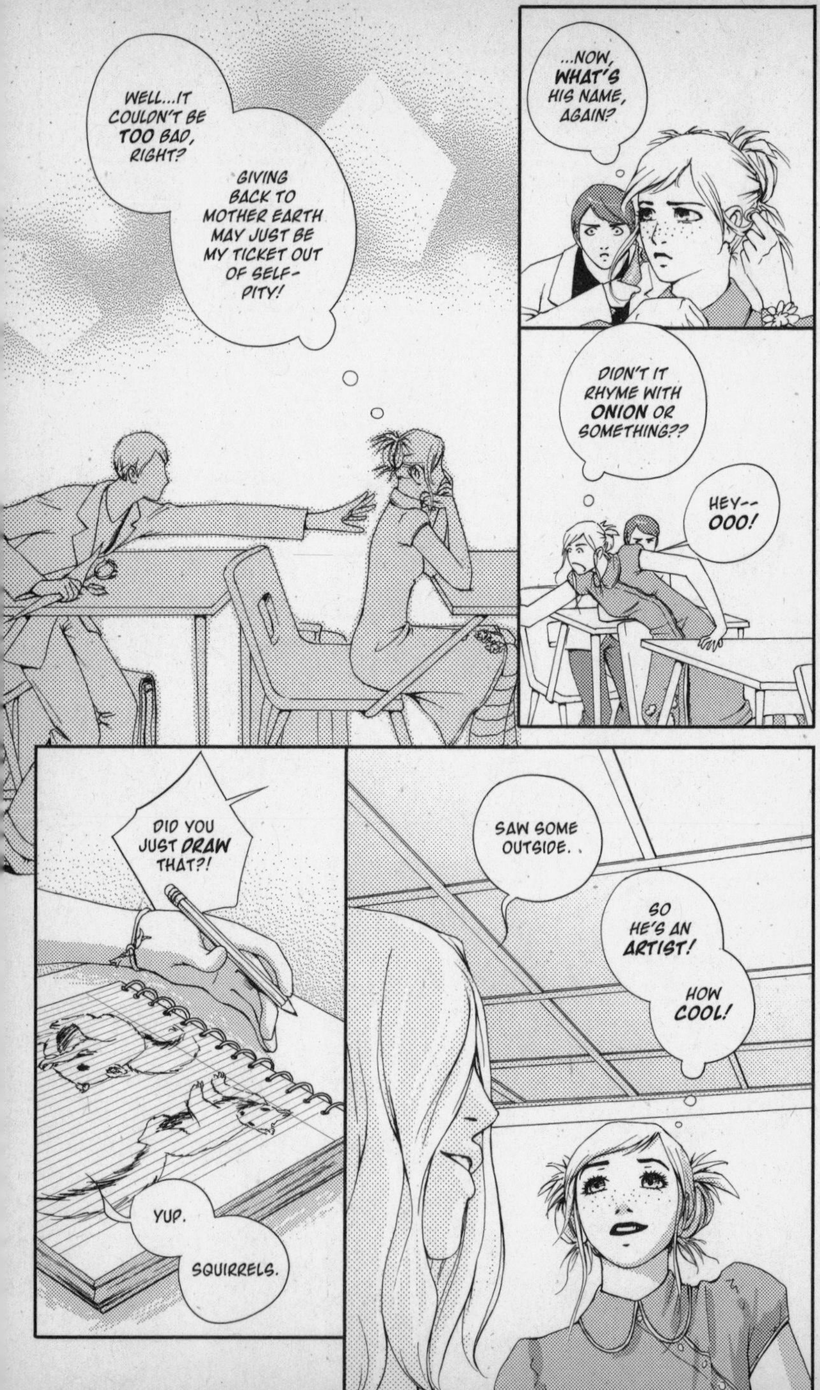
WELL...IT COULDN'T BE TOO BAD, RIGHT?
GIVING BACK TO MOTHER EARTH MAY JUST BE MY TICKET OUT OF SELF-PITY!
...NOW, WHAT'S HIS NAME, AGAIN?
DIDN'T IT RHYME WITH ONION OR SOMETHING??
HEY--OOO!
DID YOU JUST DRAW THAT?!
YUP.
SQUIRRELS.
SAW SOME OUTSIDE.
SO HE'S AN ARTIST!
HOW COOL!

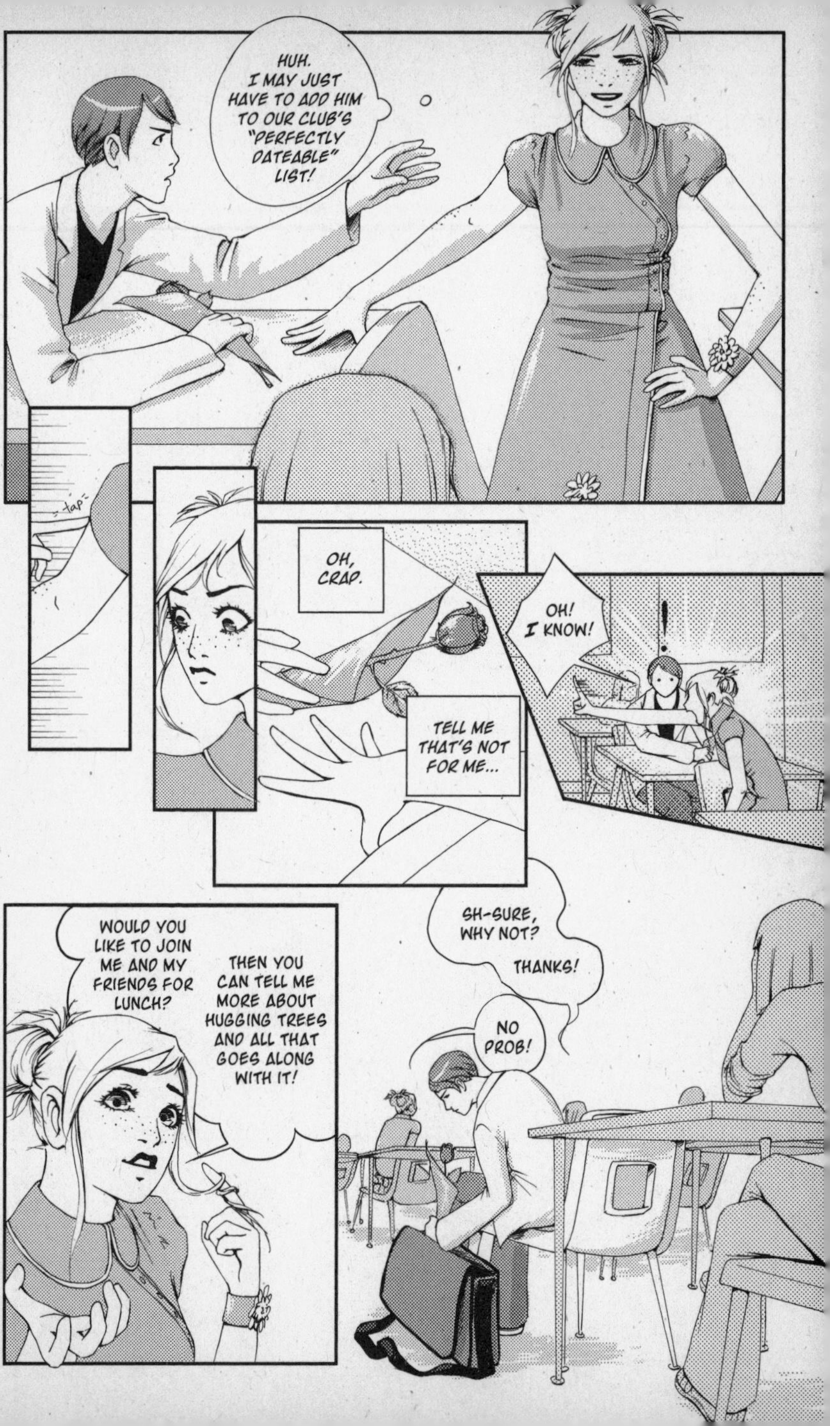
HUH. I MAY JUST HAVE TO ADD HIM TO OUR CLUB'S "PERFECTLY DATEABLE" LIST!
tap
OH, CRAP.
TELL ME THAT'S NOT FOR ME...
OH! I KNOW!
!
WOULD YOU LIKE TO JOIN ME AND MY FRIENDS FOR LUNCH?
THEN YOU CAN TELL ME MORE ABOUT HUGGING TREES AND ALL THAT GOES ALONG WITH IT!
SH-SURE, WHY NOT?
THANKS!
NO PROB!

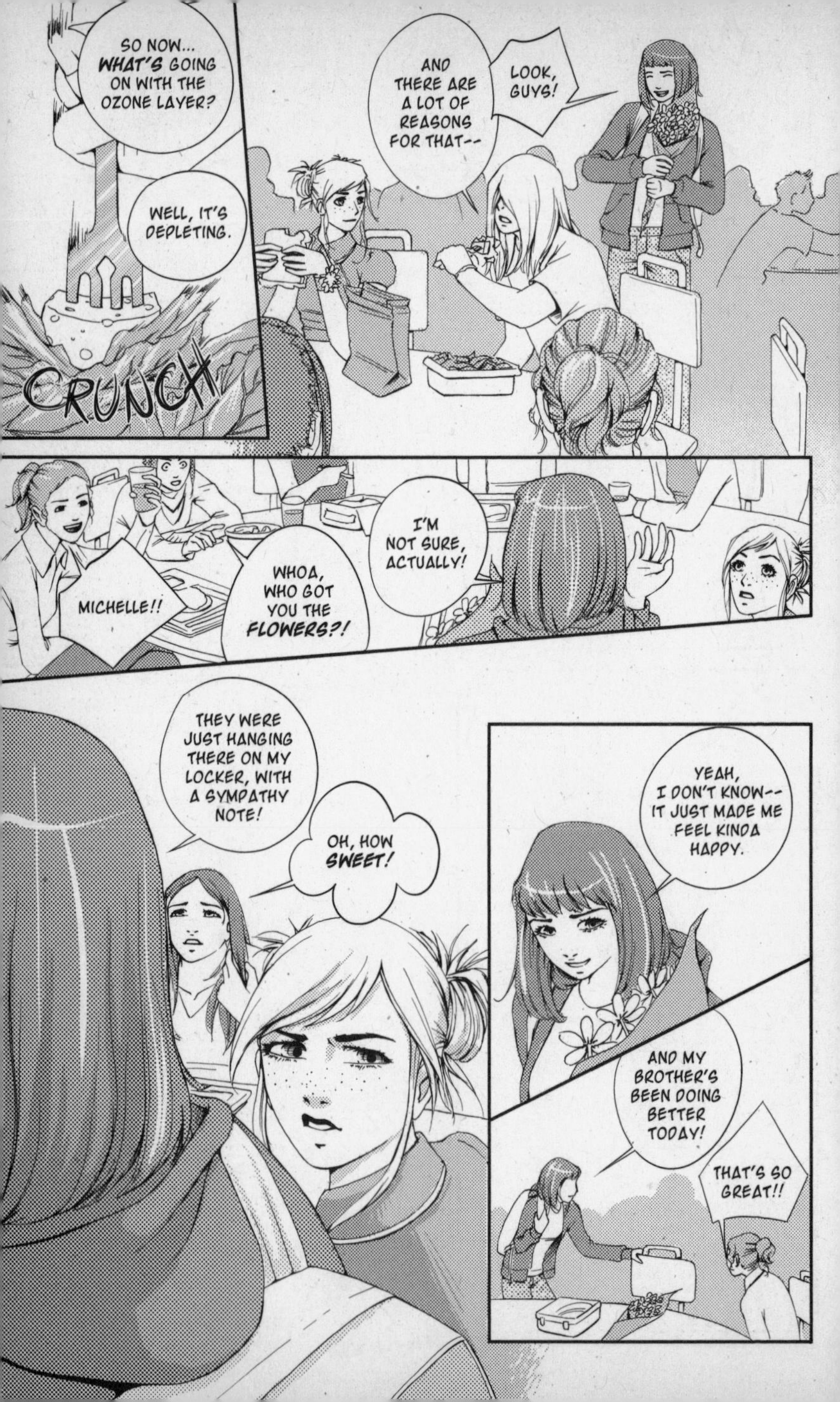
SO NOW... WHAT'S GOING ON WITH THE OZONE LAYER?
WELL, IT'S DEPLETING.
CRUNCH
AND THERE ARE A LOT OF REASONS FOR THAT--
LOOK, GUYS!
MICHELLE!!
WHOA, WHO GOT YOU THE FLOWERS?!
I'M NOT SURE, ACTUALLY!
THEY WERE JUST HANGING THERE ON MY LOCKER, WITH A SYMPATHY NOTE!
OH, HOW SWEET!
YEAH, I DON'T KNOW-- IT JUST MADE ME FEEL KINDA HAPPY.
AND MY BROTHER'S BEEN DOING BETTER TODAY!
THAT'S SO GREAT!!

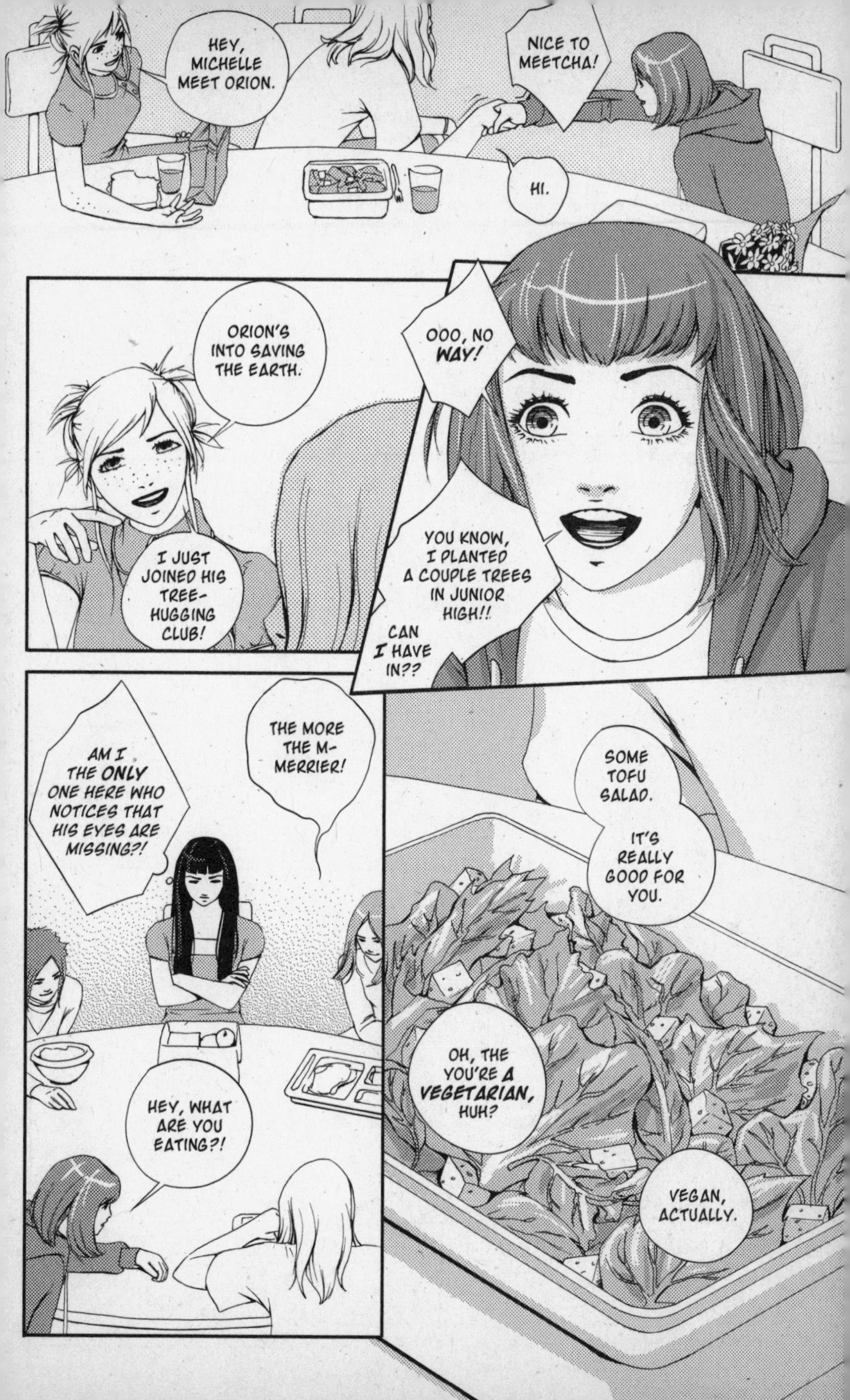

HEY, MICHELLE MEET ORION.
NICE TO MEETCHA!
HI.
ORION'S INTO SAVING THE EARTH.
I JUST JOINED HIS TREE-HUGGING CLUB!
OOO, NO **WAY!**
YOU KNOW, I PLANTED A COUPLE TREES IN JUNIOR HIGH!!
CAN **I** HAVE IN??
THE MORE THE M-MERRIER!
AM I THE **ONLY** ONE HERE WHO NOTICES THAT HIS EYES ARE MISSING?!
HEY, WHAT ARE YOU EATING?!
SOME TOFU SALAD.
IT'S REALLY GOOD FOR YOU.
OH, THE YOU'RE A **VEGETARIAN,** HUH?
VEGAN, ACTUALLY.

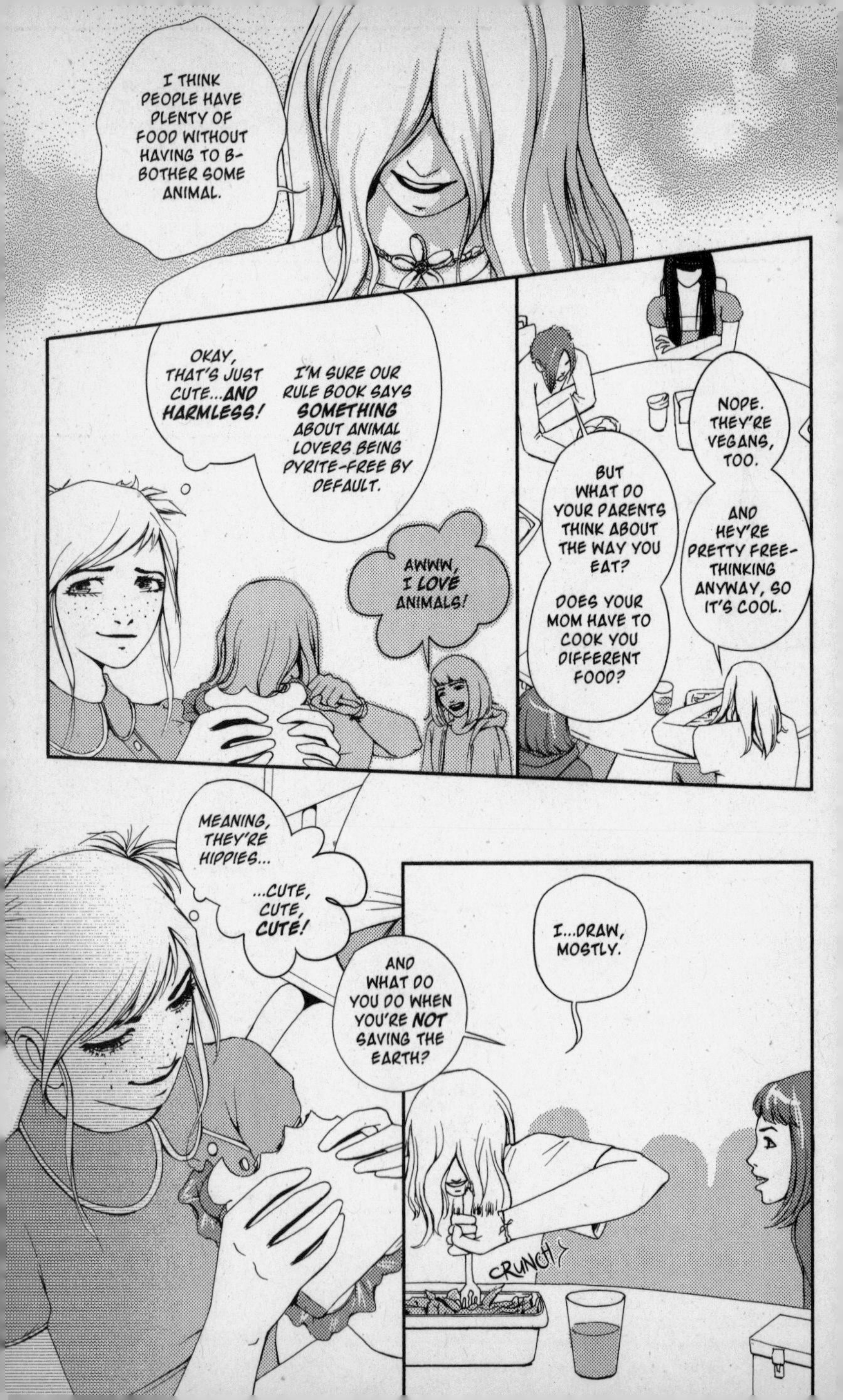
I THINK PEOPLE HAVE PLENTY OF FOOD WITHOUT HAVING TO B-BOTHER SOME ANIMAL.
OKAY, THAT'S JUST CUTE...**AND HARMLESS!**
I'M SURE OUR RULE BOOK SAYS **SOMETHING** ABOUT ANIMAL LOVERS BEING PYRITE-FREE BY DEFAULT.
AWWW, ***I LOVE*** ANIMALS!
BUT WHAT DO YOUR PARENTS THINK ABOUT THE WAY YOU EAT?
DOES YOUR MOM HAVE TO COOK YOU DIFFERENT FOOD?
NOPE. THEY'RE VEGANS, TOO.
AND HEY'RE PRETTY FREE-THINKING ANYWAY, SO IT'S COOL.
MEANING, THEY'RE HIPPIES...
...CUTE, CUTE, ***CUTE!***
AND WHAT DO YOU DO WHEN YOU'RE **NOT** SAVING THE EARTH?
I...DRAW, MOSTLY.
CRUNCH

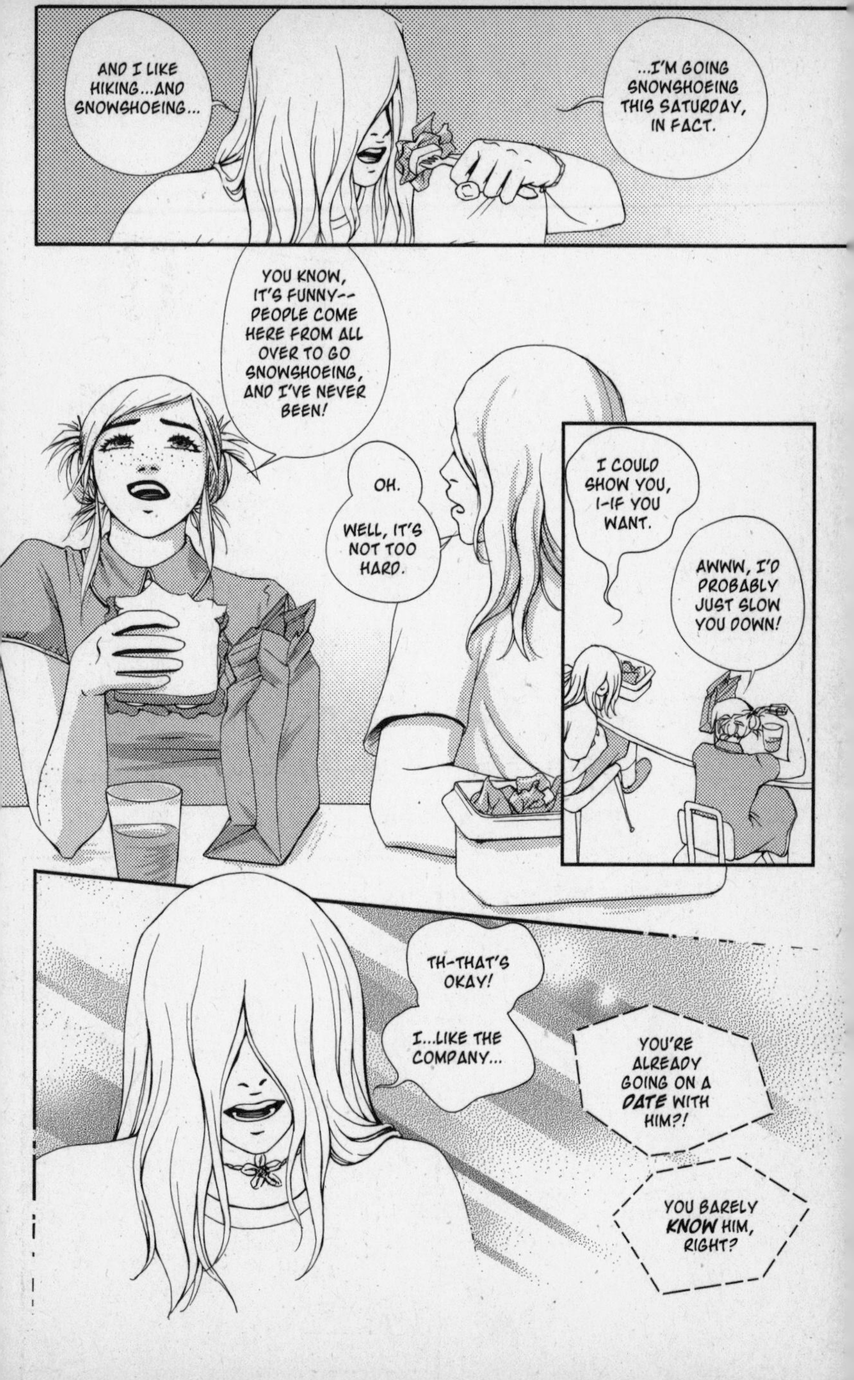
AND I LIKE HIKING...AND SNOWSHOEING...
...I'M GOING SNOWSHOEING THIS SATURDAY, IN FACT.
YOU KNOW, IT'S FUNNY-- PEOPLE COME HERE FROM ALL OVER TO GO SNOWSHOEING, AND I'VE NEVER BEEN!
OH.
WELL, IT'S NOT TOO HARD.
I COULD SHOW YOU, I-IF YOU WANT.
AWWW, I'D PROBABLY JUST SLOW YOU DOWN!
TH-THAT'S OKAY!
I...LIKE THE COMPANY...
YOU'RE ALREADY GOING ON A *DATE* WITH HIM?!
YOU BARELY ***KNOW*** HIM, RIGHT?

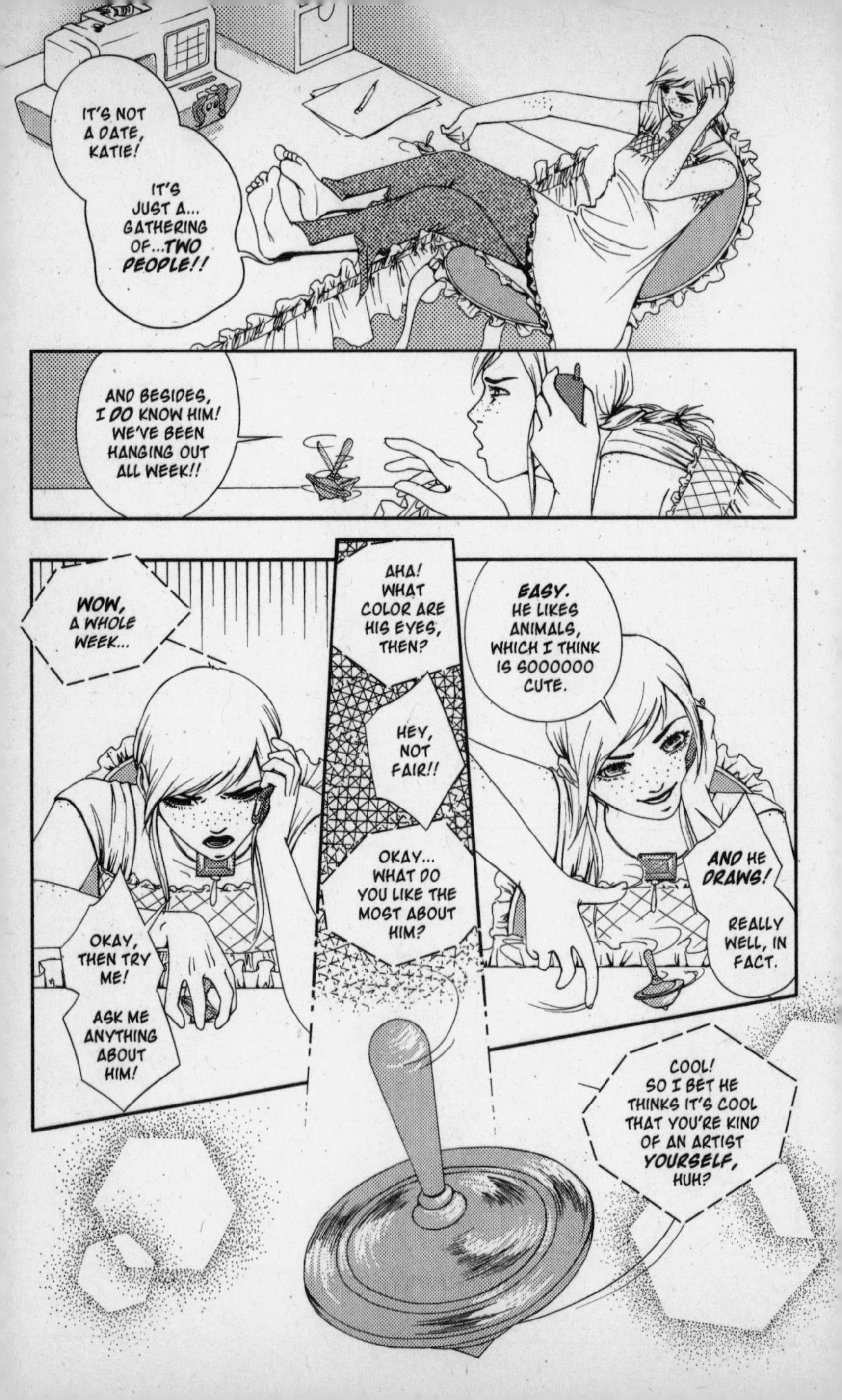
IT'S NOT A DATE, KATIE!
IT'S JUST A... GATHERING OF...TWO PEOPLE!!
AND BESIDES, I DO KNOW HIM! WE'VE BEEN HANGING OUT ALL WEEK!!
WOW, A WHOLE WEEK...
OKAY, THEN TRY ME!
ASK ME ANYTHING ABOUT HIM!
AHA! WHAT COLOR ARE HIS EYES, THEN?
HEY, NOT FAIR!!
OKAY... WHAT DO YOU LIKE THE MOST ABOUT HIM?
EASY. HE LIKES ANIMALS, WHICH I THINK IS SOOOOOO CUTE.
AND HE DRAWS!
REALLY WELL, IN FACT.
COOL! SO I BET HE THINKS IT'S COOL THAT YOU'RE KIND OF AN ARTIST YOURSELF, HUH?

SMACK!
PENNY?
...ARE YOU FIDGETING WITH SOMETHING AGAIN?
COME TO THINK OF IT, WE'VE NEVER EVEN *TALKED* ABOUT ME AND MY SEWING!
BUT THAT'S LIKE, *WHO YOU ARE!*
YEAH, I KNOW.
I'VE GOTTA ADMIT...HE'S STILL A BIG MYSTERY TO ME.
BUT HOW COME YOU'RE SO DOWN ON HIM, ANYWAY?

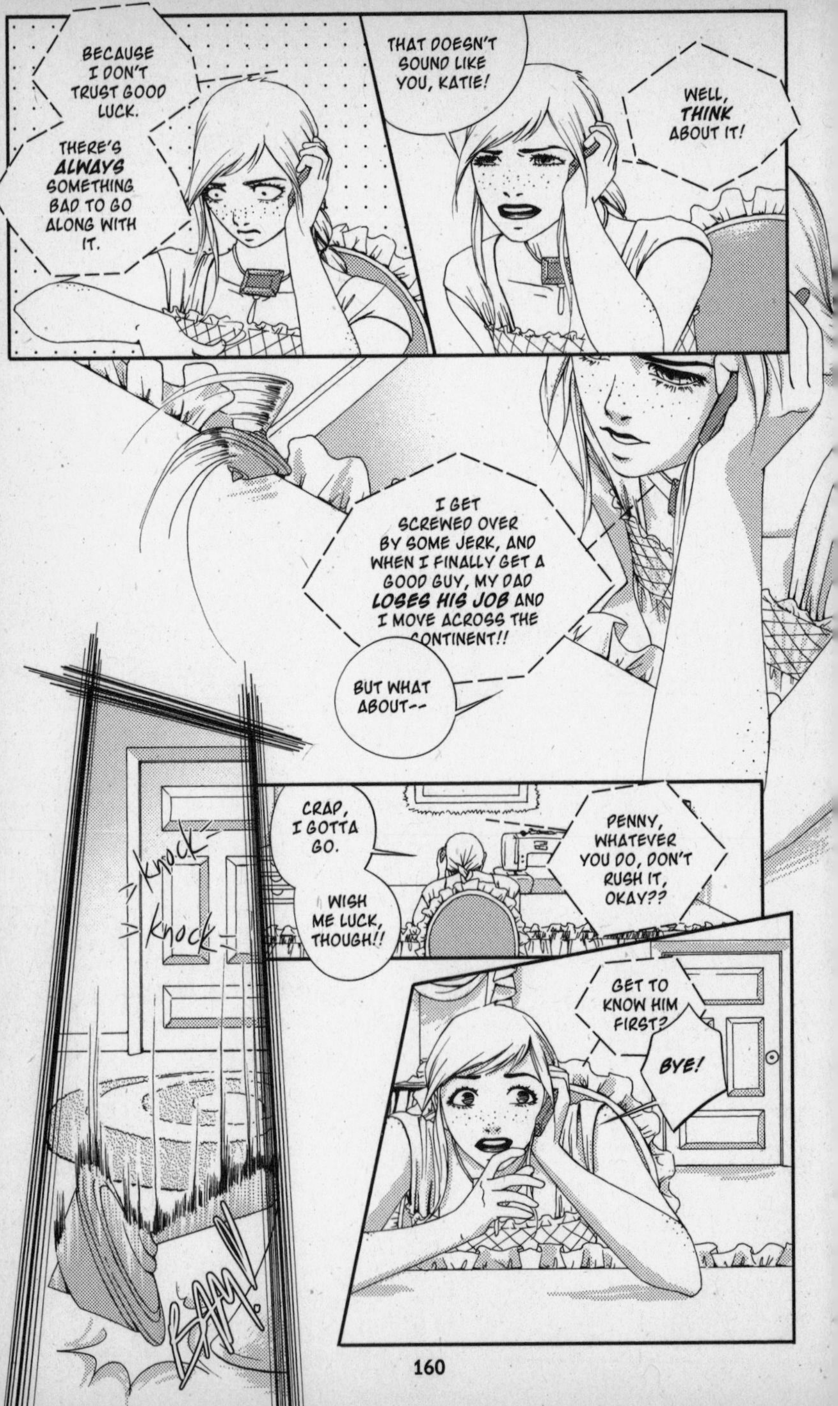
BECAUSE I DON'T TRUST GOOD LUCK.
THERE'S ALWAYS SOMETHING BAD TO GO ALONG WITH IT.
THAT DOESN'T SOUND LIKE YOU, KATIE!
WELL, THINK ABOUT IT!
I GET SCREWED OVER BY SOME JERK, AND WHEN I FINALLY GET A GOOD GUY, MY DAD LOSES HIS JOB AND I MOVE ACROSS THE CONTINENT!!
BUT WHAT ABOUT--
KNOCK
KNOCK
CRAP, I GOTTA GO.
WISH ME LUCK, THOUGH!!
PENNY, WHATEVER YOU DO, DON'T RUSH IT, OKAY??
GET TO KNOW HIM FIRST?
BYE!
BAM!!

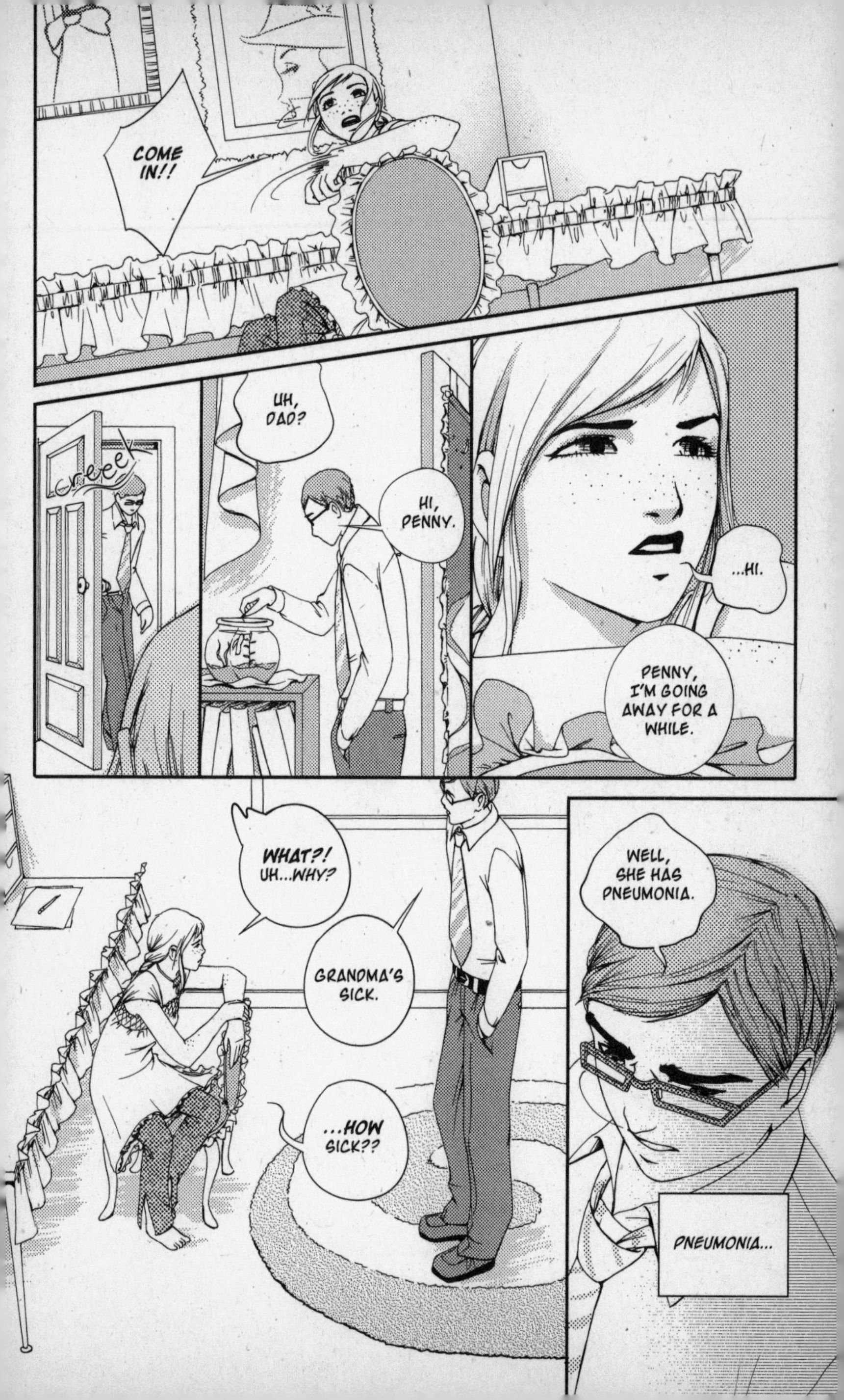
COME IN!!
creeee
UH, DAD?
HI, PENNY.
...HI.
PENNY, I'M GOING AWAY FOR A WHILE.
WHAT?! UH...WHY?
GRANDMA'S SICK.
...HOW SICK??
WELL, SHE HAS PNEUMONIA.
PNEUMONIA...

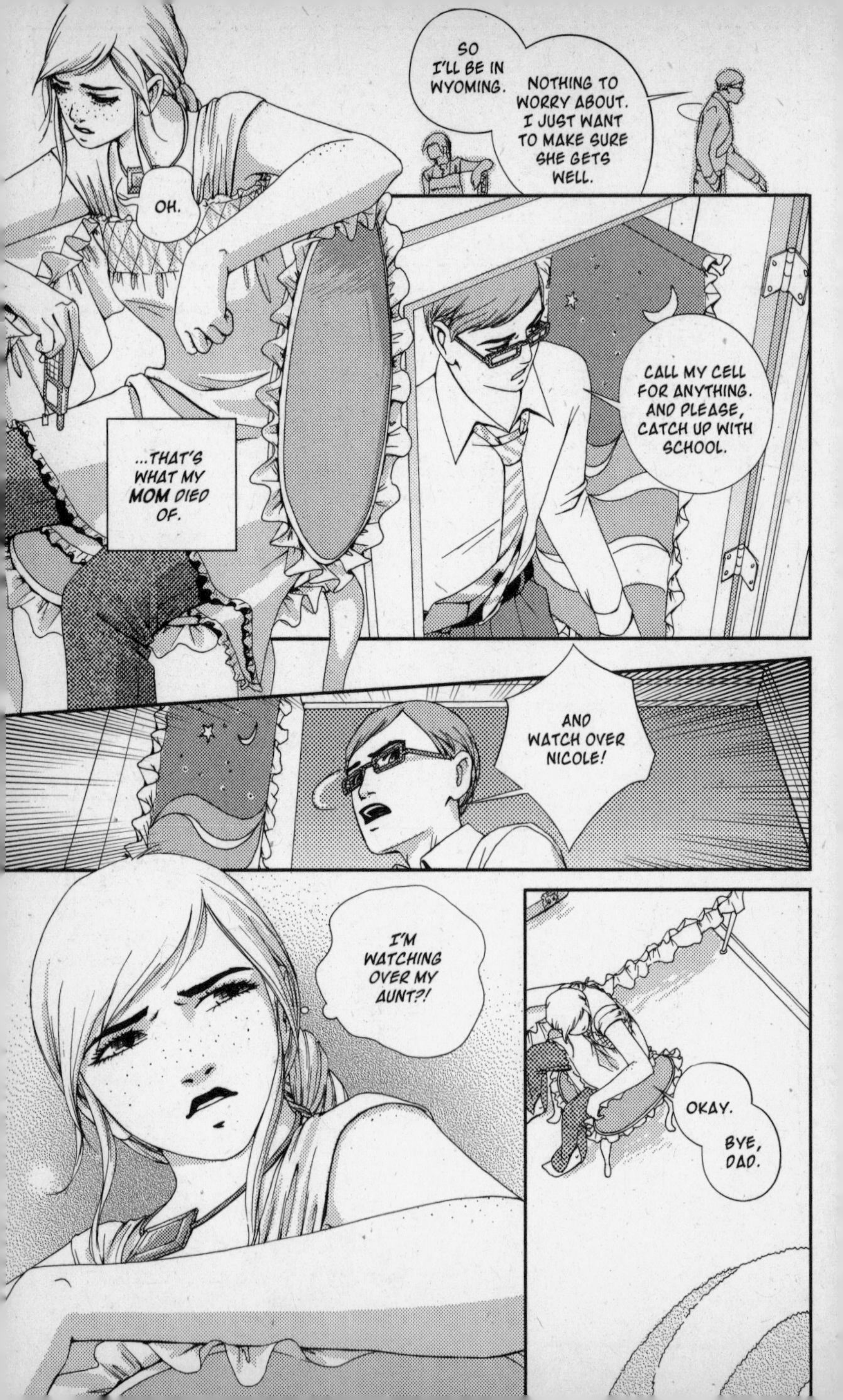
SO I'LL BE IN WYOMING.
NOTHING TO WORRY ABOUT. I JUST WANT TO MAKE SURE SHE GETS WELL.
OH.
...THAT'S WHAT MY MOM DIED OF.
CALL MY CELL FOR ANYTHING. AND PLEASE, CATCH UP WITH SCHOOL.
AND WATCH OVER NICOLE!
I'M WATCHING OVER MY AUNT?!
OKAY.
BYE, DAD.

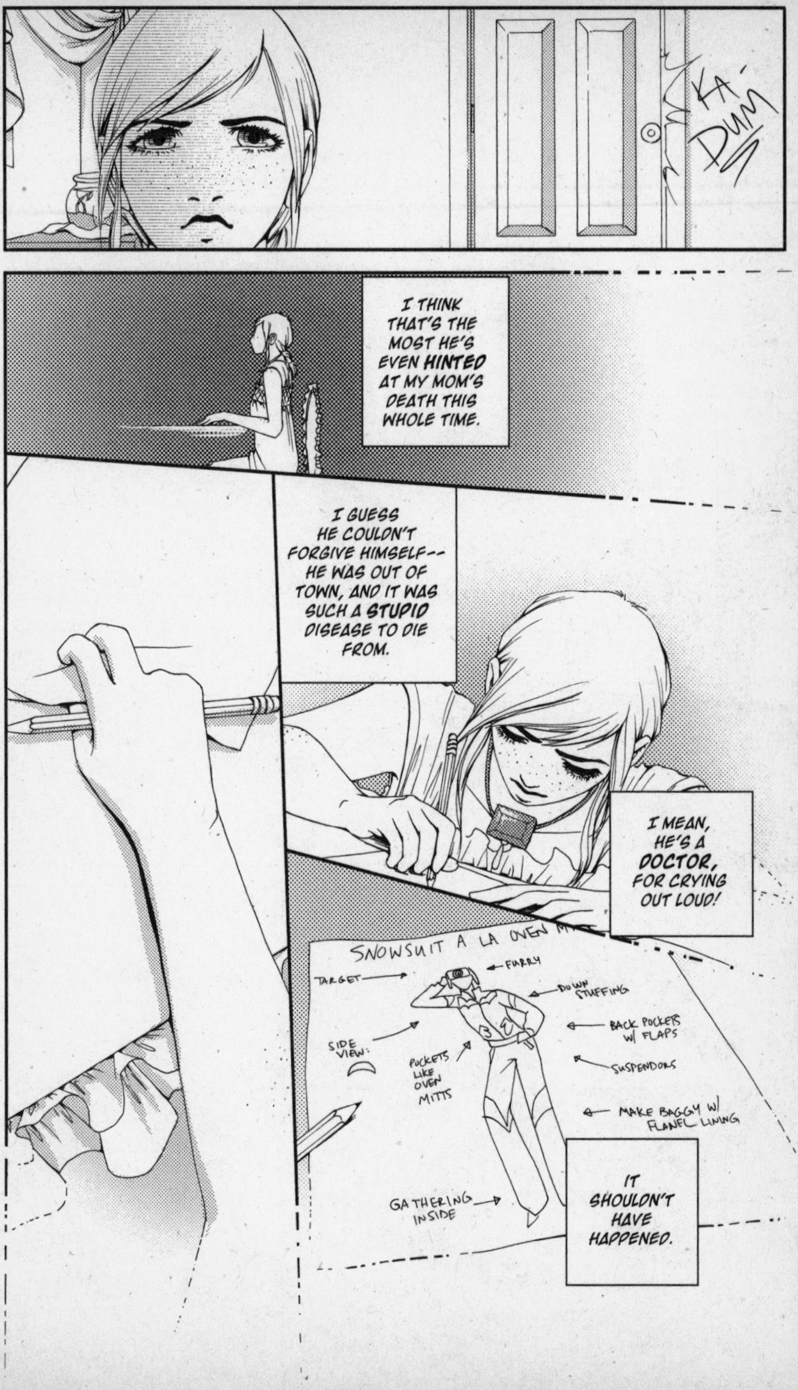
KA-DUM
I THINK THAT'S THE MOST HE'S EVEN **HINTED** AT MY MOM'S DEATH THIS WHOLE TIME.
I GUESS HE COULDN'T FORGIVE HIMSELF-- HE WAS OUT OF TOWN, AND IT WAS SUCH A **STUPID** DISEASE TO DIE FROM.
I MEAN, HE'S A **DOCTOR**, FOR CRYING OUT LOUD!
SNOWSUIT A LA OVEN
TARGET
FURRY
DOWN STUFFING
BACK POCKETS W/ FLAPS
SIDE VIEW:
POCKETS LIKE OVEN MITTS
SUSPENDORS
MAKE BAGGY W/ FLANEL LINING
GATHERING INSIDE
IT SHOULDN'T HAVE HAPPENED.

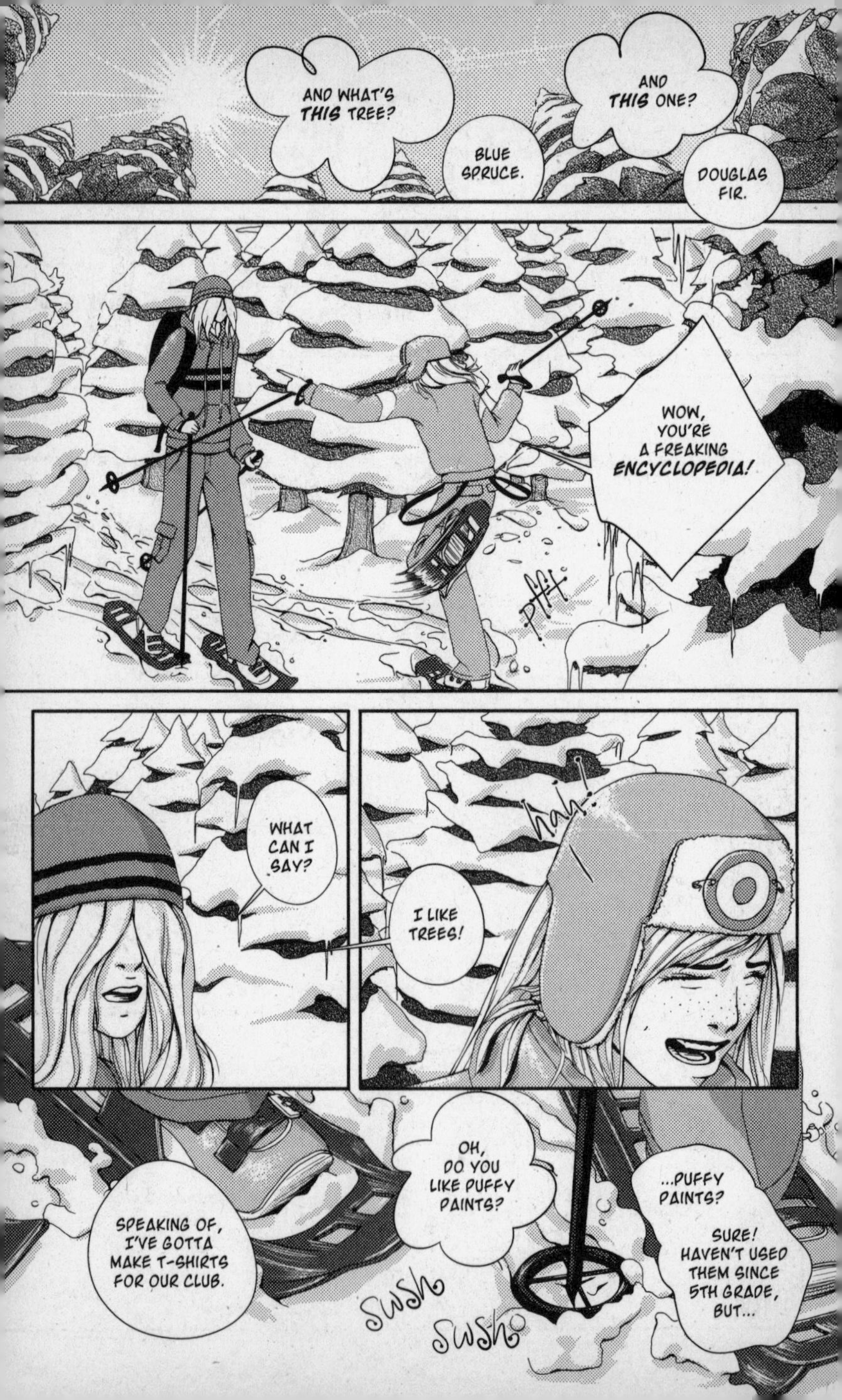
AND WHAT'S THIS TREE?
BLUE SPRUCE.
AND THIS ONE?
DOUGLAS FIR.
WOW, YOU'RE A FREAKING ENCYCLOPEDIA!
pfft
WHAT CAN I SAY?
I LIKE TREES!
hah!
SPEAKING OF, I'VE GOTTA MAKE T-SHIRTS FOR OUR CLUB.
OH, DO YOU LIKE PUFFY PAINTS?
...PUFFY PAINTS?
SURE! HAVEN'T USED THEM SINCE 5TH GRADE, BUT...
swsh
swsh

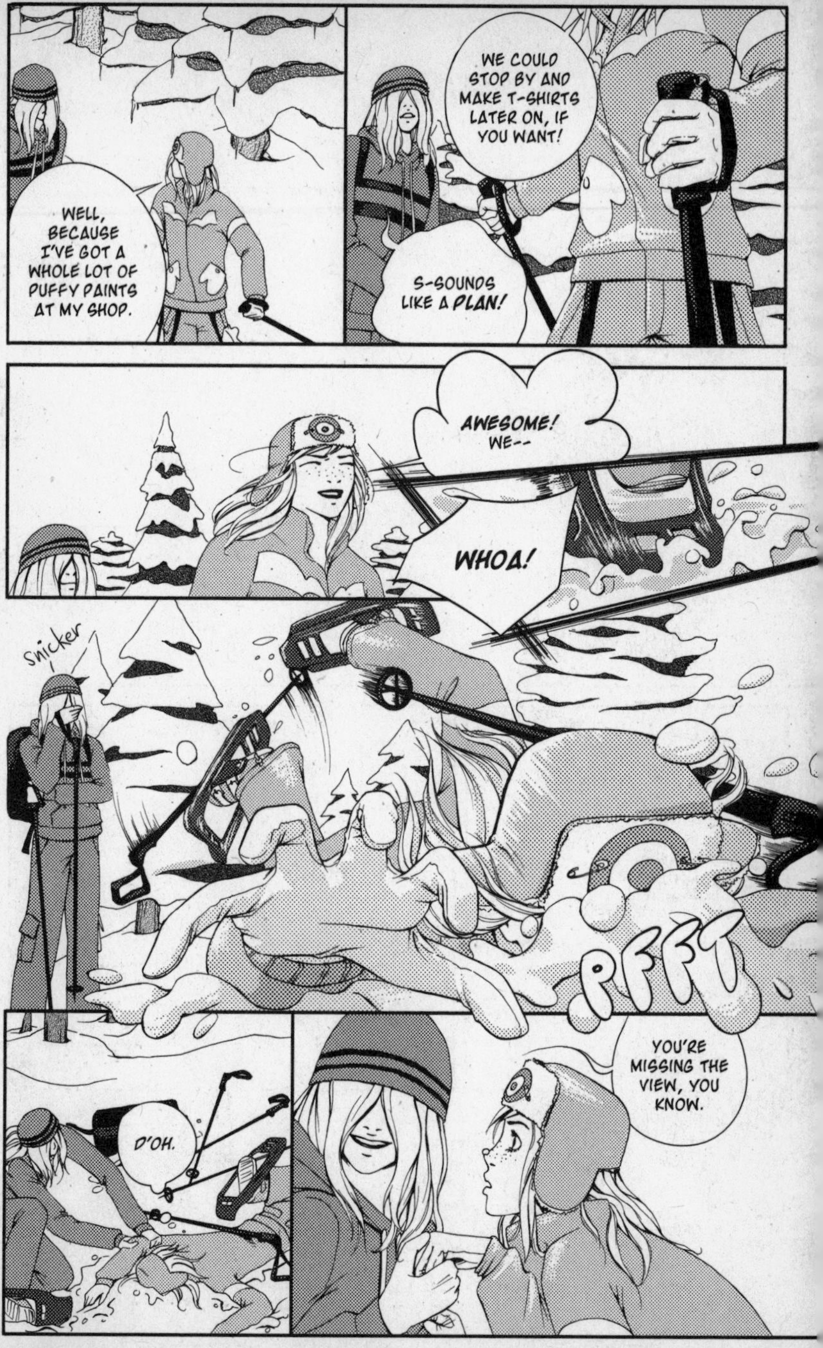
WELL, BECAUSE I'VE GOT A WHOLE LOT OF PUFFY PAINTS AT MY SHOP.
WE COULD STOP BY AND MAKE T-SHIRTS LATER ON, IF YOU WANT!
S-SOUNDS LIKE A PLAN!
AWESOME! WE--
WHOA!
snicker
PFFT
D'OH.
YOU'RE MISSING THE VIEW, YOU KNOW.

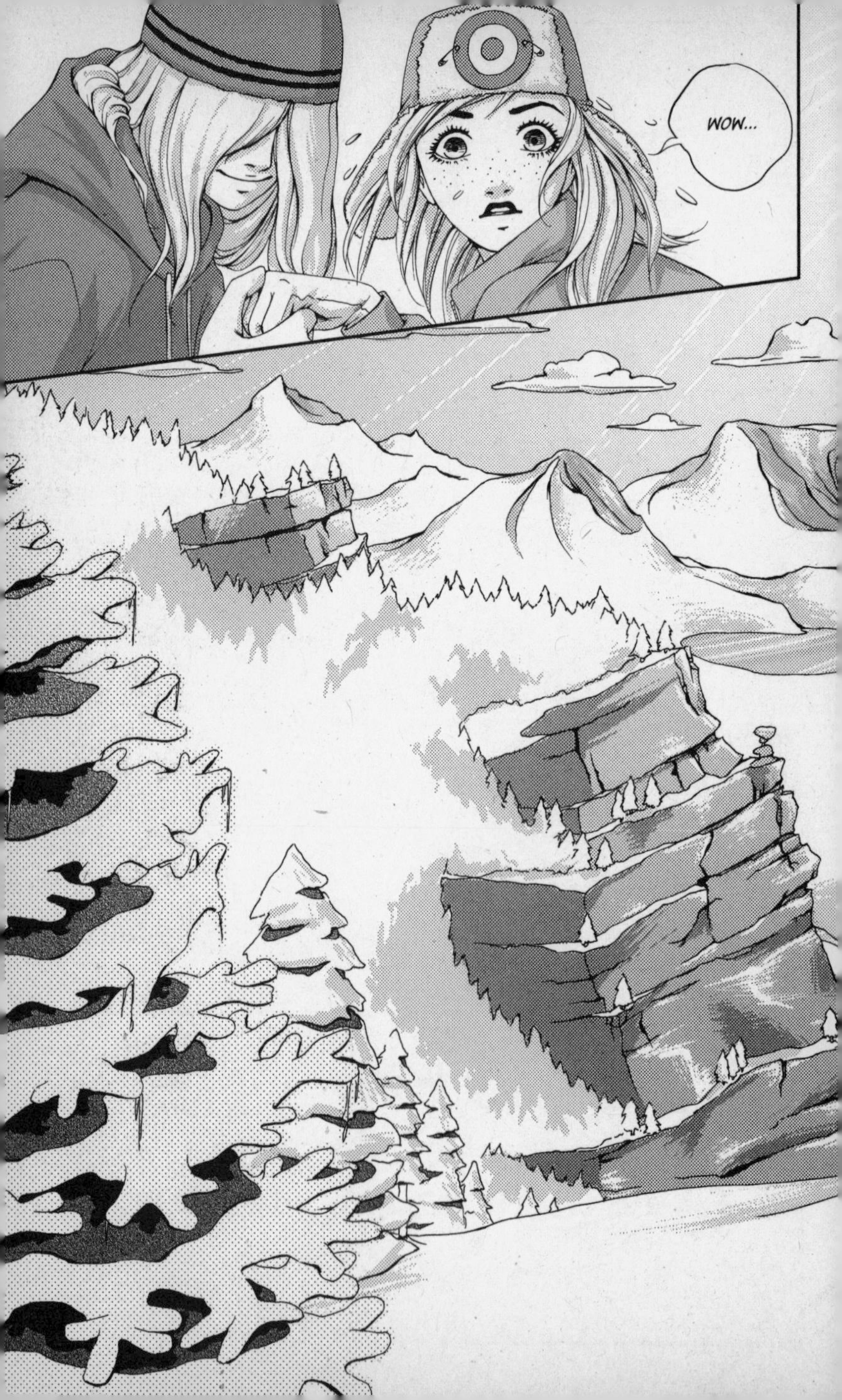
WOW...

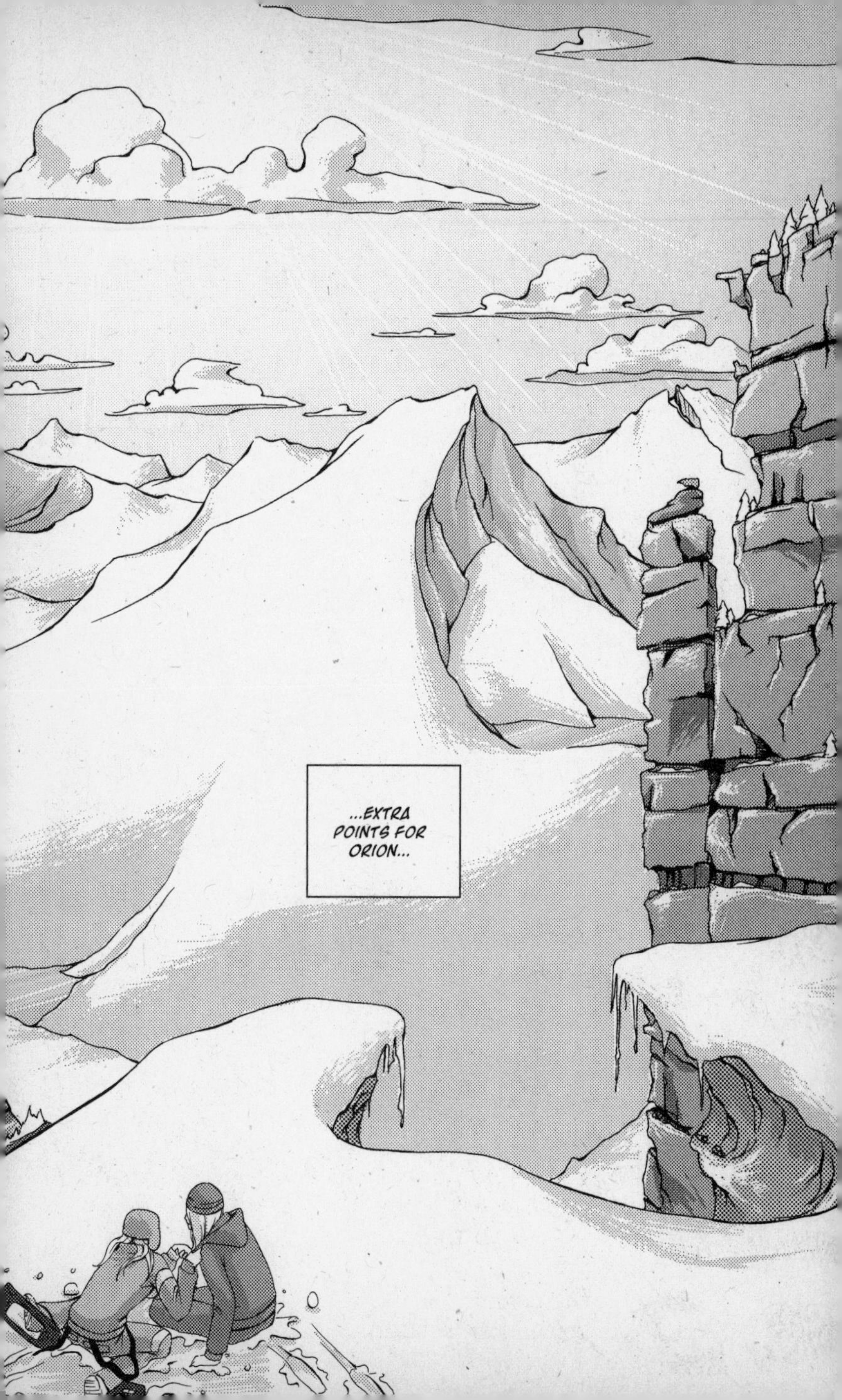
...EXTRA POINTS FOR ORION...

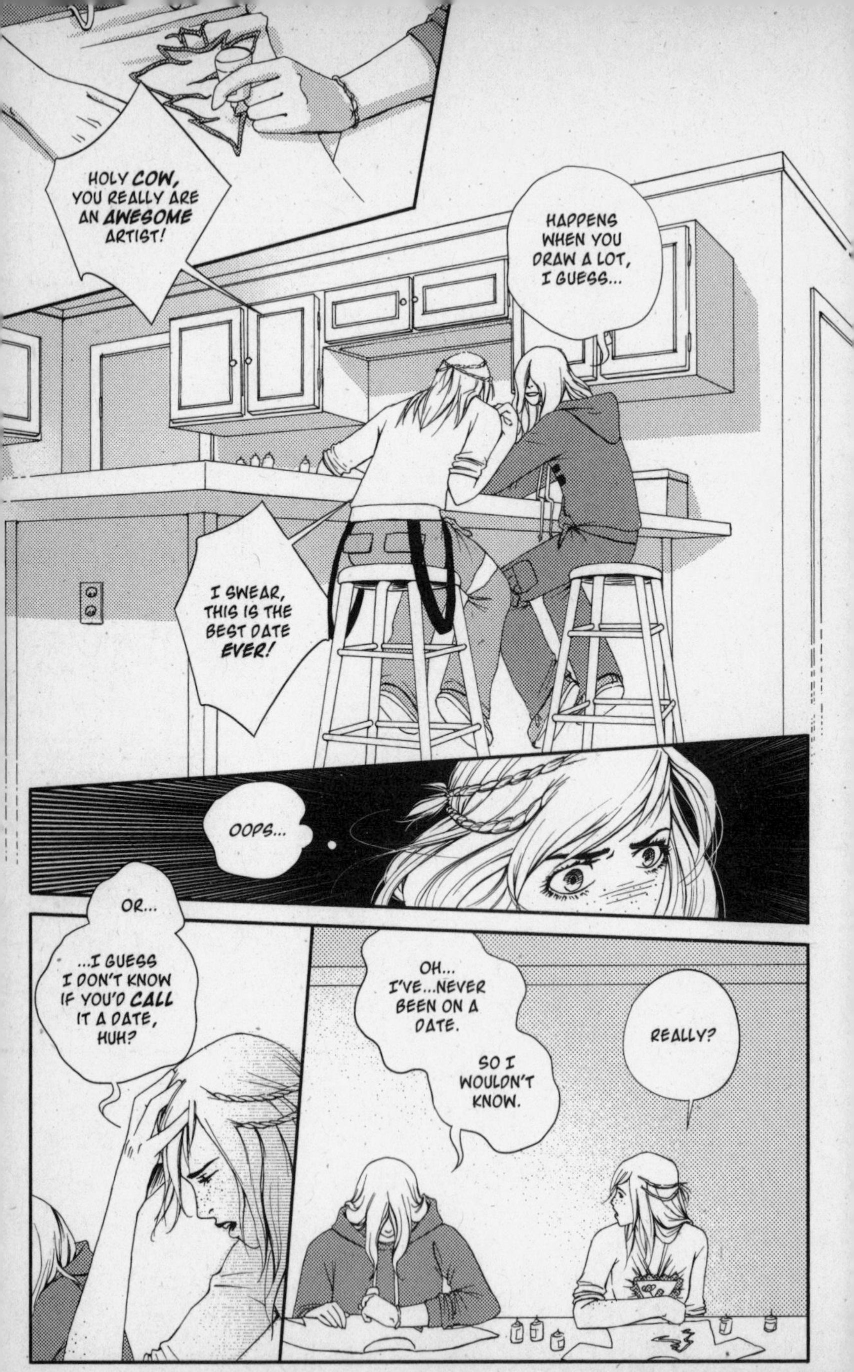
HOLY COW, YOU REALLY ARE AN AWESOME ARTIST!
HAPPENS WHEN YOU DRAW A LOT, I GUESS...
I SWEAR, THIS IS THE BEST DATE EVER!
OOPS...
OR...
...I GUESS I DON'T KNOW IF YOU'D CALL IT A DATE, HUH?
OH... I'VE...NEVER BEEN ON A DATE.
SO I WOULDN'T KNOW.
REALLY?

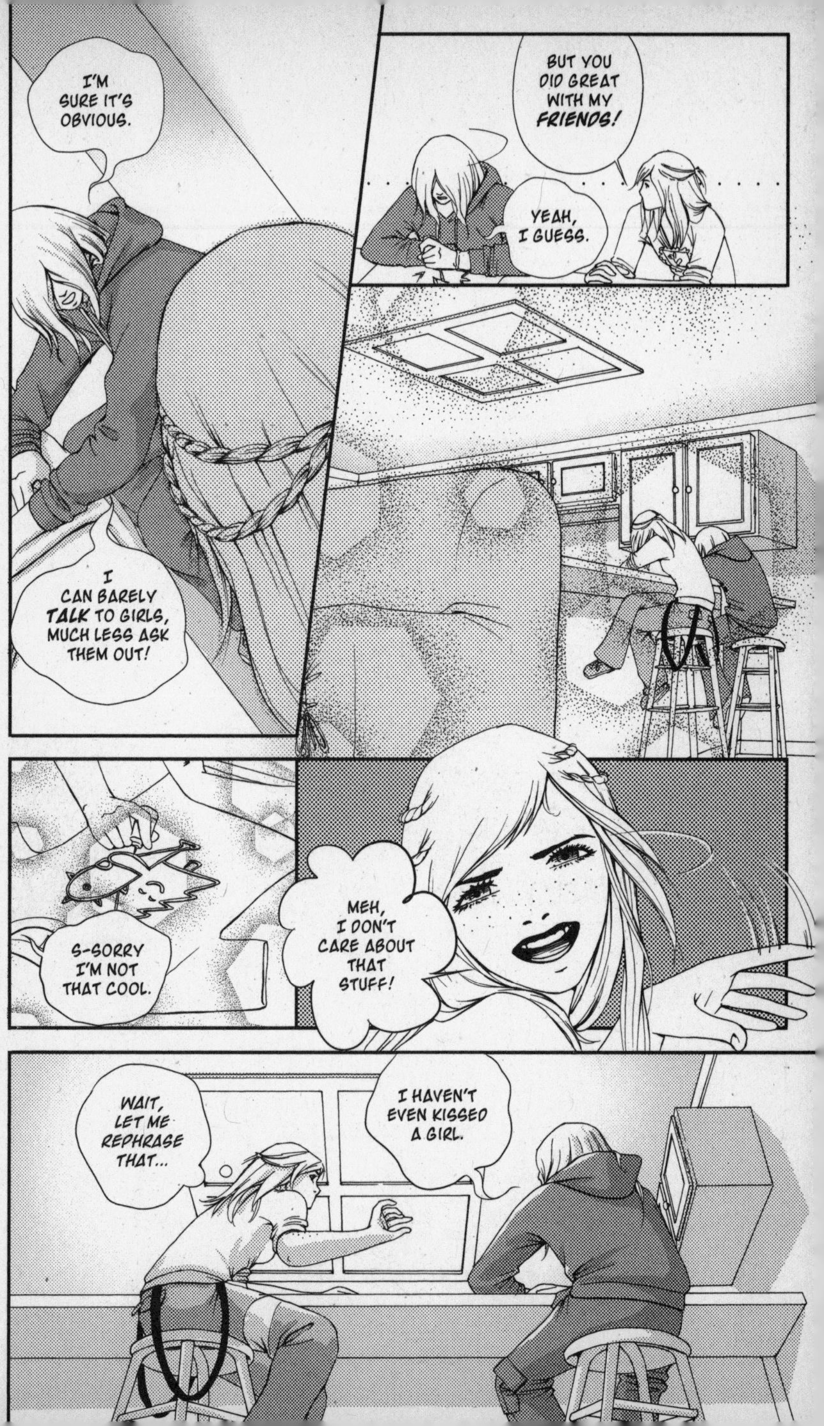
I'M SURE IT'S OBVIOUS.
I CAN BARELY TALK TO GIRLS, MUCH LESS ASK THEM OUT!
BUT YOU DID GREAT WITH MY FRIENDS!
YEAH, I GUESS.
S-SORRY I'M NOT THAT COOL.
MEH, I DON'T CARE ABOUT THAT STUFF!
WAIT, LET ME REPHRASE THAT...
I HAVEN'T EVEN KISSED A GIRL.

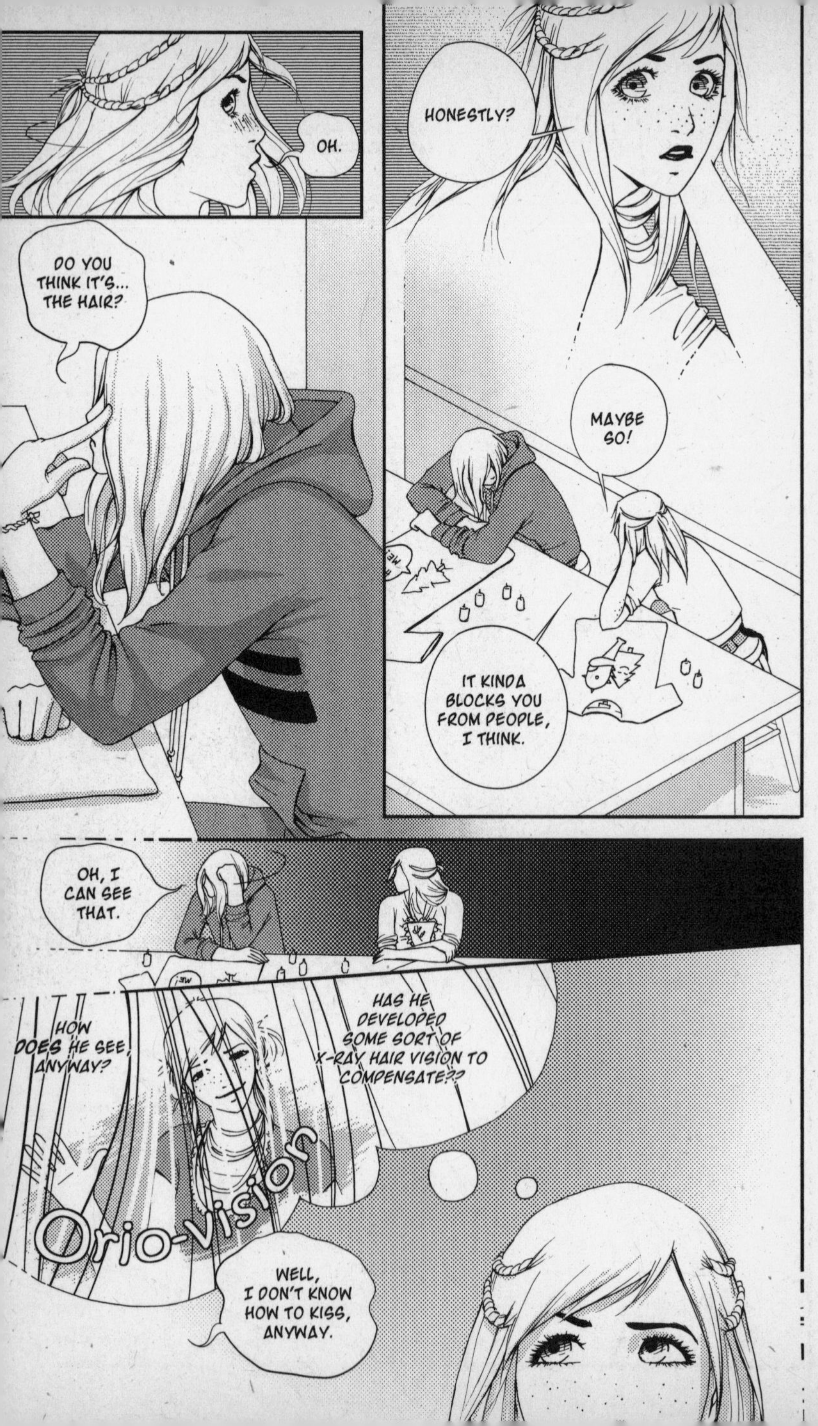
OH.
DO YOU THINK IT'S... THE HAIR?
HONESTLY?
MAYBE SO!
IT KINDA BLOCKS YOU FROM PEOPLE, I THINK.
OH, I CAN SEE THAT.
HOW DOES HE SEE, ANYWAY?
HAS HE DEVELOPED SOME SORT OF X-RAY HAIR VISION TO COMPENSATE??
Orio-vision
WELL, I DON'T KNOW HOW TO KISS, ANYWAY.

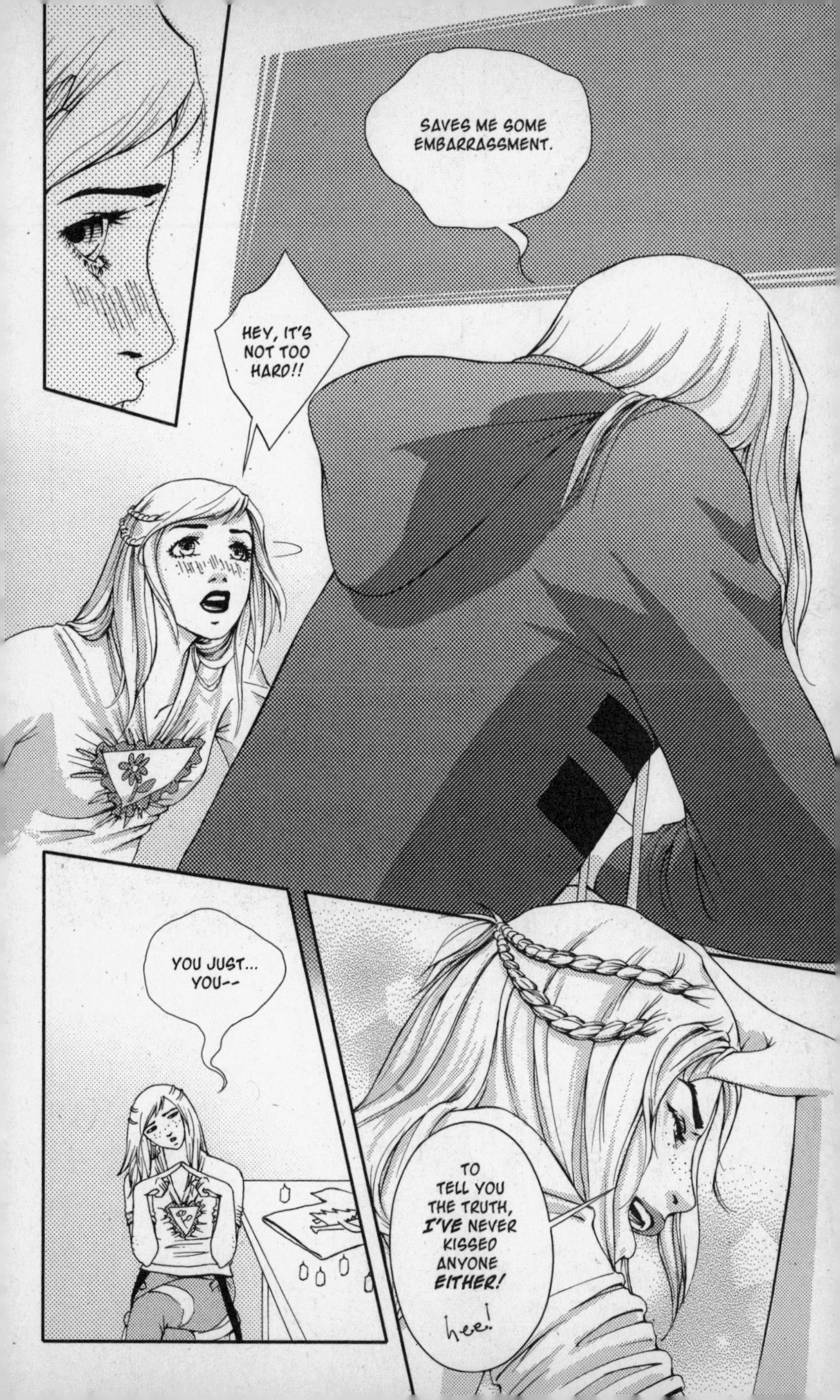
SAVES ME SOME EMBARRASSMENT.
HEY, IT'S NOT TOO HARD!!
YOU JUST... YOU--
TO TELL YOU THE TRUTH, *I'VE* NEVER KISSED ANYONE *EITHER!*
hee!

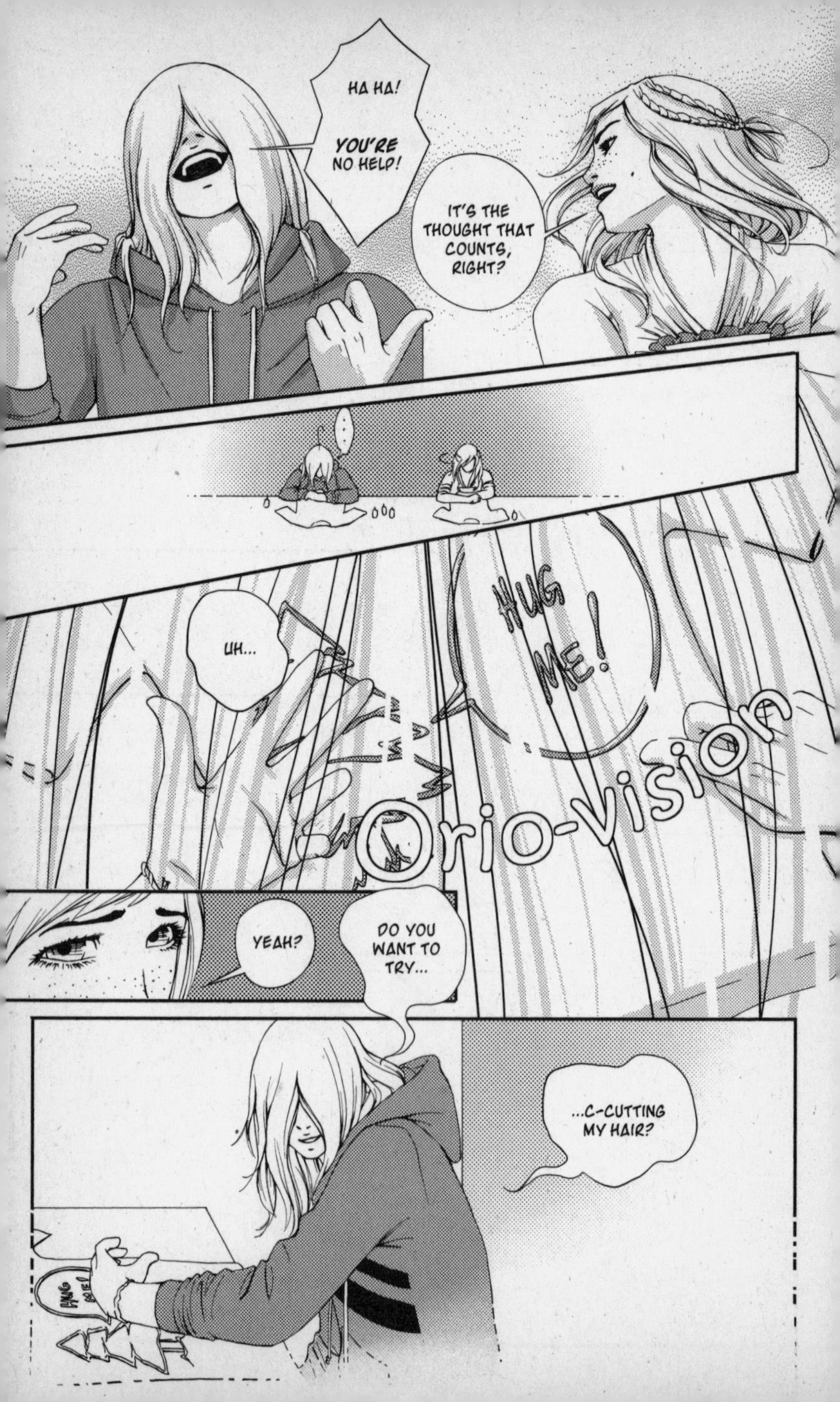
HA HA!
YOU'RE NO HELP!
IT'S THE THOUGHT THAT COUNTS, RIGHT?
UH...
HUG ME!
Orio-vision
YEAH?
DO YOU WANT TO TRY...
...C-CUTTING MY HAIR?
HUG ME!

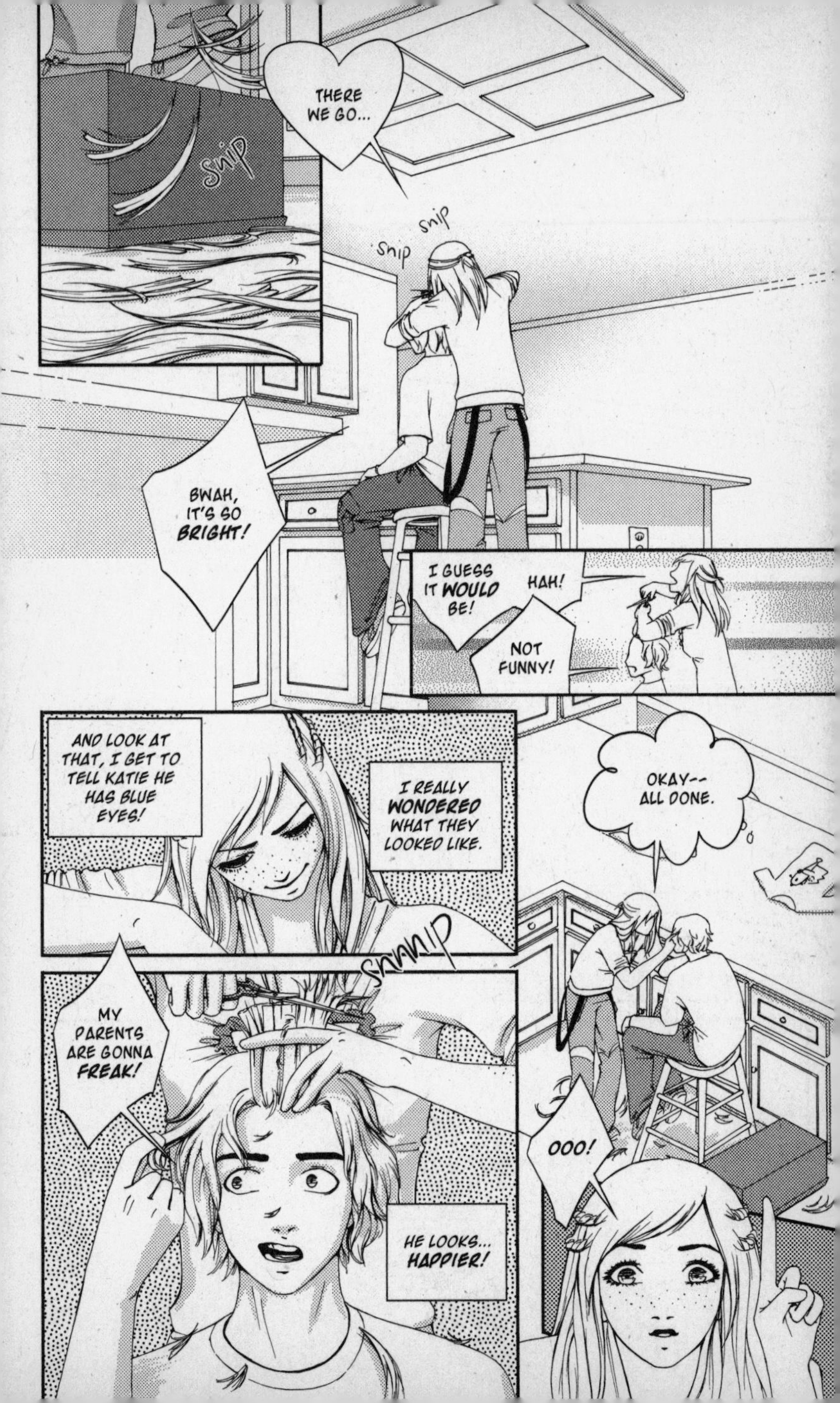

snip
THERE WE GO...
snip
snip
BWAH, IT'S SO BRIGHT!
I GUESS IT WOULD BE!
HAH!
NOT FUNNY!
AND LOOK AT THAT, I GET TO TELL KATIE HE HAS BLUE EYES!
I REALLY WONDERED WHAT THEY LOOKED LIKE.
OKAY-- ALL DONE.
SNANIP
MY PARENTS ARE GONNA FREAK!
HE LOOKS... HAPPIER!
OOO!

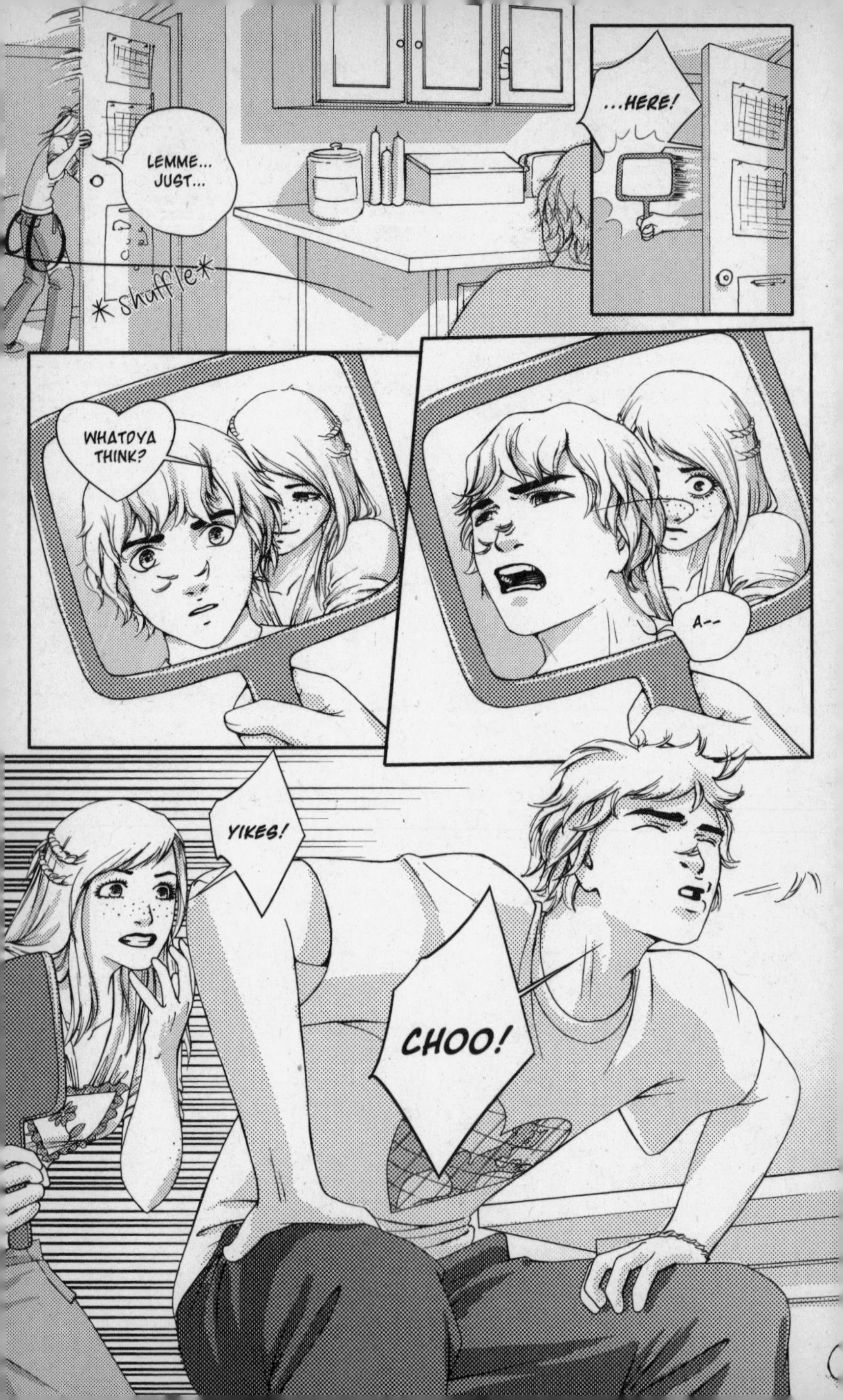
LEMME... JUST...
shuffle
...HERE!
WHATOYA THINK?
A--
YIKES!
CHOO!

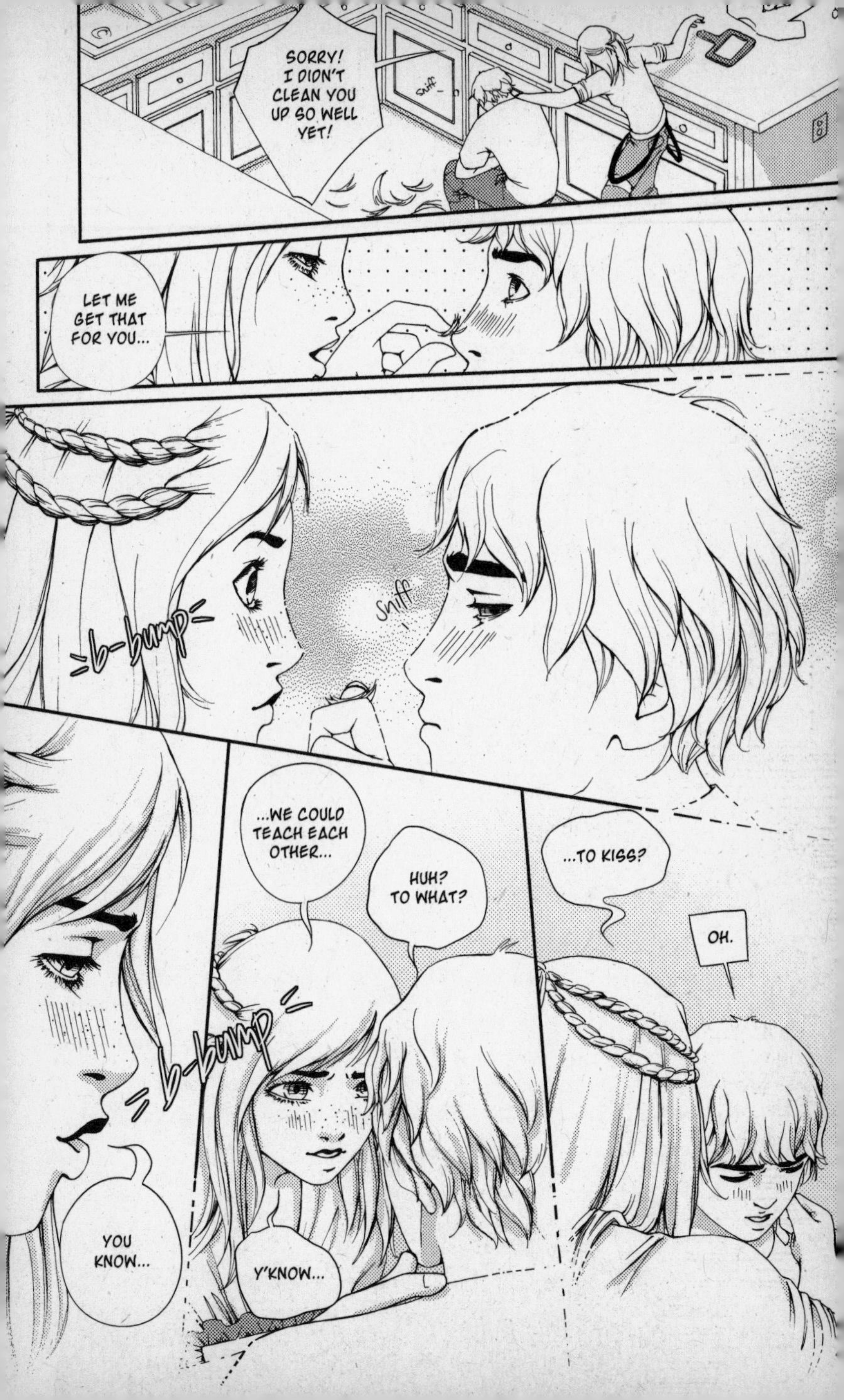
SORRY! I DIDN'T CLEAN YOU UP SO WELL YET!
sniff
LET ME GET THAT FOR YOU...
b-bump
sniff
b-bump
YOU KNOW...
...WE COULD TEACH EACH OTHER...
HUH? TO WHAT?
Y'KNOW...
...TO KISS?
OH.

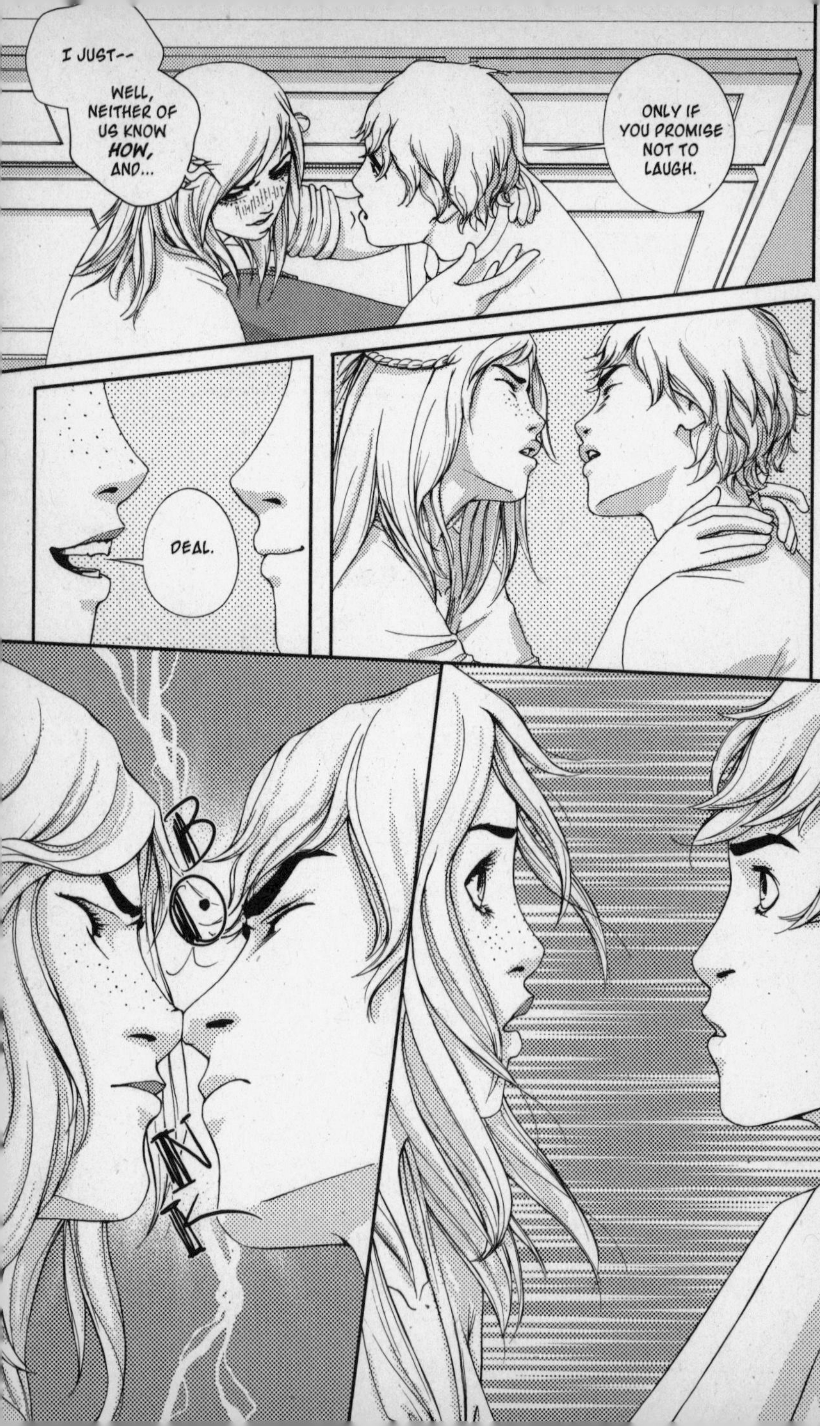
I JUST--
WELL, NEITHER OF US KNOW HOW, AND...
ONLY IF YOU PROMISE NOT TO LAUGH.
DEAL.
BONK

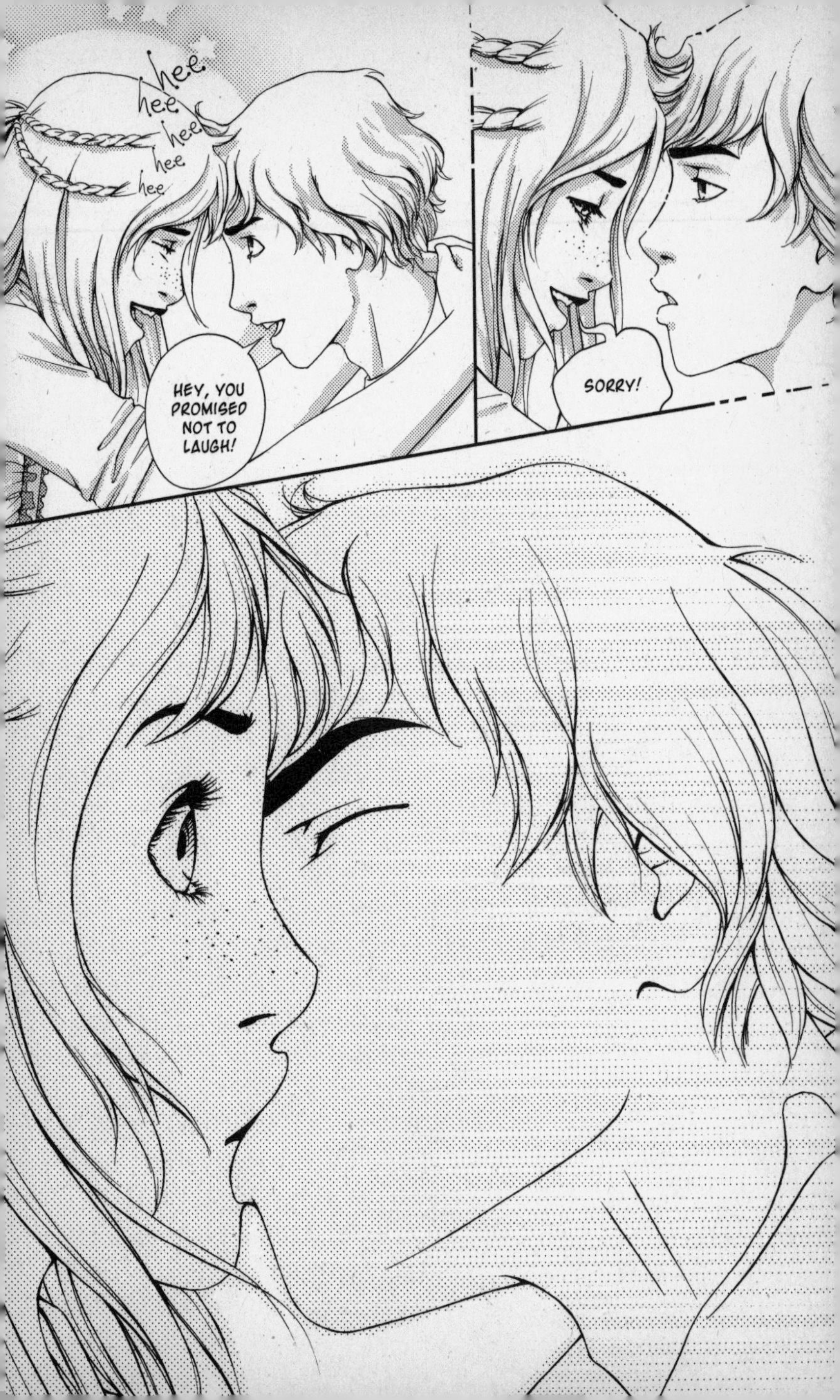
hee hee hee hee hee
HEY, YOU PROMISED NOT TO LAUGH!
SORRY!

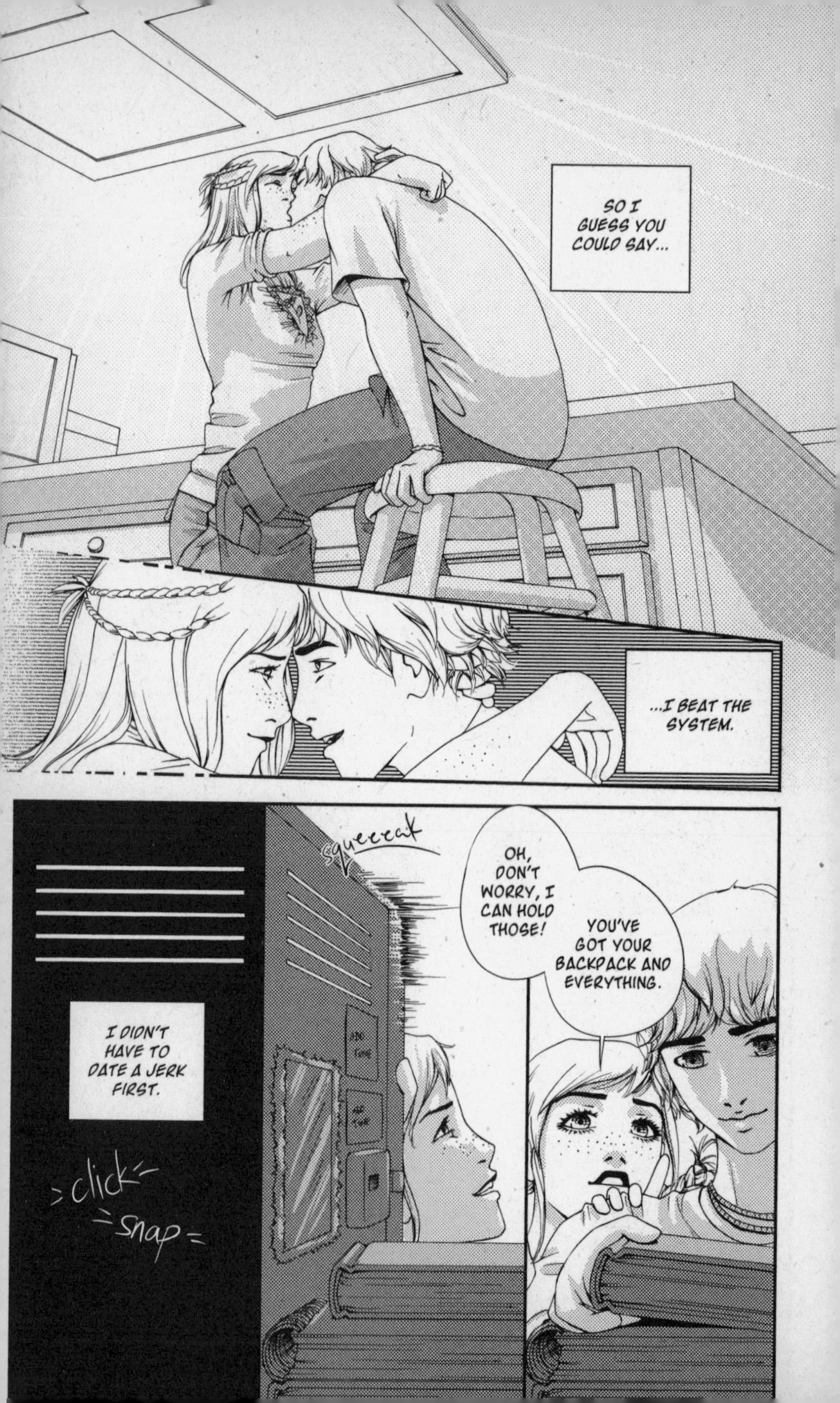
SO I GUESS YOU COULD SAY...
...I BEAT THE SYSTEM.
I DIDN'T HAVE TO DATE A JERK FIRST.
click
snap
squeeeak
OH, DON'T WORRY, I CAN HOLD THOSE!
YOU'VE GOT YOUR BACKPACK AND EVERYTHING.

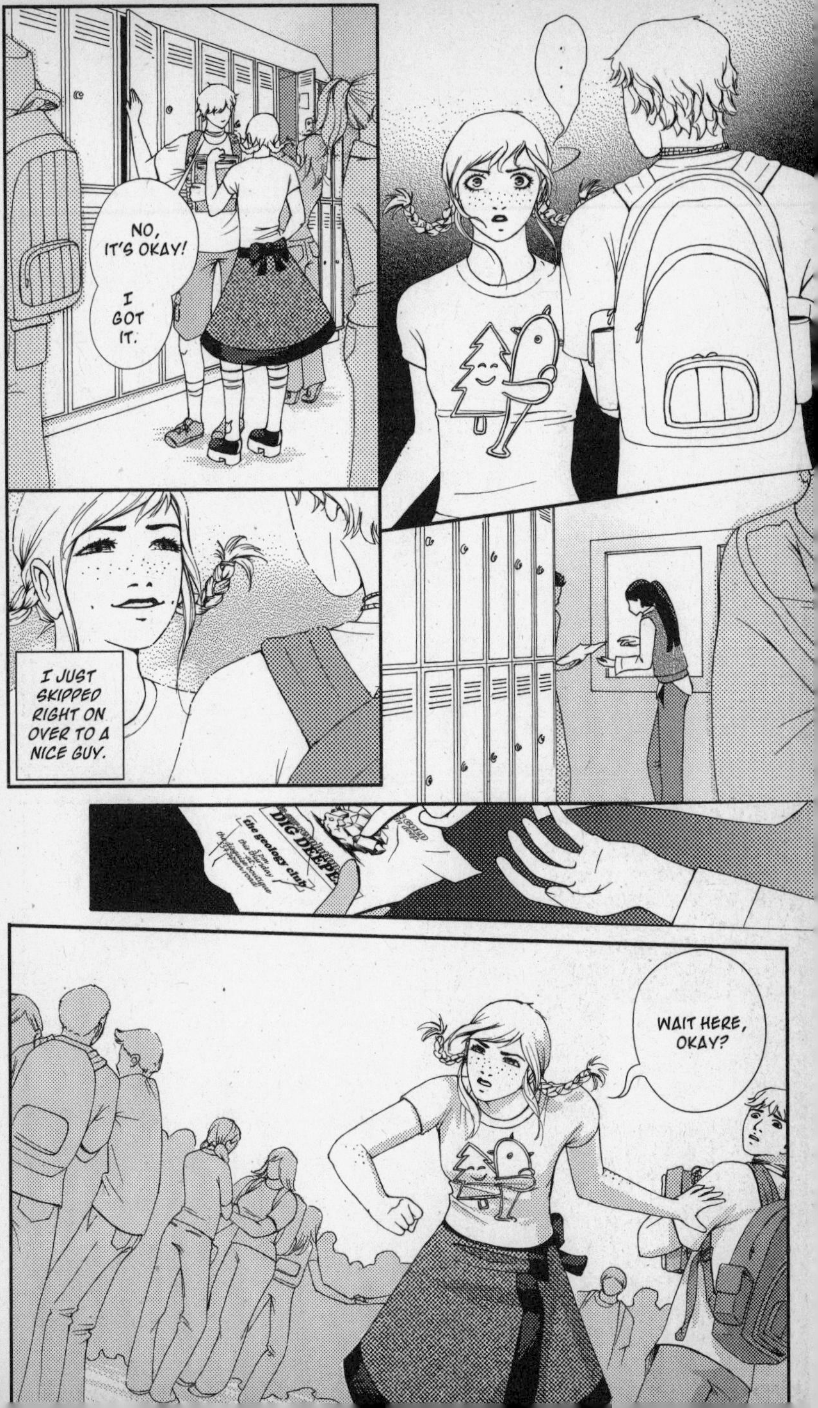
NO, IT'S OKAY!
I GOT IT.
I JUST SKIPPED RIGHT ON OVER TO A NICE GUY.
DIG DEEPE
the geology club
5 pm
this thursday
WAIT HERE, OKAY?

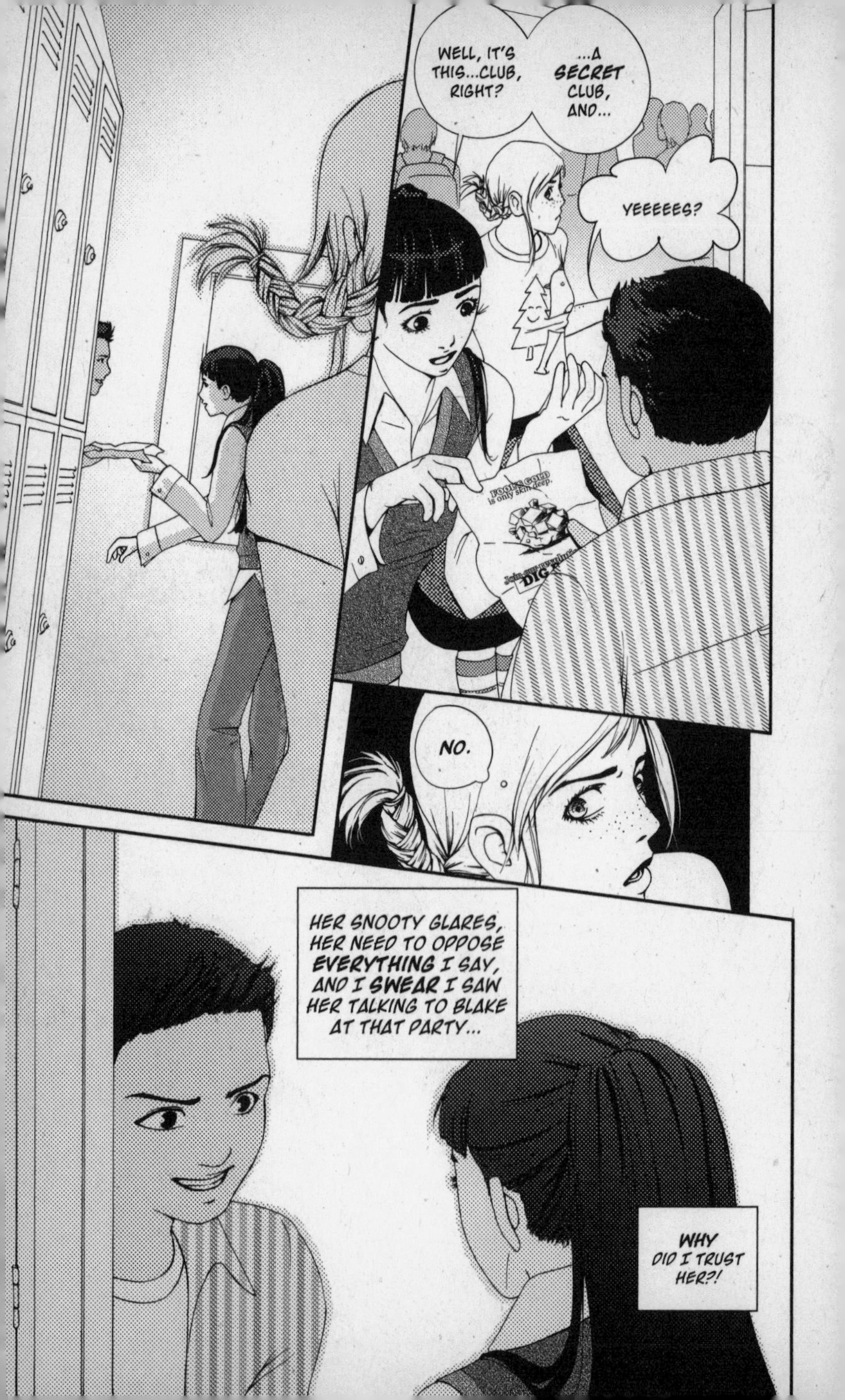
WELL, IT'S THIS...CLUB, RIGHT?
...A SECRET CLUB, AND...
YEEEEES?
FOOL'S GOLD is only skin deep.
NO.
HER SNOOTY GLARES, HER NEED TO OPPOSE EVERYTHING I SAY, AND I SWEAR I SAW HER TALKING TO BLAKE AT THAT PARTY...
WHY DID I TRUST HER?!

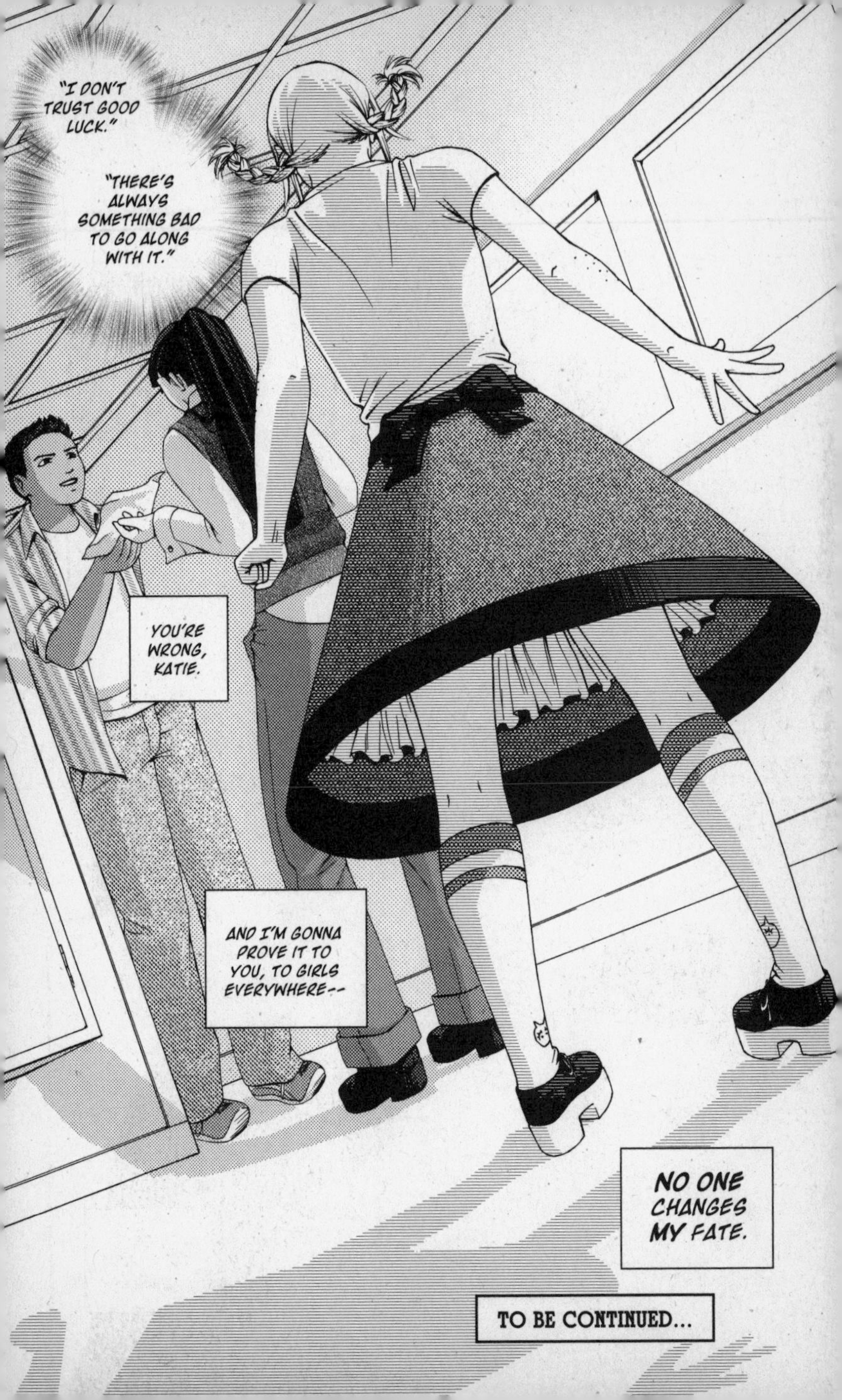
"I DON'T TRUST GOOD LUCK."
"THERE'S ALWAYS SOMETHING BAD TO GO ALONG WITH IT."
YOU'RE WRONG, KATIE.
AND I'M GONNA PROVE IT TO YOU, TO GIRLS EVERYWHERE--
NO ONE CHANGES MY FATE.
TO BE CONTINUED...

In the Next Volume of:

FOOL'S GOLD

Penny has it all: talent, confidence, power, even a new boyfriend! But Hannah's close call with a Pyrite is only a taste of many challenges to Penny's perfect life. Surrounded by a vengeful diva, probing Pyrites, gullible club members, an admiring enemy, a rebellious aunt, and a self-loathing boyfriend, Penny is in dire need of rest. Little does she know that sleep will only make her vulnerable to the greatest challenge of her existence...

Thanks

LILLIAN — I CAN'T TELL YOU HOW HAPPY I AM THAT YOU'RE MY EDITOR!! THANKS FOR EVERYTHING YOU DO, AND FOR BEING SUCH A GREAT PERSON TO WORK FOR!

JASON — FOR PUTTING UP WITH ALL THAT STRESS AND HELPING ME IN EVERY WAY POSSIBLE!! YOU ARE THE COMPLETE OPPOSITE OF A PYRITE ☺

MIKE — FOR HELPING ME PATCH UP ALL THOSE UNSIGHTLY PLOT HOLES!

MY **P**ARENTS — FOR ALL YOUR SUPPORT AND FOR GIVING ME A PLACE TO LIVE WHILE I DRAW THIS CRAZY THING!

JEANNETTE — FOR GETTING ME HOOKED ON MANGA.

MARCELLE, **E**NOS, AND **B**EAN — FOR BEING MY ✳INSPIRATION✳ FOR CHARACTERS' FACES, AND IN MARCELLE'S CASE, DEMEANOR AS WELL ☺

THANKS TO ALL MY **F**AMILY, **F**RIENDS AND **I**NTERNET **B**UDDIES (YES I AM A NERD) FOR THE MORAL SUPPORT!

AND LAST BUT **DEFINITELY** NOT LEAST, THANKS TO **E**VERYONE WHO'S READ THIS BOOK! YOU MAKE ALL THAT WORK TOTALLY WORTH IT!

♥, Amy

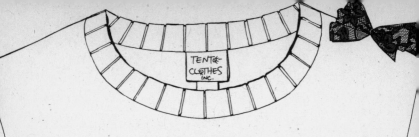

Since a large part of drawing this series involves designing clothes, I thought I'd highlight a few designs in this book. And coincidentally, they're all dresses!

I've been asked by people who have seen my art but haven't met me whether I dress like Penny. I suppose my answer is a big yes-and-no. I'm not quite as dressy and my clothes are probably plainer since I don't go out in public too much. I also don't have much time to sew! But at one point in college, most of the clothes I wore were handmade, and I loved to make goofy clothes (like skirts made of baby quilt material with cartoon characters). Also, you may have noticed Penny's last hairstyle in the book—that's actually something I used to do in college! I'd feed hanger wire into my braids and bend them up. In high school, I dressed like everyone else, because I didn't want to be made fun of (well, not more than I already was), so college was my chance to be who I'd always wanted to be. I didn't learn to sew until college, actually!

If Penny has instilled in you any desire to make your own clothes, GO FOR IT! It takes a lot of patience (and a seam ripper for when you make mistakes), but it's so much fun to LITERALLY wear your imagination on your sleeve. Take the world around you and use it for inspiration. I like to play with embroidery, buttons, pockets, cool sleeves and collars, eyelet lace, geometric patterns, animals, and fun trims. I also like stuff that reminds me of grandmas and curtains. I like to make themes and stories for my outfits. Figure out what style really speaks to you and what sorts of things you've always wanted to have in clothing! It makes life that much more fun. ☺

I drew this dress as an excuse to use kitty pockets. Once upon a time, I was making myself an apron (I *love* aprons), and I couldn't think of a creative pocket. Kitty pockets were my father-in-law's idea! It was such a great idea that I had to resurrect it for this series. And in making the dress, I put another kitty face on her chest, the ears wrapping around her neck. It clips in the back, with one side continuing on as a tail. The tail has a wire in it so you can shape it how you like! I envision the fabric being some sort of wool suiting fabric, and the whiskers are super fluffy yarn sewn into the dress. I don't really know why I've thought this through, since it only exists on paper. Maybe someday I'll make it. ☺

I really had a hard time coming up with a costume for Hannah. I wanted every costum
in chapter 5 to have some sort of meaning behind it, but with her I drew a blan
especially since hers was the last costume of many that I had to think up. I decided sh
could be a princess and just started doodling. Then, I tried to think up a necklac
and drew a spade on it, which finally got my thoughts flowing! I like to play Heart
after all, and decided that Hannah would make the perfect Queen of Spades. So
added two more spades to the dress...can you see them? And after that, I realize
that Penny had hearts all over her costume. So it only made sense to incorpora
diamonds and clubs to other clothes in the chapter. It's things like these that kee
comics interesting to make! So I've inserted lots of little symbolisms, foreshadowing
and subtle jokes in my book to make it fun for me. And some of those involve th
clothing designs!

This dress is actually one that I made at least three years ago. It's grey with pink piping and flowers, and I even knitted pink-and-grey-striped leggings to go with . The flowers snap on and off for washing. I didn't draw everything from the ctual dress, because there were little details that'd be too distracting. But I had a ink leafy embroidery pattern that went along the edge of the dress (made by my ewing machine—I'm not THAT patient!), and the buttons were white with flowers that eminded me of my grandma's dried flowers at her house. It doesn't fit me anymore, ut I've got a new goal to be able to fit into it by the time this book comes out! We'll e if I succeed...

RE: play

BY CHRISTY LIJEWSKI

HE'S THE ANSWER TO HER PRAYERS, AND THE BEGINNING OF HER NIGHTMARES!

When Cree's bass player quits her band, she's put in a tough spot—until she meets Izsak, a man without a past and, in his mind, a man without a future. Through a twist of fate, he becomes Cree's new bass player—plus a whole lot more...

FROM THE CREATOR OF NEXT EXIT!

DRAMA

T TEEN AGE 13+

READ AN ENTIRE CHAPTER FOR FREE: WWW.TOKYOPOP.COM/MANGAONLINE

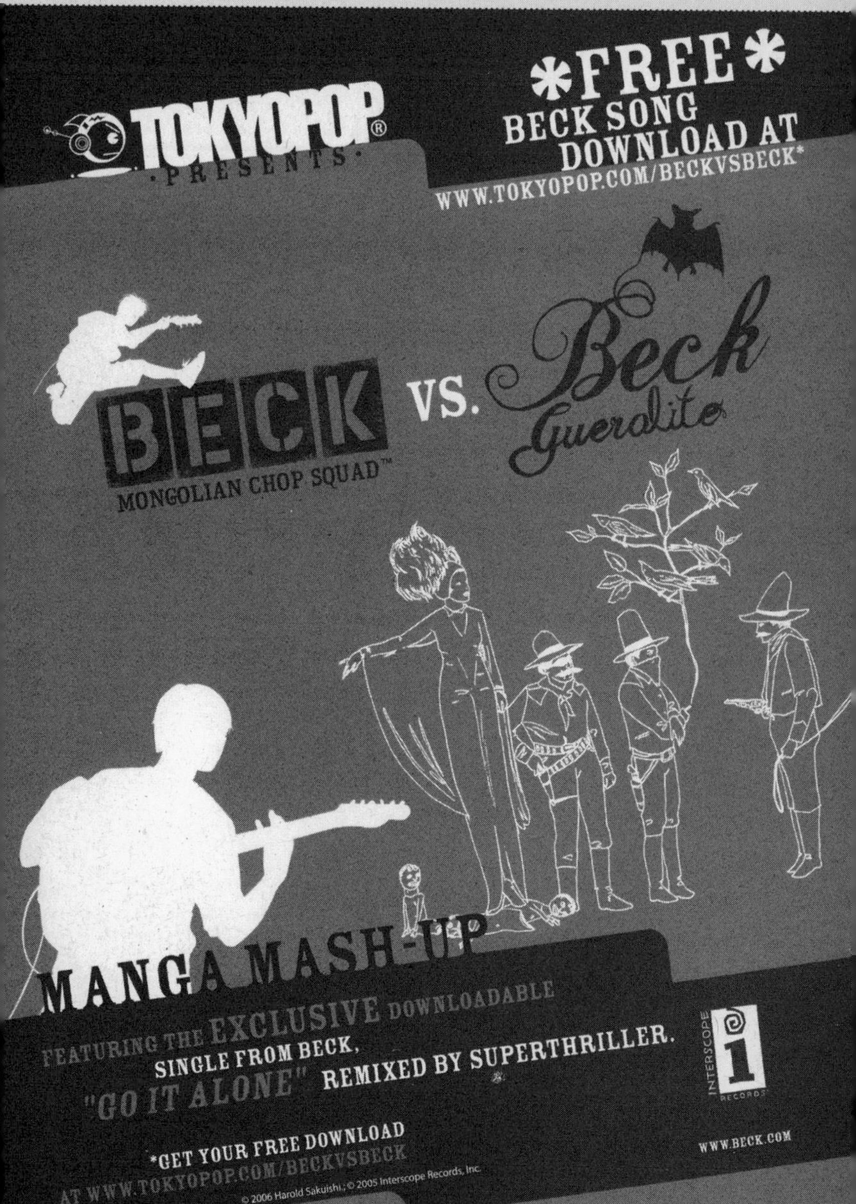
TOKYOPOP® PRESENTS
FREE
BECK SONG
DOWNLOAD AT
TOKYOPOP.COM/BECKVSBECK*
WWW.TOKYOPOP.COM/BECKVSBECK
BECK
MONGOLIAN CHOP SQUAD™
VS.
Beck
Guerolito
MANGA MASH-UP
FEATURING THE EXCLUSIVE DOWNLOADABLE
SINGLE FROM BECK,
"GO IT ALONE" REMIXED BY SUPERTHRILLER.
INTERSCOPE RECORDS
*GET YOUR FREE DOWNLOAD
AT WWW.TOKYOPOP.COM/BECKVSBECK
WWW.BECK.COM
© 2006 Harold Sakuishi, © 2005 Interscope Records, Inc.